AF575283

# THE BERLIN MASTERPIECES IN AMERICA

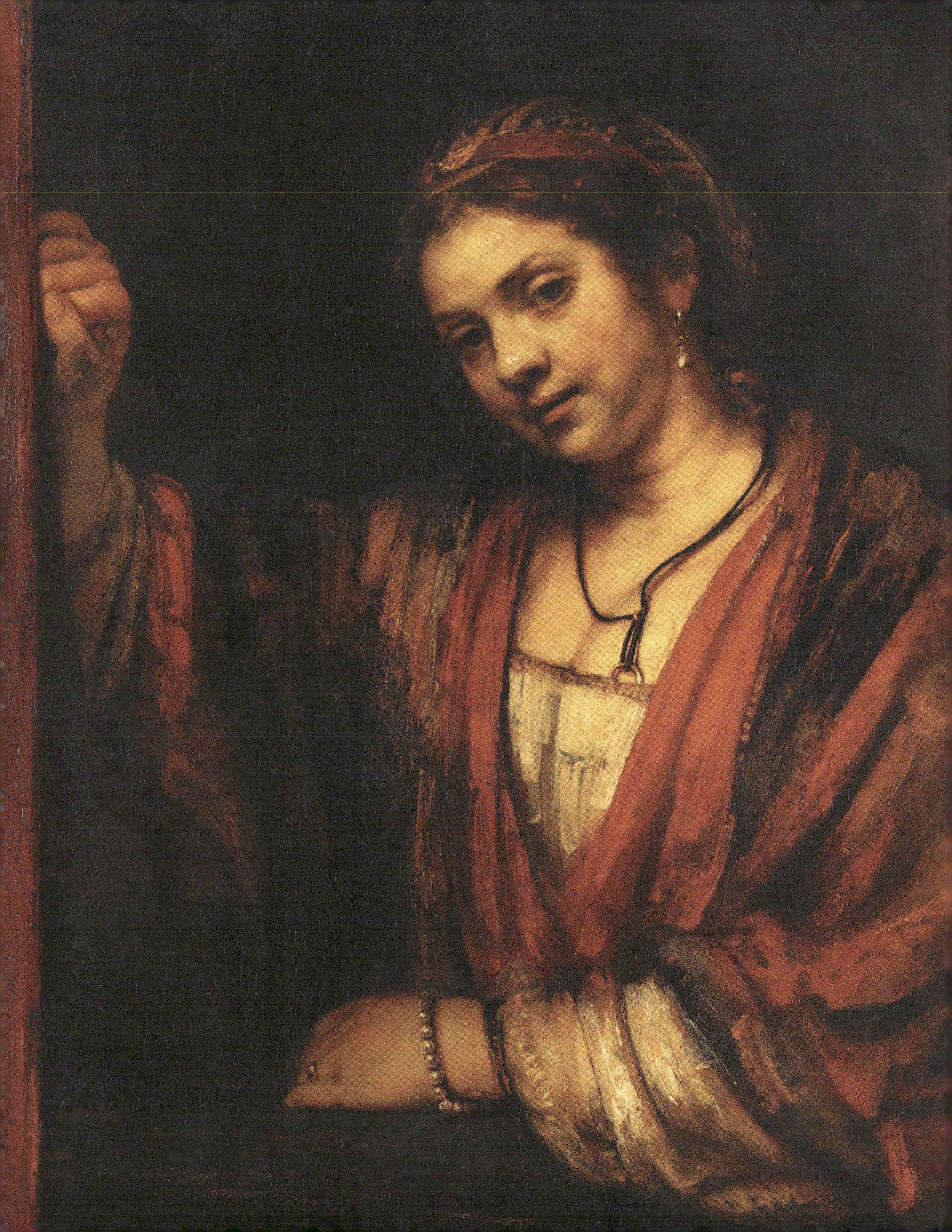

# THE BERLIN MASTERPIECES IN AMERICA

## PAINTINGS, POLITICS, AND THE MONUMENTS MEN

Peter Jonathan Bell and Kristi A. Nelson

With contributions by Tanja Bernsau, Kathryn Griffith, Neville Rowley, and Nancy Yeide

CINCINNATI ART MUSEUM
in association with D Giles Limited

cincinnati art museum g

*The Berlin Masterpieces in America: Paintings, Politics, and the Monuments Men* was made possible by the initiative, advocacy and generous support of:

Shannon and Lee Carter
Marty and Nick Ragland
Joyce and Jack Steinman

This publication accompanies the exhibition *Paintings, Politics, and the Monuments Men: The Berlin Masterpieces in America* on display at Cincinnati Art Museum, June 26, 2020–September 6, 2020, curated by Peter Jonathan Bell, Curator of European Paintings, Sculpture and Drawings, Cincinnati Art Museum and Kristi A. Nelson, Executive Vice President for Academic Affairs and Provost, University of Cincinnati.

This exhibition was organized with the generous support of the Harold C. Schott Foundation.

It was made possible by the following supporters:
Lee Carter Family Fund
Marnick Foundation
August A. Rendigs, Jr. Foundation
Charles Scott Riley III Foundation
Joyce and Jack Steinman
The Wieler Family Foundation

The Cincinnati Art Museum is grateful for the support provided by ArtsWave, the Ohio Arts Council, the City of Cincinnati, and our members.



First published in 2020 by GILES
An imprint of D Giles Limited
66 High Street,
Lewes, BN7 1XG, UK
gilesltd.com

ISBN: 978-1-911282-63-1 (hardcover edition)



For the Cincinnati Art Museum:
Edited by Peter Jonathan Bell and Kristi A. Nelson
Production management by Anne Buening
Editorial assistance from Kathryn Griffith

For D Giles Limited:
Copy-edited and proof-read by Sarah Kane
Designed by Helen Swansbourne
Produced by GILES, an imprint of D Giles Limited
Printed and bound in Slovenia

All measurements are in inches and centimeters; height precedes width.

Front cover: Members of the US Third Army discover Édouard Manet's *The Winter Garden* in the salt mines at Merkers, April 25, 1945. Photograph No. 111-SC-203453-5, Box 261, Army Signal Corps, Record Group 111, National Archives at College Park, College Park, MD

Frontispiece: Rembrandt Harmensz. van Rijn (Dutch, 1606–1669), *Woman in a Doorway* (formerly titled *Hendrickje Stoffels*), 1654–57, oil on canvas, 34⅞ × 26⅜ in. (88.6 × 67 cm), Staatliche Museen zu Berlin, Gemäldegalerie, Kat. 828 B

Library of Congress Cataloging-in-Publication Data

Names: Bell, Peter Jonathan, author. | Nelson, Kristi (Kristi A.), author. | Cincinnati Art Museum, organizer, host institution.
Title: The Berlin masterpieces in America : paintings, politics, and the Monuments Men / Peter Jonathan Bell and Kristi A. Nelson ; with contributions by Tanja Bernsau, Kathryn Griffith, Neville Rowley, and Nancy Yeide.
Description: Cincinnati : Cincinnati Art Museum ; Lewes, UK : in association with D Giles Limited, 2020. | "This catalog accompanies the exhibition Paintings, Politics, and the Monuments Men: The Berlin Masterpieces in America on display at Cincinnati Art Museum, June 26, 2020-September 6, 2020"--Colophon. | Includes bibliographical references and index.
Identifiers: LCCN 2020003317 | ISBN 9781911282631 (hardback)
Subjects: LCSH: Painting, European--Exhibitions. | Masterpieces from the Berlin Museums (Exhibition) (1948-1949 : United States) | Traveling exhibitions--Political aspects United States--History--20th century. | Cultural property--Moral and ethical aspects. | Cultural property--Repatriation.
Classification: LCC ND450 .B45 2020 | DDC 759.4--dc23
LC record available at https://lccn.loc.gov/2020003317

Authors in Catalogue section:
PJB Peter Jonathan Bell
KG Kathryn Griffith
KN Kristi A. Nelson

# CONTENTS

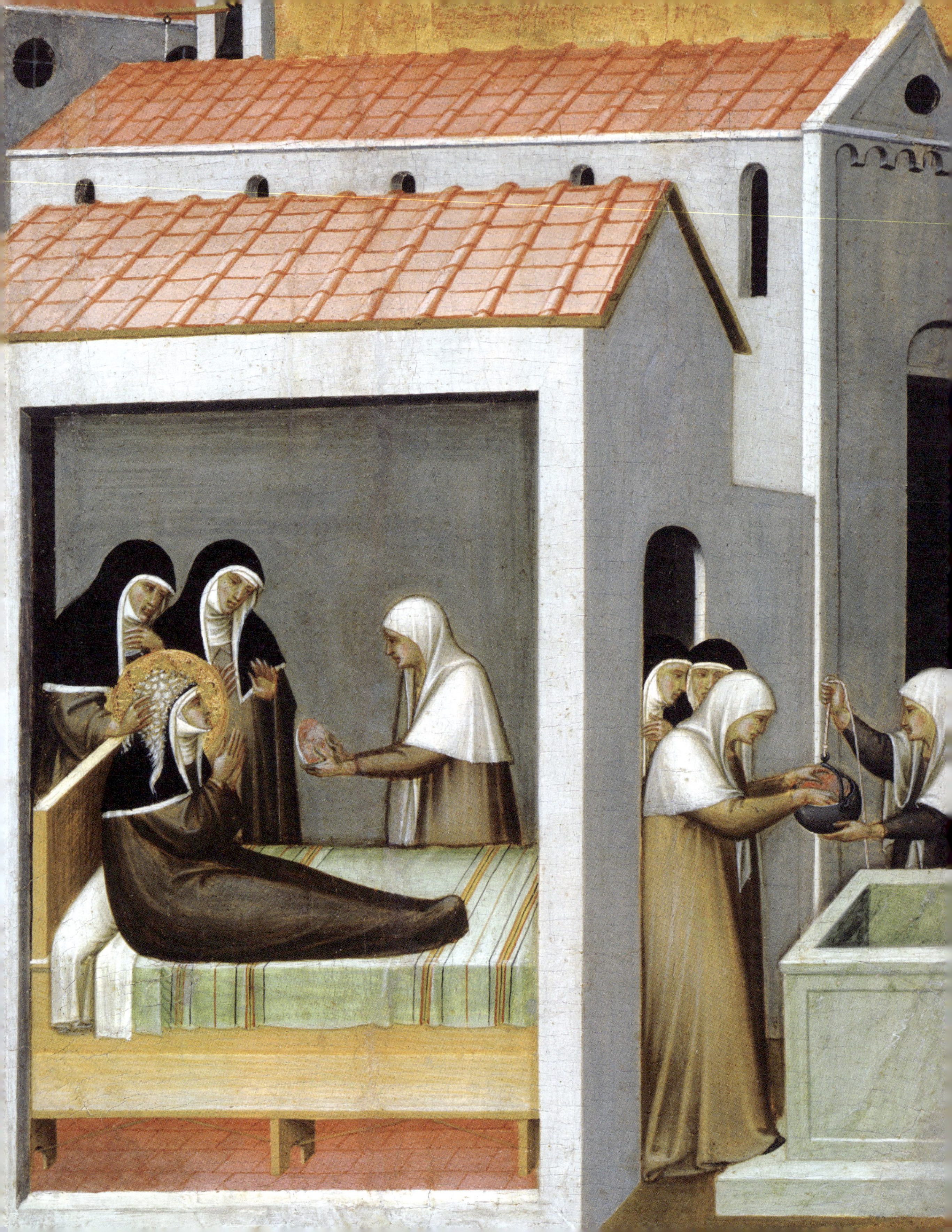

# FOREWORD

Art, scholarship, and education are harmonizing principles in the founding histories of public museums. Yet it is also true that museums carry power and effect beyond collections and galleries. Our collective choices, both of commission and omission, define history.

The storylines that underlie the exhibition *Paintings, Politics, and the Monuments Men: The Berlin Masterpieces in America*, and this accompanying catalogue, amplify the question. In 1945, a young nation was perched at the cusp of a shift in cultural power from Europe to America. Its heroic role in defeating the Third Reich and the corrupt values of the Axis powers sparked the United States' rise as a global producer and consumer of culture.

At that pivotal moment in history, the ebullience of victory coursed through every aspect of American identity. The words freedom, democracy, and power proved to be an intoxicating blend that wove through political speech in postwar America. Enlightenment became a moral calling for the United States on the world stage, furthering America's image and character in Europe and elsewhere. The value of masterpieces of art and culture in this context must never have been higher to our noble callings.

And thus the actions and bravery of a small group of safekeepers tasked with protecting shared world heritage during and after World War II transcend museology. The raised voices of the Monuments Men reminded us that who we are and what we do, not what we have and what we hold, define our morals. When Army Captain Walter Farmer cited "the dictates of a higher ethical law" in his and twenty-three other officers' objection to transferring masterpieces from the Berlin state collections to America, they articulated the conscience both of modern museum collecting and of nation building. That their calls were unheeded in November 1945, but eventually honored by 1949, further describes the complexity of the practice of art history in the heady times of postwar America.

Pietro Lorenzetti (Sienese, 1280–1348), *The Miracle of the Ice of Saint Humilitas* (formerly *Death of Saint Humilitas*), circa 1330–35, tempera on poplar panel (detail of checklist BR 104)

The journey of the 202 paintings from the Wiesbaden Collecting Point to the US heartland and back to Germany, as eloquently described in this volume by Peter Bell and Kristi Nelson with essays by Tanja Bernsau, Neville Rowley, and Nancy Yeide, is essential history for any museum director or curator. Today's headlines on art provenance, restitution, looting, and repatriation all testify to the fact that the power of art commingles unabated with political and military realms.

The circumstances change but the core questions persist. It is my hope that this exhibition and scholarly catalogue record a history, collection, and people that will help to inspire and guide our work. The safeguarding of masterpieces and great artistic accomplishments of millennia is a responsibility beyond the walls of any one museum or the borders of any single nation. That in the twenty-first century we have not dispelled the notion of targeting monuments and world heritage sites in areas of conflict tells us only that we have much more to do.

And so I return to the initial question of art museums and our role. More than a vault for art and artifacts, more than a home for authors and scholars, even more than a center for public education and interpretation of art, a museum at its best changes the very place it serves. If we alter history ourselves by our actions, we have a moral imperative to act with integrity, conscience, and principles. Thus the core story of the Berlin "202" and the *Masterpieces* exhibition, prompted by the exigencies of 1945, presages the modern age of museums.

The making of art, literature, and meaning is mysterious and miraculous. Knowing the painting, sculpture, and art forms of a people is to learn their complexities and highest aspirations and accomplishments. While museums must resist asserting an unerring account of history, the material culture of a place and time is an indispensable resource. The points of perspective on each object or thought, as it may change over time, lead us to invaluable insights.

It is with gratitude and admiration that I recall my introduction to the lessons of Walter Farmer. Shannon and Lee Carter, Marty and Nick Ragland, Joyce and Jack Steinman, John Steele, and Ellen Rieveschl called me to a lunch in January 2015 to offer the idea of a project based on the decisions of the young army officer, a Cincinnatian. I was enthralled. We were subsequently emboldened by the collaborative enthusiasm of the Gemäldegalerie team, with Neville Rowley and Michael Eissenhauer in the lead.

This project is entirely the result of generous partnership, first the spirit and remarkable trust formed between Peter Bell of the Cincinnati Art Museum and Kristi Nelson of the University of Cincinnati. The joyful scholarship threaded through this project is by way primarily of their mutual respect and affinity. Equally notable is the aforementioned gracious collegiality between the Cincinnati Art Museum and the Berlin State Museums. And finally, Walter Farmer's family, Margaret Farmer Planton and Ted Gantz, opened themselves fully to every inquiry.

On behalf of all who led this project to publication and opening day, I am pleased to share *The Berlin Masterpieces in America: Paintings, Politics, and the Monuments Men*. I hope it will add to the continuing pursuit of truth and knowledge in the crossroads of art, sociology, and our better angels.

**CAMERON KITCHIN**
Louis and Louise Dieterle Nippert Director
Cincinnati Art Museum

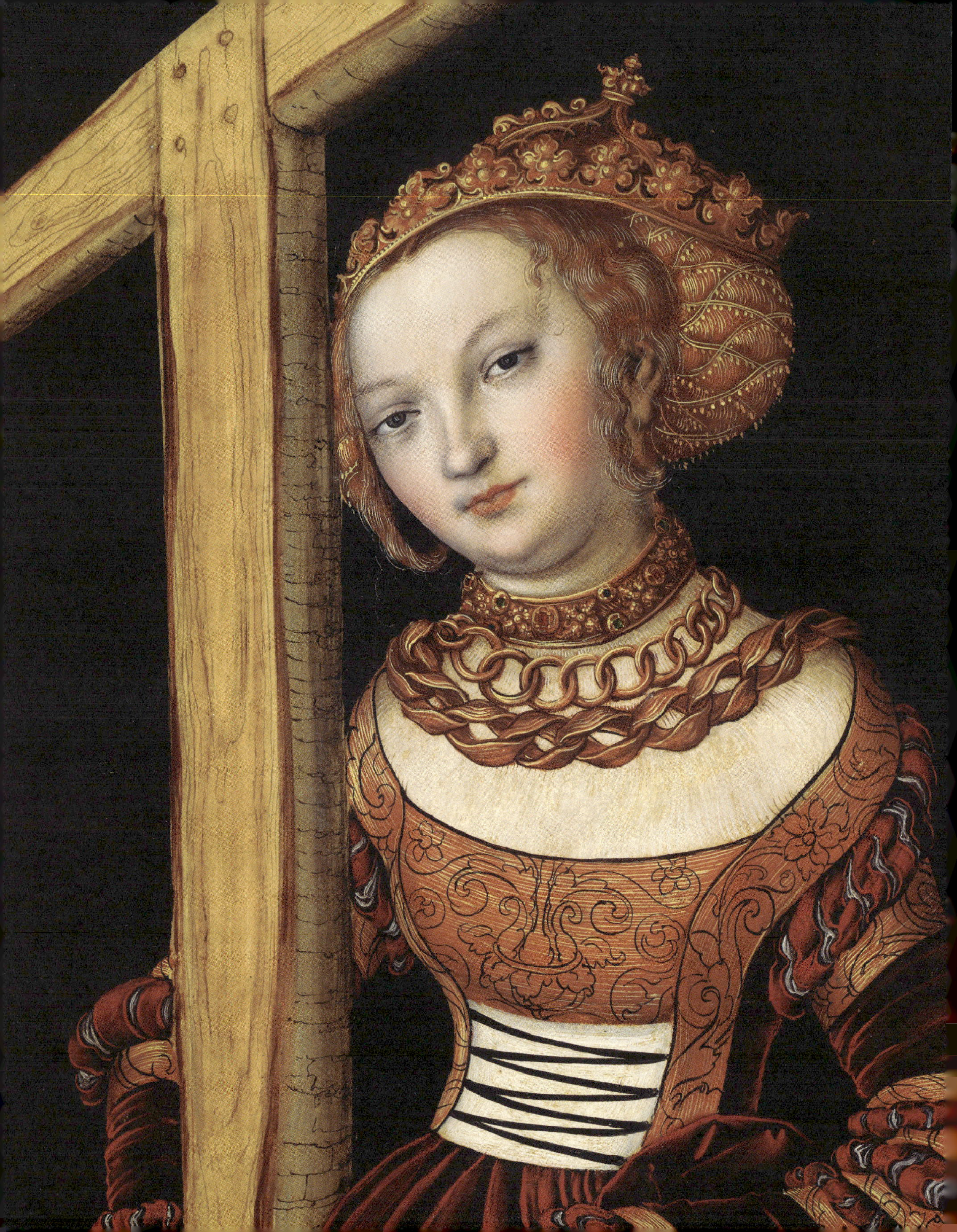

# INTRODUCTION

THE BERLIN MASTERPIECES IN AMERICA: *Paintings, Politics, and the Monuments Men* brings alive an important episode in the history of cultural patrimony and its stewardship. In so doing, it provides a timely opportunity to honor Cincinnatian Walter Ings Farmer and his role as a member of the Monuments, Fine Arts, and Archives (MFAA) organization at the Wiesbaden Collecting Point in the months following the end of World War II, a period so crucial to the fate of millions of artworks affected by that epochal conflict. Connecting the various parts of this story allows us to focus afresh on the nature of collecting, the history of museums, and the role of art in geopolitics.

Farmer was director of the Central Collecting Point in Wiesbaden, established at the end of the war to assemble and protect art and patrimony of the German State that had been dispersed during the war, and in this capacity he stands at the center of the episode addressed by this book. In November 1945, Farmer and his colleagues were ordered by the US high command to ship 202 paintings from the Berlin state collections to the United States, ostensibly for safekeeping.

Farmer and his fellow Monuments Men vehemently opposed this order (they saw their role as being one of repatriation and restitution of these artworks to the German State), and Farmer was the main instigator of an official letter of protest to their superiors signed by many of the Monuments Men, a document that became known as the Wiesbaden Manifesto. The order was nevertheless executed, and these major artworks—popularly referred to as the "Berlin 202"—were shipped to the United States and stored at the National Gallery of Art in Washington, DC, where they were put on view for six weeks in 1948; many of the paintings then embarked on a nationwide tour before their return to Germany the following year.

Lucas Cranach, the Elder (1472–1553), *Saint Helena with the Cross*, 1525, oil on panel (detail of cat. 17)

The peregrinations of these artworks, the motives behind their movements, and the effects thereof form the core of this volume. To frame the issue, Peter

Bell's essay addresses some of the ways in which artworks were utilized by the Nazis before and during the war. The essay by Tanja Bernsau provides critical background information on the role of the Central Collecting Points, Walter Farmer's work at Wiesbaden, and his call for the Wiesbaden Manifesto. In her essay, Kristi Nelson traces the "Berlin 202" through the US, drawing out the impact of their presence on American institutions and audiences. The life of the "202" in the seventy years since their return to Germany is the subject of Neville Rowley's essay; he examines their significance as diplomatic symbols in postwar Europe. An interview with Margaret Farmer Planton and Ted Gantz, the two people closest to Walter Farmer in the last twenty-five years of his life, adds an important personal dimension to our understanding of his life after the Monuments Men and the legacy of his military and civic service. An essay by provenance expert Nancy Yeide lays out the significance, timeliness, and research process required to determine the ownership history of artworks, and makes a case for supporting and expanding this work.

The catalogue section documents the works in the exhibition that make tangible the historical issues and events in question. They include several of the "Berlin 202," additional loans, and a fine selection of artworks from the collections of the Cincinnati Art Museum that have direct relevance to our topics. Finally, an illustrated checklist of the "Berlin 202" and several documents pertaining to their selection and transfer, interpreted by Kathryn Griffith, provide further context and support for the essays and catalogue.

As the topics of the core essays reflect, we wanted to bring particular attention to the complete narrative surrounding the journey of the 202 "Masterpieces from the Berlin Museums," as they were fittingly dubbed by exhibition catalogues and the press at the time—from their home in Berlin, through Germany during the war and the US and Europe in the decade that followed, before returning to Dahlem in West Berlin. The "Berlin 202" finally returned to central Berlin in 1998 following Germany's reunification, where they can be seen today at the Gemäldegalerie, Bode-Museum, and Alte Nationalgalerie.

The decision on the part of the US Army to export these paintings to the US immediately after the end of the war seems as morally dubious to us today as it did to the Monuments Men and much of the international art world that protested the action at the time. And yet it cannot be denied that the exhibition of these paintings in the United States provided the public with an exceptional opportunity. It was the first substantial showing of one of Europe's great art collections on these shores, and eager American audiences responded in force. The exhibition was visited by almost two and a half million people across the country, which means that over one and a half percent of the US population saw the Berlin paintings in 1948–49, an astonishing figure. For us the episode of the "202" thus emerges as a two-edged sword and one that resists any definitive conclusions that a moral accounting might seek to offer in hindsight.

## ACKNOWLEDGMENTS

We would like to thank the project's community support group—Shannon and Lee Carter, Marty and Nick Ragland, and Joyce and Jack Steinman—for proposing the idea of recognizing Walter Farmer and his role at the Wiesbaden Collecting Point and for providing invaluable guidance and support over the years as the project was formulated, refined, and brought to completion. Our director Cameron Kitchin saw in their suggestion the appeal, merit, and feasibility of an exhibition and publication project for the Cincinnati Art Museum. Early conversations with Robert Edsel, author of *The Monuments Men: Allied Heroes, Nazi Thieves, and the Greatest Treasure Hunt in History*, adapted as the major Hollywood movie *Monuments Men*, also offered insight into the feasibility of bringing to light this aspect of US–German history and relations. Neville Rowley has been our invaluable partner in Berlin for this exhibition and publication; we extend our sincere thanks to him for constructive dialogue that at several key points helped shape the project, for facilitating the loans from Berlin, and for contributing a key essay to the book. Curatorial Assistant Anne Buening has contributed to the project in manifold ways. We thank the Kress Foundation for supporting an Interpretive Fellow position at the Museum to help with exhibition planning and programming in the lead-up and run of the exhibition, and Kathryn Griffith, who, in filling this role, has been invaluable from her first week on the job.

We offer our deep gratitude to the two people whose lives are most deeply entwined with the history we explore—Margaret Farmer Planton, Walter and Renate Hobirk Farmer's daughter, and Ted Gantz, Walter's partner of twenty-five years—both of whom have been supportive of this project and generous with their time, memories, and archives. We have been guided throughout by Walter Farmer himself, through his memoir, *The Safekeepers*.

Special thanks go to Kristen Fleming, a Ph.D. graduate in history at the University of Cincinnati, who provided instrumental research assistance for the project, especially for Kristi Nelson's essay. It was through Juergen Czwienk that we met Tanja Bernsau in Wiesbaden and learned that she had written her dissertation on the Wiesbaden Collecting Point. We got to know Nancy Yeide at the Association of Art Museum Directors' Advanced Provenance Research Workshops, convened by Anita Difanis, where we were also able to discuss the exhibition with experts in the field. We are grateful for these fruitful connections. A special word of thanks is due to Roberto Contini, Curator at the Gemäldegalerie, Berlin, for managing the mammoth task of acquiring photos for the checklist of the "202."

It has been a delight to work with Dan Giles, who helped shape what this book offers, as well as bringing it into the world, and his team, especially Allison McCormick, Louise Ramsey, Louise Parfitt, Harry Ault, Sarah Kane, and Helen Swansbourne. We thank them for this beautiful publication.

We would like to extend our sincere appreciation to the many individuals working in archives and libraries who provided access to archival material that assisted with our research. These include Shannon Morelli, Laura Pavona, Elizabeth Walmsley, and Kathleen Williams, National Gallery of Art, Washington, DC; Melissa Bowling, Metropolitan Museum of Art, New York; Kayla Utendorf and Julie McMaster, Toledo Museum of Art; Elizabeth Tufts-Brown, Carnegie Museum of Art, Pittsburgh; Norma Sindelar, Saint Louis Art Museum; Maria R. Ketcham, Detroit Institute of Arts; Aaron Rutt, Art Institute of Chicago; Miriam Cady, Philadelphia Museum of Art; MacKenzie Mallon, The Nelson-Atkins Museum of Art, Kansas City; Beate Ebelt-Borchert, Zentralarchiv, Staatliche Museen zu Berlin; Rachael Salyer, National Archives and Records Administration, College Park; and Sim Smiley, Academic Historical Research. Our thanks also go to Matthew Shell Josephson for his translation services.

The exhibition would not have been conceivable without the participation of the Staatliche Museen zu Berlin – Preußischer Kulturbesitz, and we thank Director-General Michael Eissenhauer for supporting the loan of four of the original 202 paintings to anchor the central section of our exhibition, and curators Neville Rowley, Roberto Contini, Stephan Kemperdick, and Katja Kleinert at the Gemäldegalerie for help refining the selection of these works and presenting their collections in this publication. We thank David Alan

Brown and Gretchen Hirschauer at the National Gallery of Art and Davide Gasparotto at the J. Paul Getty Museum for recognizing the important role single paintings from each of their institutions play in the stories told here and for supporting the loans.

We thank leaders and their departments across the Cincinnati Art Museum for bringing this project in its best form to audiences in our region, including Serena Urry, Conservation; Emily Holtrop, Learning and Interpretation; Kirby Neumann, Philanthropy; and Jill Dunne, Marketing and Communications. For special praise we single out the contributions of our extraordinary Exhibitions and Collections division led by Susan Hudson: Kim Flora and her team in Installation; Lauren Walker and Victoria Karoleff, Design; Rob Deslongchamps, Photographic Services; and Jenifer Linnenberg, Registration.

**PETER JONATHAN BELL AND KRISTI A. NELSON**

# SOLD AND STOLEN: THE USE AND ABUSE OF PAINTINGS IN NAZI GERMANY AND DURING WORLD WAR II

PETER JONATHAN BELL

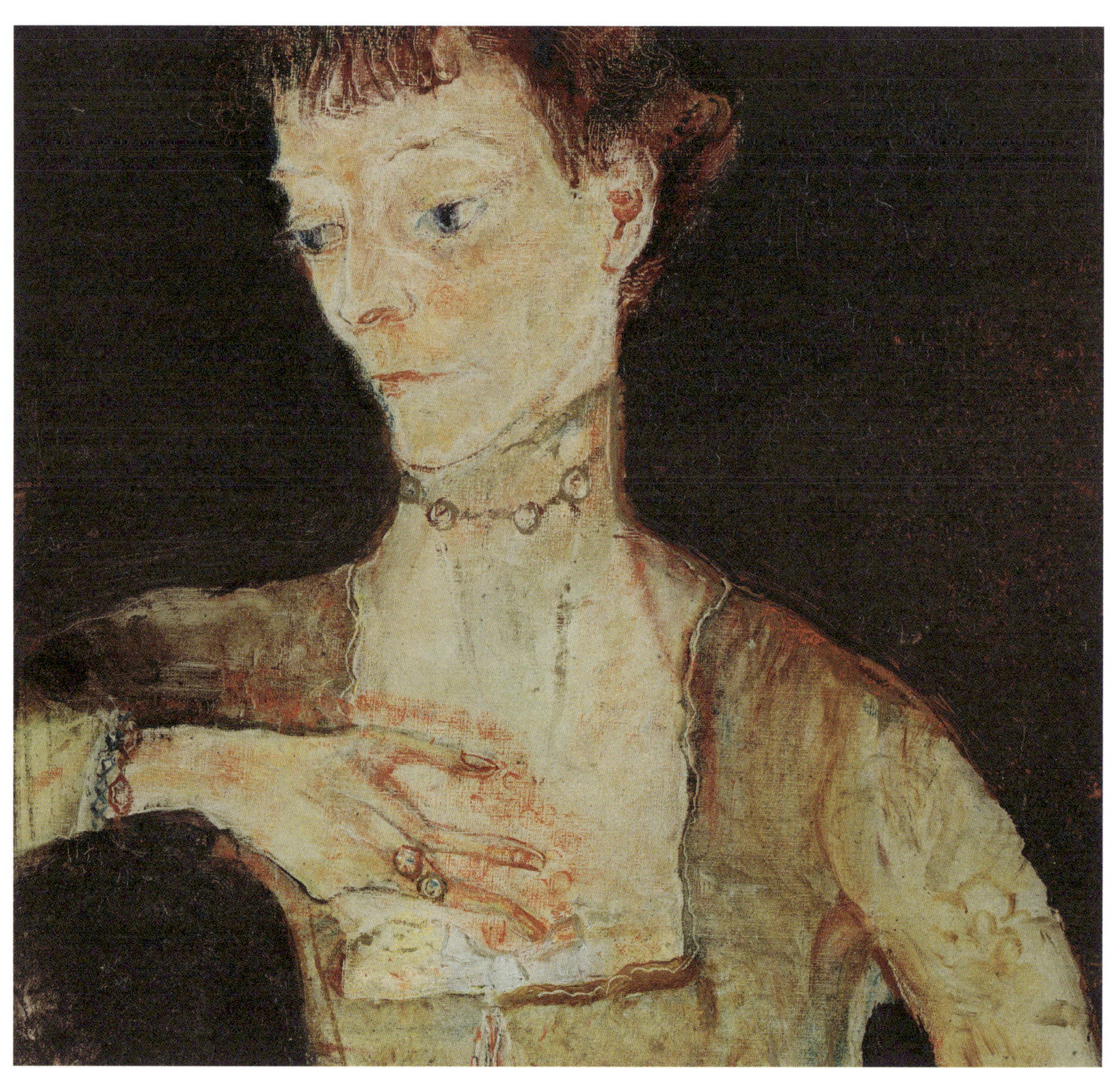

FROM EARLY IN THE NATIONAL SOCIALISTS' rise to power to the last days of World War II, cultural policy was central to Nazi ideology and artworks were used to advance the regime's larger geopolitical goals in a number of areas and through myriad tactics. As the war progressed, the tastes, ambitions, and acquisitiveness of the highest-ranking figures in the regime, Adolf Hitler and Hermann Göring foremost among them, led to the looting of artworks within Germany and occupied territories on a scale that bears no modern comparisons and has few historical precedents. Large networks of administrative bodies, groups, and individuals were involved in this state-sponsored mobilization of artworks within and without the bounds of legality and morality. The enormity and violence of the conflict, as Allied forces clawed back territory from Germany and its allies, caused destruction and displacement across areas of Europe rich in historic sites, monuments, and collections. The art history, valued possessions, and cultural identity of countless civic and religious institutions and individuals were thus scattered, compromised, or lost.

A considerable body of writing documents and analyzes different areas of impact that the Nazis and the war had on art and culture. First-hand accounts by some of the individuals most closely involved in art protection and recovery were published during and in the immediate aftermath of the war.[1] In America, the historiographical renaissance of this discipline began in the 1990s, alongside a new sensitivity to the awful variety of exploitation visited upon artworks and their owners in the 1930s and 1940s, with the Washington Conference on Holocaust-Era Assets in 1998 marking a major milestone.[2] The study of the history of artworks in the Third Reich and World War II now benefits from investigations conducted in the legal and economic spheres, as well as a plethora of new resources available to today's provenance researcher, facilitated by the organizational and distributive power of digitization and

Oskar Kokoschka (1886–1980), *The Duchess of Montesquiou-Fezensac*, 1910, oil on canvas (detail of cat. 1)

the Internet.[3] A great deal of the history of the effects of war upon artworks has been written, but its vast scale makes it difficult to offer a comprehensive treatment of the fate of art in Europe of the 1930s and 1940s.[4]

By reviewing a few strands of art ideology and commodification utilized by the Nazis and examining some case studies in greater depth, it is hoped that this essay can help position the moral and geopolitical stakes involved in the use or movement of cultural patrimony in the wake of World War II. In so doing, the goal is to offer context for the fate of the 202 paintings from Berlin in 1945 and the following years, the topic at the heart of this publication.

## MODERN ART

Actions against modern art and artists spurred by Nazi ideology reached a peak in the 1937 "Degenerate Art" exhibition, but they began as much as a decade earlier, and accelerated dramatically in 1933, when the party assumed a majority in parliament and consolidated control of Germany. The organizer of the landmark 1991 exhibition and publication on the topic summed up the situation succinctly: "The National Socialists sought to rewrite art history, to omit what we know as the avant-garde from the history of modern art."[5]

From the late 1920s, arts organizations aligned with the Nazis, including the Deutsche Kunstgesellschaft (German Art Association) and Kampfbund für deutsche Kultur (Combat League for German Culture), attacked modern art exhibitions that promoted, in their view, "corrupt art," which they contrasted with "art that was pure German, with the German soul reflecting art."[6] Abstract and expressionist art were targeted especially, as were works by Jewish artists and works or artists seen to express Bolshevism or even "Eastern European" themes. This conservative, political critique was combined with pseudo-scientific theories on artistic decadence and social decline exemplified by Max Nordau's 1892 book *Entartung* (Degeneration), which influenced Nazi ideology to a great degree. Later works on eugenics and art—Paul Schultze-Naumburg's 1928 book *Kunst und Rasse* (Art and Race), which adapted Nordau's premises—and Aryan Nordic primacy across the history of European art—Alfred Rosenberg's *Der Mythus des zwanzigsten Jahrhunderts* (The Myth of the Twentieth Century), 1930—were used to legitimize censure and seizure.[7] Critique of modern art was thus used to bolster arguments on "genetic health" and social well-being central to the nascent Nazi ideology.

Making implicit or explicit analogies between physical or mental illness and avant-garde or abstract art was a tactic with which early Nazi-sympathetic exhibition and publication makers found success in reaching a broad audience in Germany. As early as 1930, Nazi-aligned museum leaders at the regional level began systematically purging public collections of abstract art. In that year, the Schlossmuseum in Weimar moved paintings from galleries to storage and even destroyed murals by Bauhaus artist Oskar Schlemmer.[8]

When the Nazis came to power in 1933, art took a central role. Art theorist Alfred Rosenberg became the intellectual and ideological head of the party, and a range of actions in that year show the regime's deeply held belief in the power of art and its swiftness in bringing artists, professors, and museum leaders to heel. The official standing of artists who worked in avant-garde styles came under attack. For example, Oskar Kokoschka, Ernst Barlach, Käthe Kollwitz (cats. 1–3), and many other important artists were expelled from the Prussian Academy of Art, Berlin's premier arts organization. An act of parliament allowed Nazi officials to dismiss non-Aryan civil servants, which, in the cultural sector, resulted in the firing of over twenty museum directors and curators that year.[9] Artists fled. Paul Klee was pushed off the arts faculty in Düsseldorf, his home was searched by Nazis, and in December he emigrated to Switzerland. Wassily Kandinsky moved from Berlin to Paris in the same month.[10] Others were forced "underground" as they tried to continue practicing their art outside official channels, or even public notice. In Wiesbaden, for example, Alo Altripp (cat. 22) continued to paint in secret after a ban, and founded an organization, along with collector Hanna Bekker vom Rath, to provide the aging artist Alexej von Jawlensky (cat. 4) a small stipend through his last years, 1933–41.[11] Combined with earlier Nazi policies, the effects of the war could be devastating; hundreds of Jawlensky's works were destroyed in a bombing raid of Wiesbaden shortly before the end of the war.[12]

A number of so-called *Schandausstellungen* (Shame [or Abomination] Exhibitions) opened in 1933, continuing to circulate or receive new treatments through the middle years of the decade. Sometimes billed as "art chambers of horror" (*Schreckenskammern der Kunst* or *Horrorkabinetten*), they displayed art from various camps of German modern art (impressionism, social realism, expressionism, New Objectivity) as abased objects of ridicule, their makers as deficient, and the officials responsible for acquiring them with public funds as delinquent. The works were often explicitly decontextualized from art history; basic details of title and author were omitted from the display, which would instead focus on the price paid by a public institution. The press release accompanying one such exhibition, organized from the collection of the Stadtmuseum Dresden, and focusing on secessionist and expressionist artists, describes the show's goals as demonstrating "into what a morass of vulgarity, incompetence, and morbid degeneration German art—previously so lofty, pure, and noble—had sunk in fifteen years of Bolshevist Jewish intellectual domination." Through these exhibitions at regional museums, the roadmap was drawn for a "dynamically exhibitionist dramaturgy" used by the Nazis in the culmination of this cultural policy, the 1937 "Degenerate Art" exhibition.[13]

## "Degenerate Art"

In late June 1937, a commission was formed by the Nazi minister of propaganda Joseph Goebbels to "select and impound works of German art of decline since 1910 currently in the possession of the Reich, the states, and communes, from the fields of painting and sculpture, for the purposes of an exhibition [and to be labeled] degenerate art [as they] insult German sentiment or destroy or confuse natural form or obviously display a lack of sufficient craft and artistic skill in the finished product."[14]

The results of this search and seizure were trumpeted publicly as the exhibition *Entartete Kunst* (Degenerate Art), which sought to associate many schools and styles of modern art with mental and physical deficiency, moral depravity, and political and social subversion. The exhibition was first presented in Munich, opening July 19, 1937, and staged as a foil to the *Grosse Deutsche Kunstausstellung* (Great German Art Exhibition). Both exhibitions were organized by the Nazi party, the latter to showcase the strands of contemporary art sanctioned by the party—simplified figural art that was thought to exemplify the Germanic race and appealed to a conservative moral standard.[15] The combination of the two exhibitions was meant "to wipe out any hint of the modernism, Expressionism, Dada, New Objectivity, Futurism, and Cubism that had permeated the museums, galleries, journals, and press since 1910."[16]

The commission then seized another 17,500 works of art deemed similar to those exhibited in Munich, and the show was toured throughout Germany almost continuously for four years. The collections of prominent modern art museums, like the Museum Folkwang, founded and supported by the avant-garde art collector Karl Ernst Osthaus, and Kunsthalle Mannheim were particularly hard hit. In June 1939, 125 of the most valuable of these works were auctioned at Galerie Fischer in Lucerne, Switzerland.[17] During the war years, the Nazis would sell "degenerate" art abroad to raise foreign currency for the regime.

## FORCED SALES AND LOOTING

If modern art and living artists were among the early victims of Nazi cultural policies and practices, historical art became increasingly implicated as Aryanization—the systematic, forced transfer of Jewish-owned property and businesses to non-Jews—accelerated in Germany and as surrounding countries were annexed or occupied by, or capitulated to, the Nazis.

Dealers and collectors were targeted through a range of mechanisms, with the dehumanizing effects of years of institutionalized anti-Semitism and the "othering" effects that accompanied invasion, occupation, and war having lain fertile ground for these actions. Within Germany, a museum director is known to have bought looted art from the Reich for his museum.[18] Perhaps more frequently, as discussed later, museums were implicated in a gray area of morality.

Across occupied countries, old master collections were looted with particular intensity, leading to a tragic confluence of notoriety: some of the best-known prewar art collections in France and the Netherlands are now also among the best-known examples of looting. An early and well-documented case in Holland involves the stock and trade of Jacques Goudstikker (1897–1940), among the most prominent art dealers in Europe between the World Wars. Like Joseph Duveen, a generation his elder, Goudstikker's command of the market—his ability to recognize and acquire works of great rarity and importance, and to place them with collectors and institutions—made him a taste-maker and celebrity within the art world and Amsterdam high society, as well as a very successful businessman.

In May 1940, Goudstikker fled with his wife and young son to England. He had sent some paintings abroad (for example, cat. 6), but the vast majority of his stock of approximately 1,400 old master paintings remained in his Amsterdam gallery, entrusted, in an informal arrangement, along with the ongoing operation of the business, to two of his senior employees, who, not being Jewish, had less to fear from the German occupation.[19] The Goudstikkers left Holland the very day the Dutch army capitulated to the Germans, on one of the last boats to escape. With the ship completely blacked out to avoid notice by German U-boats, Jacques accidently fell through a hatch, suffering a fatal injury. With him was a black notebook documenting over one thousand of the works of art in his possession at the time of his escape from Holland.

The paintings themselves were coveted by the two most acquisitive collectors of old masters in the Reich, who were also the regime's two most powerful individuals—Adolf Hitler and Hermann Göring; Hitler, for his dreamed-of "Führermuseum" to be built in his Austrian hometown, Linz, and Göring for his own vast personal collection, most prominently displayed at his hunting estate Carinhall, northeast of Berlin. From soon after the occupation, Goudstikker's gallery was besieged by representatives of these two powerful interests. Walter Andreas Hofer (Göring's curator), Hans Posse (Hitler's curator), Kajetan Mühlmann (in charge of the Nazi authority responsible for the sale of seized Jewish property), and Alfred Rosenberg (head of the Einsatzstab Reichleiter Rosenberg, or ERR, a unit responsible for seizing art on behalf of Hitler and the Reich) were all in active pursuit. Göring himself visited the gallery within two weeks of Goudstikker's flight and death.[20]

Through a complicated arrangement, the Goudstikker firm and its stock became property of Göring and his agent, Alois Miedl.[21] Though draped in legalistic legitimacy, the "sale" of the Goudstikker stock and business was forced against the will of Goudstikker's wife and heir, through extortion of his mother, and through bribery of his principal employees.

The Nazis also scrutinized the greatest private holdings of art. The fine and decorative arts collections of the Rothschilds were targeted in several of the countries occupied by Nazi Germany.[22] Over six thousand works of art were looted from the French branches of that illustrious banking family, many intended for Hitler's Linz museum or Göring's collection.[23] These artworks included Rubens's masterful *Diana and Her Nymphs Departing for the Hunt* (fig. 1), owned by Édouard and Germaine de Rothschild and seized in 1940. It was selected by Göring in October 1942 from the depot of looted artworks set up by the ERR at the Jeu de Paume in Paris. It probably hung at his main residence, Carinhall, until spring 1945. Collected by American forces and restituted to its owners at the end of the war, the painting was later sold through a New York dealer to the Cleveland Museum of Art.[24]

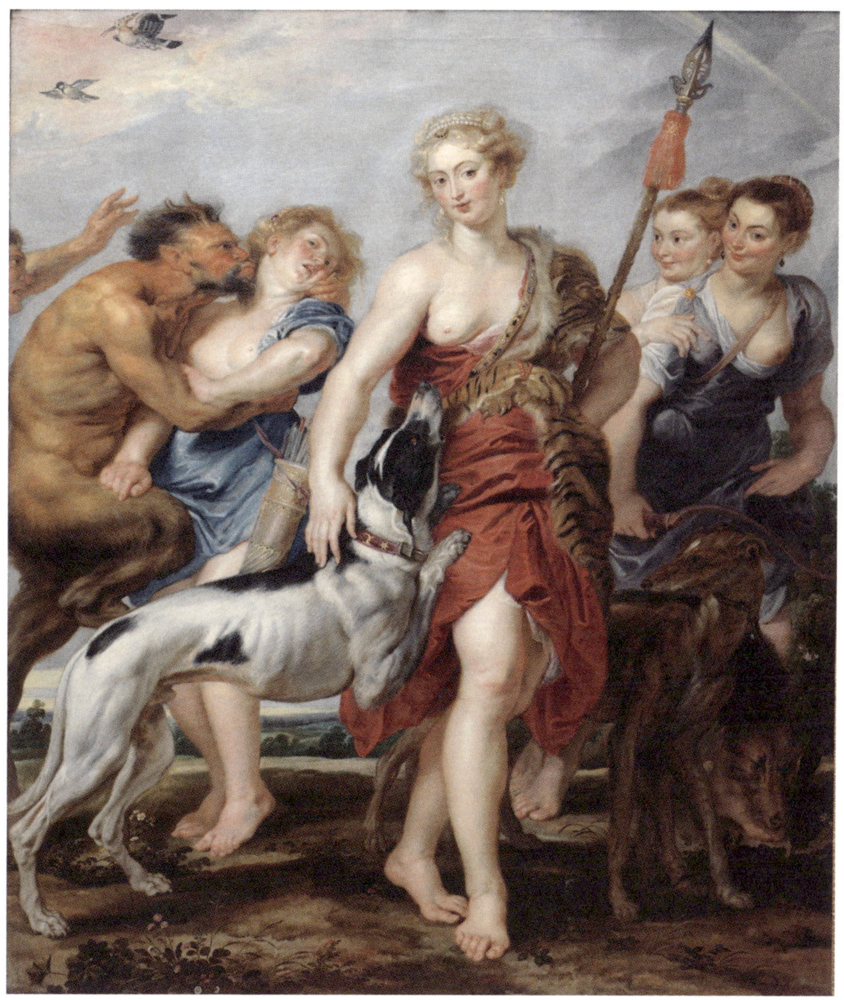

Fig. 1. Peter Paul Rubens (1577–1640), *Diana and Her Nymphs Departing for the Hunt*, circa 1615, oil on canvas, 85 1/16 × 70 3/8 in. (216 × 178.7 cm). Cleveland Museum of Art, Leonard C. Hanna, Jr. Fund, 1959.190

The Schloss collection presents another significant and illustrative case, the story of which sheds light on several of the organs of art looting active in 1940s Europe. Adolphe Schloss (1842–1910), a successful commodities broker, assembled over three hundred Dutch and Flemish paintings of the highest quality, with a particular focus on seventeenth-century masters—the greatest collection of its kind at the time. In 1939, as France became threatened by war, the collection was quietly moved from Paris to a family friend's rural estate, Chambon, in central France, where it remained hidden until the spring of 1943.[25]

The Schloss paintings were wrested from their owners through the combined and at times competing attentions of a Nazi administrative taskforce (the ERR), a high-ranking Nazi official (Göring), a division of the collaborationist Vichy government (specifically its General Commissariat for Jewish Affairs), the Nazi secret police (Gestapo, through their affiliates, the so-called Bonny-Lafont gang), and a collaborationist art dealer (Karl Haberstock). The extraordinary account of this theft is told in full elsewhere.[26] Most of the paintings were sent to Germany, and, after the war, dispersed across the art market through various avenues to museums and private collectors. Today, about half of the 333 Schloss paintings remain to be returned to heirs of Adolphe Schloss, their rightful owners.[27]

## ART MUSEUMS

The broad reach of Nazi ideology into cultural policy and the moral shift that defined the Nazi world-view had implications far and wide. Some of the most heinous practices in the art world, sketched above, include banning artists, confiscating artworks from state collections, and looting cultural property from Jewish owners. At another level, Nazi perversions of thought infected the day-to-day judgments and activities of cultural officials and governance of public museums. The effects of this, though minimal compared with the near-wholesale repudiation of modern art and the thievery of generations of beloved and valued personal property, and infinitesimal compared to the humanitarian toll of the Holocaust and the war, bear cataloguing as reminders of the pernicious potential of such a regime.

At times such practices could seem to follow naturally from precedents set in the Weimar Republic, seemingly void of prejudicial import. Such is the case for the trading of artworks by some German museums in the late 1930s. However, in those years, the practice of deaccessioning for the express purpose of acquiring other works of art (a practice very much alive in museums today) drew museum leadership into waters that seem murky through a historical-moral lens.

### Munich

In 1938 Raphael's portrait of Bindo Altoviti from the Alte Pinakothek, Munich, was traded along with two other pictures for a painting attributed to Matthias

Grünewald, recently discovered in England.[28] The British art dealer Thomas Agnew and Ernst Buchner, general director of the Bavarian State Paintings Collection, were the principal parties to this exchange. Buchner's predecessor had laid the groundwork in Munich, establishing exchange as an accepted way of refining the collections, and Buchner engaged in the practice with abandon. To appease regional cultural and finance ministries and the federal trade authorities, Buchner and Agnew found a "Swiss route" for the Munich paintings' export. In this they were aided by German dealer Hans Wendland and Swiss dealer and auctioneer Theodor Fischer, both of whom would go on to profit enormously from Nazi-confiscated and looted art in the following years. For example, at around this same time Fischer was approached by German officials to conduct the sale of "degenerate" art, which would occur in June 1939 in Lucerne.[29]

In this exchange, Buchner's role is unambiguous, but his underlying intentions can be seen in different lights. On the one hand, he was a learned scholar of early German painting, and used art exchanges repeatedly to advance that area of the Bavarian state collections, for which Grünewald was a key artist. On the other, he had an explicit understanding with Hitler about aiding the formation of the Führermuseum and reshaping the Munich paintings collection. On the one hand, he protested against the work of the "Degenerate Art" commission, succeeding in fending off to some degree their seizures of modern art from the Bavarian state collections, and fought to keep German-Jewish artist Max Liebermann's art on the walls. On the other hand, he used his access to art confiscated from Jewish owners to acquire old master works of art for his museums, acts which entailed buying the stolen art from the Gestapo.[30]

The case has been made that in this sort of exchange, Buchner was entirely focused on his own desires for the collections in his care, rather than towing a hypothetical Nazi line of systematic exchange of non-German works for German works of art.[31] Nonetheless, the episode illustrates an "increasingly Nazified world-view" in which museum leadership was heavily implicated in the 1930s and during the war years.[32] Jonathan Petropoulos adduces the alarming statistic that museum directors were among the most highly Nazified professions in the Reich, some four times the national average of ten percent party membership.[33]

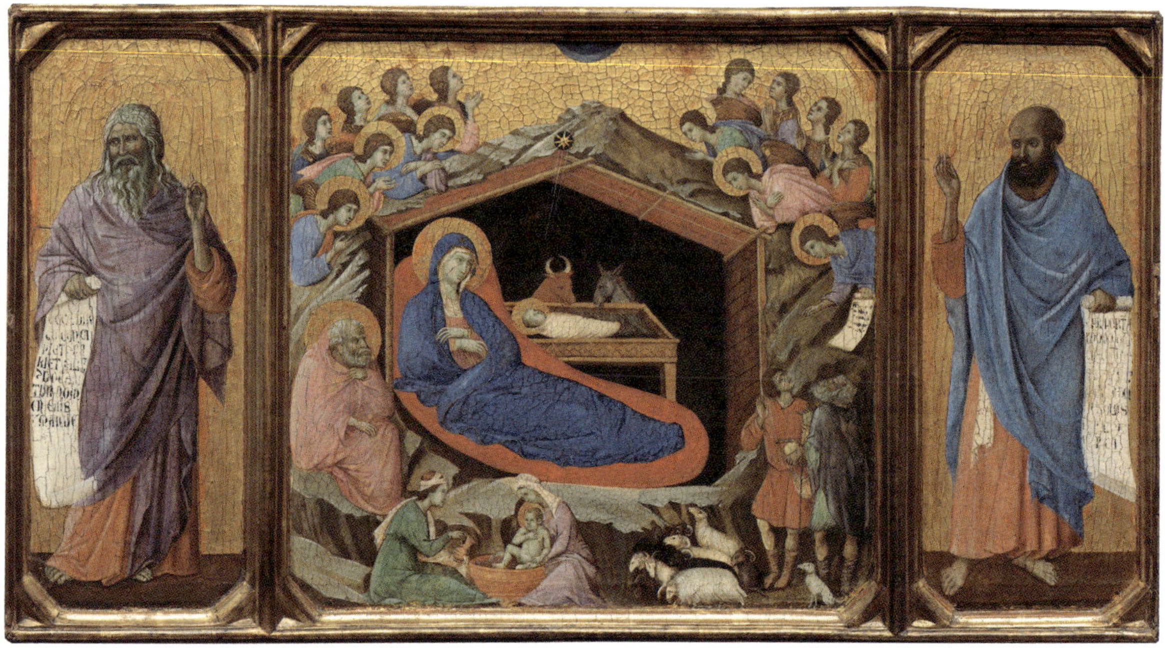

Fig. 2. Duccio di Buoninsegna (circa 1250/55–1318/19), *The Nativity with the Prophets Isaiah and Ezekiel*, 1308–11, tempera on poplar panel, overall 18⅞ × 34 1/16 in. (48 × 86.8 cm). National Gallery of Art, Washington, DC, Andrew W. Mellon Collection, 1937.1.8

## Berlin

The basic mechanism of the Grünewald–Raphael transaction, if not its multi-actor complexity, is apparent in an exchange in Berlin the previous year. A group of surviving cablegrams sketches the story of the Kaiser-Friedrich-Museum's exchange of paintings by Duccio (fig. 2) and Filippo Lippi (cat. 7) for a portrait by Hans Holbein.[34] These cables were sent in the winter and spring 1936–37 between the legendary dealer Joseph Duveen in New York and Armand Lowengard, Duveen's nephew and employee, and Edward Fowles, director of Duveen's Paris office, the latter two shuttling between Paris and Berlin.[35]

In mid-December 1936, Lowengard met with Heinrich Zimmermann, recently appointed director of the Gemäldegalerie, Berlin, who told the dealer that he was willing to exchange Italian paintings for German masterpieces.[36] Like Buchner in Munich, Zimmermann followed an established practice in the Berlin museums of paintings exchange, and built on an existing relationship with Duveen begun by his predecessor Max Friedländer.[37] A portrait attributed to Hans Holbein, the Younger had been identified for the exchange and was acquired by the dealer from the American banker and collector Henry

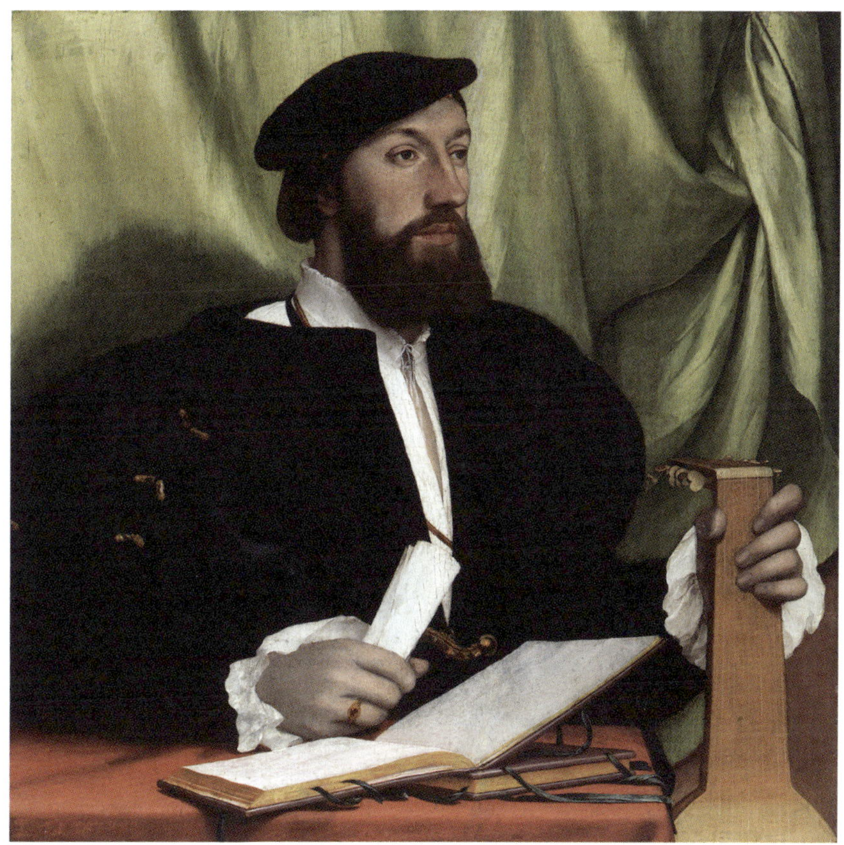

Fig. 3. Hans Holbein, the Younger (1497/98–1543), *Portrait of a Man with a Lute*, circa 1534, oil and tempera on oak panel, 17⅛ × 17⅛ in. (43.5 × 43.5 cm). Staatliche Museen zu Berlin, Gemäldegalerie, 2154

Goldman (fig. 3). The portrait was shipped to Berlin in late January 1937, and the museum was permitted to clean off its old, discolored varnish.[38]

On February 26, 1937, an official letter drafted by Duveen was dispatched from his Paris office to "The Director, Paintings Department, Kaiser-Friedrich Museum," stating the arrangement clearly:

> Dear Sir:
>
> You recently expressed a desire to obtain for the Kaiser-Friedrich Museum some great German masterpieces which by circumstance are now outside Germany. Amongst those masterpieces you mentioned particularly the HOLBEIN portrait in the Collection of Mr. Henry Goldman, New York, said to be a Portrait of Jean de Dinteville.

> We have taken up this matter diligently and can now offer you this Portrait in exchange for the following two pictures belonging to the Kaiser-Friedrich Museum, namely:-
> The Small Predella "Birth of Christ, between Two Saints", by DUCCIO DI BUONINSEGNA, No. 1062A in the Museum Catalogue;
> and
> "The Madonna and Child" by FRA FILIPPO LIPPI, No. 58 in the Museum Catalogue....[39]

The letter closes by stressing the need for confidentiality, a point made continually in discussions of the transaction within the Duveen firm.

The Gemäldegalerie advisory board approved the exchange.[40] Zimmermann subsequently relayed that the Fine Arts ministry would need to ratify the transaction, which it did in the last days of March, and the Finance ministry must have done the same in mid-April.[41] The Duccio and Lippi paintings left Europe in late April, with Duveen already expressing his intention to try to sell them to Andrew W. Mellon.[42] In the case of the Duccio, he was able to accomplish that goal handily—it seems Mellon bought it within a day or two of first seeing it.[43] Duveen sold the Lippi to Samuel H. Kress a year later.[44]

A cabled list of paintings and valuations in early March 1939, less than three months before his death and only six months before Germany invaded Poland, points to Duveen's continued efforts to pry old masters out of the Berlin state collections, and presumably his willingness to do business with state organs of Nazi Germany.[45]

The timeline of movements of this small sample of artworks affected by Nazi policy and World War II bears consideration. The "Degenerate Art" exhibition opened in Munich less than three months after the Berlin Museums' transaction with Duveen; three years after that, Goudstikker fled and died and his firm was forcibly sold; two years later, Göring was browsing the Jeu de Paume for stolen paintings from the Rothschild and Schloss collections; and two years after that the collections of the Berlin Museums were discovered by the US Army in a Thuringian salt mine, beginning the journey of the "202" that is detailed in the following pages. It is small wonder, given the intensity of art transactions under the Nazis, that the movement of these paintings after the war's end engendered controversy and ignited imaginations and passions on two continents.

NOTES

1. See, for example, Mihan 1944, Hammond 1946, and Howe 1946.
2. This historiography is described by Nancy Yeide in this volume, pp. 107–9. Groundbreaking publications of that decade include Barron 1991a; Nicholas 1994; Petropoulos 1996; Simpson 1997; Feliciano 1997.
3. See Nancy Yeide's essay in this volume.
4. Attempts continue to be made, most recently Mary Lane's *Hitler's Last Hostages* (2019), although Lynn Nicholas's *The Rape of Europa* (1994) is perhaps most successful in expressing both the scope and insidious day-to-day details of the multipronged Nazi campaign on art.
5. Barron 1991b, p. 18.
6. Barron 1991b, p. 11; see also Peters 2014b, p. 22.
7. Barron 1991b, p. 12; Peters 2014b, p. 25; Nicholas 1994, p. 8.
8. Peters 2014b, pp. 26–27.
9. Barron 1991b, p. 9.
10. Barron 1991a, pp. 264, 280.
11. "Jawlensky Gesellschaft": Mochon 1991, p. 34.
12. Letters exchanged between the Cincinnati Art Museum and Jawlensky's son; Curatorial files, Cincinnati Art Museum.
13. Zuschlag 1991, pp. 84–85.
14. Lüttichau 2014, p. 37.
15. Mosse 1991, p. 25. "National Socialism annexed neoromantic and neoclassical art, defining it as racially pure…."
16. Barron 1991b, p. 18.
17. Barron 1991c.
18. See below, note 30.
19. Shendar and Goldberg 2008, pp. 38–39; den Hollander and Müller 2009, p. 224.
20. Shendar and Goldberg 2008, p. 47.
21. See cat. 6, p. 134.
22. Members of the fourth generation of the family bore the brunt of Nazi looting. For analysis, see Feliciano 1997, pp. 43–51, and Karlsgodt 2011, pp. 214–27.
23. See https://www.errproject.org/, collection 'R'.
24. The painting's provenance is extensively documented on the website of the Cleveland Museum of Art: https://www.clevelandart.org/art/1959.190.
25. Édouard and Germaine de Rothschild also attempted to protect their collection by moving it to a property outside Paris.
26. Karlsgodt 2011, pp. 218–27; see also cat. 5, p. 132.
27. Schloss collection website.
28. David Alan Brown and Jane Van Nimmen have rivetingly described the circumstances that surrounded this episode; Brown and Van Nimmen 2005, esp. pp. 133–54.
29. Brown and Van Nimmen 2005, p. 144; see also above, note 17 and cat. 1, p. 124.
30. Petropoulos 2000, pp. 24–32.
31. Brown and Van Nimmen 2005, p. 147.
32. Petropoulos 2000, p. 33.
33. Petropoulos 2000, p. 14.
34. The cables are preserved in the Duveen Brothers records, held in the Special Collections of the Getty Research Institute, and available online through their website: https://www.getty.edu/research/tools/guides_bibliographies/duveen/.
35. In a particularly evocative message, Duveen threatens to fire both of these most relied-upon associates for not responding quickly enough to his cables; Duveen Brothers records, Kaiser Friedrich Museum folder [026].
36. Copy of December 15 telegram; Duveen Brothers records, Kaiser Friedrich Museum folder [014].
37. A November 17, 1931 letter within the firm discusses a visit to Berlin and frank discussion with Friedländer about what paintings in the museum might appeal to the American market, and thus be ripe for sale or trade; Duveen Brothers records, Kaiser Friedrich Museum folder [004]. Two examples now in the National Gallery of Art illustrate the regular practice of deaccessioning to build the Berlin collections in the 1920s and 1930s: Vittore Carpaccio's *Flight into Egypt* (1937.1.28) and a fifteenth-century bronze statuette of *Fortuna* (1957.14.9) left the Kaiser-Friedrich-Museum's collections in 1924 and 1935, respectively.
38. Copy of December 15 telegram; Duveen Brothers records, Kaiser Friedrich Museum folder [022 and 025].
39. Duveen Brothers records, Kaiser Friedrich Museum folder [035]; for the letter from Duveen Brothers to Berlin proposing the exchange, now preserved in the Central Archive of the Staatliche Museen zu Berlin, see Winter 2013, p. 273.
40. Winter 2013, p. 274.
41. Duveen Brothers records, Kaiser Friedrich Museum folder [040].
42. Duveen Brothers records, Kaiser Friedrich Museum folder [041].
43. A Duveen Paris-to-New York cable of April 9 states that the paintings cannot leave before April 21; Duveen Brothers records, Kaiser Friedrich Museum folder [040]. The Mellon Trust purchased the painting on April 26, a date confirmed by Mellon collection records in the NGA curatorial file and David Finley's notebook in the NGA archives.
44. The first published mention of the Berlin–Duveen episode may be by art restorer Helmut Ruhemann, who attributed the Duccio's selection for deaccessioning to Zimmermann's misinterpretation of Ruhemann's earlier conservation treatment, which aimed to make areas of retouching visible; Ruhemann 1968, p. 41.
45. Duveen Brothers records, Kaiser Friedrich Museum folder [043]. For Hans Wendland, see [042].

# THE MOVEMENTS OF THE "202"

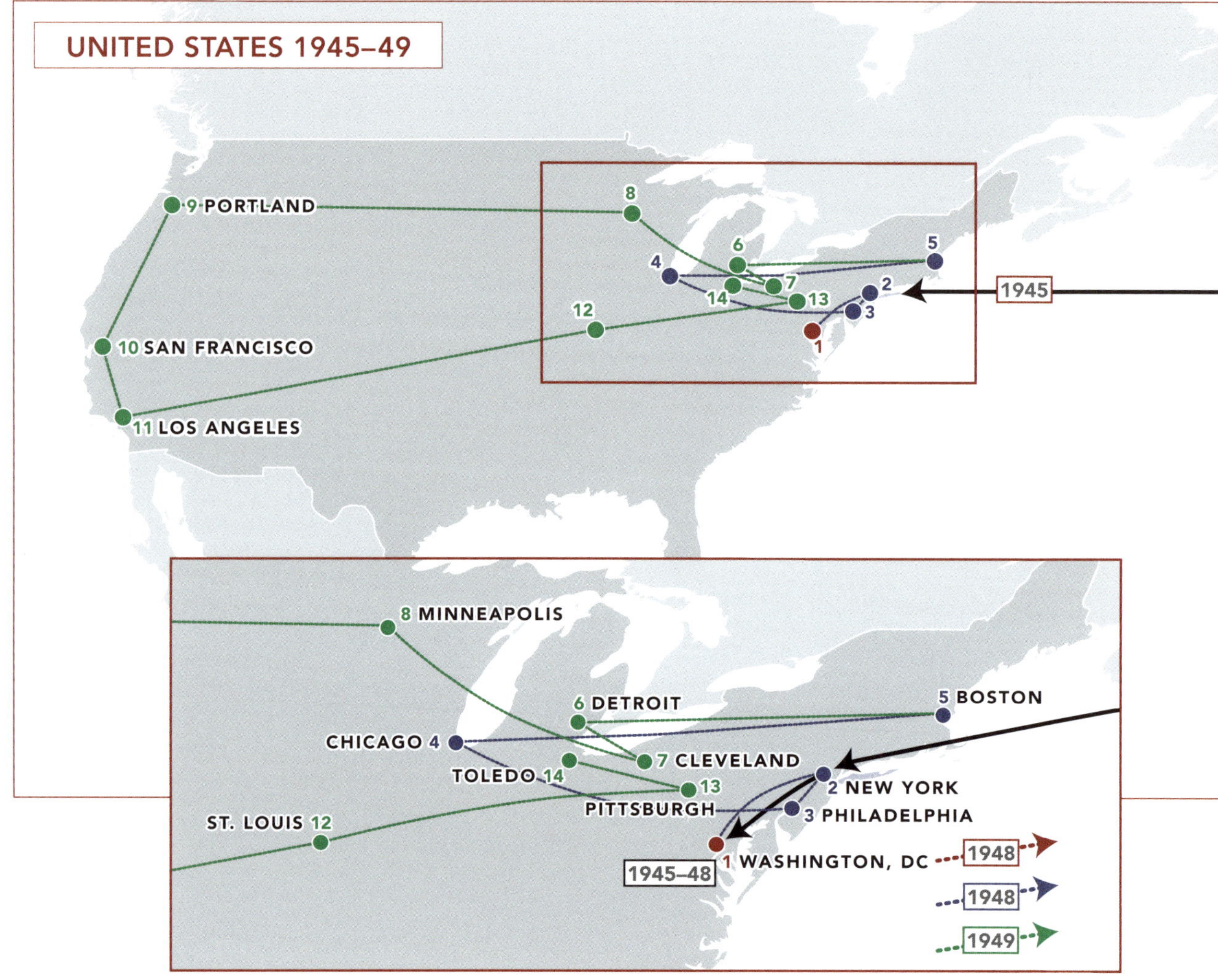


The "202" arrived in December 1945 and remained in storage until March 1948, when they were exhibited at the National Gallery of Art, and then embarked on a national tour. 53 paintings returned to Wiesbaden after Washington, DC, 52 after Boston, and the remaining 97 after the final exhibition in Toledo (see Nelson, pp. 52–71).

The Berlin Museums' collections were evacuated to salt mines near Merkers for safekeeping in March 1945. They were discovered by the US Third Army in April and moved first to Frankfurt and then to the Wiesbaden Central Collecting Point. In late November, 202 paintings were shipped to the US, sailing from Le Havre to New York (see Bernsau, pp. 32–51).

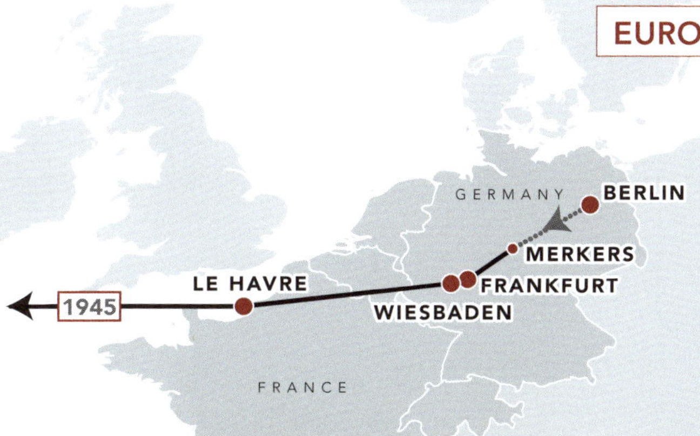


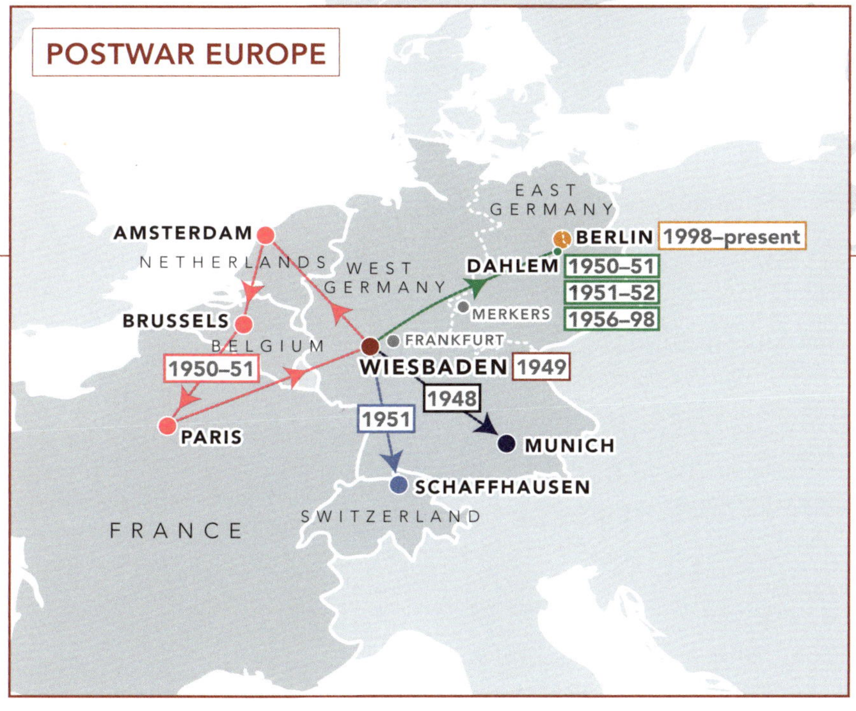


After their US sojourn, the "202" were exhibited in Wiesbaden, and many traveled for exhibitions across western Europe between 1948 and 1952. In 1956, they were transferred to their new home in divided Berlin, a museum building in Dahlem, remaining there until 1998, when they finally returned to central Berlin (see Rowley, pp. 72–93).

# WALTER FARMER AND THE CENTRAL COLLECTING POINT IN WIESBADEN

TANJA BERNSAU

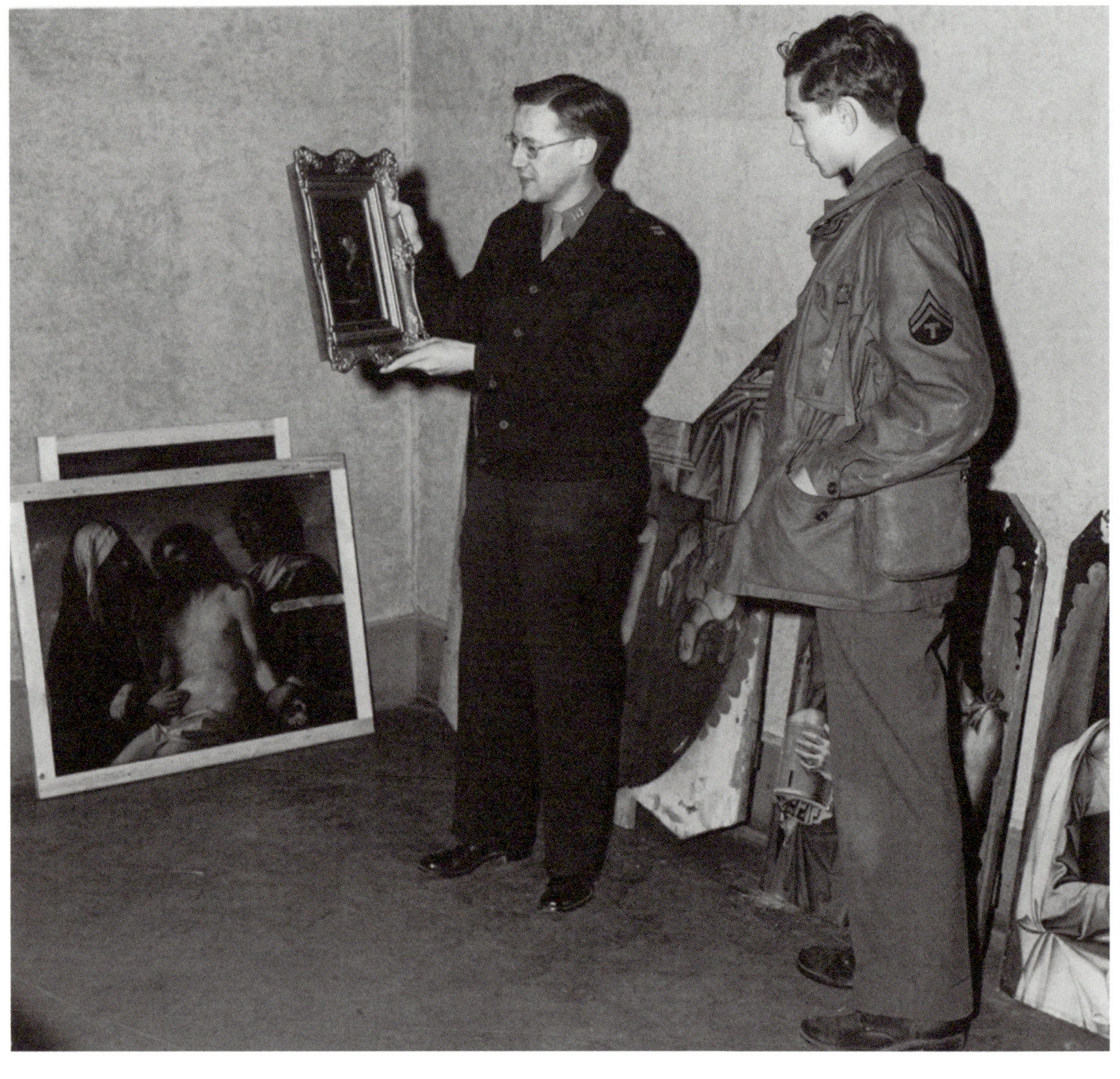

THE TRAGIC TOLL OF THE Second World War was more than sixty million deaths, countless cities in Europe largely destroyed by air raids from either side, and many millions hurt or displaced. The inhumanity of the war and the terror of the Nazi regime caused incredible suffering for millions of Europeans. When the war was over, conditions remained very difficult: bombed out, driven from their homes, facing food shortages, and often separated from their families, the majority of people struggled to meet basic needs.

Given the gravity of this humanitarian crisis, it might therefore seem strange to quibble over the protection of artistic and cultural patrimony. And yet the war also had a tremendous cost in terms of the loss, theft, displacement of, and damage to cultural heritage. The air raids destroyed architectural monuments, and archives and museums were emptied for their own protection, their contents moved to safer locations for storage. It can be said without exaggeration that, by the end of the Second World War, hardly a painting remained where it had hung in 1933.

After the war, about 700,000 of these displaced artworks were kept in the halls of the State Museum of Wiesbaden. While Wiesbaden had been a popular destination for European nobility and the well-to-do in the nineteenth century, it lost its cultural and economic prestige after the First World War. During the Second World War, this turned out to be an advantage: the provincial town was deemed strategically unimportant because it lacked heavy industry, and it sustained much less damage from air raids than other cities. In turn, because it was comparatively undamaged at the end of the war, Wiesbaden would become a storehouse of unclaimed artistic and cultural objects.

Fig. 1. Walter Farmer holding a painting at the Wiesbaden Central Collecting Point. Kenneth C. Lindsay Papers, Special Collections, Binghamton University Libraries, Binghamton University, State University of New York

This was part of the work of the "Monuments Men," an Anglo-American military unit tasked with preserving European cultural patrimony from destruction in the Second World War. A few years ago, the unit's story was made into a feature film starring George Clooney. But the story of the Monuments Men as a military institution does not end with the end of the war, as it does in the film. Arguably, the art protection unit's most important achievements concern the establishment of the Collection Points during the postwar occupation period.

## THE MONUMENTS, FINE ARTS, AND ARCHIVES SECTION

The Monuments Men, as officers from the Monuments, Fine Arts, and Archives section were known, were responsible for the preservation of artistic and cultural patrimony during the Second World War. The unit had its origins in the efforts of United States museum professionals to plan protective measures for American museum collections after the attack on Pearl Harbor. Their ideas about preventing the destruction of artwork were soon exported to Europe. On August 20, 1943, the American Commission for the Protection and Salvage of Artistic and Historic Monuments in War Areas was created. It would be known as the Roberts Commission, after its chairman, Supreme Court Justice Owen J. Roberts.[1]

As a civilian organization, the Roberts Commission had limited scope in wartime. When the Allies planned their invasion of Europe, this issue was remedied with the creation of the Monuments, Fine Arts, and Archives section (MFAA), established as a collaboration between the United States and Great Britain. From the early days of the war, concern was raised that a great deal of art would be looted and stolen in Europe, in addition to the destruction of architectural monuments. When the war was over, the rightful owners of stolen objects would have to be identified. The art protection officers established so-called Central Collecting Points (CCPs) in Marburg, Munich, Offenbach, and Wiesbaden to make it possible to organize the vast numbers of displaced artworks. The CCPs were created because of the need to move objects from the various places where they were found, which were less than optimal for their conservation, to a central repository where they could be accounted for while decisions were made about their conservation and how they were to be returned to their rightful owners.

## THE WIESBADEN COLLECTING POINT AT THE STATE MUSEUM

The history of the Wiesbaden Central Collecting Point begins in the salt mines of Merkers, Thuringia, where the Germans moved the collections of the Berlin State Museums for their protection shortly before the end of the war (fig. 2). When Allied troops discovered the artworks in 1945, officials considered a transfer to the nearby Reichsbank in Frankfurt, because the conditions in the mines were detrimental to the artworks.[2]

The Frankfurt Reichsbank building, where the US Third Army was headquartered, could safely house the artworks alongside the Reichsbank gold, which also was found in Merkers.[3] The artworks arrived on twenty-six ten-ton trucks on April 17, 1945. However, the bank vaults would not be suitable as a long-term art storage facility.[4] The sheer number of art objects made proper storage and the additional work of drawing up an inventory, plus conservation and possible restoration, not to mention restitution, impossible.[5] The artworks would have to find a new home once more.

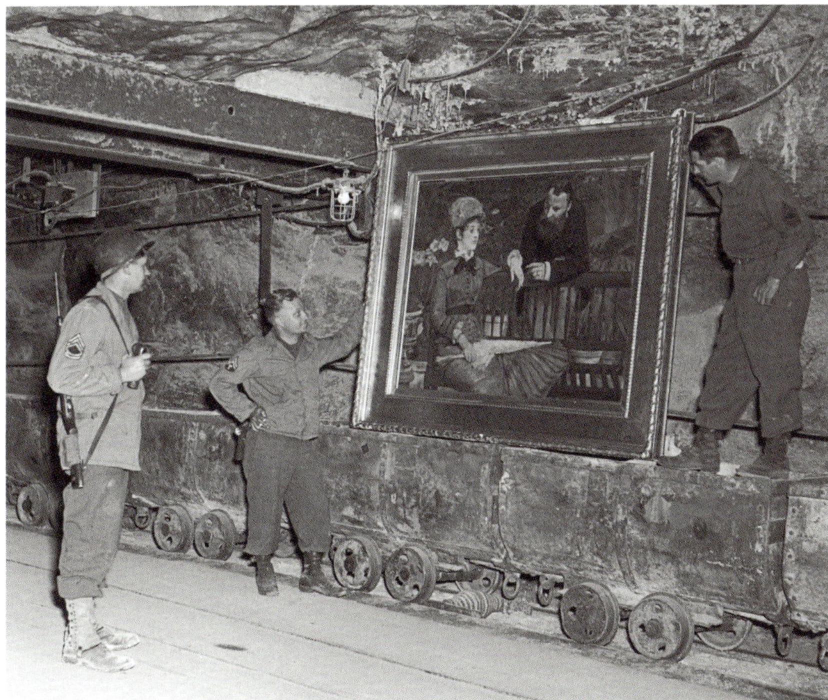

Fig. 2. Members of the US Third Army discover Édouard Manet's *The Winter Garden* in the salt mines at Merkers, April 25, 1945. Photograph No. 111-SC-203453-5, Box 261, Army Signal Corps, Record Group 111, National Archives at College Park, College Park, MD

At this point, Captain Walter I. Farmer, an architect by training, began his service as an art protection officer and was instructed to prepare the State Museum in the neighboring city of Wiesbaden to serve as a storage facility. When Farmer started on this assignment as director of the CCP in June 1945, his first task must have been to clear the building. During the war, the Luftwaffe had used the museum as a machine shop.[6] After the end of hostilities, it served as lodgings for displaced persons (DPs) and a base for various American military units, including a special unit of the US Twelfth Army that set up a clothing warehouse in the halls of the museum.[7] After clearing the building, Farmer's next priority would have been to restore and rebuild it: most windows, doors, and skylights had been destroyed by nearby detonations, and the roof had also been seriously compromised by the construction of German anti-aircraft gun emplacements.[8]

Time was short. The restoration had to be completed by August 15, 1945, when the first transports were expected to arrive from Frankfurt. The shortage of construction materials in the aftermath of the war made the task more difficult. But Farmer was able to meet the deadline by salvaging the necessary materials, such as window panes and barbed wire, from abandoned buildings. He was working under immense pressure to restore the building, convinced of the importance of his assignment. In a letter to his wife, he wrote:

> We are building a new world and want to carry over from the old everything that is good. . . . Nothing can stop my work. I'm constantly on my feet, and yet it seems to me as if it was progressing at a snail's pace.[9]

In his monthly report on his work at the Wiesbaden CCP, dated August 3, 1945, Farmer described his progress in restoring the building: two-thirds

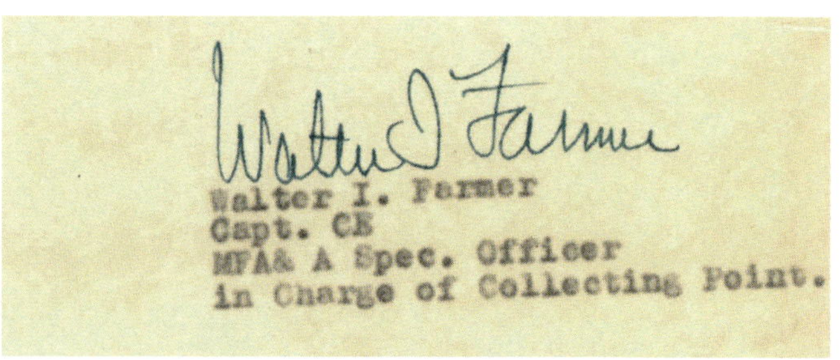
Walter I. Farmer
Capt. CE
MFA& A Spec. Officer
in Charge of Collecting Point.

Fig. 3. Walter Farmer's signature from the Monuments, Fine Arts, and Archives Status of Collecting Point report, August 3, 1945. General Records, 1945–1952, Box 67, A1 492, Records of US Occupation Headquarters, Record Group 260, National Archives at College Park, College Park, MD

U. S. GROUP, CONTROL COUNCIL
(GERMANY)
REPARATION, DELIVERIES AND RESTITUTION DIVISION
APO 742

ECR/ejb

7 August 1945.

SUBJECT: Reallocation of Custodianship of Objects Specified Herein at Present in the Reichsbank, Frankfurt a/M.

TO : Whomever itmay Concern.

I hereby direct that the custodianship of the works of art and other objects in my charge in the Reichsbank in Frankfurt a/M and listed as Inclosure 1 be transferred from the MFA&A Branch, US Group CC, represented by Lt. Col. HAMMOND and Capt E. C. RAE, to the MFA&A Subsection, RD&R Section, Economics Branch, G-5 Division, USFET, represented by Major L. B. LaFARGE and Lt. C. L. KUHN (USNR).

L. W. JEFFERSON
Colonel, GSC
Director.

1 Incl - List

Fig. 4. Letter from Col. L. W. Jefferson transferring responsibility for artworks to Maj. L. B. LaFarge and Lt. C. L. Kuhn, August 7, 1945. General Records, 1945–1952, Box 67, A1 492, Records of US Occupation Headquarters, Record Group 260, National Archives at College Park, College Park, MD

of the windows had been replaced; repairs to the roof would be completed in the next ten days; the heating would be on again within weeks; necessary piping work would be completed within the week; and one of the two elevators was already in service (fig. 3). In addition to the restoration of the building, security measures for the artworks were being put in place. The CCP was initially protected by three American and three German guards, plus a night watchman, which was more than Farmer's superiors required.[10] The whole building was surrounded by a barbed wire fence, and searchlights were used after nightfall. There was only one entrance, and no one was allowed to access the building without authorization from the director.[11]

On August 7, custodianship of the artworks was officially transferred within the US occupation government, as part of the preparations for their shipment to Wiesbaden (fig. 4). When the CCP began to receive art objects from Frankfurt on August 20, 1945, seventy-six of the State Museum's galleries had been restored and were ready for use.[12]

## WESTWARD HO! – PRESERVATION OF CULTURAL PATRIMONY, OR SPOILS OF WAR?

The American occupying forces took great care to protect German artistic patrimony in occupied Germany. However, one action taken by the US Army undermined and seemed to contradict this approach: the decision in 1945 to transport a selection of artworks from Wiesbaden to the United States. This operation, which was dubbed "Westward Ho!"—borrowing the cliché of westward expansion in the continental United States—had the unpleasant flavor of treating art as spoils of war. The Monuments Men and other American art specialists protested loudly.

### Preparations in the USA and in Germany

The plan for Operation "Westward Ho" was developed during the war. As early as March 1945, General Lucius D. Clay mentioned that he would like to bring the German state collections to the United States. At this point, the Allies had only a vague idea of the number of artworks they would find, where they were located, their storage requirements, or the state of Germany's museums. Concrete plans could not be made until the war was over.[13]

After the invasions of Italy and France, the Allies must have had a clearer idea of the quantity and quality of artworks they would encounter. A report from US Group Control Council Headquarters of July 1945 described American plans for handling works of art found in the occupied territories.[14] First, a system of classification was developed for art objects based on their provenance:

- Class A Art Objects: works of art taken by the Germans from territories they occupied which originated in public collections or were stolen from private hands without their owners receiving compensation.
- Class B Art Objects: works of art taken by the Germans from private owners in occupied territories who did receive compensation.
- Class C Art Objects: works of art that had been stored in the US Zone for their protection and were bona fide German state property.[15]

This report deemed the storage facilities in Germany to be extremely unsuitable, as neither trained personnel nor adequate storage was available.[16] The report therefore proposed that Germany's artworks be transported to a

Fig. 5. A representative from the Netherlands at the Wiesbaden CCP with paintings looted from Holland, April 26, 1946. 260-WAE-50, Photographs of Activities and Exhibits, Records Concerning the Central Collecting Points ("Ardelia Hall Collection"): Wiesbaden Central Collecting Point, 1945–1952, Records of US Occupation Headquarters, Record Group 260, National Archives at College Park, College Park, MD

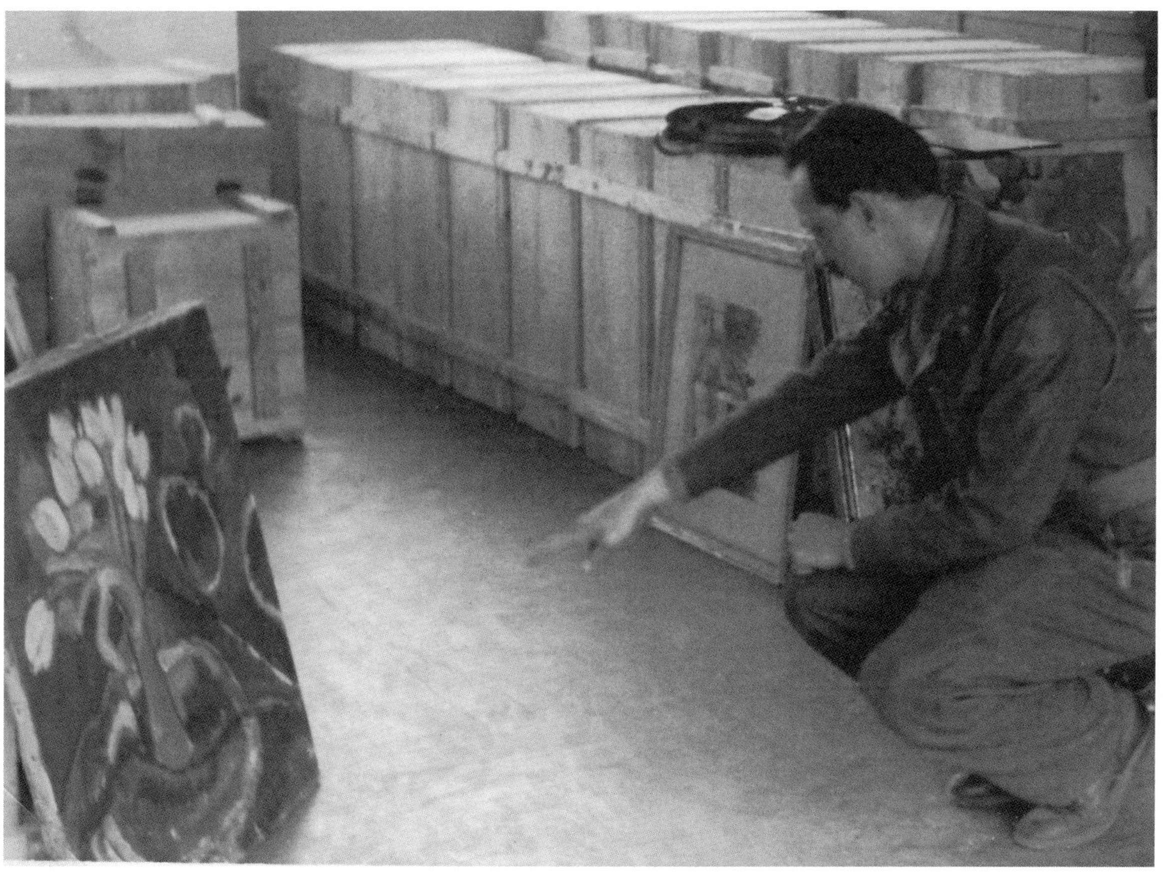

location where the proper personnel could inventory, identify, and provide adequate care for them as soon as possible. There was no question that Class A artworks should be returned to their owners (fig. 5). Class B artworks were to be returned to their countries of origin, where their ownership status would be investigated. The report stated that Class C artworks should not be taken as reparations for war damage, divided between a great number of nations. Instead, they should be placed under United States control for safekeeping, and be returned to Germany after a few years. This led to the recommendation that these artworks be brought to the United States.[17]

At this point, the Americans still had no clear idea how many Class C artworks there were, or where they were stored in Germany. John Nicholas Brown, a cultural advisor to the White House and Monuments Officer, spoke out within the administration and military in August 1945, against the plans to remove the Class C artworks. He argued in detail that the question of ownership was not clearly settled, since not all German museums were state-owned, and thus not all works of art were the property of the German State. In contrast to the report of July 1945, Brown considered storage conditions to be adequate in terms of personnel and buildings. His report gave the Monuments Men particularly high marks for their knowledge of art and museum practices, and noted that shipping all these art objects represented a greater risk than leaving them in Germany. He went on to write that because of the enormous number of artworks, which reached the tens of thousands, it was impossible to consider removing them all to the United States for inventory, identification, and safekeeping. This meant that a selection would have to be made, and, as a result, the artworks would have to be researched and identified in Germany. The situation was further complicated, Brown writes, by the works of art stored in the US Zone belonging to institutions located in the other occupation zones. Removing them could endanger relations with the other Allies. Brown argued that the removal of German cultural patrimony from the country would be viewed with mistrust and disapproval by the Germans and the other Allies; it would arouse the suspicion that the works of art were being treated as spoils of war. Finally, many works of art labeled Class C were in fact church property, and thus should not be removed.[18]

With regard to the Wiesbaden Central Collecting Point, the argument that storage conditions were inadequate cannot be taken seriously from an objective point of view. True, a significant proportion of German museum buildings had been damaged during the war, and storage conditions in the CCPs were initially far from ideal. For example some photographs and film, as well as paintings, had to be stored without protective boxes, stacked one on top of another as the work of identification took place at the Central Collecting Points in Wiesbaden and Munich (fig. 6).[19] But in Wiesbaden, Farmer and his team were making great efforts to store the artworks entrusted to them according to the best professional practice.[20]

The argument that personnel was insufficient is also untenable. It is true that a significant number of Germany's art specialists were unemployable because of denazification. However, Farmer was able to find suitable personnel in Wiesbaden quite early on—research specialists, restorers, photographers, and typists.[21] Furthermore, in Farmer's own case as director of the CCP, it was

Fig. 6. Paintings in storage at the Wiesbaden Central Collecting Point: part of a shipment of approximately 1,000 looted household furnishings and objects identified as French, April 24, 1946. 260-WAE-51, Photographs of Activities and Exhibits, Records Concerning the Central Collecting Points ("Ardelia Hall Collection"): Wiesbaden Central Collecting Point, 1945–1952, Records of US Occupation Headquarters, Record Group 260, National Archives at College Park, College Park, MD

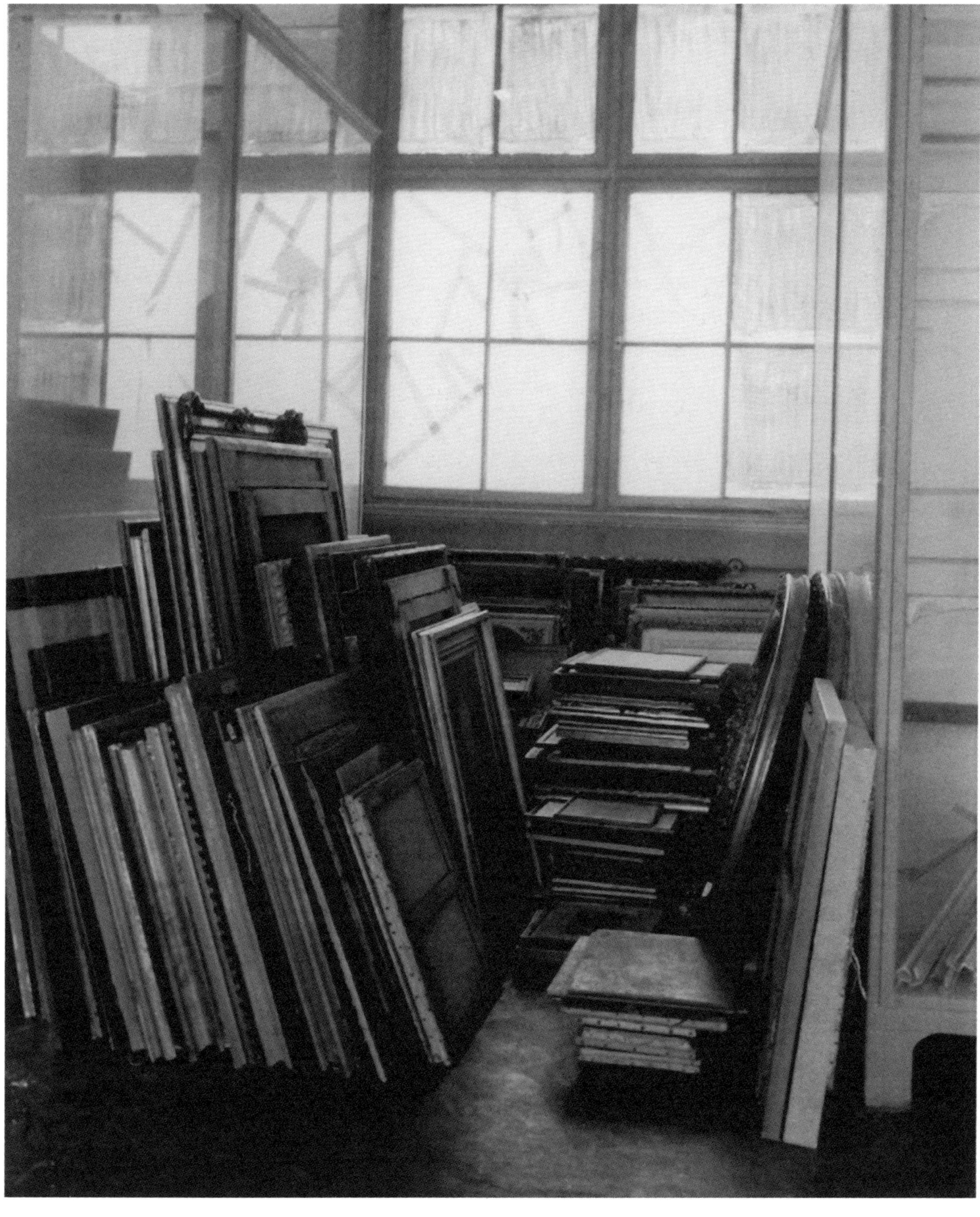

his commitment and enthusiasm for his work that allowed him to complete the task, rather than his professional qualifications.[22]

In October 1945, the American military government sent Colonel Harry A. McBride to Wiesbaden to report on the conditions and holdings of the art storage facility.[23] At this time, it seems that General Clay was planning a first shipment of 200 paintings:

> Col McBride arrived 1 November and left for Frankfurt Saturday to make selections of paintings to be moved and check plans made for this movement prior to his arrival. Unable to contact him today. Estimate at least 200 paintings can be moved within a month, if proper shipping space can be obtained. Will cable more details when Col McBride can be reached on Monday.[24]

Colonel McBride inspected the Central Collecting Point in Wiesbaden in person in early November 1945.[25] He was not convinced by Farmer's efforts to make the Wiesbaden CCP a safe art storage facility. In his account of the visit in a later essay, Farmer expressed astonishment that his work was unsatisfactory to the inspecting colonel. In retrospect, Farmer guessed that McBride's report was designed to show the CCP in a poor light in order to justify the removal of the artworks to the United States.[26] Farmer's collaborator Sergeant Kenneth Lindsay also later wrote that McBride interpreted his findings according to the goal he had in mind: for example, the museum staff had set up water receptacles in the exhibition halls to maintain a certain level of humidity, but McBride explained their presence the other way around. In his report on the state of the CCPs, the water receptacles were described as vessels to catch rainwater from a leaking roof, and given as proof that the building was unsuitable for art storage.[27]

On November 6, 1945, shortly after McBride's visit to the Collecting Point, General Clay issued the following official request for the immediate shipment of two hundred paintings to the National Gallery of Art, Washington, DC, for safekeeping:

> Take immediate steps to select, pack and ship to port 200 paintings for safekeeping at national gallery in confirmation of telephone discussion of Lt Col HARRIS this Headquarters with Col MC BRIDE. Also arrange with TSFET shipping allocation from whatever port they deem proper.[28]

The message about the planned shipment reached the Collecting Point in Wiesbaden the same day, in the form of a telegram from the US Seventh Army. Provisions were to be made as quickly as possible to ship "a selection of at least two zero zero german works of art of greatest importance" to the United States.[29] Second Lieutenant Lamont Moore was informed ten days later that he would be in charge of the shipment.[30] In a memorandum on his preparations, Moore reported that on November 6 he met in Frankfurt with Colonel McBride and Commander Keith Merrill, who was supposed to help him plan the shipment. On November 7 the three men drove to the CCP in Wiesbaden to make arrangements with Farmer and Captain James Rorimer. Two German Red Cross railway cars were made available for transport. Guards accompanied the artworks on trucks to Frankfurt, where they were loaded onto the railway cars. The shipment continued to Le Havre by rail, where the artworks were brought on board the troopship *James Parker*, which would carry them to New York.[31]

This operation stands in opposition to the principles of the MFAA on the protection of cultural patrimony, since they had been established to protect patrimonial objects on behalf of the nations to which they belonged. Treating art as the spoils of war was alien to that project. As a result, Farmer felt obliged to take action.

## The Wiesbaden Manifesto

In his memoir, Walter Farmer described his feeling of shock as he read the telegram about the removal of the artworks:

> Reading the telegram I collapsed into my chair and broke into tears. . . . My outrage was so personal because . . . I had been developing such good relations with Dr. Ernst Holzinger, Frau Dr. Schoppa, Frau Flinsch and other German museum professionals who were profoundly grateful for the work that was being done to preserve their national heritage. . . . A mockery was being made of our entire operation. Not only was there no need to "safeguard" these paintings in the United States, but in transporting them on the open seas in the dead of winter these panel paintings and canvases would be exposed to the most pernicious climatic conditions that one could imagine.[32]

For Farmer, this decision immediately brought to mind the *modus operandi* of the Einsatzstab Reichsleiter Rosenberg (ERR), a Nazi taskforce which had justified looting as the "preservation of abandoned cultural patrimony."[33] A memorandum written in November 1945, likely by Farmer, documented his stance toward the plan. It stated reasons why the removal should not go forward: transferring the artworks, which originally came from other occupation zones, could annoy other Allies and damage the reputation of the MFAA and its work in Germany, and the shipment could only endanger or do physical harm to the works of art.[34]

As Farmer reports, on November 6, immediately upon receiving the telegram containing the removal order, he summoned his MFAA colleagues to take action against the decision.[35] The seizure order also met with almost unanimous resistance from the other American art protection officers; they responded to Farmer's call and met in Wiesbaden on November 7, 1945. That meeting produced the document that would come to be known as the Wiesbaden Manifesto. Signatories included twenty-four art protection officers with an additional eight officers who expressed support for the protest. The manifesto vehemently opposed the removal of the artworks, stating that, as German cultural patrimony, the art should not be removed from Germany:

> We are unanimously agreed that the transportation of these works of art, undertaken by the United States Army, upon direction from the highest national authority, establishes a precedent which is neither morally tenable nor trustworthy. . . . We wish to state that from our own knowledge, no historical grievance will rankle so long, or be the cause of so much justified bitterness, as the removal, for any reason, of a part of the heritage of any nation, even if that heritage may be interpreted as a prize of war.[36]

Since the Monuments Men were military officers, this letter has to be understood as a kind of insubordination, which could have led to a court martial.[37] But since the letter never reached its addressees, the signatories never faced court martial and were able to keep their assignments. As an intervention by officers within the US Army on behalf of German cultural patrimony, the Wiesbaden Manifesto had absolutely no effect. Kenneth Lindsay later mentioned that the manifesto was kept by Major Bancel LaFarge, the Monuments Men's superior officer, to protect the signatories until they had been discharged from military service and returned to their civilian occupations.[38]

It is clear that the manifesto has become more important in retrospect than it was at the time. Most of the scholarship on the manifesto has been published recently, long after the document itself was written. This literature often glorifies the manifesto, facilely portraying it as a revolt by the Monuments Men against their superior officers, which it was not. Furthermore, there is a discrepancy between the chronological sequence and the way the story is often presented: McBride and Lamont Moore conducted their inspection in Wiesbaden in early November 1945 (probably on the 5th). The telegram to Farmer about the removal arrived on November 6. Farmer reported that he summoned the art protection officers to Wiesbaden the following day. His colleagues were working in a variety of locations all over Europe, most in the field, which is to say that they were traveling and could not have been reached at short notice, even by telephone. Travel was also quite complicated during this period, and it is unlikely that they could all have reached Wiesbaden in one day. It is, therefore, possible, and this author's opinion, that the manifesto was backdated in order to emphasize the speed of Farmer's response.

Even if the manifesto did not reach MFAA superior officers, it is still a testament to the posture of the Monuments Men towards "Operation Westward Ho," and it did not go unnoticed. Its early effects were felt first back in the United States, in civilian spheres. The Wiesbaden Manifesto quickly became public knowledge through the work of journalist Janet Flanner, among others. Flanner visited Wiesbaden in November and reported on the situation in *The New Yorker* on November 17, 1945.[39] In her later publication *Men and Monuments*, about the art protection officers' protest, Flanner wrote that some Monuments Men had even asked to be transferred so that they would not have to comply with the removal order.[40]

The officers' stance was supported by an article written by fellow Monuments officer Lieutenant Commander Charles Kuhn in January 1946, which also stated in print that the American art protection officers disapproved of the operation.[41]

Since the Wiesbaden Manifesto and related protest did not prevent the removal of the "202," the artworks would soon begin their long journey.[42]

## FARMER'S WORK IN WIESBADEN

### Protecting Cultural Patrimony

Walter Farmer did not stay long in Wiesbaden. In March 1946, he handed the CCP director's baton to his successor, Captain Edith A. Standen (fig. 7). But in only a few months (June 1945 to March 1946) he had been able to accomplish a great deal. Under his watch, the Wiesbaden Central Collecting Point was established and many artworks that came to Wiesbaden from the surrounding area were received and safely stored.

Each individual work of art was inventoried by CCP staff, which means they were recorded on index cards in triplicate, their condition assessed, and carefully restored if necessary. CCP staff members made every effort to research the provenance of each object and return works of art to their rightful owners, which they succeeded in doing for the majority of the works in their care. At the end of the American occupation, the Hessian Trust took control of the artworks whose owners could not be identified. A number of these objects now remain in the care of the German Federal Government, identified as "remaining stock of the CCP," and administered through the Federal Office for Central Services and Unresolved Property Issues (Bundesamt für zentrale Dienste und offene Vermögensfragen).

### Art in the Ruins

It was Walter Famer's initiative to mount the first art exhibition at the Central Collecting Point. After he had spoken out in vain against the removal of the "202," he was especially concerned to show the citizens of Wiesbaden and his German colleagues and staff that the Monuments Men were taking meticulous care with the many artworks that remained. Furthermore, according to his memoir, Farmer felt that an exhibition in the CCP's own halls would foster a spirit of cooperation with the German museum staff.

> Morale at the Collecting Point was very low after the departure of the 202. To, in some way, redeem our honor and to reassure the German people that significant art treasures remained in Germany, I put my staff to work arranging an exhibition.[43]

Fig. 7. Edith A. Standen and Rose Valland with Kenneth Lindsay at the Wiesbaden Central Collecting Point. 260-WAE-48, Photographs of Activities and Exhibits, Records Concerning the Central Collecting Points ("Ardelia Hall Collection"): Wiesbaden Central Collecting Point, 1945–1952, Records of US Occupation Headquarters, Record Group 260, National Archives at College Park, College Park, MD

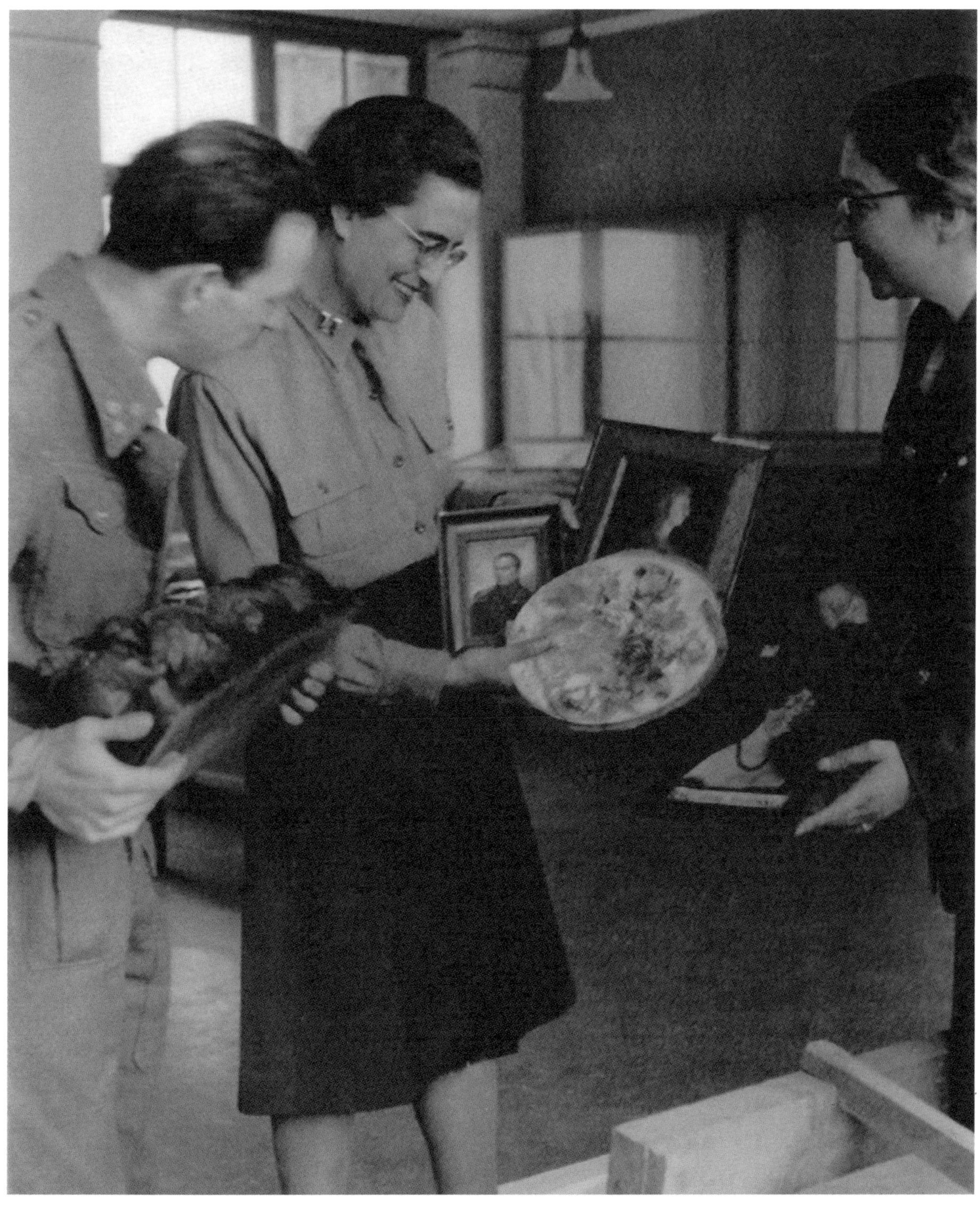

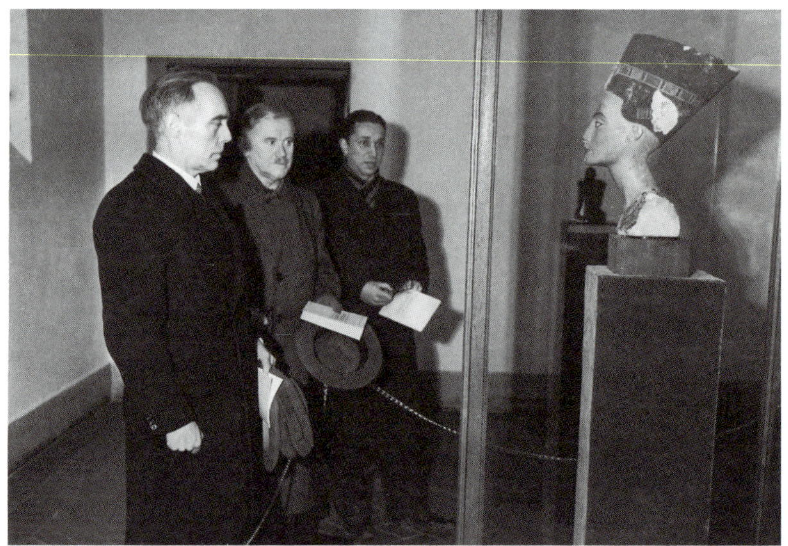

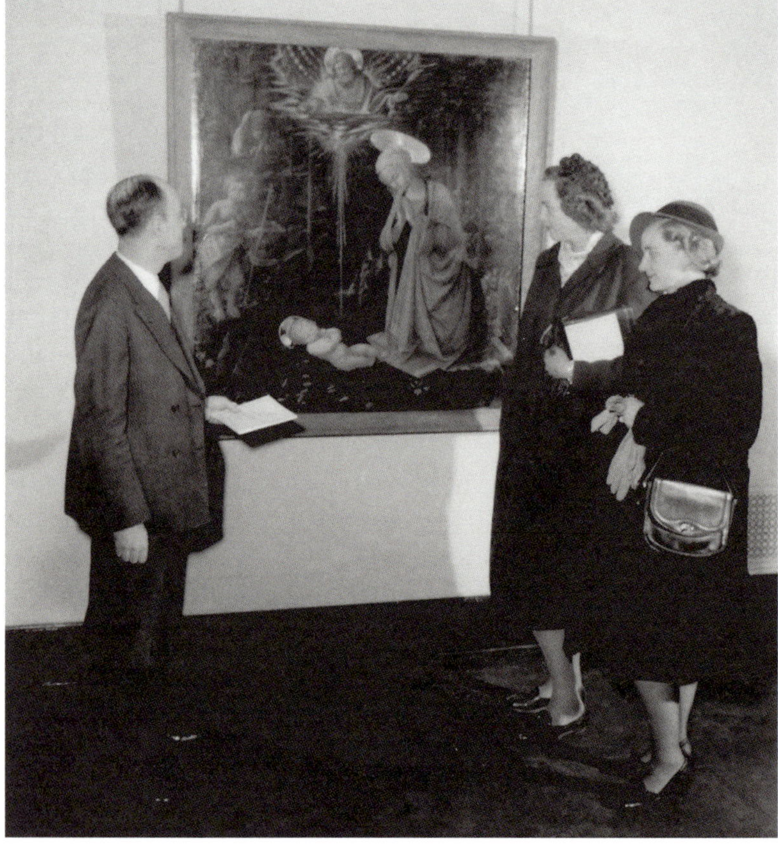

Fig. 8. Exhibition of German-owned works of art held at the Wiesbaden Central Collecting Point, February 1946. National Gallery of Art, Washington, DC, Gallery Archives, 28MFAA-C7_13788_01

Fig. 9. Theodore Heinrich, a later director of the Wiesbaden Collecting Point, explains the painting *The Madonna Adoring the Christ Child* by Lippi to Princess Hubertus of Prussia and Princess Wittgenstein during an exhibition at the Wiesbaden Central Collecting Point. Photograph No. 111-SC-310539, Box 643, folder 4626, Army Signal Corps, Record Group 111, National Archives at College Park, College Park, MD

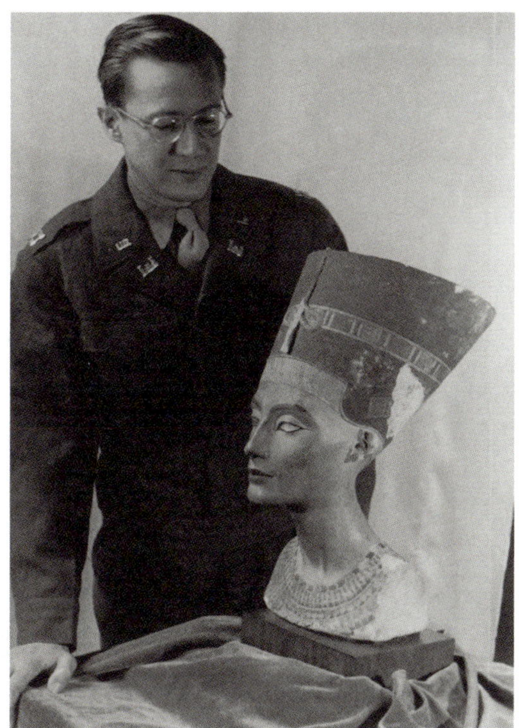

Fig. 10. Walter Farmer with the bust of Nefertiti from the Neues Museum, Berlin. National Gallery of Art, Washington, DC, Gallery Archives, 28MFAA-C, Walter Farmer Papers

The *Exhibition of German-Owned Old Masters*, which included eighty-nine paintings, grew out of Farmer's consideration of this issue. A total of 63,196 visitors attended the exhibition during the short time that it was open, from February 12 to April 23, 1946. It soon became clear that the most popular item on display was the bust of Nefertiti (fig. 8), which would be shown in all subsequent exhibitions at the CCP even when it did not fit the exhibition's theme. Later exhibitions also presented thematic displays of works from the CCP stock. These made it possible for the citizens of Wiesbaden to see high-quality artworks from a variety of German collections in the early postwar days (fig. 9).

## Supporting Contemporary German Art

Although the CCP exhibitions focused on old masters, Farmer also cultivated a personal interest in contemporary art. Since there were very few contemporary art pieces among those that he and his team handled, it was essentially a private pursuit for his own pleasure. However, Farmer made considerable efforts on behalf of the Wiesbaden artist Alo Altripp. He had become acquainted with Altripp through his work at the CCP, where Altripp worked as a draftsman, assisting with the registration and inventory of the stock. In return, he received a room in the museum for use as his studio. Farmer visited him there, and Altripp introduced him to contemporary art, for which he had no previous affinity. According to Farmer's recollection, Altripp had been persecuted as a "degenerate" artist during the Nazi period, which is why he felt a sort of duty to make amends by supporting the artist.[44] Farmer bought some of Altripp's works and arranged exhibitions and sales for the artist in the United States upon his return. As Farmer learned about contemporary art, he also became acquainted with the work of Alexej von Jawlensky, and even planned an exhibition of some of his paintings which were also stored at the CCP—however, the exhibition did not come to fruition during Farmer's time in Wiesbaden.[45]

Farmer's efforts at the Wiesbaden Central Collecting Point fostered the relationship of the local citizenry with the occupying American army. Just as important, if not more so, was his work setting the groundwork for the return of German artworks to their original museums, which aided the reconstruction of the German museum world after the Second World War. Due to his and the other Monuments Men's efforts, many artworks returned to their previous owners—private persons as well as museums. This afforded the German people the opportunity to experience art and culture after the terrors of the Third Reich and the war, and was an important part of the re-education process.

NOTES

Essay translated by Matthew Shell Josephson.

1. For the establishment of the Roberts Commission and the Monuments, Fine Arts, and Archives section, see Bernsau 2013 and Edsel 2009.
2. "United States Forces European Theater: Monthly Report on Monuments, Fine Arts, and Archives May–June 1945," a report by Leslie W. Jefferson [Chief R&D Section] to the Assistant Chief of Staff, July 10, 1945, NARA, M1947, Roll 54.
3. Zulauf 1995, p. 146.
4. Farmer 2000, p. 31.
5. Zulauf 1995, p. 146.
6. Farmer 2000, p. 29.
7. Nicholas 1994, p. 376.
8. Farmer 1996, p. 94.
9. Hildebrand 1995, p. 28.
10. Monuments, Fine Arts, and Archives Status of Collecting Point report of August 3, 1945 to "Commanding General, Western Military District APO 758, US Army," in the folder Reports: Monthly Reports, May 1945–Nov. 1945, NARA, M1947, Roll 15.
11. "Wiesbaden Collecting Point, Wiesbaden, Germany: History. Wiesbaden Collection Point 13th of July 1945–5th of March 1946" (undated report), p. 5, NARA, M1947, Roll 14. The report

is archived without an author's name, but Farmer mentions in his memoirs that he published a report with this title at the end of his term; cf. Farmer 2000, p. 27 (note 1).

12. Hildebrand 1989; Farmer 2000, p. 46.
13. Kuhn 1946, p. 78.
14. "Art Objects in US Zone," undated report from the headquarters of the US Group Control Council, in the folder Shipment of Works of Art to the United States ("202"), July 1945–October 1946, NARA, M1947, Roll 70; the report bears no date, but refers to a memorandum dated July 30, 1945 on the report which was filed after it in the archive, such that a creation date of July 30 can be assumed (cf. memorandum from Edwin Pauley and W. L. Clayton to General Clay, in the folder Shipment of Works of Art to the United States ("202"), July 1945–October 1946, NARA, M1947, Roll 70).
15. "Art Objects in US Zone," undated report from the headquarters of the US Group Control Council, in the folder Shipment of Works of Art to the United States ("202"), July 1945–October 1946, NARA, M1947, Roll 70.
16. Ibid.
17. Ibid.
18. John Nicholas Brown, Advisor on Cultural Matters, "Comments on Document 'Art Objects in US Zone,' transmitted by C of S to Col. Jefferson, RD&R Division, US Group CC, under date 29 July 1945, to Deputy Military Governor, US Group CC (Germany)," of August 9, 1945, in the folder Shipment of Works of Art to the United States ("202"), July 1945–October 1946, NARA, M1947, Roll 70.
19. For interesting images of storage in the Wiesbaden CCP, see the 3Sat documentary "Die 434 oder das Geheimnis des Bunkers." Eighth part of a documentary series for the "Jahrhundertprojekt Museumsinsel," ZDF History, May 11, 2008; for the Munich CCP, see Edsel 2009, p. 212.
20. A letter from Colonel L. W. Jefferson dated September 24, 1945 confirms that the majority of the artworks could remain in suitable storage and that their safekeeping under German supervision was guaranteed. However, a final review of all Collecting Points was still in progress; reply to cable on "Removal of German-owned Art (The following is submitted as a draft reply to the cable from Mr. McCloy W-66436 to the Deputy Military Governor)," dated September 24, 1945, in the folder Shipment of Works of Art to the United States ("202"), July 1945–October 1946, NARA, M1947, Roll 70.
21. Kuhn 1946, p. 81. Lindsay also questioned the argument that there was a lack of personnel. See Lindsay 1998, p. 127.
22. He described himself in this way: "I was not a 'museum man.' I was an engineer with a lively interest in art history." Farmer 1996, p. 93; see also Lindsay 1998, p. 91ff. and 116ff.
23. Message from "AGWAR from Hilldring to OMGGUS [sic] for Clay Personal, Oct. 1945," in the folder Shipment of Works of Art to the United States ("202"), July 1945–October 1946, NARA, M1947, Roll 70.
24. Communication from "OMGUS signed Clay" to "AGWAR for WARCAD for Clay," dated November 5, 1945, in the folder Shipment of Works of Art to the United States ("202"), July 1945–October 1946, NARA, M1947, Roll 70.
25. The dates of McBride's visit to the Wiesbaden CCP cannot be precisely reconstructed. The telegram was received by Clay, who confirms that McBride arrived in Frankfurt on November 1. Unfortunately, no report from McBride on his inspection has been preserved. In a memorandum of October 19, 1945, however, the removal of the works of art is already a closed matter – perhaps after his inspection McBride merely gave the "green light" by telegraph rather than producing a detailed report; see Colonel Raymond Marsh's "Memorandum to Deputy Director of Military Government (US Zone): Removal of German Works of Art to the United States," dated October 19, 1945, in the folder Shipment of Works of Art to the United States ("202"), July 1945–October 1946," NARA, M1947, Roll 70.
26. Farmer 1997, p. 132.
27. Lindsay 1998, p. 126; according to Lindsay, the fuel shortage reported by McBride, the inadequacy of security measures, and the lack of suitable personnel were also not accurate.
28. Communication from "Office of Mil Gov for Germany (US Restitution Branch Economics Division signed Clay 'Shipment of Paintings to US' for action: Office of Mil Gov (US Zone)," dated November 6, 1945, in the folder Shipment of Works of Art to the United States ("202"), July 1945–October 1946," NARA, M1947, Roll 70.
29. Farmer 2000, p. 56.
30. Communication from Colonel M. C. Bauer: "Movement of Paintings to Washington," to 2nd Lieutenant Lamont Moore, November 16, 1945, in the folder Shipment of Works of Art to the United States ("202"), July 1945–October 1946, NARA, M1947, Roll 70.
31. Memorandum from 2nd Lieutenant Lamont Moore: "Report on Shipment of Paintings," to CG Civil Affairs Division, War Department, Washington, DC, December 14, 1945, in the folder Shipment of Works of Art to the United States ("202"), July 1945–October 1946, NARA, M1947, Roll 70.
32. Farmer 2000, p. 57.
33. Koop 2006, p. 82.
34. "Shipping Works of Art to the US," undated and unsigned memorandum in the folder Shipment of Works of Art to the United States ("202"), July 1945–October 1946 (chronologically sorted November 1945), NARA, M1947, Roll 70.
35. Farmer 1997, p. 133.
36. Wiesbaden Manifesto, November 7, 1945, printed in Farmer 2000, pp. 147–52.
37. See also Goldmann 1997, p. 7ff.
38. Lindsay 1998, p. 123.
39. This is the last part of a three-part series of articles dealing with the theme of looted art, Collecting Points, and the Monuments Men; see Flanner 1947, pp. 38–55.
40. Flanner 1957, p. 288ff.
41. Kuhn 1946.
42. See essay by Kristi Nelson, pp. 52–71.
43. Farmer 1996, p. 105.
44. Altripp was not prohibited from painting during the Nazi era, but was drafted into military service and was not active as an artist during this period; Museum Wiesbaden 1988, p. 8.
45. Farmer 2000, pp. 40–43.

# MAKING ART HISTORY: THE MASTERPIECES' POSTWAR TOUR

KRISTI A. NELSON

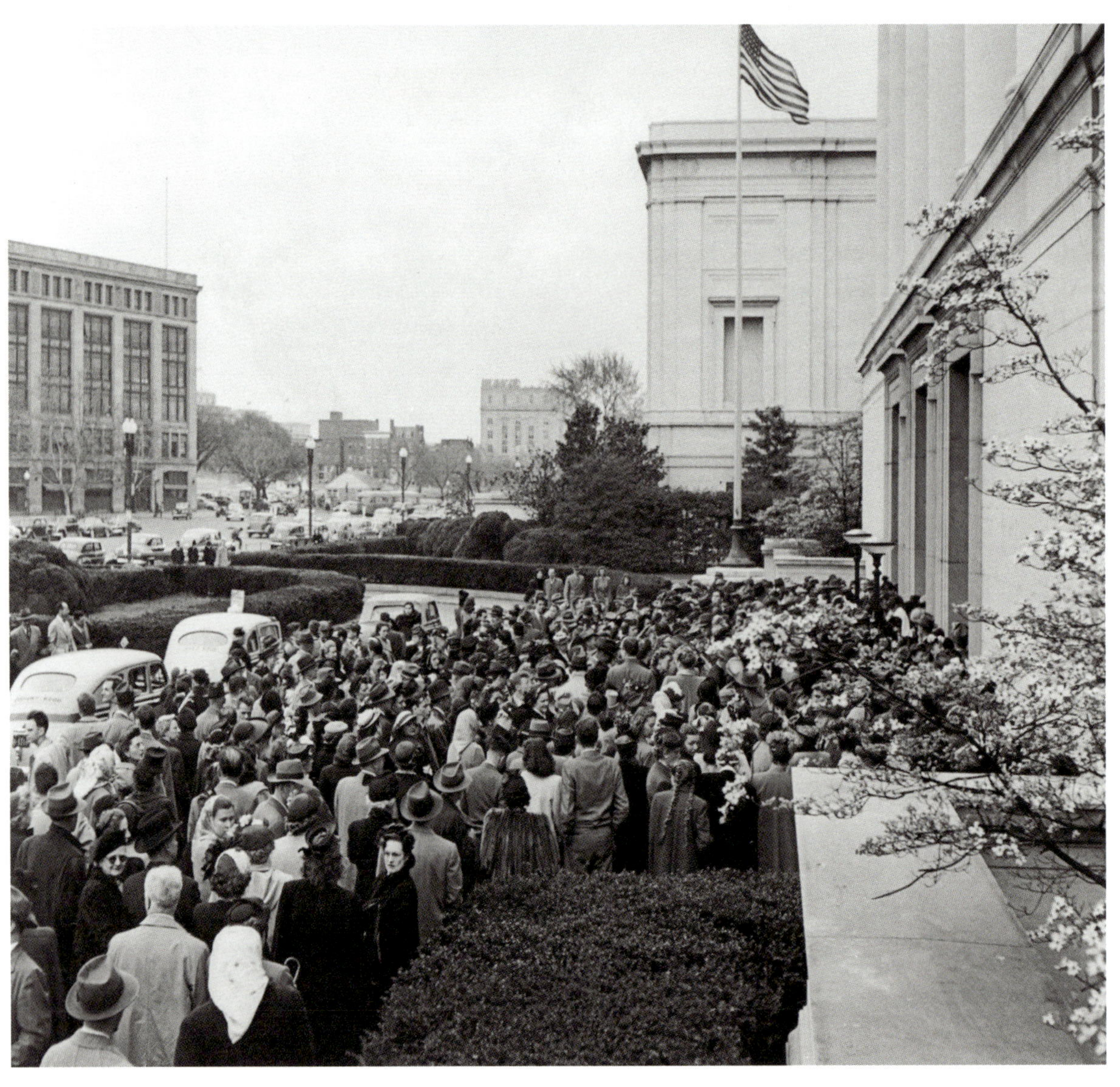

*Painting, like music, speaks a universal language.*
*We need no interpreter for our communication with the*
*artist of another time and another tongue.*

Dr. Blake-More Godwin[1]

On September 26, 1945, in the aftermath of World War II, the White House announced plans to bring German artworks to the United States. Under the assumption that neither expert personnel nor adequate facilities were available in postwar Germany, this move apparently had the "sole intention of keeping such treasures safe and in trust for the people of Germany or other rightful owners."[2]

The National Gallery of Art, Washington, DC, founded only eight years earlier, agreed to house the works and quickly made plans for the move. John Walker, chief curator, asked staff to prepare a list of Germany's top masterpieces, while administrator Colonel Harry A. McBride agreed to travel to Germany to organize the transfer.[3] Meanwhile, many in the art world opposed the decision, or hoped it would never come to fruition.

Nevertheless, on November 6, 1945, Cincinnatian Walter Ings Farmer, director of the Wiesbaden Central Collecting Point (CCP), received a hand-delivered telegram from Seventh Army Headquarters ordering that "immediate preparations be made for prompt shipment to the US of a selection of at least 200 German works of art of greatest importance." He was tremendously upset by this command and protested that such action would make the US "no better than the Nazis." With other Monuments, Fine Arts, and Archives (MFAA) officers in Europe, he drafted and signed the Wiesbaden Manifesto, which called for the masterpieces to remain in Germany.[4]

Fig. 1. Crowds waiting outside the National Gallery of Art for the exhibition *Paintings from the Berlin Museums* (March 17–April 25, 1948). National Gallery of Art, Washington, DC, Gallery Archives, 26B4_29_001

Despite Farmer's efforts and the Wiesbaden Manifesto, Colonel McBride arrived in Wiesbaden in early November. Piecing different accounts together, we can deduce that ultimately the decision was made to ship a selection of paintings housed in Wiesbaden only (not implicating other CCPs), with the final selection made by McBride and Lamont Moore, who had worked as a curator at the National Gallery of Art before enlisting.[5] Thus, the National Gallery's list of paintings was supplemented with additional choices, bringing the total to 202. All were from state collections in Berlin: two hundred from the Kaiser-Friedrich-Museum and two from the Nationalgalerie. These masterpieces—representing six centuries of art history—were not artworks confiscated by the Nazis, but had been discovered by the US Third Army in the Kaiseroda salt mines at Merkers (Bernsau, fig. 2). The selection included superior paintings of diverse subject matter dating from the thirteenth century (Giotto) to the late nineteenth century (Édouard Manet), among them five paintings by Van Eyck, fifteen by Rembrandt, six by Frans Hals, five by Titian, three by Raphael, two by Vermeer, six by Rubens, eight by Masaccio, a Caravaggio, a Fouquet and more: a roll call of major old master artists from across Europe. The works were on canvas and panel, ranging in size from Orazio Gentileschi's *Landscape with Saint Christopher* (BR 62, as Adam Elsheimer) at 8¼ inches tall to Carpaccio's *Preparation of Christ's Tomb* (BR 35), over six feet wide.[6]

## WESTWARD HO, WATTEAU!

Moore, who was familiar with museum protocols from his prior work at the National Gallery of Art, attentively supervised the packing of the masterpieces and personally escorted them to Washington, DC. The operation received the code name *Westward Ho!*, to which Farmer and his team added the alliterative name *Watteau*, the eighteenth-century French artist represented by three lovely canvases among the "202," including *The French Comedians* (BR 190; cat. 11).[7] Between November 12 and 17, the artworks were packed in forty-five cases. They left Wiesbaden on the 19th and traveled by train through Frankfurt to Paris, arriving in Le Havre on the 21st. There the shipment was loaded onto the carrier *James Parker*, which departed November 28, and arrived in New York on December 6.[8] The works were then transferred to storage at the National Gallery of Art for safekeeping.

## THE "202" IN THE UNITED STATES

The American and German press eagerly shared news of the shipment. Janet Flanner, writing as Genêt in *The New Yorker*, was skeptical of the stated need to provide proper care for the paintings in the steam-heated United States.[9] *Die Neue Zeitung*, a German-American newspaper, reaffirmed the misconception that Wiesbaden did not have sufficient heating fuel to care for the paintings,[10] and on December 7 the headline "$80 Million Paintings Arrive from Europe on Army Transport" appeared in *The New York Times*, declaring that the pictures were Nazi loot, a statement that had to be corrected by Chief Justice and National Gallery of Art Board Chairman Harlan Fiske Stone when the paintings were taken into the gallery's custody.[11]

Response to the removal of the paintings from Wiesbaden varied. In January 1946, Charles Kuhn published the manifesto in the *College Art Journal*,[12] and, in an open letter to Secretary of State James F. Byrnes, Rensselaer W. Lee, president of the College Art Association, argued that the integrity of US policy abroad had been questioned and urged no further shipments. Adhering to party line, the State Department responded that adequate facilities did not exist in Germany at this time, and repeated President Truman's unequivocal statement that the pictures would return to Germany eventually.[13] In May, an additional ninety-five museum officials and academicians, led by Juliana Force and Frederick Clapp, directors of the Whitney Museum of American Art and The Frick Collection, sent a letter of protest to the president requesting immediate return of the paintings, cancellation of plans to exhibit them, and confirmation that no further shipments of this kind should be contemplated. Among the signatories to this letter was the director of the Cincinnati Art Museum, Philip Adams.[14]

Once the "202" arrived in Washington, the museum prepared photographs and condition reports and placed the paintings in air-conditioned storerooms, where they remained under the technical control of the US Army. Although they were not displayed publicly before 1948, David E. Finley, director of the National Gallery of Art, and Walker accommodated numerous requests from museum directors, curators, and professors to view the pictures while they were in storage.[15] In October 1946, the army cabled General Lucius D. Clay, military governor of US-occupied Germany, to determine if the paintings could be returned. Clay was unwilling, fearing they would be siezed by the

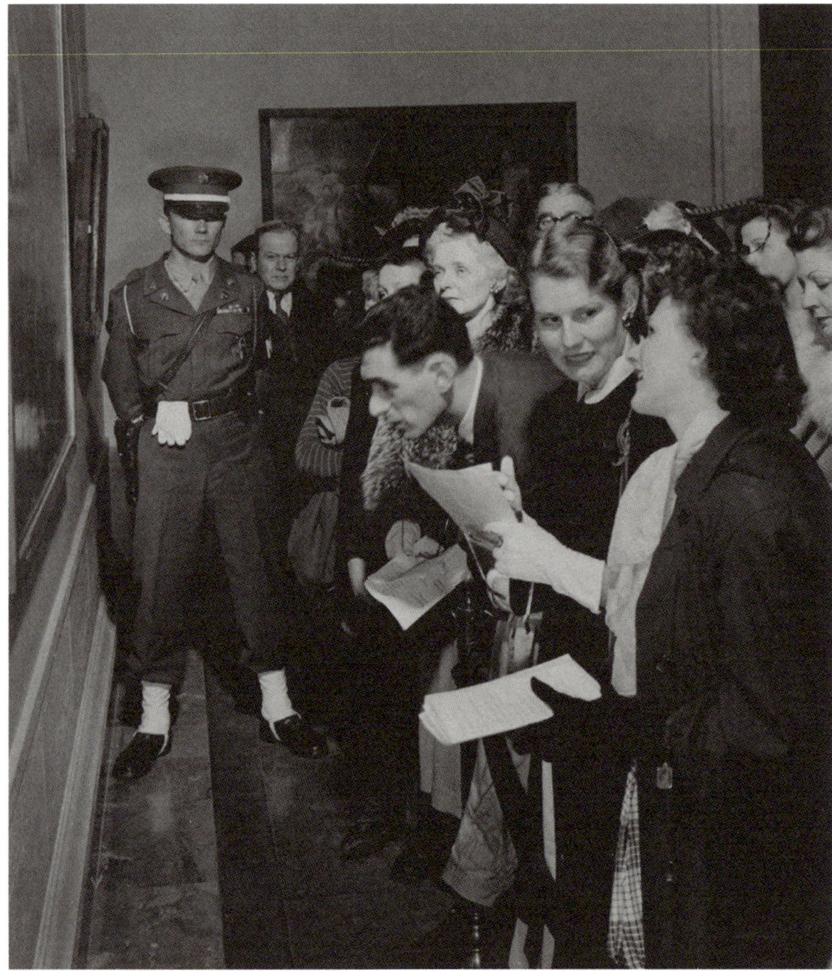

Fig. 2. Crowds attending the National Gallery of Art's exhibition *Paintings from the Berlin Museums* (March 17–April 25, 1948). National Gallery of Art, Washington, DC, Gallery Archives, 26B4_29_019

Fig. 3. Hans Holbein, the Younger (1497/98–1543), *Portrait of Georg Gisze*, 1532, oil on oak panel, 38⅜ × 33¹⁵⁄₁₆ in. (97.5 × 86.2 cm). Staatliche Museen zu Berlin, Gemäldegalerie, 586

Russians. As a compromise, he recommended an exhibit in Washington, but the War Department held back. A year and a half later, on February 6, 1948, Clay informed the US Army that conditions in Wiesbaden and Munich were appropriate for the return of the pictures. Twenty days after that, President Truman ordered the masterpieces be repatriated to Germany, following their exhibition at the National Gallery of Art.[16]

The museum prepared the display in just three weeks, and the public response was overwhelming; nearly one million people visited over the short span of the show.[17] Even a month into the exhibition, on April 11, crowds swelled to over 67,000 before an afternoon opening (fig. 1).[18] To guard the

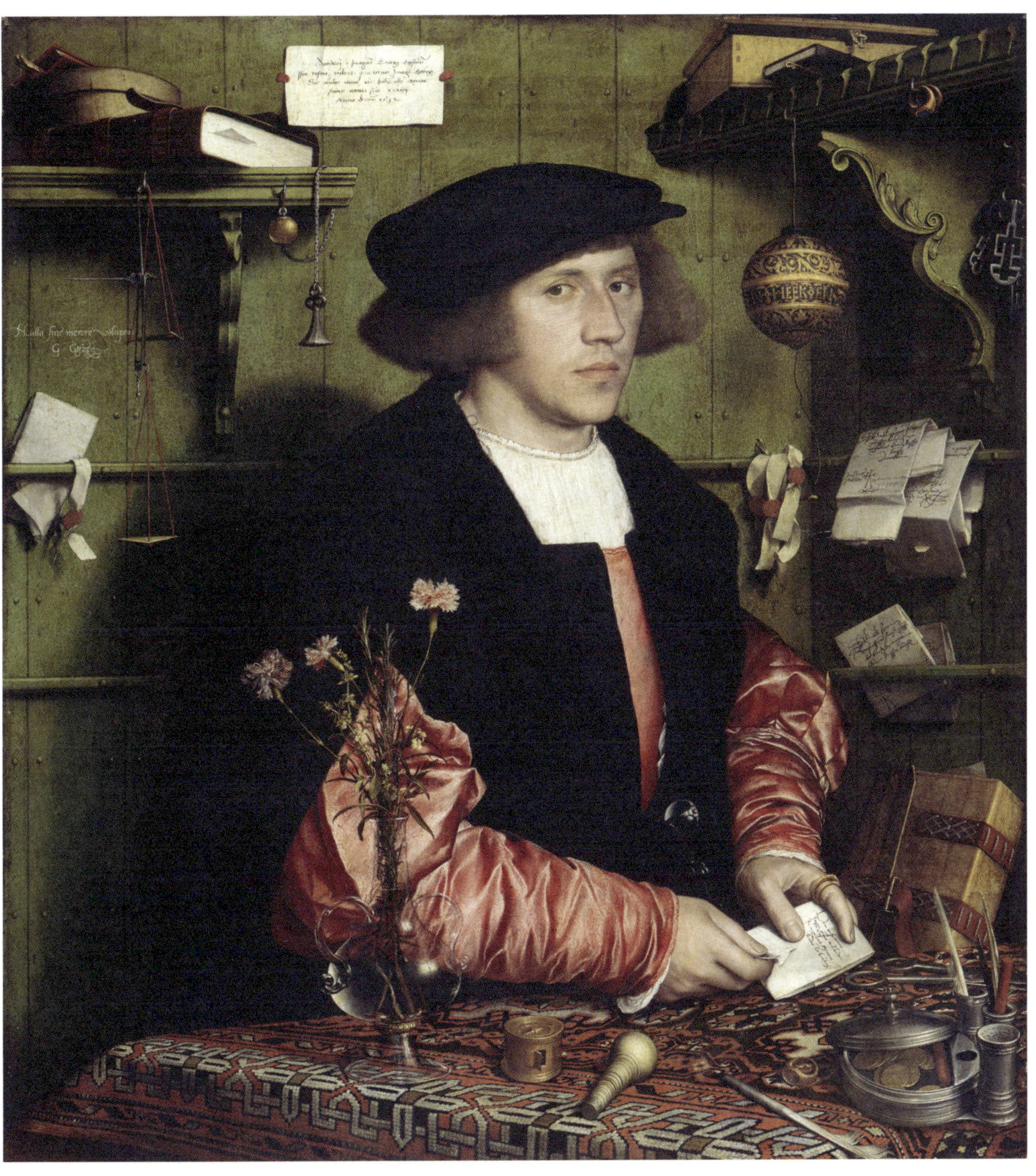

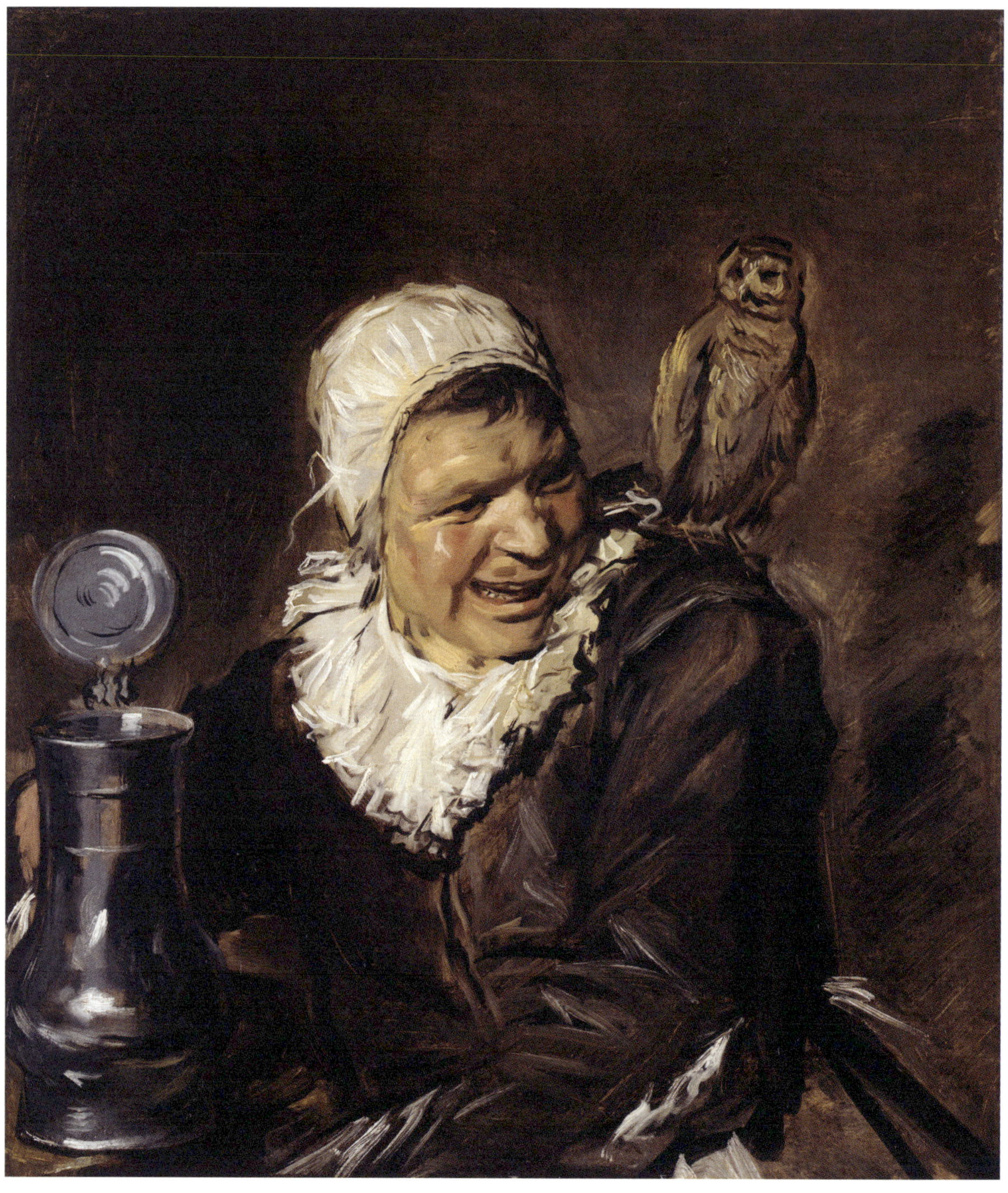

Fig. 4. Frans Hals (1582/83–1666), "*Malle Babbe*," 1629–30, oil on canvas, 30⅞ × 26¹⁄₁₆ in. (78.5 × 66.2 cm). Staatliche Museen zu Berlin, Gemäldegalerie, 801 C

paintings, the army assigned a detail of well-trained military police (fig. 2).[19] President Truman visited on two occasions and picked his favorite pictures: Rembrandt's *Moses Breaking the Tablets of the Law* (BR 138), Titian's *Self-Portrait* (BR 178), Holbein's *Portrait of Georg Gisze* (BR 91; fig. 3) and the works of Frans Hals (BR 83–88; fig. 4). The press splashed these choices in coast-to-coast publications. Much of the public probably commended the taste of the president, who once expressed his disdain for modern art, calling it the "kind of 'ham and egg art' that looks as if the painter had thrown his breakfast at the canvas."[20]

With such significant response to the exhibition in the nation's capital, national interest was expressed in Congress. Between March 4 and April 16, 1948, meetings of the Subcommittee on Armed Forces considered Senator James William Fulbright's (D-Ark) bill to temporarily retain the "202" for a tour across the nation.[21] The army, anxious to relieve itself of the burden of custodianship, was for the most part not in favor of a traveling exhibition. General Clay believed that the "German multimillion dollar art treasures" on display should be returned and that any delay would "play directly into the hands of the Communists with their constantly reiterated propaganda of American exploitation."[22] However, further support came from William C. Bullitt, former US ambassador to Russia, and Senator Wayne L. Morse (R-Ore), with expert testimony from Perry T. Rathbone, director of the Saint Louis Art Museum, who asserted, "It would be of untold advantage to our entire country if these works of art could be brought within reasonable reach of every American."[23] One newspaper asked, "A lot of Americans would enjoy a look at [the paintings]. Don't we get even that much out of the war?"[24]

## ART TOUR

Persistent effort by leading senators and widespread interest in the collection led to passage of the Fulbright bill, with the stipulation that the paintings be returned to Germany within one year in three shipments: one of roughly fifty pictures following the exhibition at the National Gallery of Art, a second of fifty in September 1948, with the remaining hundred pictures at the conclusion of the tour in April 1949.[25] A group of museum directors met at the National Gallery of Art on April 29 to determine the first shipment and finalize the schedule for the nationwide tour (see fig. 12 and appendix). Two German curators—Dr. Kurt Martin, director of the Kunsthalle in Karlsruhe (Baden), and Dr. Karl M. Birkmeyer, chief adviser to the MFAA—traveled to the US to "keep a constant check on the condition of the paintings" and accompany the paintings on tour, while the German conservator Dr. Irene Kühnel-Kunze served as technical expert.[26]

The logistics behind moving over one hundred paintings to thirteen venues were incredible and hardly imaginable today. The exhibition lasted about three weeks at each venue, with a week in between to take down, transport, and reinstall it in the next city. To prepare the paintings for exhibit, the National Gallery of Art made simple wooden frames, as many of the originals had burned in a Berlin fire.[27] Security Storage of Washington developed an elaborate packaging process that required approximately thirty to forty minutes for a medium painting, a task Birkmeyer changed in Cleveland by substituting special cardboard containers and using B.F. Goodrich Co. rubber as cushion.[28] Participating museums paid a deposit of two thousand dollars to cover overhead expenses for the entire tour; transportation from the place of previous exhibit to the next institution was at the expense of the latter; and each museum was responsible for its own unpacking and installation costs.[29] Museums were allowed to charge a reasonable admission fee, the proceeds of which went to relief of German children in the United States Zone in Germany, and to produce catalogues, reprints, and other souvenirs to recoup expenses and build public interest.

The first exhibition after the initial showing at the National Gallery of Art was at the Metropolitan Museum of Art in New York. Aline Louchheim, writing in *The New York Times*, noted the unique opportunity for New Yorkers to see "little known" German masters, including Konrad Witz, whose *Crucifixion* (BR 200; cat. 8) shows "grief-stricken figures, ingeniously arranged around the cross, [asserting] themselves as sculptural solids against the spacious landscape."[30]

Between Washington, New York, and the third venue, the Philadelphia Museum of Art, the paintings were transported in closed vans heavily guarded by the army (fig. 5).[31] After the exhibition in Philadelphia, special rail cars, typically reserved for the transport of thoroughbred horses, were deployed for the remainder of the tour. These heated and heavily padded cars were designed so that, once the crates were loaded, military police guards could keep a constant watch on the paintings.[32]

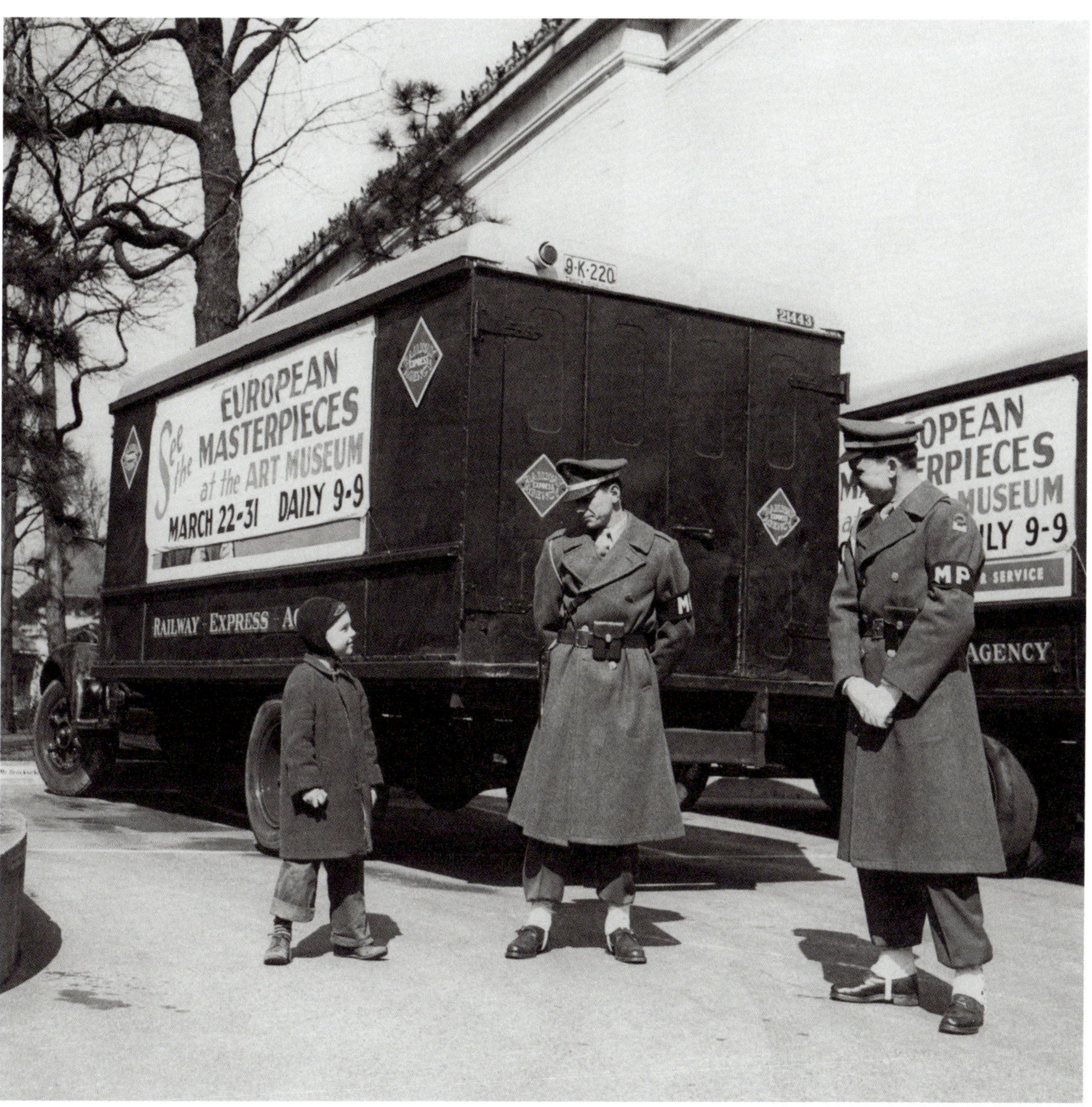


Fig. 5. Transporting the exhibition *Paintings from the Berlin Museums* in vans. Toledo Museum of Art Archives, 7837-13

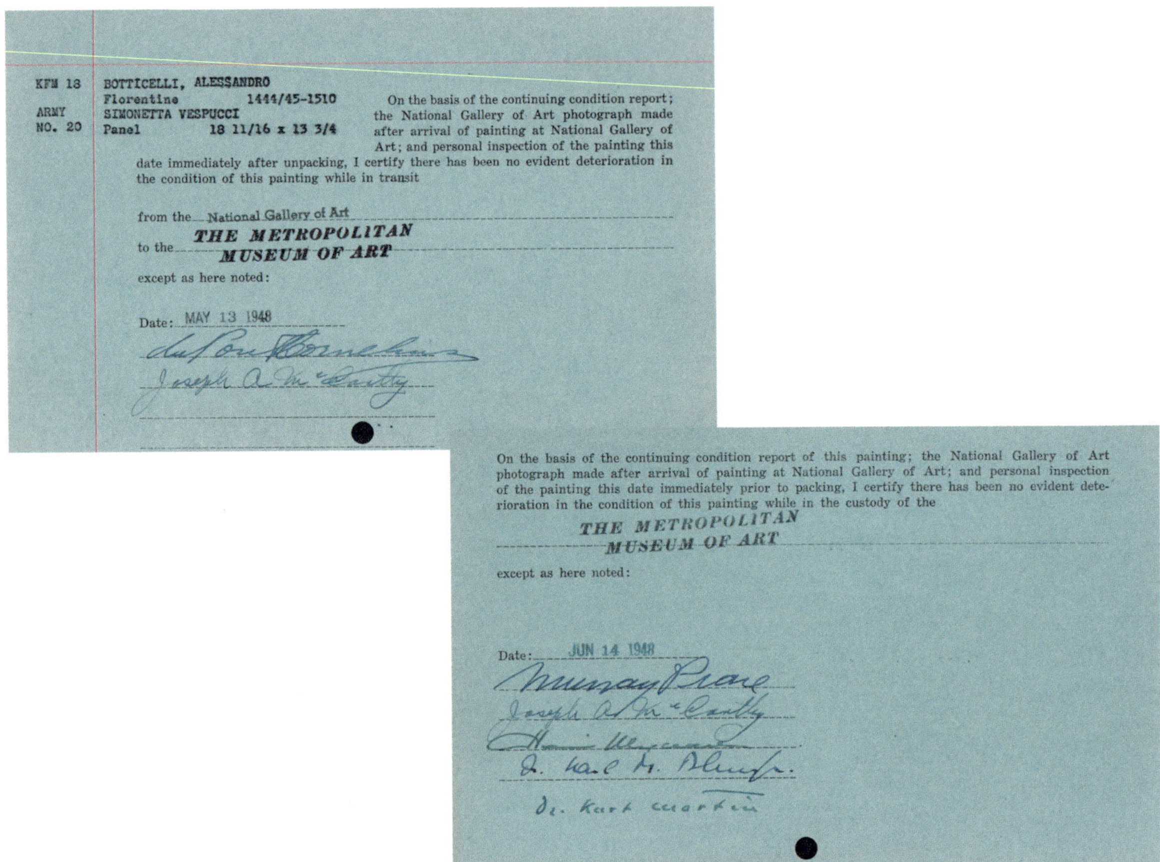

KFM 18
ARMY
NO. 20

BOTTICELLI, ALESSANDRO
Florentine 1444/45-1510
SIMONETTA VESPUCCI
Panel 18 11/16 x 13 3/4

On the basis of the continuing condition report; the National Gallery of Art photograph made after arrival of painting at National Gallery of Art; and personal inspection of the painting this date immediately after unpacking, I certify there has been no evident deterioration in the condition of this painting while in transit

from the National Gallery of Art

to the THE METROPOLITAN MUSEUM OF ART

except as here noted:

Date: MAY 13 1948

On the basis of the continuing condition report of this painting; the National Gallery of Art photograph made after arrival of painting at National Gallery of Art; and personal inspection of the painting this date immediately prior to packing, I certify there has been no evident deterioration in the condition of this painting while in the custody of the

THE METROPOLITAN MUSEUM OF ART

except as here noted:

Date: JUN 14 1948

Fig. 6. The "blue card" for Botticelli's *Ideal Portrait of a Lady ("Simonetta Vespucci")* (BR 18, cat. 9). National Gallery of Art, Washington, DC, Gallery Archives, RG17A5, Curatorial World War II Files, 1941–1953

At the conclusion of each exhibition the condition of each painting was noted on blue cards in duplicate; one copy was sent to the National Gallery of Art and a second stayed with the host museum (fig. 6). Detailed explanations of damage were recorded. Quick fixes were made with scotch tape, sponge-rubber wedges, tissue, and glue.[33] If a painting was determined unfit to be displayed, it would be sent back to Washington, DC.[34] Maximum security was exercised during packing as well as exhibition (fig. 7); Walter Heil, director of the de Young Museum, San Francisco, was locked in his office for three hours when he "unthinkingly touched the surface of a painting."[35]

Museums displayed the "202" differently, but the paintings were always organized by nationality. The time to install a gallery varied: at the Detroit Institute of Arts, four men were needed for eight hours to unpack and for

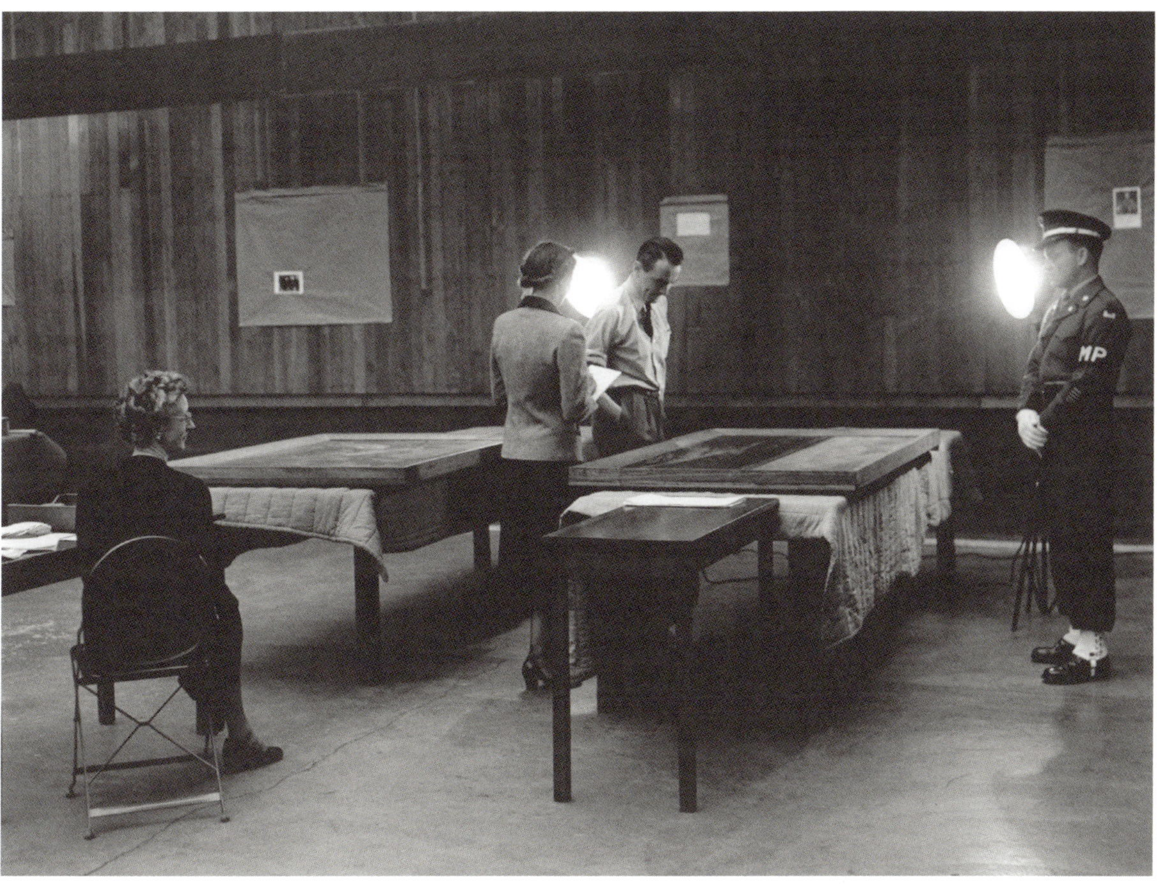


Fig. 7. Examining works in the exhibition *Paintings from the Berlin Museums.* Toledo Museum of Art Archives, Folder: Exhibitions—1949, European Masterpieces from Berlin

sixteen hours to hang the paintings. At the Saint Louis Art Museum, hanging time was reduced to nine hours, but it took six people. At the Philadelphia Museum of Art, the paintings were arranged chronologically in the European period rooms. The Art Institute of Chicago used ten galleries, whereas Detroit used only four.[36]

In total, the bulk of the paintings traveled about 12,000 miles (fig. 12). Parades and military bands often accompanied the masterpieces from rail station to museum (fig. 8).[37] In Chicago, observers noted that the artwork was "guarded and handled as if it were a cargo of crown jewels or atomic bombs." The Black Horse Troop of the National Guard and a contingent of distinguished army officers accompanied it from Union Station through the Loop.[38] Chicagoans lined the downtown streets to watch crated Rembrandts,

Rubenses, Titians, and Dürers pass by, and to see the "unpacking" of Vermeer's *Lady with a Pearl Necklace* (BR 185) in the street, as it was ceremonially presented to Art Institute president Chauncey McCormick and director Daniel Cotton Rich (fig. 9).[39] Although the museum kept the ceremony short, without a band or speeches, Detroit's director, E. P. Richardson, wrote, "The presence of the military police is one of the things that interested both the public and the newspaper people and the brief ceremony was very helpful in getting wide publicity for the opening."[40] Indeed, newspapers emphasized the presence of military police: "For the next 17 days, the Detroit Institute of Arts will be about as close to martial law as it can get. The military rule started Monday when half-tracks with machine-gun mounts conveyed $50,000,000 worth of German art treasures to the museum."[41] The general security rule was that at least one guard for every twenty paintings needed to be present during

Fig. 8. Military caravan in Toledo, Ohio. Toledo Museum of Art Archives, Box 13: Toledo Museum of Art Exhibition Archives

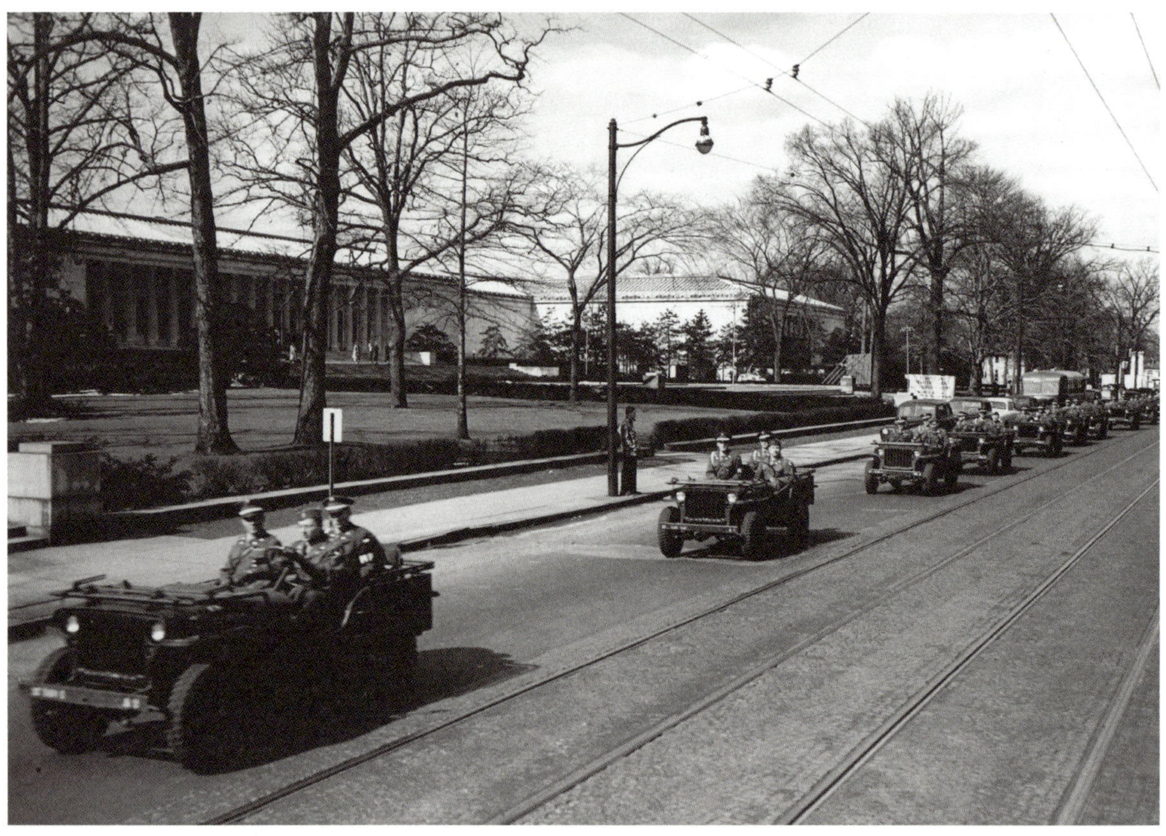

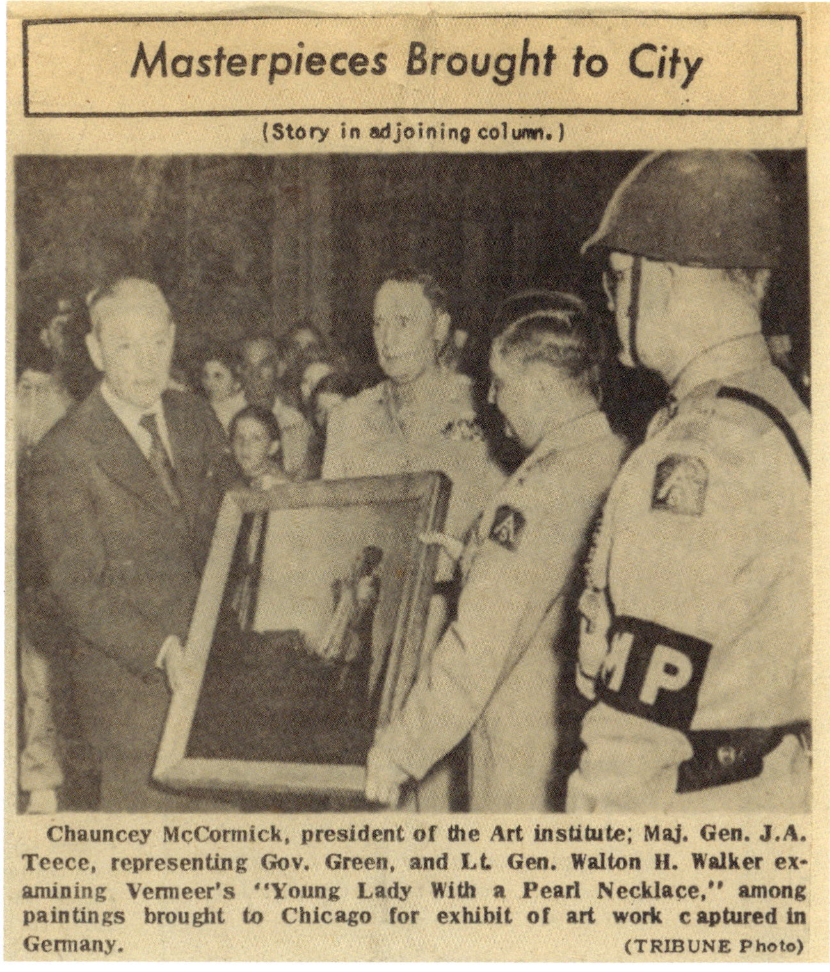

Masterpieces Brought to City

(Story in adjoining column.)



Chauncey McCormick, president of the Art institute; Maj. Gen. J.A. Teece, representing Gov. Green, and Lt. Gen. Walton H. Walker examining Vermeer's "Young Lady With a Pearl Necklace," among paintings brought to Chicago for exhibit of art work captured in Germany. (TRIBUNE Photo)

Fig. 9. Unwrapping Vermeer's *Lady with a Pearl Necklace* in Chicago, *Chicago Daily Tribune*, July 14, 1948. National Gallery of Art, Washington, DC, Gallery Archives, RG14A8 Records of the Office of Public Information, Public Information Scrapbooks, 1937–1986

exhibition hours.[42] The MPs, equipped with "Sam Brown leather equipment" and 45-caliber pistols attracted attention from press and public alike.[43]

Response to the artworks themselves across the country varied, but Rembrandt's *Man with a Golden Helmet* was often cited as a favorite (BR 137; see Rowley, fig. 5). The *Times* (Toledo, Ohio) noted that "some admired the technique and color of the helmet itself, others were impressed with the features of the man under the helmet."[44] Meanwhile, another publication in Toledo, the *Catholic Chronicle*, brought special attention to ecclesiastical art, such as Rembrandt's *Daniel's Vision* (BR 134) and *The Preaching of Saint John the Baptist* (BR 142), and noted that the figures in Rubens's *Madonna and Child*

*Enthroned with Saints* (BR 152) gave the beholder a sense of vibrant motion.[45] The wide array of visitors across the country offered an amusing variety of responses. One visitor noted that "Titian is pretty fair, but Rembrandt must have been drunk when he did his stuff."[46]

On opening day in Chicago, the Army band played light classics for the crowd.[47] For Boston's evening hours, over two thousand people were waiting in line when the gallery opened. Attendance swelled to the point that reinforcements were called in to manage the crowds, and officials had to cut off the line for fear that "more than 4600 in the building might cause damage to some of the valuable objects on display."[48] In St. Louis, the attitude of the crowds was close to reverence: "They seem[ed] to sense being in the presence of something big."[49]

Many museums were confronted with managing crowds, rerouting traffic, arranging buses, and dealing with warm temperatures. Saint Louis Art Museum director Perry Rathbone found "that what the Museum needed was not a director, but a crowd engineer."[50] This seemed to plague other locations as well. In Boston, the museum's circuitry overloaded: "Only out of the ordinary event yesterday was the momentary blackout of the Museum when lights failed because of an overloaded circuit."[51] In Philadelphia, the museum was incredibly hot. One visitor noted, "Suffering for a drink a guard also directed me to a lavatory, where the water wasn't fit to drink. The Art Museum is no fit place to visit in summer."[52] In many locations, controlling the climate within the galleries proved to be difficult for the visitor experience and the paintings alike. Chicago's museum was a warm and muggy eighty degrees, and many visitors brought paper fans for gallery viewing.[53] Los Angeles, in extraordinary climatic conditions, experienced the opposite in April: cold and snow greeted many of the 161,141 visitors to the Los Angeles County Museum of Art.[54] In St. Louis humidifiers were needed to control air quality; at the Carnegie Institute in Pittsburgh, a new gadget was installed in the air heating system to send cold air into the galleries to protect the paintings; while the Los Angeles museum's heating system caused air dryness, leading to slight warping of a couple of paintings.[55]

Along with the pageantry planned for exhibition openings, museums hired publicity firms to bring attention to the exhibit. *The Detroit News* claimed the exhibit was "the most important and widely publicized art event to hit America."[56] As Birkmeyer wrote in reflection, "All papers reported almost daily on the paintings. All radio stations mentioned the exhibition again and

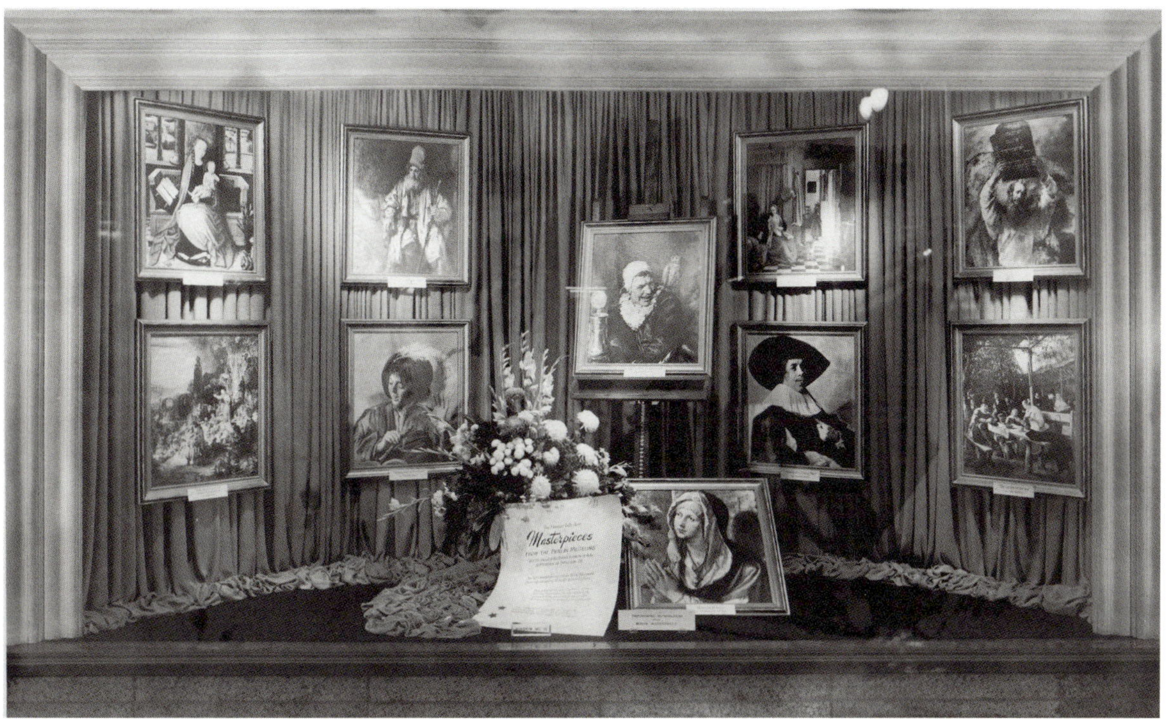


Fig. 10. J.L. Hudson Department Store window display in Detroit, September 1948. Detroit Institute of Art Archives, Folder: Exhibitions of Paintings from the Berlin Museums, September 10–26, 1948, RCH 66/12

again. Hundreds of signs appeared in department stores, shops, hotels and on public traffic systems."[57] Newspapers like the *Toledo Sunday Blade* helped build anticipation by featuring paintings once a week, with beautiful, full-color reprints. Detroit's publicity task list included the following: car cards, posters, Sunday newspapers, photographs of arrival of parade and unpacking of paintings, mailed calendar of lectures, store windows (fig. 10), outdoor displays, signs for Railways Express trucks, and display for windows of Manufacturers National Bank.[58] The Minneapolis Institute of Arts reported that almost all of the department stores in town devoted all or part of their windows to publicizing the exhibition.[59]

Host cities felt it very important that school children experience the exhibition. The St. Louis Parent Teacher Association stated that it was a "parental obligation" to take children to the exhibition.[60] In Toledo, the community pooled funds to pay for bus transportation, and the Cleveland Museum of Art reached out to colleges all over the region, including the University of Cincinnati (fig. 11).[61]

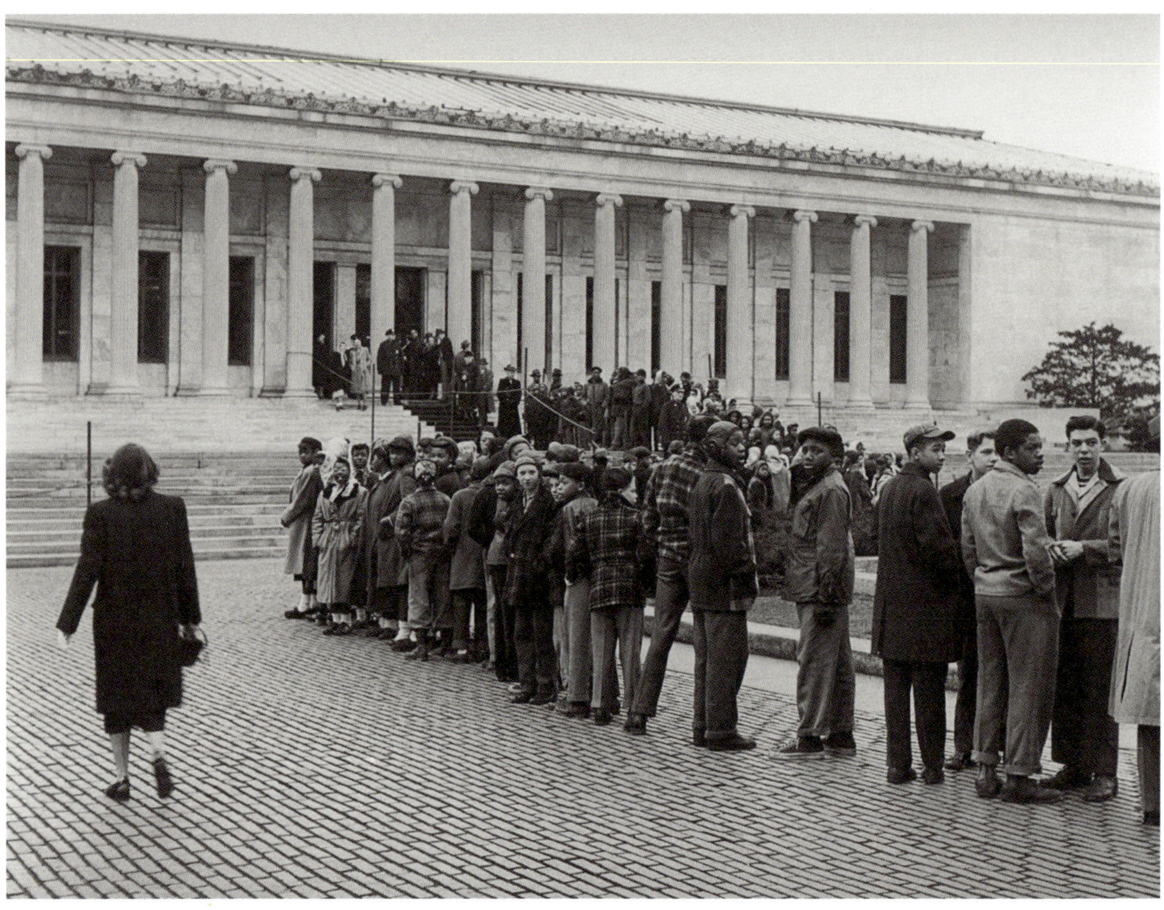

From the exhibition's final venue, at the Toledo Museum of Art, thirty-eight boxes of paintings were transported in closed vans to Washington, DC, then to New York, where they were loaded onto the Army transporter *General Alexander M. Patch*, which departed New York harbor on April 22, 1949, accompanied by Dr. Ernst Troche, German art curator, and Commander Keith Merrill.[62] On May 14, the paintings arrived in Wiesbaden and remained based there until 1958, when all were returned to West Berlin. Today two hundred of the works reside in the Gemäldegalerie and the Bode-Museum and two in the Alte Nationalgalerie, Berlin.[63]

Fig. 11. Lines outside the Toledo Museum of Art waiting to see *Paintings from the Berlin Museums*. Toledo Museum of Art Archives, 2837-137

## The "202" in America

| Venue | Dates | Attendance | Receipts | Miles to next site |
|---|---|---|---|---|
| WASHINGTON | March 17 – April 25, 1948 | 964,970 | n.a. | 228 miles |
| NEW YORK | May 17 – June 11, 1948 | 146,388 | $58,398.00 | 91 miles |
| PHILADELPHIA | June 19 – July 7, 1948 | 38,282 | $14,013.34 | 821 miles |
| CHICAGO | July 17 – August 3, 1948 | 144,785 | $30,297.25 | 1,034 miles |
| BOSTON | August 14–31, 1948 | 127,546 | $22,225.14 | 750 miles |
| DETROIT | September 10–25, 1948 | 84,073 | $21,240.80 | 137 miles |
| CLEVELAND | October 6–24, 1948 | 84,634 | $18, 646.42 | 777 miles |
| MINNEAPOLIS | November 2–17, 1948 | 108,008 | $14,731.82 | 2,042 miles |
| PORTLAND | November 26 – December 3, 1948 | 64,160 | $11,914.06 | 772 miles |
| SAN FRANCISCO | December 11–28, 1948 | 86,047 | $21,654.45 | 475 miles |
| LOS ANGELES | January 4–22, 1949 | 161,141 | $40,969.91 | 2,084 miles |
| ST. LOUIS | January 30 – February 17, 1949 | 227,414 | $24,514.42 | 621 miles |
| PITTSBURGH | February 27 – March 14, 1949 | 58,574 | $10,620.67 | 261 miles |
| TOLEDO | March 22–31, 1949 | 101,828 | $14,379.07 | 723 miles |

Fig. 12. Paintings returned to Germany in three shipments: after Washington, after Boston, and after Toledo (see Map, pp. 30–31)

## POST-WAR REFLECTIONS

The episode of the "202" assumed important geopolitical dimensions in the postwar era. Press coverage and speeches frequently took the moral high road, characterizing the exhibition tour as a mission in diplomacy, trust building, and international goodwill, the admissions proceeds from which were committed to German children.[64] Nearly $200,000 was raised for the Council of Relief Agencies Licensed to Operate in Germany; $10,000 was earmarked for the Danish Red Cross to continue the vaccination program in the US Zone of Germany, and $19,000 for bedding for children's institutions in the western sector of Berlin.[65] Whether the United States can be seen as a savior of the precious masterpieces is much more debatable, even though the art treasures were ultimately returned to their rightful owners, the German people.

It would be difficult to argue, however, that Americans did not benefit from the tour, through education, edification, and inspiration. As Rathbone so elegantly noted when the show opened in Toledo: "This is the beginning of knowledge. For many the exhibition will be a discovery, a revelation; the beginning of a life-long pleasure in the contemplation of works of art. . . . I am confident that the exhibition has already greatly elevated the place that art occupies in the public mind as no other event in the art history of this country has done."[66]

NOTES

*The author wishes to express her sincere thanks to Kristen Fleming, a Ph.D. graduate in History at the University of Cincinnati, for her invaluable assistance with the preparation of this essay.*

1. Radio interview. Folder: Masterpieces from Berlin Museums – Publicity, TMA Library and Archives.
2. Nicholas 1994, pp. 391–92; "Reich Art Objects to be Shipped Here," *The New York Times*, September 28, 1945.
3. Nicholas 1994, p. 392. In particular, Hanns Swarzenski—working from memory, prewar catalogues, and microfilmed copy of Berlin evacuation documents—compiled a list of 254 paintings, 73 sculptures and 30 objects, including 102 works from the Kaiser-Friedrich-Museum in Berlin.
4. Farmer 2000, pp. 56–59. The manifesto was forwarded to Major Bancel LaFarge, and no further action was taken on it. See Bernsau 2013 and her essay in this volume for a thorough account of the Wiesbaden Collecting Point.
5. Nicholas 1994, pp. 395–96 and Lindsay 1998, p. 127. Lamont Moore, "Report on Shipment of Paintings," December 14, 1945, Shipment of Works of Art to the United States ("202"), July 1945–1946, NARA M1947, Roll 70.
6. There were 103 biblical subjects, 52 portraits, 11 landscapes, 15 genre scenes, 17 subjects from literature, and 3 still lifes. See Exhibition Checklist, p. 174ff., for current attributions and titles. This checklist follows the inventory of the "202" prepared by Karl M. Birkmeyer, "Report on 202 Paintings Belonging to the Berlin Museums in the United States of America," April 22, 1949, Folder: Loan Exhibitions – Held – 1948. Office of the Secretary Subject Files, 1870–1950, Metropolitan Museum of Art (MMA) Archives, pp. 1–6 (hereafter, Birkmeyer, "Report"). Another list was published in Farmer 2000, Appendix IId; this list is based on that prepared by the National Gallery of Art when the paintings arrived in Washington, DC.
7. Farmer 2000, p. 72.
8. Farmer 2000, p. 73.
9. Flanner 1945, p. 74. See Farmer 2000, p. 56, about this misconception. Farmer was adamant that under his leadership the conditions in Wiesbaden were more than adequate to care for the paintings.
10. *Die Neue Zeitung*, November 30, 1945 (Munich: Pub. Operations Section, Information Control Division, USFET, US Army).
11. *New York Times Weekly*, December 9, 1945. National Gallery of Art press release, December 14, 1945: https://www.nga.gov/content/dam/ngaweb/research/gallery-archives/PressReleases/1949-1940/1945/14A11_43633_19451214.pdf.
12. Kuhn 1946, pp. 78–79; Hamlin 1946a.
13. Lee and Riddleberger 1946, pp. 83–84. Copy in NGA Archives, Record Group 17, Records of the Curatorial Departments, General Curatorial, World War II Files, 1941–1953, Series 17A5, Box 9, Folder: German Paintings, General Correspondence, 1945–April 1947.
14. Howe 1946, p. 305. *The Washington Post*, May 18, 1945, called the petition an "absurd accusation."
15. Record Group 2, Records of the Office of the Director, David Finley Office Files, Series 2A1, Box 8, File: German Paintings, General Correspondence 1945–April 1947, NGA Archives.
16. Birkmeyer, "Report," p. 6. National Gallery of Art press release, March 7, 1948. https://www.nga.gov/content/dam/ngaweb/research/gallery-archives/PressReleases/1949-1940/1948/14A11_43672_19480307.pdf.
17. *Paintings from the Berlin Museums* was on display at the National Gallery of Art, March 17 to April 25, 1948—less than six weeks. In that time 964,970 visitors attended the exhibition: https://www.nga.gov/exhibitions/1948/berlin_paintings.html.
18. McBride 1948, p. 748. Folder: Masterpieces from Berlin Museums – Catalog, *Art News Picturebook*, April 1948, Color Reproductions, TMA Library and Archives.
19. Folder: Masterpieces from Berlin Museums – Negotiations and Official Documents, TMA Library and Archives.
20. Hakanson 1948.
21. *Temporary Retention in the United States of Certain German Paintings: Hearings before a Subcommittee of the Committee on the Armed Services, United States Senate, Eightieth Congress, Second Session, on S.2439, March 4, April 16, 1948*, United States Government Printing Office, Washington, 1948.
22. "Gen. Clay Sees US Black Eye on German Art," *Daily News* (New York), April 17, 1948; "No Rush about that Art," *Daily News* (New York), April 17, 1948; "National Showing of Reich Art Asked," *Philadelphia Inquirer*, April 4, 1948; "Germans See Art Returned by US," *Philadelphia Inquirer*, June 14, 1948.
23. "Statement of Mr. Perry T. Rathbone, Director of the City Art Museum of St. Louis, Missouri, Before the Senate Armed Services Committee in Support of S.2439, April 16, 1948," copy in Archives, Saint Louis Art Museum. See also *Temporary Retention in the United States of Certain German Paintings*.
24. "No Rush about that Art," *Daily News* (New York), April 17, 1948.
25. Birkmeyer, "Report," pp. 7–8. "Captured German Art Treasures To Be Shown in New York City," *Star-Gazette* (Elmira, New York), April 28, 1948; "Experts Reject Plea for Return of German Art," *New York Herald Tribune*, June 11, 1948, Folder: German Paintings – Publicity, 1948, Office of the Secretary Records, MMA Archives.
26. Birkmeyer, "Report," pp. 7, 9.
27. Birkmeyer, "Report," p. 20; the paintings were stored without their frames in the salt mine, and the original frames burned in the Friedrichshain "Flak" tower. See also Nicholas 1994, pp. 362–63.
28. Birkmeyer, "Report," p. 30.
29. While not required by the terms of the tour, about half of the museums took out additional liability insurance for the time the paintings were within their museums; Birkmeyer, "Report," p. 11.
30. Aline B. Louchheim, "The German Pictures: Unique Items," *New York Times*, May 16, 1948, Clippings scrapbook, NGA Archives.
31. "German Art Gems at Museum Here," *Daily News* (New York), May 14, 1948.
32. Birkmeyer, "Report," p. 21.
33. "Part I: Final Packing and Shipment from Toledo to Washington," Folder: Masterpieces from Berlin Museums – Packing Lists, etc., TMA Library and Archives.
34. Birkmeyer, "Report," p. 34, for example when John Walker visited St. Louis for the exhibition there he took the Rogier van der Weyden *Miraflores Altarpiece* (BR 198) back to Washington with him.
35. Letter from Director to Messers. Ce. E. Heath and Company, Ltd., February 14, 1949, Folder: Masterpieces from Berlin Museums – Insurance. "German Art – St. Louis by Earl Zeke Retenlion," Folder: Masterpieces from Berlin Museums – Publicity, TMA Library and Archives.

36. Telegram from E. P. Richardson to Walter Heil, September 20, 1948, The Edgar P. Richardson Records, Series IX Exhibitions, 1936–1961, Folder: Exhibitions of Paintings from the Berlin Museums, Sept. 10–26, 1948 (RCH 66/12), DIA Archives. Memo to Mr. Wittman from Mr. Brockseker regarding "The Berlin Painting Exhibition at St. Louis," February 2, 1949, Folder: Masterpieces from Berlin Museums – Record of Operations, TMA Library and Archives. "Philadelphians Will See Captured German Art," *Philadelphia Inquirer*, June 13, 1948. Evelyn Griffin, "Berlin Masterpieces Cover Four Galleries," *Times* (Toledo, Ohio), September 12, 1948.
37. Letter to Otto Wittman from H. D. M. Grier, assistant director of the Minneapolis Institute of Arts, January 12, 1949, Folder: Masterpieces from Berlin Museums – Record of Operations, TMA Library and Archives.
38. John Thompson, "Seized German Art Treasures Arrive in City," *Chicago Tribune*, July 14, 1948.
39. Hakanson 1948.
40. Letter to Ted [no last name] from E. P. Richardson, September 30, 1948, The Edgar P. Richardson Records, Series IX Exhibitions, 1936–1961, Folder: Exhibitions of Paintings from the Berlin Museums, Sept. 10–26, 1948 (RCH 66/12), DIA Archives.
41. "100 Masterpieces of Art Convoyed to Institute," F. P. 8/7/1948, Scrapbook, 1948–1950, p. 4, DIA Archives.
42. Birkmeyer, "Report," p. 12.
43. "The guards—those good-looking stalwart MP's who had seen the handling of the exhibit in other places and who ranked second only to the paintings themselves in the interest of the audiences—found the Toledo presentation and the Toledo crowd to their liking." Ruth Elgutter, "Shifting Scenes: Even MPs Praise Handling of German Art by Museum," *Times* (Toledo, Ohio), March 23, 1949, Scrapbook November 1938 – May 1949, TMA Library and Archives.
44. "'Man with Gold Helmet' Favorite Painting," *Times* (Toledo, Ohio), March 24, 1949. Today this work is not regarded as a genuine Rembrandt and is attributed to his circle.
45. The *Catholic Chronicle* noted as well *Madonna and Child* by Geertgen tot Sint Jans (BR 72); *Madonna and Child* by Hans Memling (BR 117); *The Rest on the Flight into Egypt* by Joachim Patinir (BR 126); *The Holy Family with Young Saint John* by Hans Burgkmair (BR 30); and two paintings by Giovanni Tiepolo, *Christ Bearing the Cross* (BR 173) and *The Martyrdom of Saint Agatha* (BR 171) (Flournoy & Gibbs, "Art Museum – Berlin Paintings, Catholic Chronicle – For Immediate Release," Folder: Masterpieces from Berlin Museums – Publicity, TMA Library and Archives).
46. *Chicago Tribune*, July 30, 1948, Scrapbook, p.13, Art Institute of Chicago.
47. Hakanson 1948.
48. "Museum," *The Boston Globe*, August 18, 1948.
49. "German Art – St. Louis by Earl Zeke Retenlion," Folder: Masterpieces from Berlin Museums – Publicity, TMA Library and Archives.
50. Perry T. Rathbone, "The Berlin Masterpieces," Folder: Masterpieces from Berlin Museums – Publicity, TMA Library and Archives; "Study Traffic Arteries to Museum: Treasures Hitler Seized will End US Visit Here; Traffic Problem is Feared," *Times* (Toledo, Ohio), March 4, 1949, p. 1, sec. 2, Scrapbook November 1938 – May 1949, TMA Library and Archives.
51. "Record Throngs of 128,018 See German Art Here," *Boston Globe*, September 1, 1948.
52. "Art Museum in Summer," *Philadelphia Inquirer*, July 18 1948.
53. Hakanson 1948.
54. Birkmeyer, "Report," p. 33.
55. Birkmeyer, "Report," pp. 33–34.
56. Hakanson 1948.
57. Birkmeyer, "Report," p. 38.
58. "Publicity Schedule for Berlin Masterpieces Exhibition," The Edgar P. Richardson Records, Series IX Exhibitions, 1936–1961, Folder: Exhibitions of Paintings from the Berlin Museums, Sept. 10–26, 1948 (RCH 66/12), DIA Archives.
59. Letter to Otto Wittman, from H. D. M. Grier, assistant director of the Minneapolis Institute of Arts, January 12, 1949, Folder: Masterpieces from Berlin Museums – Record of Operations, TMA Library and Archives.
60. "German Art – St. Louis by Earl Zeke Retenlion," Folder: Masterpieces from Berlin Museums – Publicity, TMA Library and Archives.
61. Letter from the director of the Toledo Museum of Art, April 14, 1949, Folder: Masterpieces from Berlin Museums – Contributors to Bus Fund, TMA Library and Archives.
62. "Part I: Final Packing and Shipment from Toledo to Washington," Folder: Masterpieces from Berlin Museums – Packing Lists, etc., TMA Library and Archives.
63. See Neville Rowley's essay in this volume, pp. 72–93, for details of the paintings' movements following their return to Germany.
64. Otto Wittman, February 7, 1949, speech to the Luncheon Club, Folder: Masterpieces from Berlin Museums – Record of Operations, TMA Library and Archives.
65. Birkmeyer, "Report," p. 42.
66. "Address by Perry T. Rathbone, opening of Berlin Masterpieces Exhibit, Toledo Art Museum," Folder: Masterpieces from Berlin Museums – Publicity, TMA Library and Archives.

# THE ROAD (BACK) TO BERLIN: THE ENDLESS JOURNEY OF THE "202"

NEVILLE ROWLEY

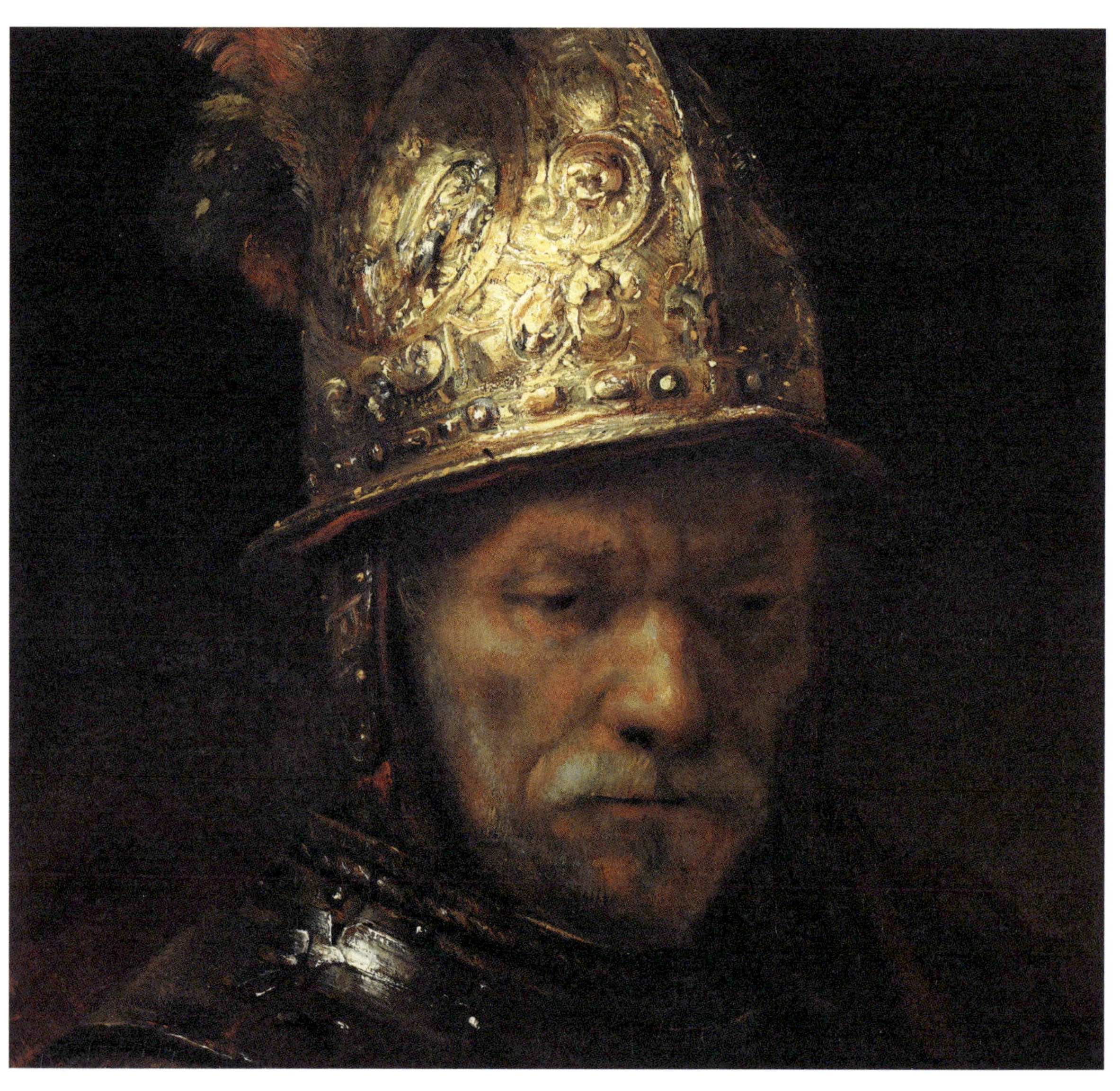

In November 1945, the departure for Washington of two hundred of the most important works from Berlin's Kaiser-Friedrich-Museum—together with two paintings by Manet and Daumier from the city's Nationalgalerie—had given rise to legitimate concern from US Army Captain Walter Farmer, who was responsible for the conservation of these works at the Central Collecting Point in Wiesbaden. Farmer saw in this operation not so much a conservation measure, as it had been described, as a thinly veiled attempt at plunder.[1] The "Wiesbaden Manifesto," immediately drawn up under his initiative, clearly denounced this transfer and helped prevent appropriation by the United States of the Berlin paintings: promise was soon made to "return [them] to the German people."[2] Alongside this controversial transfer and the subsequent American tour of the Berlin paintings between 1948 and 1949—the subjects of the previous essays in this catalogue—the return to Germany discussed in the present text is an equally interesting chapter in the history of the "202." Here, as in those earlier episodes, we see that the noblest intents of conservation and restitution of cultural property are often intimately linked to more base political maneuvers.

## A PROBLEMATIC RETURN TO A DIFFERENT GERMANY

For the United States, agreeing to "returning [the Berlin paintings] to the German people" was one thing; deciding precisely to whom to restitute them and where they were going to be exhibited was another. By the end of the Second World War, Germany had changed immeasurably. The neighboring countries that had been annexed by the Nazis (Austria, Czechoslovakia) returned to their pre-1938 borders, while Poland shifted towards the West and the USSR gained a lot of ground, all of which caused the influx of millions of German refugees from the former Eastern territories. What remained of Germany was not a

Detail of Fig. 5. Circle of Rembrandt Harmensz. van Rijn (1606–1669), *Man with a Golden Helmet*, circa 1650 sovereign country, but an occupied one, shared among the victorious Allied armies: the United States, the United Kingdom, France, and the Soviet Union. Berlin, the former capital of Hitler's "Third Reich," had become an enclave in the middle of the Soviet Zone. Like almost every major German city, it had been massively bombed by Anglo-American air raids; furthermore, it had been divided into four sectors of occupation (mirroring the whole country), and was soon to be parted into two hermetically sealed worlds, that of the Western powers and that of the "Eastern Bloc," dominated by the Soviet Union.[3] In the two and a half years between the transfer of the "202" to Washington at the end of 1945 and the return of the first group of them in the spring of 1948, this emerging Cold War context had already considerably complicated the restitution of the Berlin paintings. The original museums displaying the "202," the Kaiser-Friedrich-Museum and the Nationalgalerie, were located on Museumsinsel (Museum Island), in the Soviet sector of the city. Although the United States had decided to return the "202" to "the German people," it would not be acceptable to hand over so many masterpieces to the Soviets. The restitution would therefore have to employ other means.[4]

At the end of 1945, the official reason for the transfer of the "202" to Washington had been the safekeeping of the artworks (although there were political reasons for the operation, and in spite of the material risks involved in such a project). So, at the time of their return, it was appropriate for the Americans to mention conservation first: the fifty-three paintings that were shipped to Germany in the spring of 1948 were considered the most fragile ones.[5] These were mainly fourteenth- and fifteenth-century wooden panels, which might have suffered from humidity and climate changes during an American tour. Among this shipment was also a work on canvas, the *Presentation of Christ in the Temple* by Andrea Mantegna (BR 109; fig. 1), which is still fixed on its original wooden support—a likely reason for the early return of the painting.[6] However, this shipment did not include all the works on panel transferred to the United States, which would have constituted a coherent conservation measure: a hundred of them would be allowed to travel across America. This was the case, for example, for the other painting by Mantegna among the "202," the *Portrait of Cardinal Ludovico Trevisan* (BR 108).

After crossing the Atlantic in a military vessel, the first group of returned paintings did not immediately reach its planned destination, the Central Collecting Point in Wiesbaden. First they were shown at the Haus der Kunst

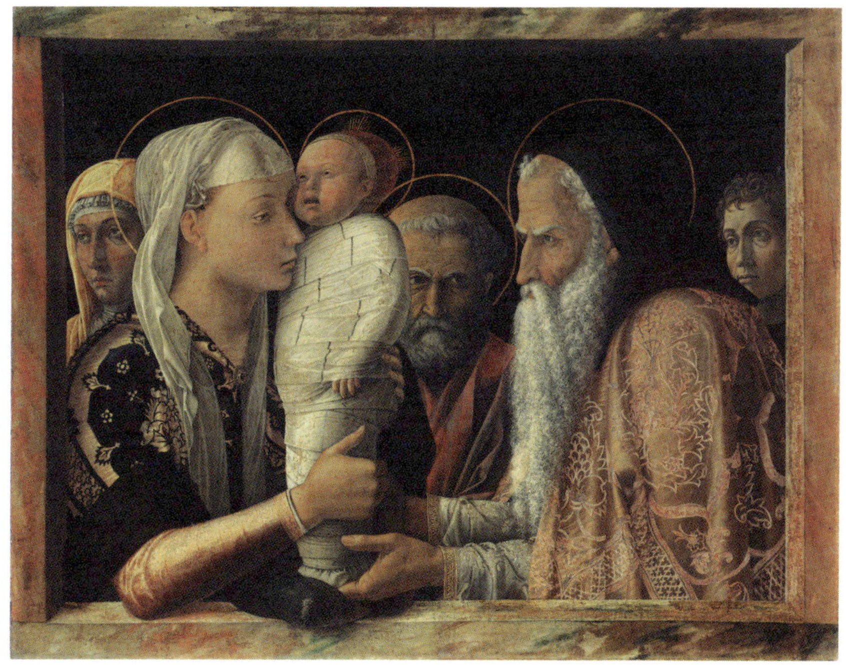

Fig. 1. Andrea Mantegna (circa 1431–1506), *Presentation of Christ in the Temple*, circa 1454, tempera on canvas, 30⅜ × 37³⁄₁₆ in. (77.1 × 94.4 cm). Staatliche Museen zu Berlin, Gemäldegalerie, 29

in Munich.[7] After the groundbreaking success of the Washington exhibition of the "202" earlier that year, the American occupying authorities tried to use the Berlin masterpieces to rally to their cause the former German enemy. US General Lucius Clay, military governor of US-occupied Germany, wrote in the Munich exhibition catalogue that he "hope[d] that our mutual appreciation of these works of art will help toward mutual understanding between our nations."[8] (This stated intention is rather ironic as General Clay had been one of the officials most responsible for the transfer of the paintings to America in 1945.[9]) The question of conservation, which had been considered important enough to justify the early return of these works to German soil, had become secondary in comparison to the political gain in exhibiting them.

For the city of Munich, presenting the "masterpieces of the Kaiser-Friedrich-Museum [in] Berlin" (as the exhibition title stated) was an exceptional opportunity to turn one's back on the horrors of the war. The works exhibited referred to a common European past not marked by guilt, unlike the exhibitions held in the same building—the Haus der Kunst—during the Nazi era, especially the one dedicated to "Degenerate Art" in 1937.[10] The paintings of the old masters were not controversial in the way that twentieth-century art was: this was exactly what the city needed, all the more since the exhibited paintings were (for the largest part) not among the millions of works of art looted by the Nazis, the problematic restitutions of which were just beginning.[11] Given this situation, it is not surprising that the museums of Karlsruhe and Stuttgart expressed their interest in showing the Berlin pictures after the Munich venue.

The prospect of a German tour immediately following the American one was, however, of great concern to those who considered themselves the legitimate owners of the paintings, the new museums in West Berlin. At the end of the war, the political tension between East and West had forced officials of the "former State Museums of Berlin" (as they were now called) to choose sides. While the East German museums remained in the historic heart of Museum Island, new museums covering the same areas of collecting were established in Bruno Paul's largely intact Museum of Asian Art (built 1914–25) in the southwest suburb of Dahlem, in the American sector. Yet very few works were still preserved in Berlin, East or West: the Red Army had transferred to the USSR 2.5 million cultural assets from German territories (including the monumental frieze from the Pergamon Altar, dating from the second century BCE), while the Western Allies had gathered the Berlin works found during their military advance at the Central Collecting Points in Wiesbaden, capital of the State of Hesse, and Celle in Lower Saxony.[12] The West Berlin Museums considered themselves owners of the works once in Berlin stored in these Collecting Points (without which these museums would have no reason to exist), and of the 202 paintings that had left for the United States in 1945, and had been partly returned in spring 1948.

At the beginning of July 1948, the director of the Gemäldegalerie (the Berlin Painting Collection), Heinrich Zimmermann, wrote to his counterparts in Karlsruhe and Stuttgart to advise them not to proceed any further with plans for a traveling exhibition of the Berlin paintings, which would have disastrous consequences for the condition of the works and would also probably extend the stay in the United States of the remaining ones.[13] A few days earlier, Zimmermann had written to the director of the Haus der Kunst in Munich to express his dissatisfaction about not having been informed of the current exhibition.[14] He also lamented not being able to plead his case in person: since June 24, 1948, eleven days after the opening of the Munich exhibition, the roads leading to the American, British, and French sectors of Berlin had been cut off by the Soviet Union. This was the beginning of the "Berlin Blockade," during which the Western part of the city was supplied only by air. The Haus der Kunst in Munich replied to Zimmermann that the show had been entirely planned by the US occupying forces.[15] However, the concerns that he formally expressed had some utility, as the Karlsruhe and Stuttgart exhibitions never happened. The West Berliners had been taken seriously, even if the Berlin Blockade was a serious military obstacle to the restitution of the paintings to their city.

The legal aspect of a restitution of the paintings to Berlin was not an easy one either: until the end of World War II, the works of the Berlin Museums had belonged to the State of Prussia, the largest territorial entity in Germany. As Prussia had been dissolved by the Allies on February 25, 1947, the return of some of the "202" to German soil in 1948 could not constitute a restitution to their original owner. Returning the Berlin works to the museums from which they came would have meant transferring the majority of them—and especially the old master paintings—into Soviet territory. The chosen method of restitution thus implied no movement of works of art, but rather a prudent transfer of custody from an Allied control to a German one. In June 1948, the works of art from Berlin stored in Wiesbaden were transferred in trust to the Hessian state.[16] Even though Hesse had been part of the immense Prussian state since 1866, Berliners could only interpret this decision, which was dictated by political circumstances, as an injustice.

In September 1948, a second group of the "202" returned to Wiesbaden after the exhibition in Boston; the third and final group would arrive in April 1949.[17] In the summer of 1949, an exhibition in Wiesbaden celebrated this event.[18] The return of the paintings after almost four years in America could have been seen as completed. But for at least one observer, MFAA officer Ardelia R. Hall, it was a mere step. On May 1, 1949, she declared, "The final chapter of the long hegira of the 'returned masterpieces' will not be written before they are restored once more to their rightful owners, the people of Berlin."[19]

In comparison to the preceding year, something had changed from the American perspective. West Berlin was no longer a territory at risk of being lost; it had become a real part of West Germany, and a symbol for which the global West had to fight. On May 12, 1949, the Soviet Union ended the Berlin Blockade, and the Western part of the city became accessible again by land after almost a year. This was a resounding victory for the United States, which had refused to leave the "people of Berlin" to fall under communist rule. Even if the city soon lost its status as German capital when the new Federal Republic of Germany was founded in Bonn later that month, West Berlin had gained a new image, that of the "showcase of the free world."[20] The return of the paintings to West Berlin could thus not only be considered a legitimate decision for the "people of Berlin;" it also had become a political weapon.

## AN EPHEMERAL EXHIBITION IN WEST BERLIN

In the years that followed, West Berliners did their utmost to recover works that remained in trust in West Germany. In February 1950, Mayor Ernst Reuter and City Councilor for Popular Education Walter May wrote a joint letter to the Allied High Commission for Germany, requesting the physical and legal transfer to West Berlin of the works preserved in the city before the war.[21] The answer came three months later: if security conditions did not allow all the collections to be sent to West Berlin, it was suggested (and implicitly authorized) that some works be selected for temporary display in Dahlem, a proposition not without merit for Berliners.[22] A few days later, however, they would be disappointed to learn that another exhibition of "their" masterpieces was soon to be held at the Rijksmuseum in Amsterdam, at the Palais des Beaux-Arts in Brussels, and at the Petit Palais in Paris.[23] For a whole year, 120 paintings from Berlin (almost all of them having been part of the "202") were once more involved in a diplomatic mission, namely to reconcile West European countries and to unite them against communist danger.[24] Unlike the Munich exhibition in 1948, the tour had not been decreed by the US Army: the new trustees of the paintings, the State of Hesse, but also the Federal Republic of Germany, had understood that this operation was a way to rebuild links between potential economic partners. It was in that very moment, in early May 1950, that France and West Germany took the first steps toward what would become the European Union.[25]

If West Germany was working to build a popular image outside its borders, the situation within the country was quite complicated. The West Berliners of Dahlem considered themselves the legitimate owners of works formerly shown in the Eastern sector; the State of Hesse would not mind a prolonged stay of so many masterpieces under its jurisdiction; while the government of Bonn, in particular the Finance Ministry, considered a return to Berlin senseless despite the end of the Blockade and dreamt of a West German national museum, with,

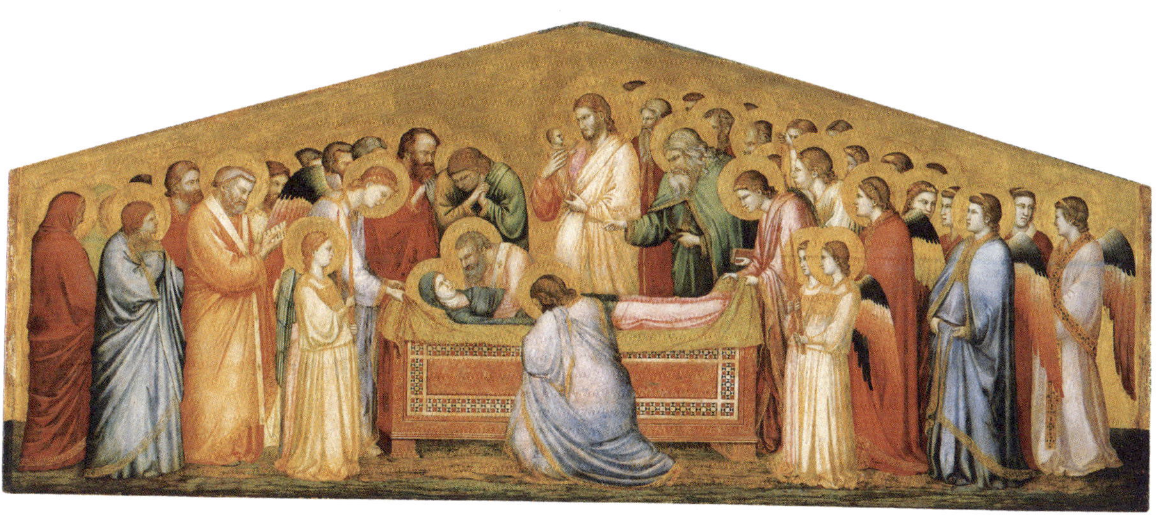

Fig. 2. Giotto (1266–1337), *Death of the Virgin*, circa 1310, tempera and gold on poplar panel, 29¹³⁄₁₆ × 70¾ in. (75.8 × 179.7 cm). Staatliche Museen zu Berlin, Gemäldegalerie, 1884

at its core, the Berlin pictures.[26] On June 25, 1950, the beginning of the Korean War revived the fear of an invasion by Soviet troops, not only of West Berlin, but of the whole country.[27] In August, the West German government refused to authorize the exhibition which had been suggested to the West Berlin Museums by the Americans a few months earlier. This time, Mayor Reuter decided to write directly to German chancellor Konrad Adenauer to express his frustration, and to state in vivid terms that a renunciation of the planned shipment would be perceived as a clear signal of weakness towards the East.[28] The argument hit its mark: on September 21, Adenauer authorized a three-month exhibition of the Berlin paintings in Dahlem.

The selection of the works, however, was not easy to make, as 120 first-class paintings were traveling at that moment from Amsterdam to Brussels, and there was no question of canceling this diplomatic exhibition. Sending second-rate paintings to West Berlin was no more of an option, so the most fragile works, which had been spared the tours in America and Western Europe, were requisitioned, including Giotto's monumental panel, *Death of the Virgin* (BR 74; fig. 2). The Berlin curators, who had been so critical of the movements of "their" works, did not have the same concerns in this case. For them, this transfer was not yet another exhibition, but a return home.[29] In late September 1950, 176 works were brought to West Berlin by plane, as the roads were still considered unsafe. On October 2, the exhibition opened to the public.[30]

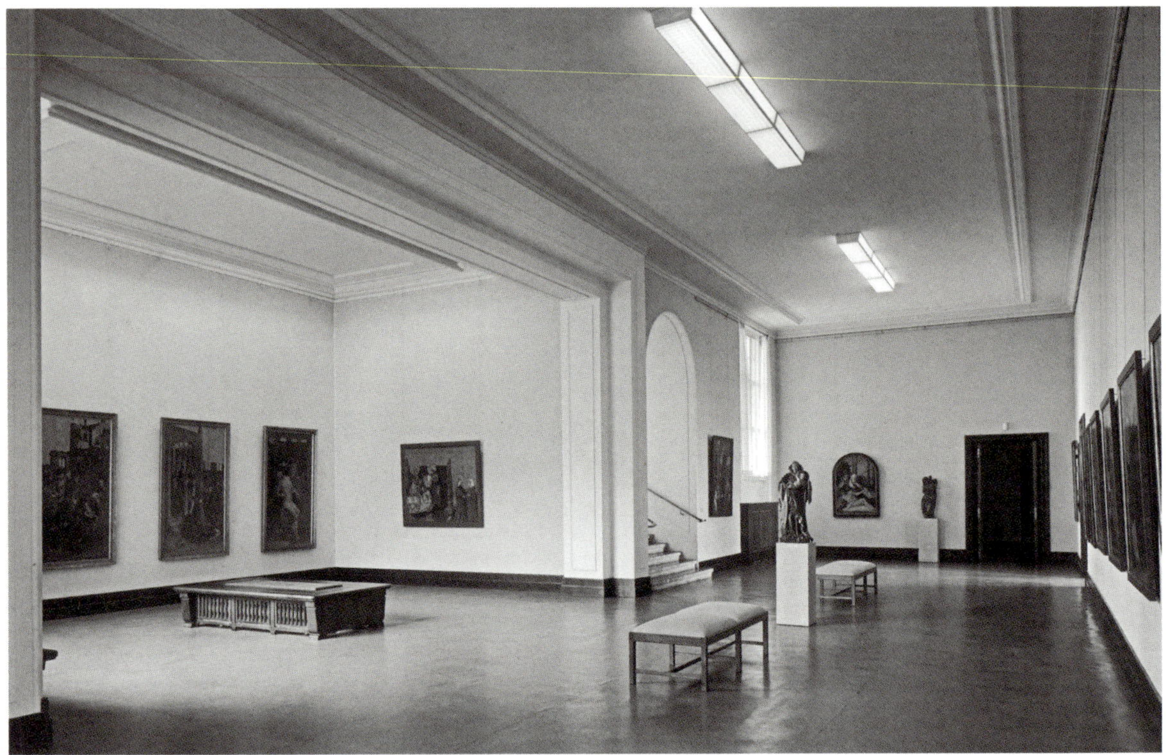

Fig. 3. View of the exhibition "Masterpieces of the Berlin Museums: German, Italian and Netherlandish Painting of the 13th to 16th Centuries," Dahlem Museum, West Berlin, Fall 1950–Winter 1951. Zentralarchiv der Staatlichen Museen zu Berlin, SMB-ZA, V/Fotoslg

The importance of this event cannot be overestimated: since September 1, 1939, and the invasion of Poland by the German army, Berlin's collections had been hidden from its citizens. A total of four hundred and thirty-four paintings had been destroyed in two unexplained fires in a Berlin bunker in May 1945.[31] The works that survived the war were seized by the victors (Americans or Soviets), the majority of them dispatched far from Berlin, from Washington to Moscow. In late 1945, a return of the Berlin works to the city seemed hypothetical at best; five years later, some paintings were back, and it was a cause for celebration. The abstracted classicism of Bruno Paul's museum building in Dahlem had little to do with the neo-renaissance rooms of the Kaiser-Friedrich-Museum, but the spirit of this institution, once directed by Wilhelm von Bode, with its mixed display of paintings and sculptures, inspired the aesthetic of the 1950 exhibition. This can be seen in the room of the Gothic paintings, which was installed notably with the four panels of the altarpiece of the Master of the Darmstadt Passion (BR 50–51), with the splendid wooden sculpture known as the *Dangolsheim Madonna* at the center (fig. 3).[32] "It is as if the works of Dürer and Titian, the works of the German Primitives of the Quattrocento and of the Netherlands had emerged like a phoenix from a rain of fire and ashes," described journalist Will Grohmann.[33] Berlin had burnt, Berlin had died, but Berlin had come back to life—thanks to its works of art. Ernst Reuter, who as mayor had played such a major role in this operation, concluded his opening speech with the statement: "It is the most beautiful day since I have lived in Berlin."[34]

## "THE PAINTINGS QUARREL"[35]

There was one thing, however, that Reuter regretted in this exhibition: the responsibility for the transfer of the works had not been entrusted to the West Berlin Museums, but to their legal trustees at that moment, the State of Hesse.[36] Still, it was hoped in Berlin that the temporary loans could be extended until the political solution of a legal return had been agreed. In fact, the exhibition initially planned for three months was extended for three more. On February 25, 1951, however, the West Berliners learned with great surprise that they would soon have to part with "their" paintings again, as the Museum zu Allerheiligen of Schaffhausen, Switzerland, was planning to show them in a few months. The initial reason for this curious loan, prepared in great secrecy by the West German Ministry of Finance, in agreement with the Hessian state, was not so much to display the paintings in another museum, but above all to evacuate them from a military threat.[37] The exhibition in Schaffhausen, which opened on July 14, would most certainly have been an unremarkable stay for the Berlin paintings, had it not given rise to a brilliant review by one of the greatest specialists of Italian painting of the time, Roberto Longhi.[38] It was all very well for him to criticize some inconsistent choices of the works selected from Berlin, which were presented alongside a few major international loans, and lament the lack of acknowledgement of the past two decades of scientific literature; the exhibition had much less to do with scholarship than with postwar diplomacy.[39]

A further wrinkle in the history of ownership meant that not all of the works previously shown in West Berlin were moved to Switzerland as planned. A legal issue arose concerning the paintings listed in the Berlin exhibition catalogue as "property of the Kaiser-Friedrich-Museums-Verein." Founded in 1896–97, the Association of the Friends of the Kaiser-Friedrich-Museum had acquired over the years significant paintings and sculptures for the Berlin collections, while remaining the owner of the works. This provision constituted a legal breach: the Kaiser-Friedrich-Museums-Verein, reconstituted in West Berlin after the war, considered itself the legitimate owner of seven paintings and five sculptures lent to Dahlem at the end of 1950 (the most important one being Giotto's *Death of the Virgin*; see fig. 2). The decision was taken to leave these works in Berlin until their situation had been clarified.

For the Berliners, this was the beginning of a run of good news, as the general principle of the works' return to West Berlin was adopted shortly thereafter, in November 1951—even if no date was provided for the actual transfer of property.[40] From then on, temporary exhibitions of the pictures would only be organized in one place: Berlin Dahlem.[41] The first one was dedicated to European paintings of the seventeenth and eighteenth centuries,

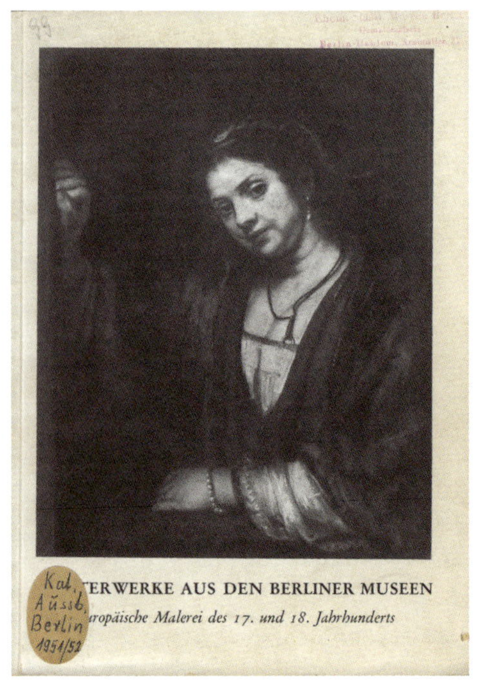


Fig. 4. Cover of the exhibition catalogue "Masterpieces of the Berlin Museums: European Painting of the 17th and 18th Centuries," Dahlem Museum, West Berlin, Fall 1951–Winter 1952. Staatliche Museen zu Berlin, Gemäldegalerie, Inv. Kat.Ausst. Berlin 1951/52

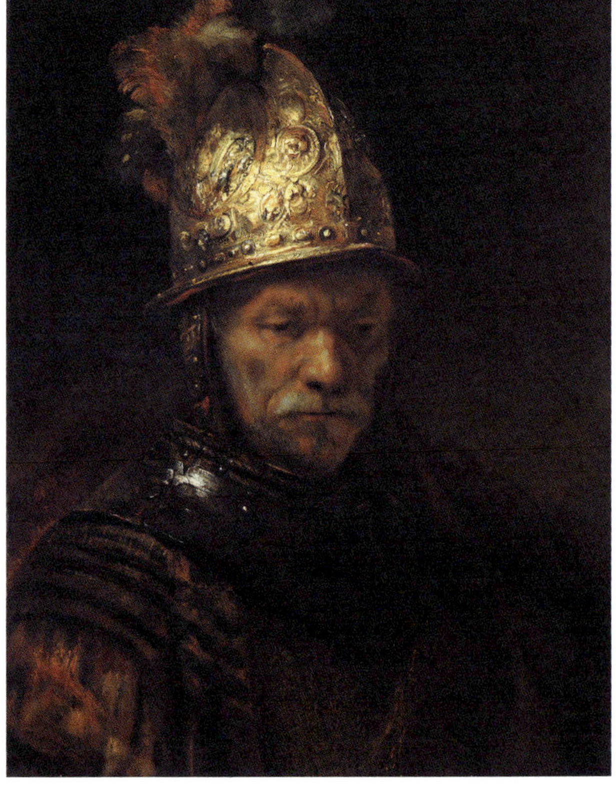

Fig. 5. Circle of Rembrandt Harmensz. van Rijn (1606–1669), *Man with a Golden Helmet*, circa 1650, oil on canvas, $29\frac{9}{16} \times 19\frac{15}{16}$ in. (67.5 × 50.7 cm). Staatliche Museen zu Berlin, Gemäldegalerie, 811 A

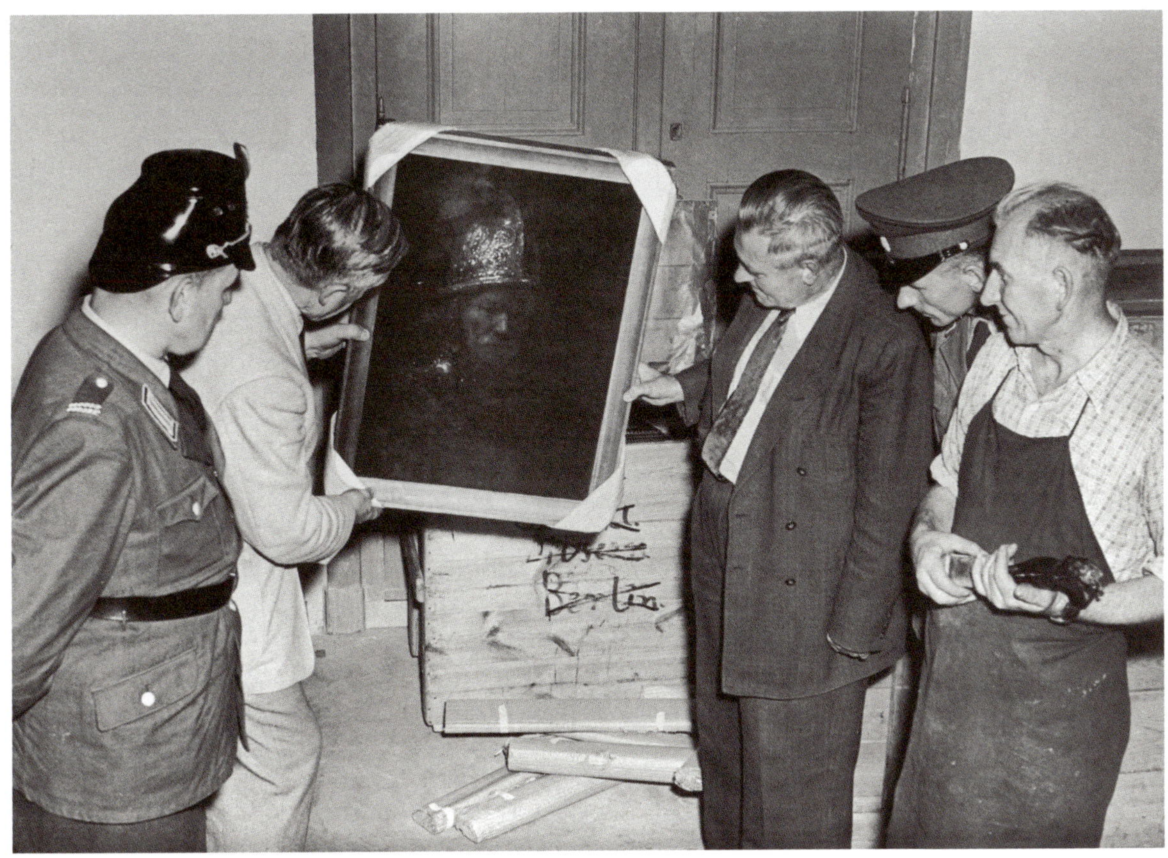

Fig. 6. Return of the paintings and sculptures owned by the Kaiser-Friedrich-Museums-Verein: unpacking the *Man with a Golden Helmet* at the Dahlem Museum, West Berlin, 1953. Zentralarchiv der Staatlichen Museen zu Berlin

which allowed for a display of artists not shown in 1950, due to the exhibition organized in Amsterdam, Brussels, and Paris. More than any other, one painter had been missed by the public: Rembrandt. His *Woman in a Doorway*, once considered a portrait of Hendrickje Stoffels (BR 135) was illustrated on the cover of the catalogue (fig. 4), while the exhibition listed no fewer than thirteen works by the master.[42] However, his most famous painting from the Berlin collection was not there: the *Man with a Golden Helmet* (BR 137; fig. 5) had been acquired in 1897 through the Kaiser-Friedrich-Museums-Verein, and had to wait in Wiesbaden for the settlement of its legal situation before being sent anywhere. In 1953, the Kaiser-Friedrich-Museums-Verein was recognized as the legal owner of the works it had financed before the war: all of them were then transferred to the Dahlem Museum and proudly exhibited.[43] The publicity around this return to Berlin was skillfully orchestrated, notably by a photograph of the *Man with a Golden Helmet* when it was unpacked (fig. 6). For Berliners, this return was even more important than the recent ones, as it was known to be definitive.

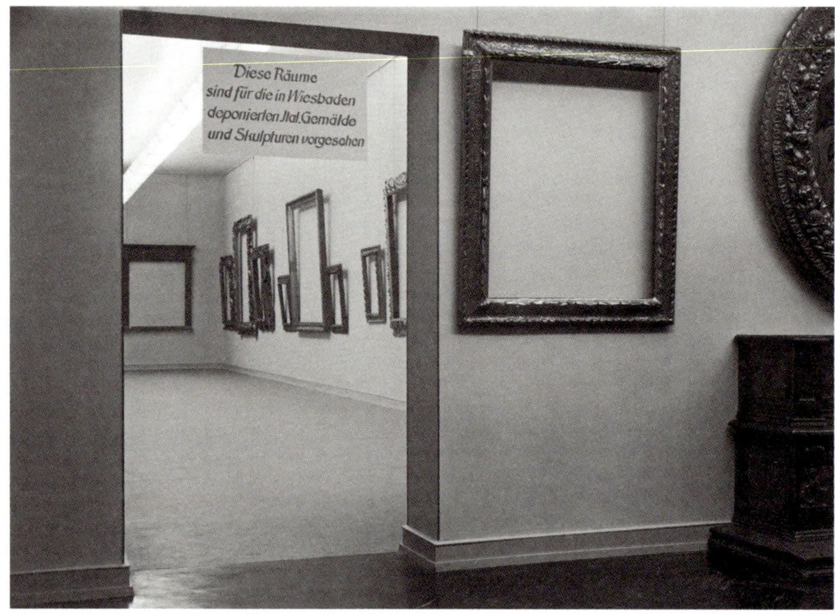


Fig. 7. View of the Dahlem Museum, West Berlin, with empty picture frames and a sign that reads "These rooms are intended for Italian paintings and sculptures deposited in Wiesbaden," 1954. Zentralarchiv der Staatlichen Museen zu Berlin, ZA 2.4.103499

If a few significant works from Wiesbaden had come back permanently, this was not the case for the majority of them—a situation that the Dahlem Museum could not accept. Besides publications and press campaigns, the most spectacular manifestation of the pressure that West Berliners exerted on the federal authorities in order to recover "their" paintings was the establishment in 1954 of a suite of galleries of the Dahlem Museum entirely hung with empty frames and introduced in the starkest terms: "These rooms are intended for Italian paintings and sculptures deposited in Wiesbaden" (fig. 7).[44] In fact, the Italian paintings (and sculptures) had never been shown in Dahlem before the war, and the exhibited frames had nothing to do with those of the "missing" pictures, but the message was clear: the rightful place of the paintings unjustly retained in Wiesbaden was on the walls of the Dahlem Museum. Once again, legitimate motivations for restitution were intimately linked to propagandistic operations.

At the far right of the photograph of the "empty frames" installation, one can see the extremity of a major work that had just returned to Berlin in an unquestionably legal way: Sandro Botticelli's *Madonna and Child with Singing Angels* (BR 19; fig. 8), named the *Raczynski tondo* because of its round shape and its former owners, the Raczynski family. Rather than donating the work

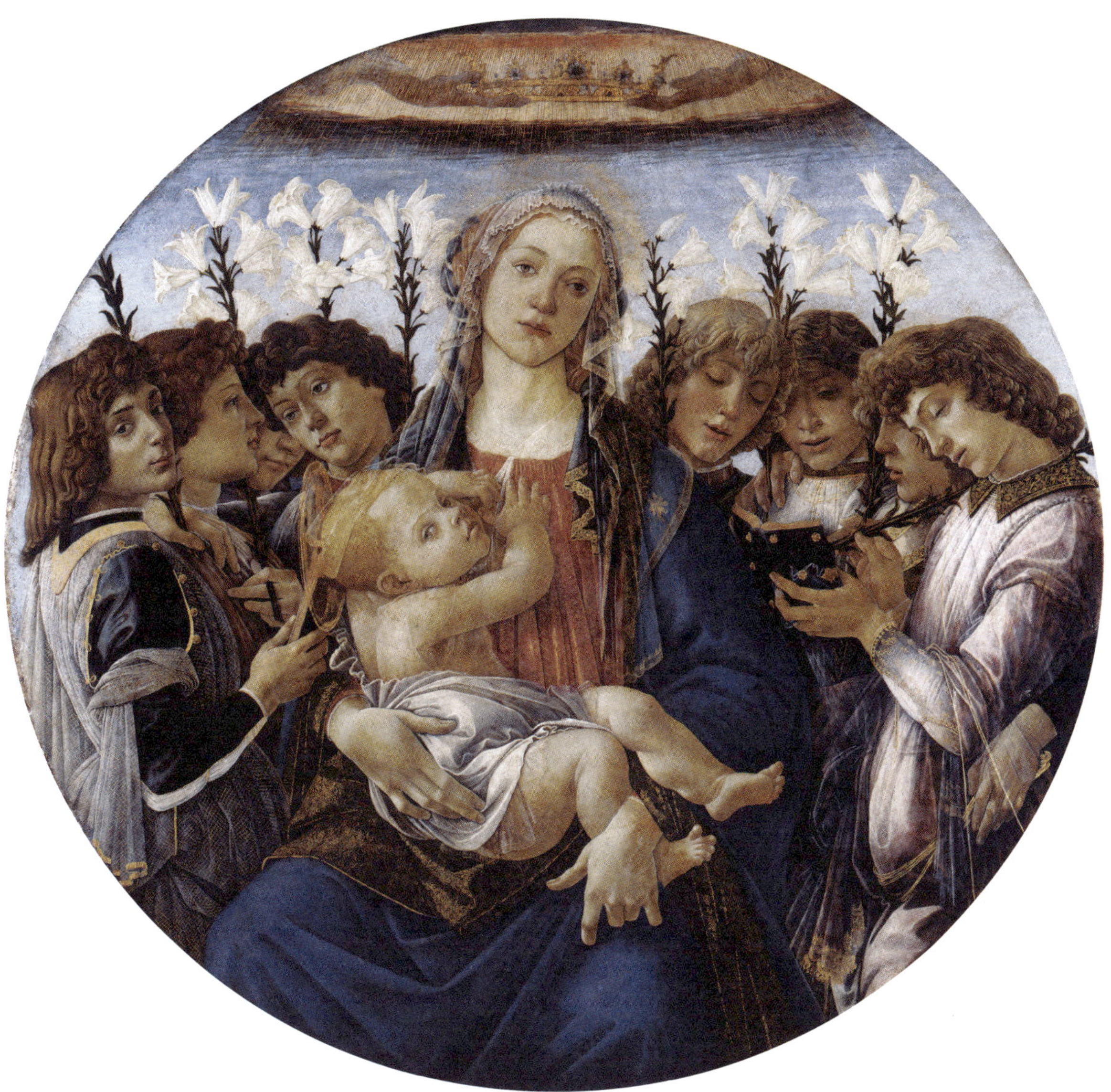

Fig. 8. Sandro Botticelli (1445–1510), *Madonna and Child with Singing Angels (Raczynski tondo)*, circa 1477, tempera on poplar panel, diam. 53¾ in. (136.5 cm). Staatliche Museen zu Berlin, Gemäldegalerie, 102 A

to their home city of Posen (now Poznań) with the rest of their collection, the Raczynskis had decided in 1903 to lend it on a long-term basis to the soon-to-be-opened Kaiser-Friedrich-Museum in Berlin. After World War II, the work had been sent to Washington as part of the "202" and had returned to Germany in spring 1948; two years later, the Raczynski heirs took legal action to obtain its restitution. The *tondo* was then bought from them in 1954 by the West German government, thanks to contributions from almost all of the German states, and immediately sent to the Dahlem Museum to be exhibited.[45] In a booming West Germany, it was no longer a time for internal disputes: the whole country had agreed to provide its former capital with a painting as much emblematic of the Italian Renaissance as of its museum history. The definitive restitution of the remaining paintings to Berlin would soon follow.

## THE END OF THE STORY?

On January 11, 1956, the decision to transfer definitively to West Berlin the paintings from Wiesbaden was finally enacted:[46] three months later, another exhibition opened in the Dahlem Museum, in which many of the masterpieces that had traveled throughout America and had already come to West Berlin in the preceding years were to be seen, no more as temporary loans but as part of the permanent display (fig. 9).[47] In 1949, the return of the "202" from America to Wiesbaden was thought of as a mere step before their return to Berlin.[48] Now that the complete contents of the Gemäldegalerie preserved in the Western Bloc had reached its city of origin, it was time to plan a step further: at the opening of the exhibition, Ernst Reuter's successor as mayor of West Berlin, Otto Suhr, vowed to see all the Berlin paintings (that is to say from the Eastern and Western Blocs) displayed again in five years' time in their original location on Museum Island, in a free and united Berlin.[49] Such a statement was already optimistic considering the international situation in 1956; it would have looked positively utopian five years later, since after August 13, 1961, Berlin was divided by a wall. Yet one of Otto Suhr's wishes made on that day in 1956 was soon granted: as a consequence of the return of the works to West Berlin, the Soviet Union decided to transfer to the German Democratic Republic 1.5 million works—over half of the cultural assets taken in 1945–46.[50] If the partition of Berlin and of the former Prussian Museums seemed definitive, at least the majority of the works had returned home.

The story of the "202" could have ended quietly in Dahlem, where the paintings were to be displayed for more than three decades. At the end of the 1950s, however, the administration of the West Berlin Museums was already planning to create a new museum complex closer to the city center: this "Kulturforum" would be located a stone's throw from the Wall and the divided Potsdamer Platz, once the most animated square of prewar Berlin.[51] When the Wall fell, on November 9, 1989, a structure had not yet been built for the paintings and sculptures of Dahlem, even though the project for a new museum had been fully funded. It was decided that the Skulpturensammlung (Sculpture Collection) would again be displayed in the former Kaiser-Friedrich-Museum, which had been renamed Bode-Museum in 1956, while the reunified Gemäldegalerie would be transferred to the new building of the

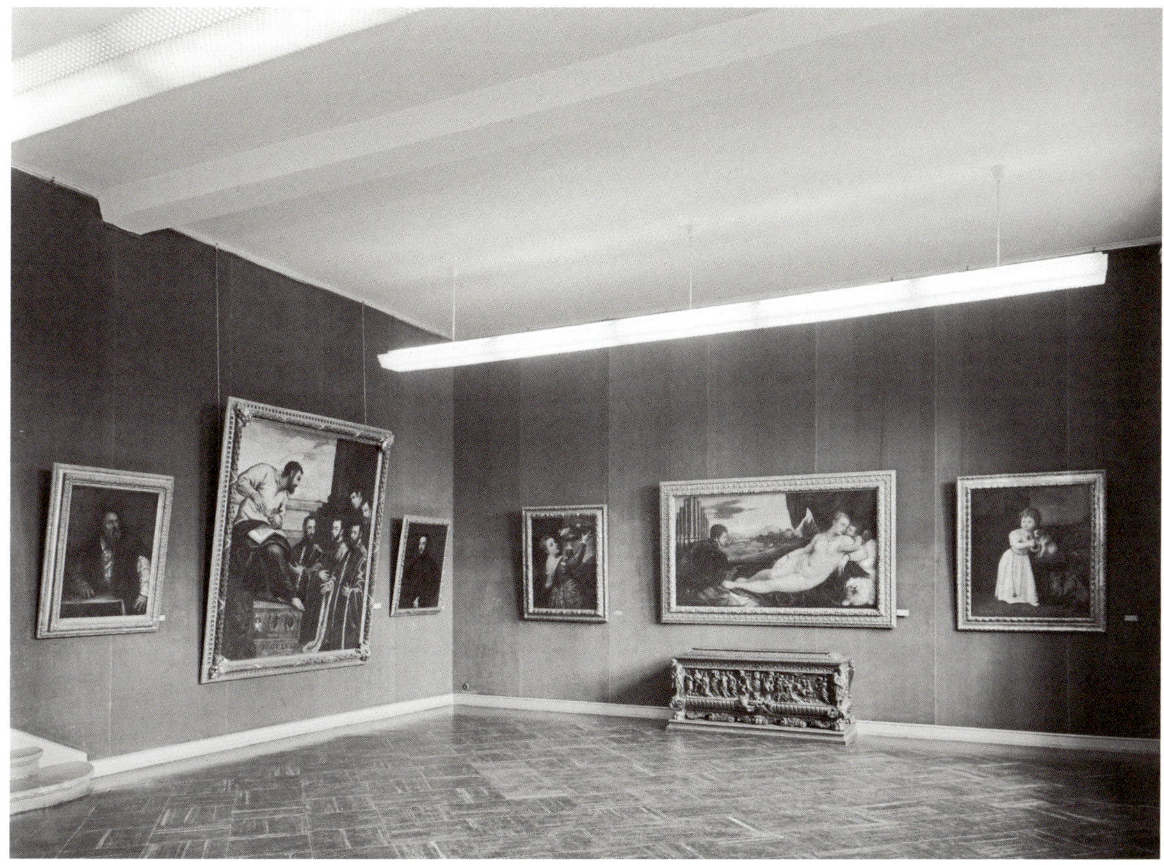

Fig. 9. View of the Titian Room, Dahlem Museum, West Berlin, 1956. Zentralarchiv der Staatlichen Museen zu Berlin, SMB-ZA, V/Fotoslg

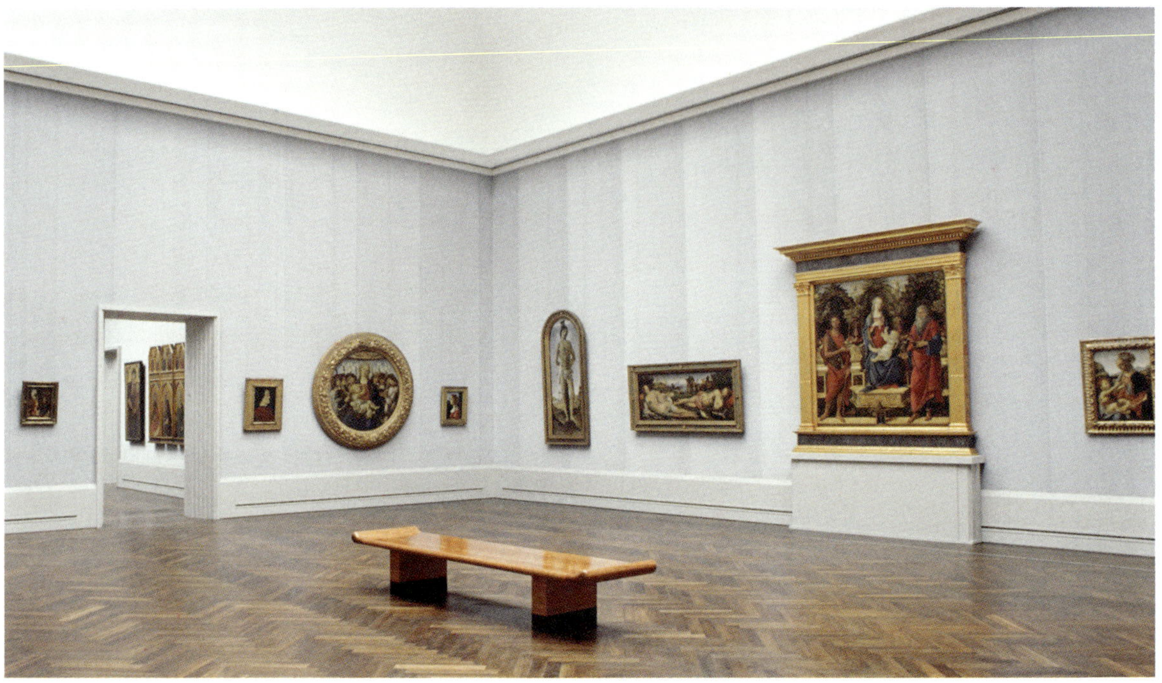

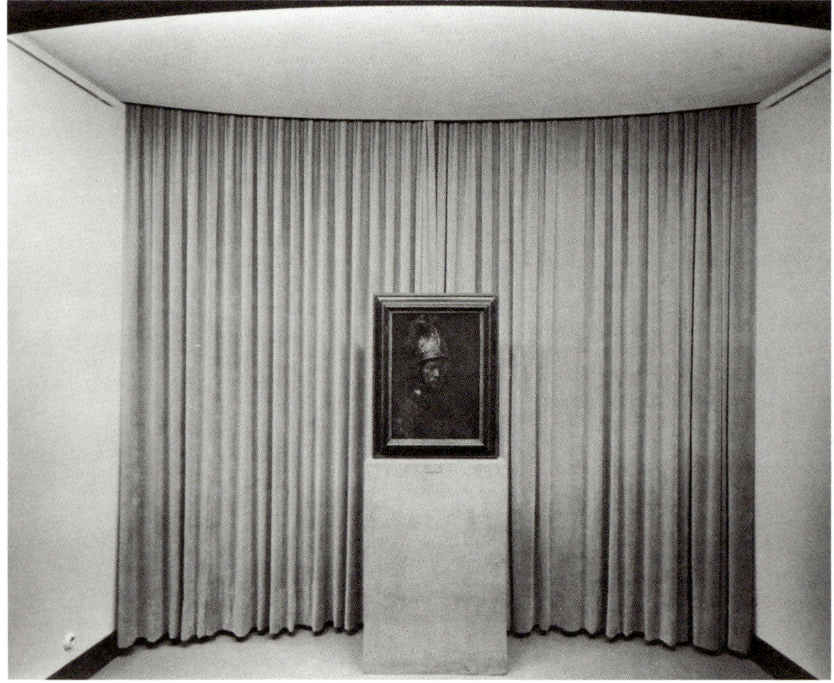

Fig. 10. View of the Botticelli Room, Gemäldegalerie, Berlin, June 11, 1998. Zentralarchiv der Staatlichen Museen zu Berlin, SMB-ZA, V/Fotoslg

Fig. 11. View of the *Man with a Golden Helmet* in the Dahlem Museum, West Berlin, 1991. Zentralarchiv der Staatlichen Museen zu Berlin, SMB-ZA, V/Fotoslg

Kulturforum. As Otto Suhr had wished in 1956, the prewar paintings collection would once again be shown in a free and reunified Berlin—even if not in its entirety due to the losses of the war, and not in its former building, the Kaiser-Friedrich-Museum.

Today, most of the "202" are visible at the Gemäldegalerie in the Kulturforum. The vast majority of them are still considered masterpieces central to the collection (fig. 10).[52] One painting has however suffered a spectacular setback: the *Man with a Golden Helmet*, which had long been considered as a masterpiece by Rembrandt and had been one of the first paintings to return permanently to Berlin due to the fact that it belonged to the Kaiser-Friedrich-Museums-Verein. In 1986, based on scientific analysis, the museum downgraded its attribution to a collaborator of Rembrandt;[53] the preeminent exhibition of the work in Dahlem as "the" masterpiece of the Berlin collection could no longer be sustained in the new building (fig. 11).

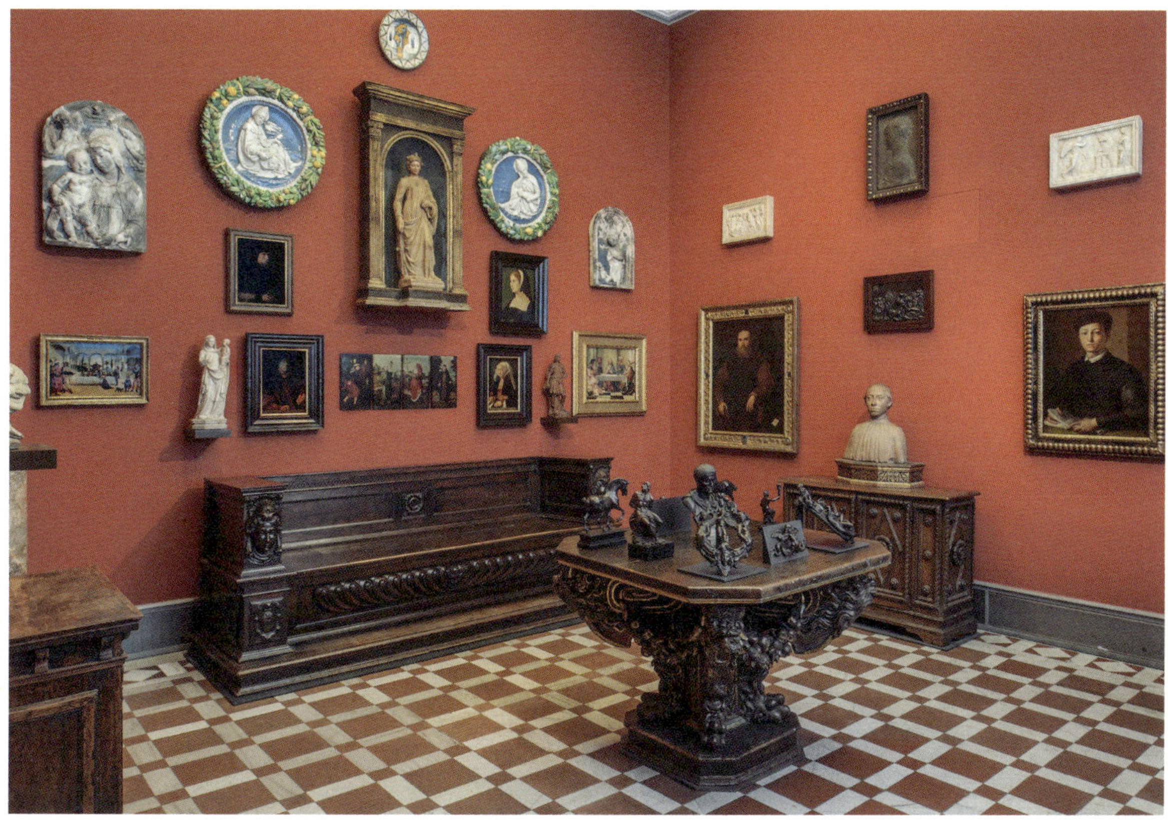

Fig. 12. View of the James Simon Cabinet in the Bode-Museum, 2019

If it has lost its place among the greatest masterpieces of the collection, the painting is at least still exhibited at the Gemäldegalerie. This is not the case for a small handful of paintings from the "202," such as a *Madonna and Child* formerly attributed to Dieric Bouts (BR 24), which are now consigned to storage. Some works from the "202" are also exhibited at the Bode-Museum, in dialogue with the Sculpture Collection. *Portrait of a Young Man* attributed to Agnolo Bronzino (BR 25), for example, has been displayed there since 2019 in a gallery recreating the Renaissance collection of the greatest donor in the history of the Berlin Museums, James Simon (fig. 12).[54] At present, this is the only painting of the "202" that is hung in the same room—and even on the very same wall—in which it was displayed before World War II.[55]

Upon the return of the "202" to West Berlin, many of the paintings that had toured so extensively in the previous decades were not allowed to travel for exhibition. This condition continues to prevail, especially for large works on panel, such as Giotto's *Death of the Virgin* or Botticelli's *Raczynski tondo* (figs. 2 and 8).[56] Some of the works, however, are in sufficiently good condition to be presented in exhibitions of significant scholarly interest. This has been the case for several events held at the National Gallery of Art in Washington, DC, to which a few of the "202" have been willingly returned after their forced stay between 1945 and 1948. The latest examples are two paintings of the *Madonna and Child* (BR 187–188) lent in fall 2019 to an exhibition dedicated to Leonardo da Vinci's master, Andrea del Verrocchio. In his review of the exhibition held in 1951 in Schaffhausen, Roberto Longhi disparaged both of them: the first (BR 187) was Verrocchio's work, but it was "mediocre" in comparison to the second (BR 188; fig. 13), which "shall be ascribed to [Verrocchio's pupil] Pietro Perugino," Longhi wrote peremptorily.[57] Six decades later, the world is still divided on the attribution: the Berlin paintings continue to be a subject of dispute, at least mostly in the field of scholarship.[58] But with their return to Berlin, not all the paintings had come back to where they belonged. Among the "202" were two paintings that their Jewish owner had been forced to sell during the Nazi era: *The Ordination of Saint Clara of Assisi* and *Saint Clara Aids the Shipwrecked* by Giovanni di Paolo (BR 76–77). In 2019, they were returned to the heirs of the entrepreneur Harry Fuld, Sr.[59]

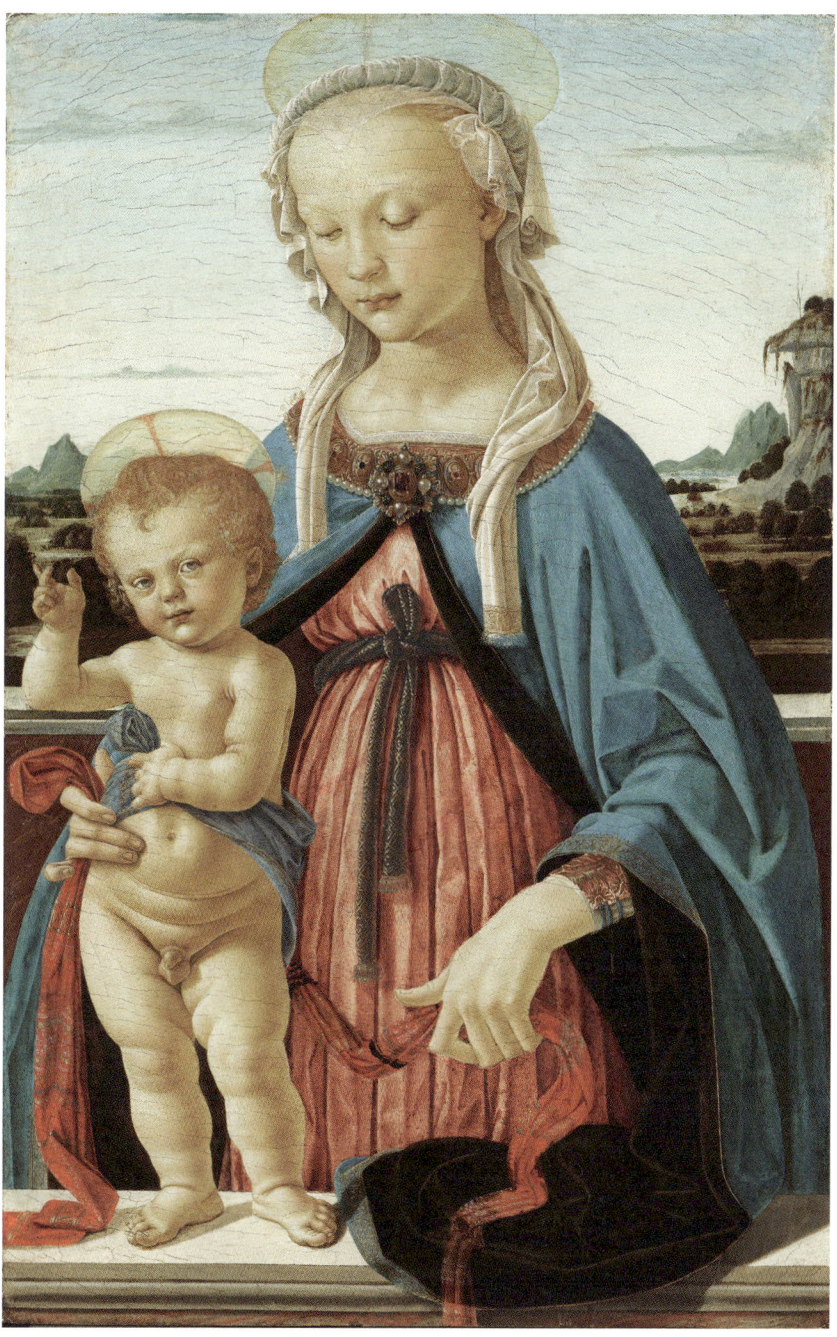

Fig. 13. Andrea del Verrocchio (1435/36–1488), *Madonna and Child*, circa 1473, tempera and gold on poplar panel, 29 13/16 × 18 7/8 in. (75.8 × 47.9 cm). Staatliche Museen zu Berlin, Gemäldegalerie, 108

## NOTES

*My warmest thanks to Peter Bell, Julien Chapuis, Douglas Kline, Kristi Nelson, and Petra Winter.*

1. Farmer 2000, p. 56: "Plunder is the only word."
2. Press release from the US armed forces in Germany on November 24, 1945 (cited by Kühnel-Kunze 1984, p. 103).
3. The effective partition of Berlin happened on November 30, 1948.
4. The most important sources on the events described in this essay are Kühnel-Kunze 1984 and Winter 2008. On the Central Collecting Point in Wiesbaden, see Bernsau 2013.
5. The order in which the paintings were restituted is indicated in the Exhibition Checklist, pp. 174–208. On the official motivations of this operation, see the press release issued by the National Gallery of Art on April 29, 1948 (cited by Kühnel-Kunze 1984, pp. 383–85, esp. p. 383).
6. On the critical fortunes and physical condition of this work, see respectively Rowley 2018 and Hartwieg 2018. Among the paintings of this group was also *The Holy Family with Angels and Infant Saint John* by Adam Elsheimer (BR 60), which is painted on copper.
7. The exhibition was open from June 13 to August 15, 1948; see Bayerische Staatsgemälde-Sammlungen 1948.
8. Cited by Kühnel-Kunze 1984, p. 387.
9. Farmer 2000, esp. pp. 67–70.
10. On this exhibition, see Peter Bell's essay and catalogue numbers 1–4.
11. See, however, the conclusion of this essay.
12. Wiesbaden was located in the American-occupied zone of Germany, while Celle was under British jurisdiction.
13. Letters from Heinrich Zimmermann, both dated July 3, 1948 (Staatliche Museen zu Berlin, Zentralarchiv, II B/GD 9).
14. Letter from Heinrich Zimmermann, June 30, 1948 (Staatliche Museen zu Berlin, Zentralarchiv, II B/GD 9).
15. Letter from Andreas Sessig to Heinrich Zimmermann, July 7, 1948 (Staatliche Museen zu Berlin, Zentralarchiv, II B/GD 9).
16. Kühnel-Kunze 1984, p. 121. See also Winter 2008, p. 124, with a slightly later date. The works from Berlin stored in Celle were likewise placed in the custody of the State of Lower Saxony.
17. See Exhibition Checklist, pp. 174–208, and Kristi Nelson's essay for further discussion of the groups of paintings returning from America.
18. *Returned Masterworks* 1949.
19. The article is cited by Kühnel-Kunze 1984, pp. 387–91, Appendix 13; the quote is on p. 388.
20. The expression was apparently coined for the first edition of the Berlin Film Festival in 1951: see https://www.berlinale.de/en/archiv/jahresarchive/1951/01_jahresblatt_1951/01_Jahresblatt_1951.html (accessed on August 5, 2019).
21. The letter is reproduced by Kühnel-Kunze 1984, pp. 411–12, Appendix 21.
22. Kühnel-Kunze 1984, p. 162 (letter of May 10, 1950).
23. The exhibitions took place in Amsterdam, June 17–September 17; Brussels, September 27–December 27; and Paris, February 2–May 9. For the catalogues, see Rijksmuseum 1950, Palais des Beaux-Arts 1950, and Musée du Petit Palais 1951.
24. The cover of the Paris exhibition catalogue was Jean-Antoine Watteau's *L'Enseigne de Gersaint*, a picture from the Charlottenburg Palace that was not part of the Berlin Painting Collection, and hence not one of the "202." Such "diplomatic" exhibitions were not restricted to the Berlin pictures: in the same years, the collections of the Alte Pinakothek in Munich and of the Kunsthistorisches Museum in Vienna also went on international tour, and were shown, for instance, at the Petit Palais in Paris.
25. On May 9, 1950, French foreign minister Robert Schuman proposed that German and French coal and steel production be placed under one common High Authority, a proposition seen today as the real starting point for European integration.
26. See Kühnel-Kunze 1984, p. 261.
27. See for instance the testimony of French politician and economist Jean Monnet: "The fate of the world is not playing out in Korea [said Adenauer] but in the heart of Europe. I am convinced that Stalin has the same plan for Germany as for Korea. What is happening over there is a rehearsal of what awaits us here." See Monnet 1976, p. 395.
28. The letter is cited by Kühnel-Kunze 1984, pp. 163–64.
29. See Kühnel-Kunze 1984, p. 178. Besides the *Adoration of the Magi* by Hugo van der Goes (strangely not included in the "202"), four works initially slated to travel—but kept back in Wiesbaden for conservation reasons—were from the "202": the *Enthroned Madonna and Child with Donor (Glatz Madonna)* (BR 16); *Netherlandish Proverbs* by Pieter Bruegel (BR 28); the *Madonna and Child in a Church* by Jan van Eyck (BR 64); and the *Portrait of Georg Gisze* by Hans Holbein (BR 91). Sandro Botticelli's *Raczynski tondo* (BR 19) could not travel for legal reasons (see later in this essay).
30. Gemäldegalerie 1950.
31. Michaelis 1995; Chapuis and Kemperdick 2015.
32. This variation between paintings and sculptures inherited from Bode was explicitly defended in the Dahlem exhibition catalogue; see Kühnel-Kunze 1950, p. 7. The *Dangolsheim Madonna* was catalogued as anonymous in 1950; it is now ascribed to Nikolaus Gerhaert.
33. Cited by Winter 2008, p. 140: "Es ist, als seien die Werke Dürers und Tizians, die Werke der deutschen Primitiven des Quattrocento und der Niederländer wie ein Phoenix aus Feuer- und Aschenregen hervorgegangen."
34. The speech is reproduced in Kühnel-Kunze 1984, pp. 416–19, Appendix 24 (the quote is on p. 419: "Es ist der schönste Tag, seitdem ich in Berlin bin."). Ernst Reuter had first moved to Berlin in 1913.
35. The expression "Berliner Bildstreit" (Berlin paintings quarrel) was coined by West Berlin's Senator for Popular Education Joachim Tiburtius in a report given in June 1951 (its foreword is reprinted in Kühnel-Kunze 1984, p. 424, Appendix 26).
36. Kühnel-Kunze 1984, p. 169.
37. Tisa Francini, Heuss, and Kreis 2001, pp. 461–63.
38. Museum zu Allerheiligen Schaffhausen 1951; the exhibition lasted until October 28, 1951. See Longhi 1952 (1985).
39. Longhi was not always just in his reproaches, as when he found it regrettable that the exhibition attributed a painting of the *Three Archangels* to Giovanni Boccati and not to the Master of Pratovecchio; at that time, no one but Longhi knew this master, to whom he would dedicate a famous article later that year (see Longhi 1952 [1975]).
40. Winter 2008, p. 148.

41. For a list of the exhibitions held during this period, see Kühnel-Kunze 1984, pp. 432–40, Appendix 30.
42. The exhibition lasted from September 1951 to March 1952. See Gemäldegalerie 1951.
43. The title of the exhibition catalogue is a clear statement on the propriety of the pictures: "Catalogue of the works of art of the Kaiser-Friedrich-Museums-Verein which have been delivered to the Dahlem Museum on loan" (see Gemäldegalerie 1953). On this episode, see Schoenebeck and Bloch 1972, p. 9; and Kühnel-Kunze 1984, p. 228.
44. "Diese Räume sind für die in Wiesbaden deponierten Ital. Gemälde und Skulpturen vorgesehen." For the press campaign, see the forum organized by the *Tagesspiegel* on May 23, 1951 (mentioned by Kühnel-Kunze 1984, p. 185). See also the short pamphlet published once again by the Kaiser-Friedrich-Museums-Verein with the eloquent title "Save the Berlin Museums" (see *Rettet die Berliner Museen. . .* 1954).
45. See Zimmermann 1954; and Kühnel-Kunze 1984, pp. 232–36.
46. Kühnel-Kunze 1984. This decision was taken one year and a half before the creation of the entity that would own the State Museums of Berlin, the Stiftung Preußischer Kulturbesitz (Prussian Cultural Heritage Foundation).
47. Staatliche Museen Berlin 1957.
48. See note 19 above.
49. This text is reproduced in Kühnel-Kunze 1984, pp. 482–85, Appendix 40 (esp. p. 485). Ernst Reuter had died in 1953.
50. Winter 2008, pp. 202–4.
51. Winter 2008, p. 207.
52. Half of a recent publication dedicated to the "200 masterpieces of the Gemäldegalerie" (Eissenhauer 2019) is taken up by paintings from the "202" (including the cover, Vermeer's *Lady with a Pearl Necklace*, BR 185); the rest of the pictures are works that were preserved in the Eastern Bloc during the Cold War, but also acquisitions made after World War II. The differences reflect also the changes of taste between the 1940s and 2019.
53. See Kelch 1986.
54. See Rowley 2020.
55. Other paintings from the "202" exhibited at the Bode-Museum are Masaccio and Fra Filippo Lippi's *Four Saints* from the Pisa Altarpiece (BR 114, all four panels were attributed to Masaccio in 1945; the *Young Carmelite* is now attributed to Fra Filippo Lippi) and Alessandro Allori's *Portrait of a Young Man* (BR 27, attributed to Bronzino in 1945).
56. The *Raczynski tondo* was shown at the Berlin venue of an exhibition dedicated to "The Botticelli Renaissance" in 2015–16, but did not travel to the Victoria and Albert Museum in London for the second leg of the exhibition (Evans and Weppelmann 2015).
57. Longhi 1952 (1985), p. 313. Longhi's attribution was, however, made in the absence of the work (BR 188), whereas the other *Madonna* (BR 187) had traveled to the exhibition.
58. On the various positions on this work see Aldo Galli in Caglioti and De Marchi 2019, pp. 124–27, cat. 3.4 (listed as Verrocchio); and Neville Rowley in Butterfield 2019, pp. 208–211, cat. 26 (listed as attributed to Verrocchio or Perugino). I am now convinced that the work is by Verrocchio.
59. See http://www.preussischer-kulturbesitz.de/pressemitteilung/article/2019/08/29/pressemeldung-spk-restituiert-zwei-predellentafeln-aus-der-sammlung-fuld/ (accessed on September 17, 2019). Both works were sold at Christie's London on December 3, 2019, for the record price of £9 million. Another debated provenance for one of the 202 paintings is *Doge Alvise Mocenigo* by the workshop of Jacopo Tintoretto (BR 174), acquired in 1935 by the Prussian state from the art possessions of the Dresdner Bank and transferred to the Berlin State Museums (formerly in possession of Anne Caspari in Munich).

# WALTER INGS FARMER: MEMORIES OF A LIFE

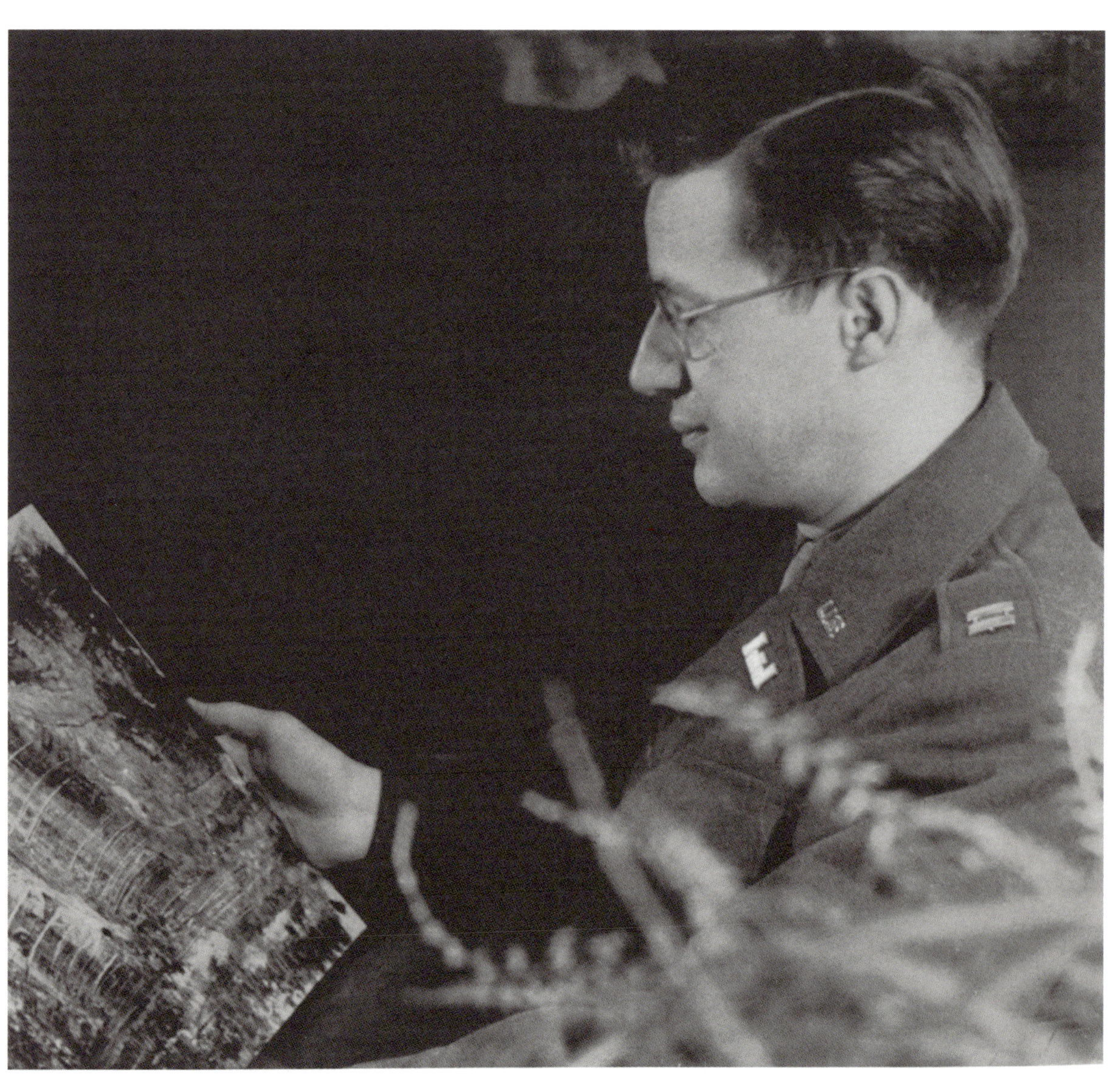

Fig. 1. Walter Farmer at the Wiesbaden CCP examining Alo Altripp's *Bank of Spring Flowers*, one of five of the artist's paintings Farmer gave to the Cincinnati Art Museum. National Gallery of Art, Washington, DC, Gallery Archives, 28MFAA-C, Walter Farmer Papers

Walter Farmer was born in 1911 in northern Ohio, son of a steel factory executive. In his own words, he "moved with rapidity into a precocious adolescence. I had discovered reading, music and collecting at a very early age and for my interest in these pursuits I was rewarded with adult friendships and encouragement."[1] As a young man he was introduced to art collecting and interior design by a relative, Kenyon Painter, who also provided Farmer with entrée to the cultural life of New York City, which had a profound effect. He then studied architecture at Miami University in Oxford, Ohio, and moved to Cincinnati in 1935 to work for the A. B. Closson Company, a large decorating and interior design firm. Soon he began teaching courses on interior design and the decorative arts at the Cincinnati Art Museum and University of Cincinnati.

With war looming, Farmer attempted to enter the armed services several times in 1941, but was rejected due to poor eyesight. He was engaged to Josselyn Liszniewska, the worldly daughter of a diplomat and a musician, at Christmas time that year, and they married two months later.[2] Five weeks after that, in March 1942, Farmer was successfully drafted into the Medical Corps. He quickly rose through the ranks, graduating from the Officers Candidate School, and making first lieutenant in July 1943. He joined the 373rd Engineers General Service Regiment, which shipped to England that fall. In February 1944, while under fire from German aircraft, Farmer's back was broken in a jeep accident near his regimental headquarters in Wales. During his convalescence in Bristol, he visited bookstores and antique shops, shipping home his finds.

Crossing the English Channel with his regiment in late August 1944, Farmer witnessed the destruction of war-ravaged Normandy. As adjutant to Colonel Bell, he supervised initial rebuilding efforts in Le Havre, and on into western and southern Germany as the Allied forces advanced. Not long after V-E Day, the 373rd Engineers was ordered to return to the US in June 1945, at which point Farmer applied to join the Monuments, Fine Arts, and Archives (MFAA) branch of the Army. Farmer sought out this transfer, hoping it would be, in his words, "a kind of personal redemption . . . , an opportunity to work for something I believed in," to assuage the horror he felt in the previous months, witnessing the destruction of cultural patrimony across Europe—the "carelessness and even viciousness the troops, ours and theirs, [exhibited] when confronted with beautiful objects and when quartered in wonderful historic surroundings."[3]

Farmer's efforts as an MFAA officer in Wiesbaden are discussed in the essays by Tanja Bernsau and Kristi Nelson in this book. Walter Farmer and Renate Hobirk were at the center of activities in the initial months of the Wiesbaden Central Collecting Point in 1945 and 1946. They would marry several years later, and have a daughter, Margaret Farmer Planton. They divorced in 1966, and in 1972 Farmer began a committed relationship with Ted Gantz that would last the rest of his life. Margaret grew up with Walter and Renate, and Margaret and Ted were the two people closest to Walter during the last thirty years of his life. They were interviewed in summer 2019 with the goal of giving some context to Walter Farmer's life after the war and Wiesbaden.

* * *

| *After he returned from Europe, Walter Farmer moved to Houston.*

**Ted Gantz**: Walter had worked, before the war, with Closson's, which was this fancy decorating firm, in Cincinnati. But the owner was a man that Walter said under no circumstances would he ever go back to work for. And so when the war ended Walter started looking around, and he was offered a job at Foley's department store, in Houston. So he goes to Houston, at which point he writes to Renate and says, "Do you want to marry?" She writes back and says, "I mean, I'm desperate to get out of Germany." And Margaret was born in Houston.

**Margaret Planton**: There actually was a Cincinnati connection [in Houston]—somebody was related to somebody else that owned Foley's. Then Walter got in there and worked there quite a number of years and had the little house. The address shows up even before Mother did, because they must have corresponded. Well, he asked her to marry him, and then the process to come

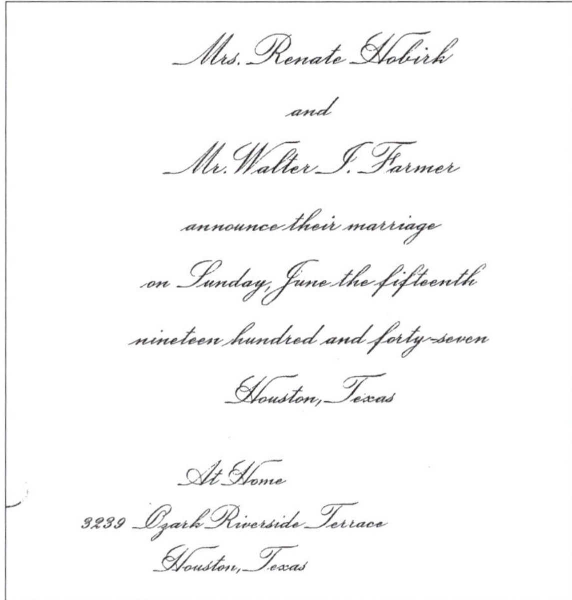

Mrs. Renate Hobirk

and

Mr. Walter I. Farmer

announce their marriage

on Sunday, June the fifteenth

nineteen hundred and forty-seven

Houston, Texas

At Home

3239 Ozark Riverside Terrace

Houston, Texas

Fig. 2. Marriage announcement for Walter Farmer and Renate Hobirk. Administrative Records, 1944–1951, Box 85, A1 493, Records of US Occupation Headquarters, Record Group 260, National Archives at College Park, College Park, MD

over involved all of these approvals and all these letters. There are three letters about Mother by this group of Monuments Men, about her character—references, vouching for her. I have a whole folder of her paperwork. Then the stuff Walter had to show: that he had some money, where he had been born, and that he had a job. So, to get her visa and to get the ship arranged took quite a while. Then there's some letters in there: Edith Standen wrote, "Oh, I'm sad and sorry for you this is taking so long."[4] Just charming. So, these people all became friends.

| *After Houston, Walter and Renate moved to Cincinnati.*

**TG**: And then Walter decided he wanted to come back to Cincinnati. I'm not sure exactly why. He came back and went to work for Greenwich House, which was owned by the Fleischmanns.[5]

**MP**: It was right at the turn of 1950 that they moved to Cincinnati. I think there was a first rental, and then there was Collins Avenue.[6] "Gin Row" is the other name for it. It's just this whole group of condos, apartments—Collins Avenue. I guess they're still going. It was fantastic. Artist Bob Smith of the Cincinnati Art Academy and his family lived there, and many other interesting people. So it was a first step for Mother meeting people in Cincinnati, and developing new friendships.

***What were your early years like with them?***

**MP**: They were both teaching art. He was running the store. There was the house that they bought, I believe in '52, on Observatory Place.[7] They spent years working together to fix the house and garden. It became filled with furniture from my mom that was shipped over from Germany, in '53, '54. The house was also an extension of the store. Walter was chasing his dream [as a decorator, collector], and Mother was doing a good job teaching, being an art history teacher, and I went to school there.[8]

**TG**: The garden was Walter's true love, and it was the reason that he was never going to give the house up for the divorce. And Renate didn't want the house, anyway.

**MP**: And what a magical house and garden it was! There were huge amazing parties all over the house and garden for friends and clients.

He was building this business, working at it incredibly hard, even weekends, and then the teaching at nights—I don't know that Mother had ever experienced that. They used to fight over how to celebrate Christmas. They never really learned to talk to each other, but talking to each other wasn't the thing then either.

Such very, very different life flow and assumptions, and I guess I came to grips at one point that they stayed together longer because they both loved me. It was, "Well, we also have this child that we are enjoying."

### *Ted, how did you get to know Walter?*

**TG**: We met at a party, a big party the Fleischmanns had thrown, about '72. I had started working pretty extensively for Skip [Charles] Fleischmann a few years before.

I was a practicing sculptor. I lived at home with my parents. Traveled to Europe two or three times a year, did all that sort of thing. I had no real interest in owning a property or anything like that.

I knew his [Walter's] ex-wife, Renate, because she taught at the Academy.[9] So I knew her from around '64, but I had never met Walter. And then Walter came along, and after a year or so, I moved into Walter's house. And we lived together until '90.

## BUSINESS

> *Walter's professional life as a decorator was bound up in Greenwich House Interiors from the moment he returned to Cincinnati for the rest of his career – almost forty years.*

**TG**: He came back [to Cincinnati] and went to work for Greenwich House. The manager had very little interest in what it cost to run [the business], because the bill was being footed by the Fleischmanns. And so Walter, at a certain point, says to the Fleischmanns, "Would you sell it?" Walter had developed a nice business friend relationship with Oliver Bardes, who was an industrialist here in Cincinnati. He dealt in diamonds, and had an international business. When he went to visit one of his companies in Europe, he took Walter with him, to see some museums, to see a little bit of cultural life. And so when Walter wanted to buy Greenwich House, Oliver Bardes backed him, became his silent partner.

So that got Walter started in Greenwich House, which was a firm that, like Closson's, had its own upholstery department, its own drapery department, several delivery trucks. It was like a complete firm. There was almost nothing that they outsourced. It was all in-house. And that's what he bought.

***How did his business in Cincinnati evolve? Was his work in Cincinnati successful?***

**TG**: It worked through the '60s. The difficult period was the recession of '79, '80. That really affected Walter's business, and so he struggled to be as successful in the '80s as he had been in the '60s and '70s. People were saying, "Oh, we go to the young people."

And he struggled with that in the '80s, and then all of a sudden, in the '90s, he became the grand old man of decorating. And so people came back to him, and he very much was successful working until the day he died.

**MP**: The clientele was a wide range, but then mostly professional people, people of society.

**TG**: He was social with his clients, but it also built his business. He wanted to be part of the crowd, as much as possible. And he liked to have prestigious jobs to do, the public rooms in the Cincinnati Country Club, the public rooms at the Woman's Club, at the Cincinnati Queen City Club. He did all of those public spaces, and then he enjoyed doing the major corporate clients.

## COLLECTING

*Photographs of his Observatory Place home and his gifts to the Cincinnati Art Museum document a wide range of interests – European drawings and prints, antique glass and ceramics, Asian porcelain, Pre-Columbian art, and abstract paintings.*

### *How do you think of Walter as a collector?*

**TG**: Well, I think the thing that's interesting about the time that Walter was collecting, is how much was available. This was certainly true at the point Walter was collecting in the '50s and '60s, when the big houses of people in Cincinnati were being scaled down.

A lot of the big families, the old families, were dying and closing their mansions. So [there were sales at] auction houses like Aronoff, which no longer exists. But, I mean, I remember in the late '60s and the '70s, it was just like a treasure trove. There was much more material available regionally, it didn't just all go to New York.

Even in England, when Walter was stationed there before D-Day, he was buying books and things. And, apparently, you could get wooden ration boxes as they emptied them, and pack things up and send them back free. So Walter was acquiring library books and things of that sort, in England.

I don't think he found any objects, particularly. Although, knowing Walter, God knows. Where all that stuff came from, I just have no idea. I just know what we bought together, from the '70s on.

*In his memoir he does mention the ration boxes, especially when he was convalescing in Bristol, and that his previous employer, Closson's, set a whole room aside to store the things he was shipping back.*[10]

**TG**: And then, in '72, when Walter came into my life, Walter and I did a number of trips to Italy together, and bought things. Not so much for Greenwich House. I don't think we did that. We did flower pots and terra cotta garden-y things, but I don't think Walter ever bought antiques in Europe.

We would do antiquing trips around the United States. There used to be a number of big import houses; one up in Pennsylvania, called Merritt's, and one in Winston-Salem, which we never bought from. But then there was a place up in Ypsilanti, Michigan, called Schmidt's. They were bringing in things from England. Merritt's brought in things from Germany, so a lot of Biedermeier. It was mostly household furniture, things like that, but antique, not grand things. We would go up with a van and bring things back for the store. And if we saw things for ourselves, that would fit in.

### *Was Walter interested in contemporary art?*

**MP**: Not in the earlier part of his life. It really was the experience in Wiesbaden of getting to know Alo Altripp, and a few of the other artists who were coming to the museum, or their families saying, "Please save the Jawlenskys. I think they were hauled out of the basement somewhere, please save these things." And then Ernst Nay also was part of the circle.

Realizing that Alo had been painting, but was not allowed to paint under the Nazi regime because he was labeled "degenerate." And so he had to keep painting furtively. I mean, his pieces at that point were very modern, and bright, and bold—abstract. So it gave Walter that insight that somebody was so determined to do that, to risk their lives, to paint. That just made it all of a sudden seem real, not just maybe like kid stuff, or whatever he really had thought of it before. Walter sent lists home for Alo and for Ernst Nay to his first wife who sent paints to Wiesbaden. And my mom was the one transcribing these lists into English.[11] Walter felt that the process was amazing. He was just so impressed by the sincerity of this, that it really turned his attitude.

## PHILANTHROPY

> *Walter Farmer was one of seven Houston citizens that came together to found the Contemporary Arts Museum Houston in 1948, which flourished and has become integral to the culture of that city. He was also a catalyst for the founding of Miami University Art Museum, in Oxford, Ohio, and its greatest donor.*

**TG**: One of his teachers, who is mentioned in the foundation of the museum, Orpha Webster, I think [on her initiative] evolved the idea of starting a museum at Oxford. And then Walter started giving things, and I think other people started giving things, at that point.

Walter's position [as a potential donor of artworks] was strong enough that he was able to dictate what the building would be. Miami felt Walter was important enough that Walter was able to say "I will give it if a contemporary architect is the designer."

They sent Walter around the state, looking at Ohio architects. Then Walter came back and just sort of said, "You've got to be kidding." And they said, "Well, who do you recommend?" And Walter said, "I. M. Pei, Skidmore [Skidmore, Owings and Merrill], and Philip Johnson."

**TG:** So it ended up with Skidmore and Walter Netsch [as lead architect]. Miami certainly had enough of a sense of Walter, and what he was giving, to allow him to have that kind of sway over the building.

> *Walter Farmer was a supporter of the Taft Museum of Art and other Cincinnati arts organizations. The Cincinnati Art Museum benefited from gifts of art from Farmer over the course of forty-five years. This aspect of his patronage is addressed in section three of the catalogue.*

## THE AFTERLIFE OF THE WIESBADEN COLLECTING POINT

### *Did Walter and Renate talk about their experiences in Wiesbaden?*

**MP**: From the get-go there were Monuments Men that visited, friendships that continued. There was also this whole array of books and folios. It was pretty marbled paper boxes with [photos of the artworks that moved through the Collecting Point at] Wiesbaden that he had brought back. I'm assuming copies, of copies, of copies, and I played with them. The whole discussion of art and what happened in Germany. I heard conversations, the Monuments Men visited. I was very much an only child who was always right there and included, and just part of getting to know some of these people. I even visited Edith Standen in New York at one point.

### *You were growing up with this history.*

**MP**: Right. I can still hear the dinner-table conversation. They both loved to cook, they loved having dinner, so, lively dinner-time conversation. I can still hear, in my mind, my dad expressing how he felt when that telegram arrived to ship these pieces to America. I mean, the outrage. I could feel it, I could hear it, I can still hear it. It was such a profound experience to him that he had to speak up. Literally the next day he had put out a call to all nearby Monuments Men and Women. Together they debated and wrote the manifesto, and my mom was the one that typed it. She was the one German in the room with all of this.

### *What prompted Walter to talk publicly about his work in Wiesbaden?*

**MP**: The story of what they had done was hardly talked about out in the world. I did find one little thing at the University of Cincinnati, where I believe he'd actually lectured on it. Then he did give a series of lectures for the Literary Club—three or four of them—which I later helped him smooth out when he started being asked questions.

**TG**: The problem was, he was denigrated. Everybody just considered it a fantasy tale that he was telling. In the '70s and '80s, when he talked about this, there were some . . . I mean, decorators can be bitchy queens, to put it mildly. And there was one in particular, one here, that just said this was all lies and foolishness, and, "He's on that story again." And it really made Walter quite upset.

**MP**: Then all of a sudden, in the later '80s, Klaus Goldmann from Berlin found him and was like, "Okay, where's the Trojan gold I'm looking for? I've been looking, and looking, and looking, and not finding it, and I'm thinking you maybe might know where it is." Father was like, "Sorry. No, I don't know. Can I tell you about the Collecting Point?" "What's that?" Goldmann didn't know. That is really when I got involved. The divorce was long behind us. Mother still had friendships with people from the Collecting Point time, too, but there I was all of a sudden thrown into helping Dad answer questions. So, it got me busy translating.

**TG**: Yes, and then Klaus Goldmann, from Germany, comes over and contacts Walter, and says, "I'm doing this research. Could I interview you?" And that's what got Walter back into seriously starting to think about this. Walter and I went up to Washington, DC, and Klaus Goldmann interviewed Walter.

*And then in the 1990s came a surge of international interest in art looting and recovery during and after World War II.*

**MP**: Edith Standen was still alive at the symposium in '95 in New York.[12] Walter and I were there. And everybody was standing up and talking about different things—there was a panel of Monuments Men, and it was fantastic. There were Russians there, there were people from all over the world there, talking about all of this, and where things are now.

That symposium was really where Germany focused and said, "Wow, this is what the protests did and said." They were, I think, really realizing the significance of this. So that's what the manifesto had meant, and that Walter was the one that really started that. That's what led to the award trip, and the Groβes Verdienstkreuz in '96.[13] And in 1997 was the Mason's humanitarian award.[14]

The whole history was coming out, and that's when the first publications came out. There was Lynn Nicholas's book, she was there.[15]

*And so Walter's memoir became part of that literature and surge of interest, scholarship, and documentation.*[16]

**MP**: The follow-through of finishing the book happened after he passed away. Once in a while I'd be back and forth with the publisher in Berlin. Ruth Meyer had worked for Walter to start writing the book. She'd written a full first draft and much of it got quite rewritten. Walter and I started editing, and then Dr. Klaus Goldman and I worked on the final editing of the book. So there are several voices.

### *And you are still working to continue the legacy?*

**MP**: I'm probably the only one of the children of a Monuments person, because they were women too, obviously, that learned so much [about the period] because both of my parents were there. I mean, if it was just one [parent], well there was a box packed away somewhere and life went on. But for Walter and Renate the Monuments Men phase carried through their whole lives.

So it was actually at the Monuments Awards Ceremony that the German architect who was part of the staff of Wiesbaden asked me what [Renate] had told me about witnessing the opening of a concentration camp. And I had to say "nothing"—I had tried to ask her and I got nothing. So, she absolutely refused to talk about it.

### *You are now working to research your mother's life before and during the war years.*

**MP**: She didn't want me to be burdened with it, and yet I am. And there's actually writing in Germany about that, how my generation actually still feels a weight, even though we weren't part of it. I was with her as she passed away, and her last words were, "Do not forget, do not forget." And part of my question was, "What am I not . . . what is it I'm not to be forgetting?" So, I'm working on it.

NOTES

1. Farmer 2000, p. 5. This biographical sketch is drawn from the first two chapters of Farmer's memoir.
2. The marriage would not survive the strains of wartime separation.
3. Farmer 2000, p. 25.
4. Before the war, Edith Standen worked for art collector and National Gallery of Art patron Joseph E. Widener. Following her service as an MFAA officer, she became long-time curator of tapestries at the Metropolitan Museum of Art.
5. A long-standing Cincinnati family of industrialists, politicians, and philanthropists.
6. Collins Avenue is in the East Walnut Hills neighborhood of Cincinnati.
7. Observatory Place is in the Hyde Park neighborhood of Cincinnati.
8. Renate Hobirk taught at the College Preparatory School, now the Seven Hills School.
9. The Art Academy of Cincinnati was affiliated with the Cincinnati Art Museum until 1998, and located adjacent to it until 2005.
10. Farmer 2000, p. 18.
11. The lists are held in the Cincinnati Art Museum archives.
12. Bard Graduate Center, "The Spoils of War"; see Simpson 1997.
13. The Bundesverdienstkreuz, or Federal Cross of Merit, signifies the only federal decoration awarded by the German State. The honor was awarded to Farmer by Minister of Foreign Affairs Klaus Krinkel in Bonn, February 9, 1996.
14. Farmer was presented with the Prize of German Freemasons for "exemplary, ennobling humanitarian achievements" in Fürth, May 10, 1997.
15. Nicholas 1994.
16. Farmer 2000.

# WHAT'S PAST IS PROLOGUE: PROVENANCE RESEARCH IN AMERICAN MUSEUMS

NANCY YEIDE

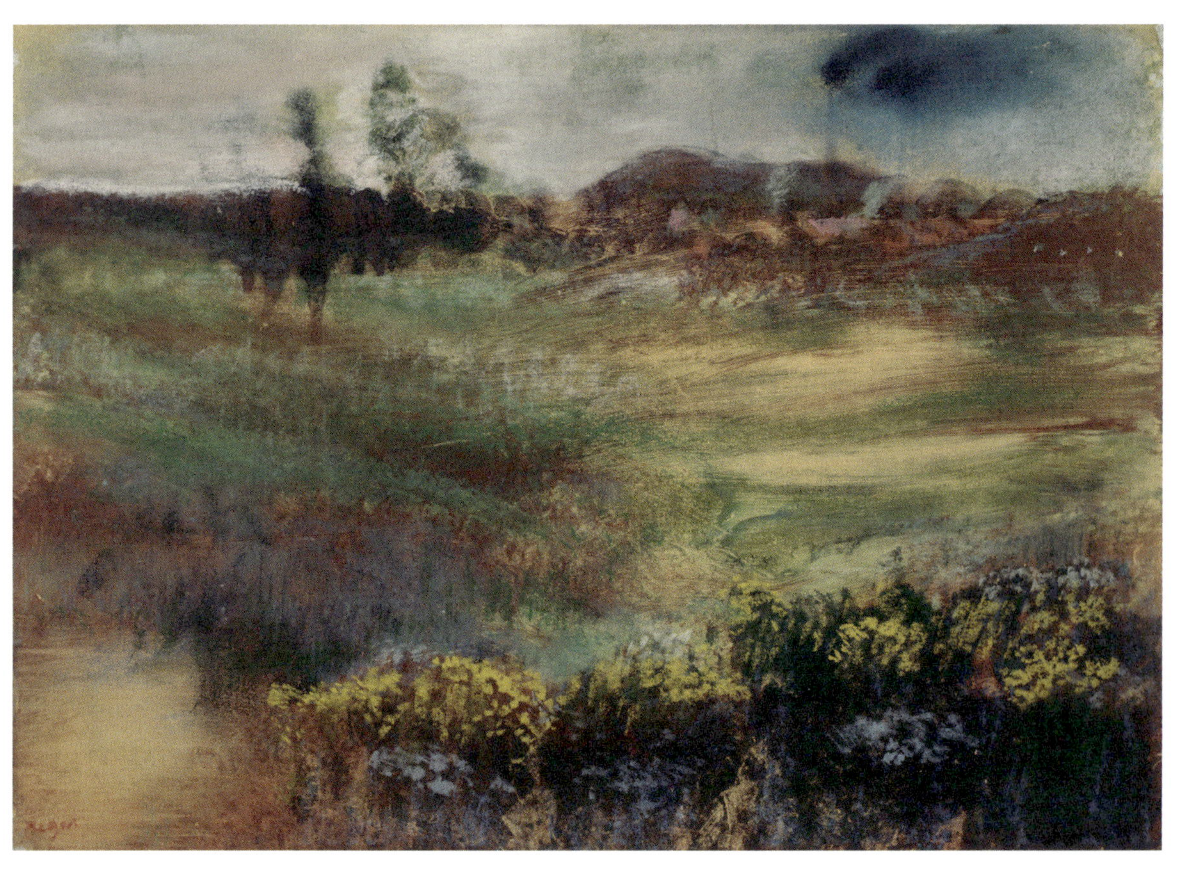

*What's Past is Prologue*
*What to come*
*In your and my discharge.*

*The Tempest*, Act 2, Scene 1

## A RESURGENCE OF INTEREST

IN 1998, THE AMERICAN MUSEUM COMMUNITY was reminded of an issue that had been dormant for some forty years: the possibility that art looted during World War II had inadvertently wound up in public collections. A variety of factors, a confluence of events, led to this reawakening.

Bolstered by recent successful negotiations for compensation to victims and their families for missing gold assets and forgotten Swiss bank accounts, in 1998 the US Department of State convened the Washington Conference on Holocaust-Era Assets. Forty-four nations participated, culminating in an international agreement on the eleven tenets of the Washington Conference Principles on Nazi-Confiscated Art.[1] The Washington Principles were deceptively simple, crafted deliberately to achieve international consensus. Sovereignty was respected, allowing each country to enforce the principles according to its own laws. This naturally led to disparity in effectiveness and awareness, but the principles were nonetheless a pivotal starting point for the reevaluation of an issue that had been forgotten for so long.

In the United States, with very few exceptions, museums are private institutions, not under the jurisdiction of the government. Consequently, best practices in museum stewardship generally evolve via the two main professional associations: the American Alliance of Museums (AAM), formerly

Fig. 1. Edgar Degas (1834–1917), *Landscape with Smokestacks*, circa 1890, pastel over monotype, on textured cream wove paper, 12½ × 16⅜ in. (31.7 × 41.6 cm). Art Institute of Chicago; Purchased from the collection of Friedrich and Louise Gutmann, and gift of Daniel C. Searle, 1998.915

the American Association of Museums, and the Association of Art Museum Directors (AAMD). At about the same time as the Washington Principles, both organizations issued guidelines regarding potential unrestituted Nazi-confiscated art in public collections.[2] Similar to the Washington Principles, these guidelines were general suggestions concerning research, publication of results, and dispute resolution.

The breakup of the Soviet Union in 1991 is frequently cited as leading to the Washington Principles, and indirectly to the American museum guidelines. This is partially true, but not because of the so-called "opening" of previously inaccessible archives, as is often suggested. Arguably the most important archival sources for researching Nazi confiscations and postwar restitutions are at the United States National Archives, part of the National Archives and Records Administration (NARA). The documents on this topic at the National Archives had been accessible, if underutilized, since the late 1970s. The breakup of the Soviet Union made it possible for victims or heirs to pursue claims for property confiscated or nationalized in the former East Germany. This led reunified Germany to enact laws and protocols that have been used as models in other countries.

Coincidental scholarly and popular publications contributed to a new awareness of Nazi-confiscated art in the late 1990s. In 1994 Lynn H. Nicholas published *The Rape of Europa*, utilizing declassified documents in the National Archives. In 1995, the Bard Graduate Center in New York City convened a three-day conference, "The Spoils of War," to mark the fiftieth anniversary of the end of World War II.[3] Speakers from Europe and the US described the processes for restitution in their respective countries after hostilities ended, and the situation half a century later. In 1996, Jonathan Petropoulos published his dissertation as *Art as Politics in the Third Reich*.[4]

And finally, a series of high-profile claims against American museums for unrestituted Nazi-looted art galvanized institutions to reconsider an issue that had been all but forgotten since the return of the so-called "Monuments Men" to their former professions in museums and academic institutions. In 1995, a member of the board of the Art Institute of Chicago was approached regarding a Degas pastel he had purchased years earlier, with allegations that it had been looted in France. Eventually a settlement was reached, in which the Art Institute took possession of the pastel and compensated the heirs for half its value (fig. 1). In June 1999, the Seattle Art Museum returned a painting by Henri Matisse to the heirs of Parisian dealer Paul Rosenberg from whose gallery it had been looted and never recovered. And, in 2000, the North Carolina Museum of Art came to an elegant solution regarding a prized Cranach in its collection that was found to have been looted from a Viennese collection in 1940. The heirs were compensated and the painting remained in the museum with a label acknowledging its history.

## THE WHAT AND HOW OF PROVENANCE RESEARCH

These cases demonstrated the importance of archival documentation relating to World War II art looting and postwar restitution and the need for serious provenance research on extant public collections (and potential museum acquisitions). But what is provenance research? Traditionally a means used by art historians to authenticate a work, by tracing it from the creator to its current location, or to highlight its importance through the noted collections in which it had formerly resided, provenance research is of primary importance to writing art history. Museum collection catalogues, exhibition catalogues, auction house sales catalogues, and dealer brochures generally include history of ownership, with a greater or lesser degree of detail. Provenance information had not generally been interpreted as proving or disproving legal ownership, at least not until the events of the late 1990s.

At that time, the methodology of provenance research had not been seriously addressed in academic training, and all too frequently had relied on repeating previously published, often unconfirmed, information about object histories. As the utility and relevance of provenance research came into sharper focus, the need for some guidance led to *The AAM Guide to Provenance Research*, published by the American Association of Museums in 2000.[5] The *Guide* was bolstered by regular panels and workshops at the AAM annual conference. Divided into two parts, basic art historical provenance research and World War II specific resources, the *Guide* also includes case histories and an extensive bibliography.

The fundaments of provenance research are independent verification of any published provenance or information provided by an owner, collector, auction house, museum, or dealer, in tandem with art historical research. The first step, assuming the object is at hand, is physical examination, especially of the back of the painting or drawing and back or underside of a sculpture and its base. A wide variety of stamps, labels, inscriptions, and other markings can often be found, which can be important clues to previous ownership.

For example, particularly for works on paper, collectors frequently placed their personalized stamp of ownership on the reverse of the object (and occasionally on the front). These markings have been studied and catalogued for decades. First published in 1921, Dutch collector and connoisseur Frits Lugt compiled the standard dictionary of collector's marks in his *Les marques de collections de dessins & d'estampes.*[6] Now available online, the dictionary can be searched by collector name, and by a variety of descriptions of the stamp itself, which is often a monogram of some sort but also can include animals, abstract designs, heraldry, natural motifs, or anything to the owner's taste.[7] Entries for each mark include, as known, life dates and brief biographies of collectors, as well as publications or sales of the collection.

Collector's marks are just one type of clue that can be found on objects to corroborate, or confound, ownership history. Dealers generally have unique labels and a numeric or alphanumeric code that if deciphered can confirm the time of acquisition or sale. Auction houses sometimes stamp such codes directly onto the backs of canvases, stretchers, frames, or mats. Exhibitions in which the object figured frequently have labels noting the exhibition title and date and possibly the owner. Unlike collector's marks, these various stamps and labels have not been systematically catalogued and frequently require some sleuthing to decode. For major dealers, however, much progress has been made in the past twenty years to provide keys to the coding and links to stock books or sales books that have been preserved. The Getty Research Institute in Los Angeles has long been in the forefront of systematically recording not only dealer information, but also provenance information for American public collections (a project begun in the 1980s, although sadly not maintained) and individual lots from historic sales catalogues. More recently, the Getty has worked in cooperation with the Heidelberg University Library and the Kunstbibliothek–Staatliche Museen zu Berlin to catalogue individual lot descriptions and digitize catalogues for sales that took place in Germany and Austria between 1933 and 1945. Through a commitment to using technology to facilitate research, in addition to a dedication to collecting extant archives, the Getty Research Institute has made vast amounts of historical ownership and sale information available online.[8]

Other types of information that can be gleaned from the backs of objects (or, in the case of sculptures or decorative arts, the underside or base) include export stamps from European countries and, tellingly, Nazi markings regarding appropriation source.

Stamps and markings on objects elicit great interest from the general public, as well as from specialists. Not only do such markings provide a window into a hidden world, but also, more importantly, they bring home the fact that artworks are physical objects with a history—they have traveled many paths to reach their current home. Recognizing this, a small number of institutions have dedicated exhibitions to displaying artworks with their backs visible, pointing out markings, and explaining their meaning. An early example, *In Pursuit of the Past: Provenance Research at the Princeton University Art Museum*, was organized in 2003. More recently, in 2017, the Krannert Art Museum at the University of Illinois presented *Provenance: A Forensic History of Art.*[9] Some museums have approached the topic in a different way, creating online presentations of labels and markings to illuminate provenance research. For example, the Metropolitan Museum of Art published labels found on works in the Leonard A. Lauder Cubist Collection.[10] Several museums have made available online images of the reverse of paintings with particularly interesting provenance histories or described stamps, marks, and labels in their presentation of information about their permanent collection.

If extracting clues from labels, markings, and publications is the first step in documenting ownership history, a next step is to confirm this information. At the most basic level, checking exhibition catalogues in which an object is said to have been presented, as well as relevant scholarly publications, such as artist monographs, can yield vital leads. While many early exhibition catalogues are little more than checklists, there are occasionally general lists of lenders that can be pursued. Expanding the search to contemporary press coverage might also reveal the identity of lenders. Catalogues raisonnés and scholarly journal articles can provide valuable information, although they may focus on other aspects of the artist or artworks, and so can be erratic in their listing of ownership history. Auction sales catalogues references should be confirmed, as sometimes lots with different ownership history are added to a sale listed as from a certain collection.

Photograph archives—among the most important resources for provenance information—may seem somewhat "old-fashioned" in today's digital world. Often initially assembled by scholars tracking a given artist or school through scholarly publications, sales, or exhibitions, these archives consist of clippings, photographs, and even pages torn from publications. Sometimes the crumbs of information gleaned from these folders or photo "mounts," such as publication dates and locations of exhibitions, are crucial. Among the most important of these resources are the Witt Library at the Courtauld Institute of Art in London, established by British art historian Sir Robert Clermont Witt (1872–1952); the photo documentation center at what was the Rijksbureau voor Kunsthistorische Documentatie and is now the RKD–Nederlands Instituut voor Kunstgeschiedenis (Netherlands Institute for Art History), based on the research materials of collector and curator Cornelis Hofstede de Groot (1863–1930); the documentation center at the Musée d'Orsay in Paris; the Image Collections at the National Gallery of Art in Washington, DC; the Frick Art Reference Library in New York City; and the photographic collection at the Getty Research Institute in Los Angeles.

Fig. 2. Jan Steen (1625/26–1679), *As the Old Sing, So Pipe the Young (Soo de Ouden Songen, Soo Pijpen de Jongen)*, circa 1668, oil on panel, 17⅜ × 23⅞ in. (44.1 × 60.6 cm). Allentown Art Museum; Samuel H. Kress Collection, 1961, 1961.60

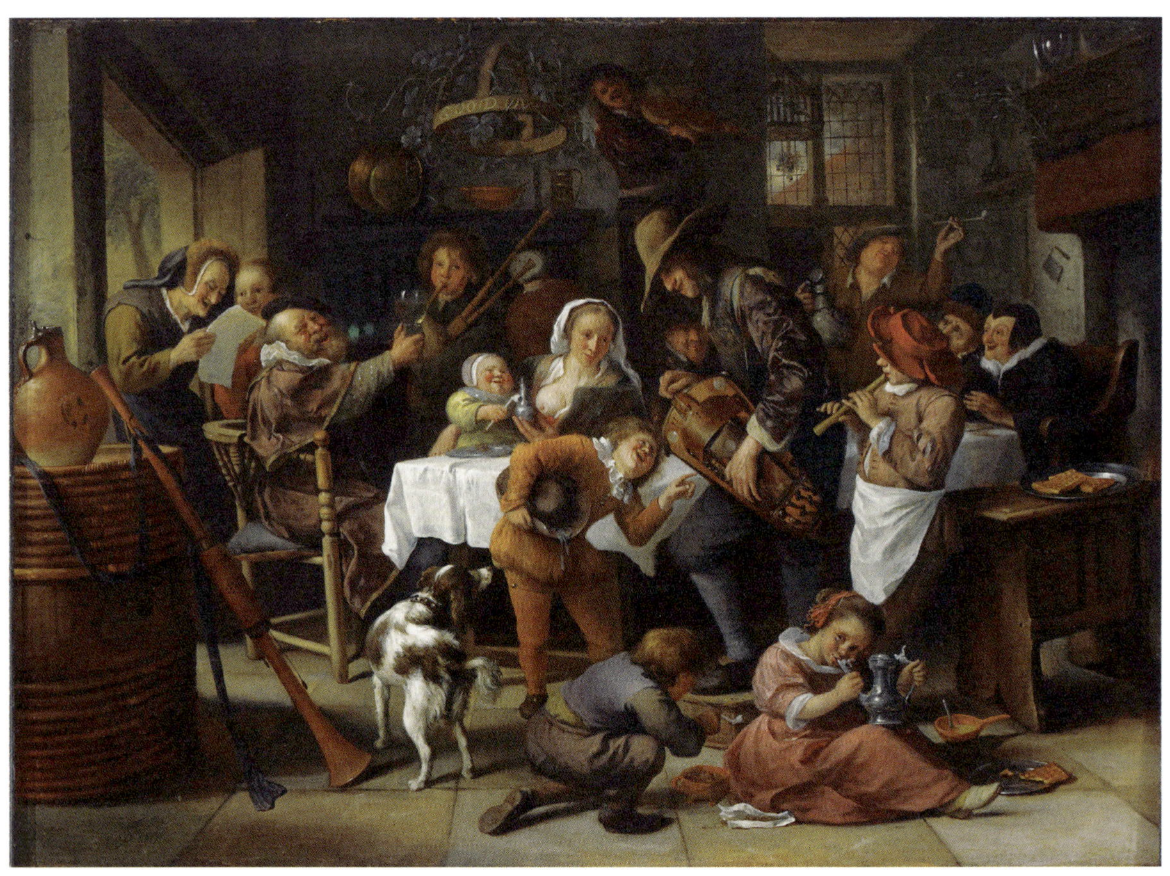

However, virtually every public museum has some type of photographic archives—whether housed in the curatorial or registrarial departments, museum library, or archives—and if one is researching a collector in a specific location, these can be extremely valuable.

Investigating names that appear in provenances is critical, and often revealing. One might come across two names in a provenance that appear to have nothing to do with one another, but a little genealogical research reveals that these two individuals were related in some way. For example, the name David Birnbaum appears in several provenances of Dutch paintings in the Kress collection followed by the name David Bingham (fig. 2). Birnbaum came from a Jewish family of Dutch origin that established itself in the United Kingdom in the 1920s, and he came to the United States in 1940. Bingham seems to have been established in New York by the mid-1940s. The two appeared to have nothing to do with one another. However, the papers of the dealer Jacques Seligmann & Co., now at the Archives of American Art, include an announcement that Birnbaum had changed his name to Bingham in 1946. Hence the two were one and the same, and the provenance information, instead of being disparate and consecutive, is continuous.

## NATIONAL ARCHIVES AND RECORDS ADMINISTRATION

The traditional art historical provenance research described above has been the stock-in-trade of trained museum professionals for generations. However, at the time of the 1998 Washington Conference, tracking ownership during World War II was *terra incognita*. An adjunct to the conference was a one-day meeting at the US National Archives facility in College Park, Maryland, just outside Washington, DC, where the records relating to World War II looting and restitution are available for consultation. While the conference had important political and diplomatic components, for those provenance researchers and museum professionals able to attend, it was a window onto a brave new world.

For those unfamiliar with archival research, the key maxim to bear in mind is that archives are not libraries. Archives generally do not include subject indices, for example. Instead, archives are organized around the principle of maintaining the structure of the organization that produced the documents, be that the Department of the Treasury, the Bureau of Land Management or, as most relevant to World War II art provenance researchers, the Office of

Military Government, United States (OMGUS), established by the US military at the end of the war to administer US-occupied Germany. Thus, art historians investigating possible Nazi-looted art were plunged not only into the unfamiliar territory of government archives, but also the somewhat obtuse and mercurial organization of the military oversight of Allied-controlled Europe.

Why are records regarding Nazi looting and subsequent Allied restitution at the US National Archives? The history of the period provides the answer. As Europe was liberated in 1944–45, the US and its Allies, including the now famed Monuments Men, discovered, and ultimately bore responsibility for, the troves of looted art and other valuables that the Germans had tried to conceal from the enemy. This material was found in the salt mines in Alt Aussee, Austria, and the Disneyland castle of Neuschwanstein in Bavaria, in addition to hundreds of lesser known repositories. As the process of identifying the art proceeded—and it must be noted this was not the most urgent task of a coalition attempting to feed, heat, and control a devastated continent—the records created by the Nazis were incorporated into the OMGUS records. As the German records had become US government records, they were eventually deposited in the US National Archives. German records included valuable inventories of art confiscated from prominent Jewish families in Germany, Austria, France, and to some extent the Netherlands. The OMGUS records also include the influx of inquiries and claims for these objects and decisions made on their postwar distribution.

The end of the restitution story, however, is not documented at the US National Archives. Allied policy was to return objects to the country of origin (France, Holland, etc.), the government of which would determine the individual owner and be responsible for the return. Thus, the records of individual returns of property reside in disparate archives across Europe. Nevertheless, the most logical place to begin a Nazi-era provenance research project is at the US National Archives.

It is understandable that most art historians would be unfamiliar with the National Archives, and overwhelmed by the prospect of it, so how to begin? Fortunately, shortly after the Washington Conference, Greg Bradsher, senior archivist and subject-area specialist, compiled *Holocaust-Era Assets: A Finding Aid to Records at the National Archives at College Park, Maryland* (the Archives has two venues: the iconic structure in downtown Washington, DC, that houses the Declaration of Independence, and the facility near the University of

Maryland that maintains most government records including those relevant to Nazi looting and restitution).[11] Bradsher's 1,300-page tome, the "Bible" of NARA provenance research, is overwhelming in itself, but it is helpful to understand that it includes all Holocaust-era assets, not just art. Winnowing the records relevant to researching an artwork's provenance was one of the purposes of the *AAM Guide to Provenance Research*.

One key document, which is frequently misinterpreted, is the final report of the Art Looting Investigation Unit (ALIU): the list of Red Flag names of individuals who appeared in any of its earlier reports. The ALIU, a branch of the Office of Strategic Services (precursor to the CIA) was tasked in 1945–46 with interrogating and describing individuals suspected of involvement in the confiscation of art or of profiting therefrom. Their terse reports on major such individuals and the transfers in which they were involved remain a key resource in provenance research during World War II. The final report, or "Red Flag" list, is a compilation of all names that surfaced during their investigations, and hence includes many individuals who were ultimately deemed not culpable. Nonetheless, consulting the "Red Flag" list is a fundamental first step in screening for problematic provenances. It is now available online in several venues.[12]

Another important document is the list of victims of confiscations assembled by the Einsatzstab Reichsleiter Rosenberg (ERR), an arm of the Nazi bureaucracy that processed confiscations, mainly from Jewish families, in France and Belgium. Through meticulous if not always comprehensive cataloguing of art objects and the owners from whom they were confiscated, the ERR created what would become a road map for future researchers. The information assembled by the ERR is also now available online.[13]

## CASE STUDIES

Henri Fantin-Latour's 1861 *Self-Portrait*, now at the National Gallery of Art in Washington, provides a good example of how useful ERR documentation can be to fleshing out the provenance of a painting (figs. 3–4). The small, intense work was known to have been in the collection of David David-Weill (1871–1952), Parisian banker, art collector, philanthropist, and president of the Conseil Artistique de la Réunion des Musées Nationaux, as he had lent it in 1936 to an exhibition in Grenoble.

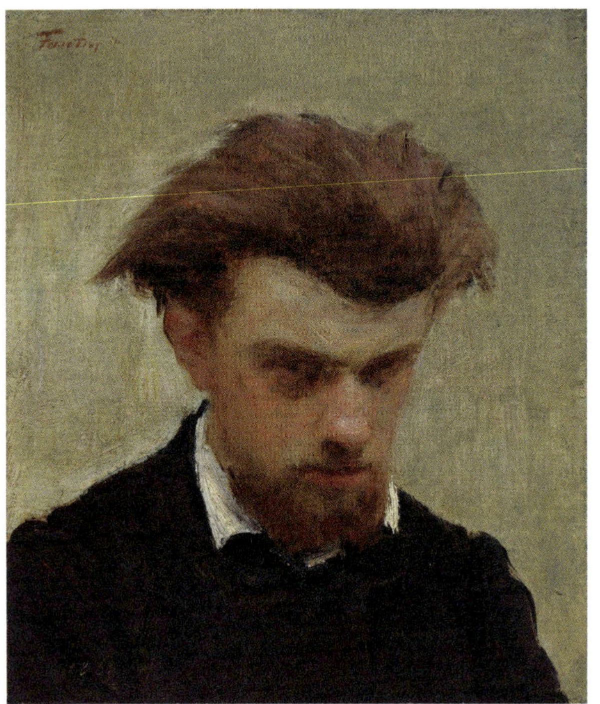

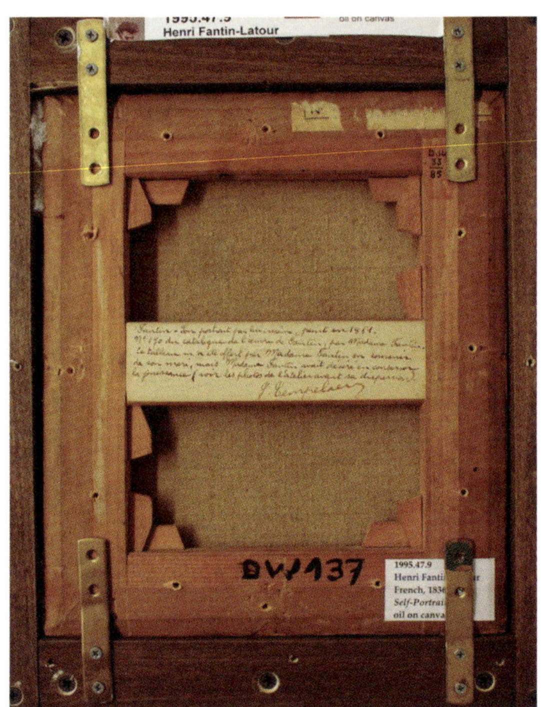


KÜNSTLER HERKUNFTSLAND: Ignace, Henri, Jean, Theodore Fantin-Latour
LEBENSZEIT: geb. 1836 in Grenoble, gest. 1902 in Buré (Orne)
LEICA-PHOTO
DATIERUNG
INVENTAR-NR.: D.-W. 137

| FILM-NR. / BILD-NR. | GROSSFOTO | AUFBEWAHRUNGSORT | WERT | INV. NR. ALTE SLG. | AUS KISTE NR. |
|---|---|---|---|---|---|
| | | Peter | | DW 33/85 | DW 56 |

THEMA BZW. GEGENSTAND: Selbstbildnis (1861)

BESCHREIBUNG: Brustbildnis in Vorderansicht, der Kopf leicht vorgeneigt. Weisser Halskragen auf schwarzer Kleidung und geknotete Krawatte. Heller Hintergrund.

| MATERIAL GRÖSSE | GERAHMT FASSUNG | BEZEICHNET SIGNATUR | VERBLEIB |
|---|---|---|---|
| Öl auf Lwd. 25 x 21 | | oben links: Fantin 61 | |

| ZUGANGSTAG | STANDORTWECHSEL | ZUSTAND BEHANDLUNG (AUCH UMSEITIG) | BEMERKUNG HERKUNFT SCHRIFTTUM (UMSEITIG) |
|---|---|---|---|
| IN PARIS :<br>IM REICH : | | | x |

EINSATZSTAB RR. Sonderstab Bildende Kunst, Berlin W 9, Bellevuestr. 3

Fig. 3. Henri Fantin-Latour (1836–1904), *Self-Portrait*, 1861, oil on canvas, 9⅞ × 8⅞ in. (25.1 × 21.4 cm). National Gallery of Art, Washington, DC, Collection of Mr. and Mrs. Paul Mellon, 1995.47.9

Fig. 4. Verso of fig. 3

Fig. 5. ERR DW-137 card. Einsatzstab Reichsleiter Rosenberg (ERR) Card Files, 1945–1945, Box 6, A1 549, Records of US Occupation Headquarters World War II, Record Group 260, National Archives at College Park, College Park, MD

On the reverse of the painting, clearly visible, is scrawled "D W 137," which is the ERR code for objects confiscated from the David-Weill collection, the Fantin-Latour being number 137 (of over three thousand). This cataloguing number is confirmed by the card produced by ERR staff at the Jeu de Paume in Paris, which clearly identifies the object and includes an accompanying photograph (fig. 5).

At the end of the war, the painting was recovered from the salt mine at Alt Aussee, Austria, where it had been sent by the Nazis for safekeeping. It was transported to one of several Allied Central Collecting Points, staffed by art historians—Monuments Men and locals—who also created a card cataloguing system. The main collecting point for objects to be restituted to formerly occupied countries was in Munich. Records there indicate that the painting was restituted to France on July 11, 1946.[14] Records in France confirm that the painting was returned to the David-Weill family in September of that year.[15] Later it was sold through a Paris dealer to Mr. and Mrs. Paul Mellon, who deeded it to the gallery.

Often documentary research is not as clear-cut as in the case of the Fantin-Latour. In 2000, the National Gallery of Art returned a seventeenth-century *Still Life with Fruit and Game* by Frans Snyders to the heirs of a French family from whom it was determined to have been looted (fig. 6). Some of the available

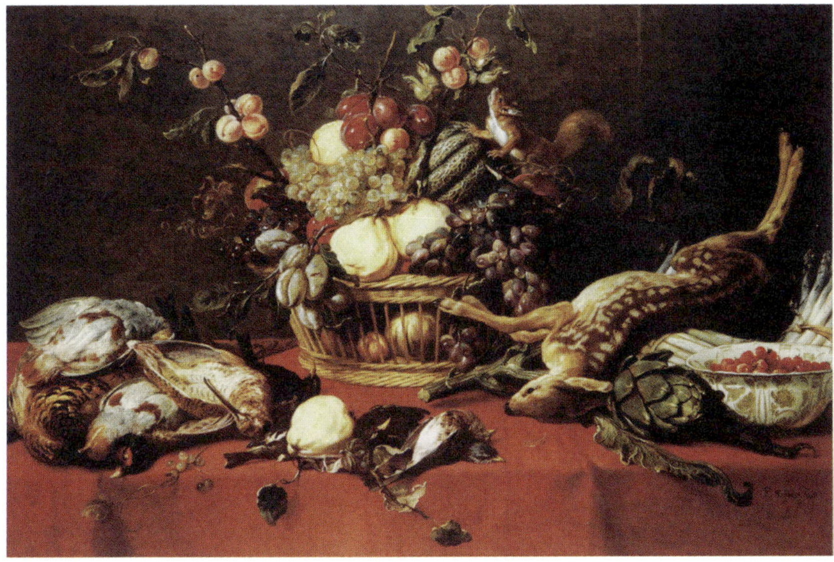

Fig. 6. Frans Snyders (1579–1657), *Still Life with Fruit and Game*, 1615–20, oil on panel, 37³⁄₁₆ × 56⁵⁄₁₆ in. (94.5 × 143 cm). Private collection

archival material documenting its chain of possession was inconsistent, but the decision to restitute was made on the basis of a preponderance of evidence and adherence to the Washington Principles, one of which states that the benefit of the doubt should be given to claimants in the case of incomplete documentation. The picture had been donated to the National Gallery in 1990, and raised no concerns at that time. Indeed, the large gaps in its known provenance were and remain quite common and unavoidable. However, in late 1998 the gallery discovered the picture reproduced in a catalogue of the Munich dealer Karl Haberstock.[16] This was a cause for concern—Haberstock was well known as one of Hitler's principal dealers. After significant research, the Snyders was tentatively linked with a *Still Life* confiscated from the Stern collection in Paris, obtained by Haberstock and traded to a German collector named Baron von Poellnitz, from whom the donor to the National Gallery of Art had obtained it decades after the war. The chain of evidence was muddied, however, by vague records giving inconsistent titles and dimensions. Only a partially legible marking on the back could connect the painting to the confiscated one. Eventually, it was determined that the most likely scenario was that the Snyders in Washington was the same as that confiscated in France, and it was returned to the Stern family.[17] The AAM and AAMD guidelines stop short of recommending that museums seek out potential heirs, as this is both impractical, in that it would require extensive and perhaps impossible genealogical research, and perilous, in that as heirs multiply through generations so does the potential for inter-family disagreement. So, how did the National Gallery of Art connect the Snyders to the legitimate heir (in this case a representative of several family branches)? It did so by adhering to the AAM and AAMD guidelines to publish known provenance information and respond appropriately to inquiries.

Thanks to the timing of the resurgence of interest in World War II provenance, publishing could be accomplished online via museum websites. The National Gallery of Art was in an enviable position when, in 1997, its first website was launched, making available all collection information known at the time, including provenance, which was drawn from years of careful cataloguing. This led directly to the gallery being approached by the claimant of the Snyders. Today most major and medium-sized American museums, and a surprising number of smaller institutions, have published collection and provenance information online.

## PROVENANCE RESEARCH IN THE DIGITAL ERA

Technological developments of the past twenty years have greatly facilitated all aspects of traditional provenance research. An explosion of online resources has made preliminary research significantly less expensive in terms of travel and logistics, although perhaps not saving as much time as many envisioned. Reviewing documents and databases now available through the internet requires no less knowledge and patience than reviewing the same materials on site. Keyword searches, while temptingly expedient, are a tool and not necessarily a quick fix.

Bradsher's *Holocaust-Era Assets* finding aid has been available online at the National Archives since 1999.[18] The finding aid is divided into sections on military and civilian records, a key distinction in these documents. For example, OMGUS is a military organization, while the Roberts Commission (officially the American Commission for the Protection and Salvage of Artistic and Historic Monuments in War Areas, established in 1943 and named for its chair, Chief Justice Owen Roberts) is a civilian agency. These sections, and others at most archives, are referred to by their "RG," or record group, number, which designates the origin of the documents, in these cases RG260 (OMGUS) and RG239 (Roberts Commission). There are several other record groups of great utility to World War II provenance research, such as RG331 (Records of the Allied Operational and Occupation Headquarters), RG59 (Records of the Department of State), and RG131 (Records of the Office of Alien Property). "RG" references are the vernacular of government archives, and it behooves researchers to learn this language and spend the time necessary to understand the sources of relevant documents.

In early 2000, National Archives staff met with art provenance and claims researchers to identify key series of records for their work and the means of making those records more accessible. Ultimately this meeting resulted in a microfilming project, which made the identified records available to researchers nationwide via the Archives' regional facilities and inter-library loan. A series of descriptive pamphlets, organized by record group, was published online.[19] The next step, digitizing the microfilms, was accomplished through a partnership between NARA and the genealogy website Ancestry. Many of these records are now freely available to researchers via Ancestry's component, Fold3.[20]

The US National Archives was not the only national repository striving to make its materials available remotely. The German Bundesarchiv, located in Koblenz, has an online finding aid to its records of postwar investigations on looted art, which is linked to digitized documents.[21] The Dutch created a website documenting the objects returned from Germany after the war and still in Dutch state possession.[22] The French did the same, and several other countries created searchable databases and finding aids to archives. Eventually the abundance of online resources became a cacophony. Researchers not only had to discover and keep track of each initiative, they also had to search them individually. Led by the US National Archives, a creative international solution was devised.

The International Research Portal for Records Related to Nazi-Era Cultural Property was launched in 2011.[23] For the first time, digital access to millions of Nazi-era cultural property–related records, from eighteen participating institutions, was available through a single internet portal. Similar to the Washington Principles, the portal respected the integrity of each participant and its access policies, while providing a single point identifying the most important resources worldwide. Researchers still had to navigate each site individually, but at least now there was a fairly comprehensive list of sources. Recognizing the impatience born of the keyword search expectations of researchers, a private organization took on the task of creating a more unified search engine. In 2017, the Digital Curation Innovation Center at the University of Maryland inaugurated the Enhanced International Research Portal for Records Related to Nazi-Era Cultural Property project (IRP2), which allowed for searches against participating members of the original portal. The IRP2 is now housed at the European Holocaust Research Infrastructure.[24]

## THE FUTURE OF PROVENANCE RESEARCH

The proliferation of resources for World War II provenance research (and provenance research in general) in recent years can be overwhelming. To address the need for training, the AAM, AAMD, and Smithsonian Institution have sponsored and organized national and international workshops and conferences to update museum professionals on the ever-evolving slate of available resources. Of particular note are the AAMD workshops held in cooperation with the National Archives, providing hands-on access to archival documentation and subject specialists, and the German-American Provenance

Exchange Program, a combined effort of the Smithsonian Institution and the Staatliche Museen zu Berlin – Preuβischer Kulturbesitz (Berlin State Museums – Prussian Cultural Heritage Foundation). These programs are aimed at current museum professionals of different levels of expertise. To move the field forward, art historical provenance research methodology, including but not limited to World War II issues, should be reintroduced into graduate-level education curricula. Anecdotal experience suggests that there is a strong interest in the topic, but a profound lack of training opportunities for graduate students and young professionals.

Provenance research informs every aspect of art history and the multiple professions touched by the discipline, including museum curators, registrars, archivists, auction house and dealer researchers, and educators. Provenance research illuminates not only legal ownership history, but also collecting history, genealogy, connoisseurship, the history of taste and valuation, and the movement of art, among other specialties. Instruction in the fundamental principles and sites of documentary provenance research—dealer archives, government archives, personal papers of art historians and scholars, literature and exhibition history, photographic archives, and burgeoning online resources—are desperately needed in higher education. Acquiring familiarity with resources and methodology contributes to the advancement of art historical knowledge as well as, in a practical sense, better preparing potential museum curators and scholars for the interdisciplinary and often unexpected requirements of the profession.

NOTES

1. https://www.state.gov/washington-conference-principles-on-nazi-confiscated-art/.
2. https://www.aam-us.org/programs/ethics-standards-and-professional-practices/unlawful-appropriation-of-objects-during-the-nazi-era/.
3. Simpson 1997.
4. Petropoulos 1996.
5. Yeide et al. 2001.
6. Lugt 1921.
7. http://www.marquesdecollections.fr.
8. http://getty.edu/research/tools/provenance/.
9. The exhibitions were accompanied by pamphlets: Reed 2003, Karrels 2017. For the latter, see also https://kam.illinois.edu/resource/provenance-forensic-history-art.
10. https://www.metmuseum.org/art/libraries-and-research-centers/leonard-lauder-research-center/cubist-collection/archival-labels.
11. Bradsher 1999.
12. https://www.lootedart.com/web_images/pdf/aliu_index_0712.pdf.
13. https://www.errproject.org/jeudepaume/.
14. Munich property card #181/6; French Receipt for Cultural Objects no. 9A, item no. 77; US National Archives, Record Group 260, Cultural Object Movement and Control Records, Custody Receipts on Restitution to France, Records 642–685, March 27 1946–Aug 23 1946.
15. Correspondence from the French Ministère des Affaires Étrangères, April–May 2000, National Gallery of Art curatorial files.
16. Haberstock 1967, plate 21.
17. https://www.nga.gov/press/archive/frans-snyder.html.
18. https://www.archives.gov/research/holocaust/finding-aid; see above, note 11.
19. https://www.archives.gov/research/holocaust/international-resources/nara.
20. https://www.fold3.com.
21. https://invenio.bundesarchiv.de/basys2-invenio/login.xhtml.
22. http://www.herkomstgezocht.nl.
23. https://www.archives.gov/research/holocaust/international-resources.
24. https://irp2.ehri-project.eu.

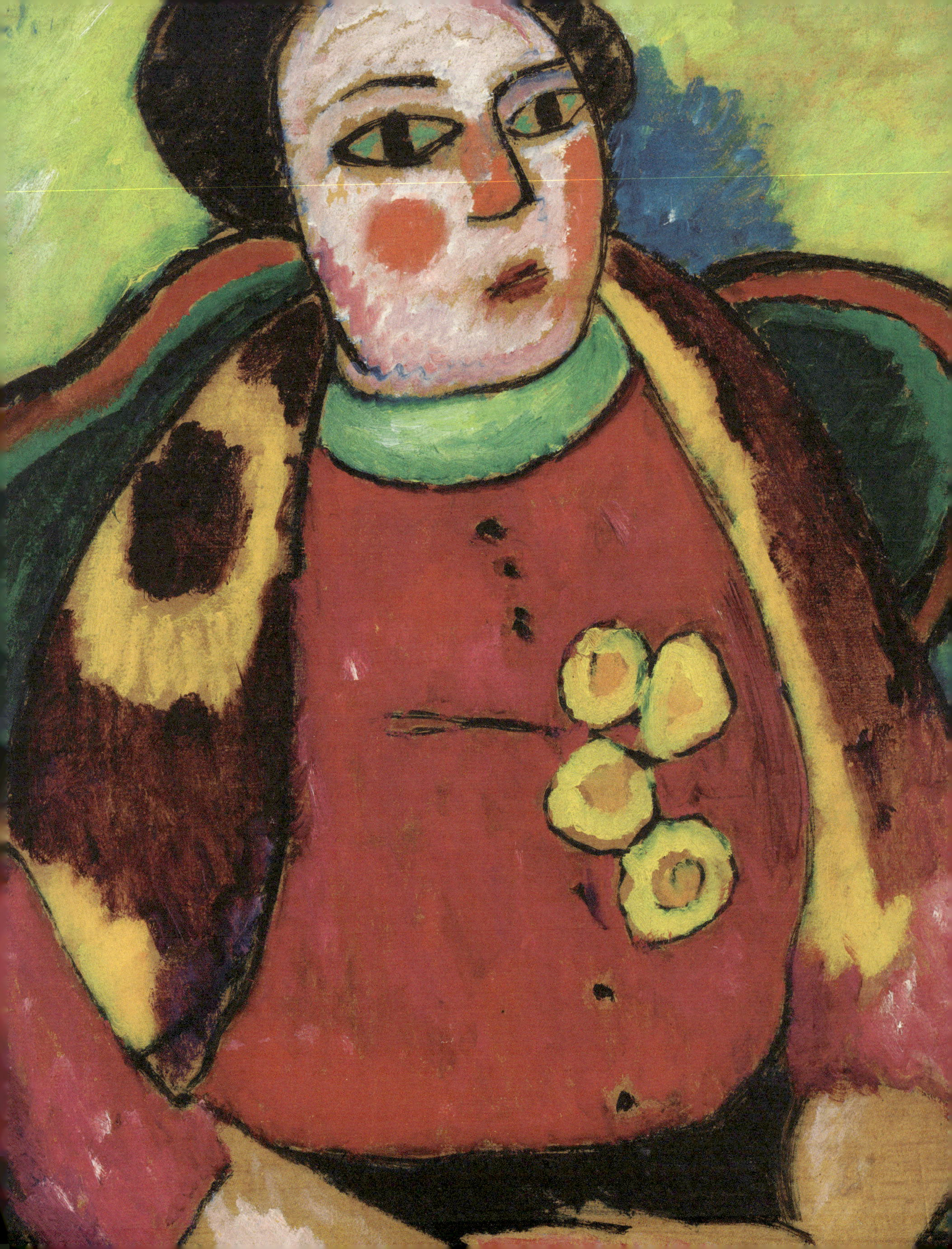

CATALOGUE

# ART AND INJUSTICE UNDER NAZI RULE

# 1

# Oskar Kokoschka (1886–1980)

## The Duchess of Montesquiou-Fezensac, 1910

oil on canvas, 37¼ × 19¼ in. (94.6 × 48.9 cm)
Cincinnati Art Museum, Bequest of Paul E. Geier, 1983.64

Oskar Kokoschka trained in Vienna in the early years of the twentieth century, where he absorbed the then-dominant style—Jugendstil—under the sway of Gustav Klimt and alongside Egon Schiele. In the 1910s, he became a leading figure in expressionist circles, as he sought to convey the inner essence of his subjects, whether a person or a landscape, through their form. Working into the early 1970s, his career encompassed set design and playwriting, and he was an active and sought-after teacher.

An early supporter, the architect and intellectual Adolph Loos, took Kokoschka to a sanatorium in Leysin, Switzerland, in 1910, where Loos's wife was being treated for tuberculosis. There, the young artist painted several patients, including Victoire Masséna d'Essling, then Marchioness of Montesquiou-Fezensac and her husband, who would become Duke of Fezensac a few years later. Kokoschka recounted his affection for her in his autobiography. "I was moved by her beauty. She reminded me of those aristocratic women who used to seek consolation in their faith, back in the days of religious upheavals when the world was so godless that only mystics still believed in a paradise, which they placed in their own hearts." Through her downturned gaze and dramatic gestures, Kokoschka makes visible the inner essence of his sitter as much as her sickened state. The artist referred to "this special painting" as "very dear to me as a souvenir of my youth, misunderstood and moneyless."

This portrait was a centerpiece of Kokoschka's first major exhibition, later that year in Berlin. It was purchased from that show for the recently founded Museum Folkwang, the first public art museum in Germany and a pioneering institutional advocate for modern art, and so became Kokoschka's first work to enter a museum collection.

In 1937, a Nazi commission was charged to "select and impound works of German art of decline since 1910. . ." from German museums, "[as they] insult German sentiment or destroy or confuse natural form. . . ." Over six hundred works were exhibited in Munich in July 1937, Kokoschka's *The Duchess of Montesquiou-Fezensac* among them, in one of history's most notorious examples of the use of artworks for political ends. The exhibition, entitled *Entartete Kunst* (Degenerate Art), set up much modern art, particularly expressionism, as the nemesis of good "German art," in much the same terms that the Nazis vilified the Jewish people, who were seen as lacking the wholesome qualities found in Aryan Germans. Statements emblazoned on the walls of the exhibition proclaimed the works "monstrous product[s] of madness [and] incompetence." Following the exhibition, the commission seized another 17,500 works of art, including over four hundred of Kokoschka's paintings.

Less than a year later, a commission was established to investigate ways to monetize "degenerate" art. One of the first results was an auction of 125 works at Galerie Fischer in Lucerne, Switzerland, in June 1939, at which *The Duchess of Montesquiou-Fezensac* was sold to a young American collector, Paul E. Geier, who later donated it to the Cincinnati Art Museum. –PJB

FURTHER READING

Kokoschka 1974; Barron 1991a; Natter 2002; Peters 2014a

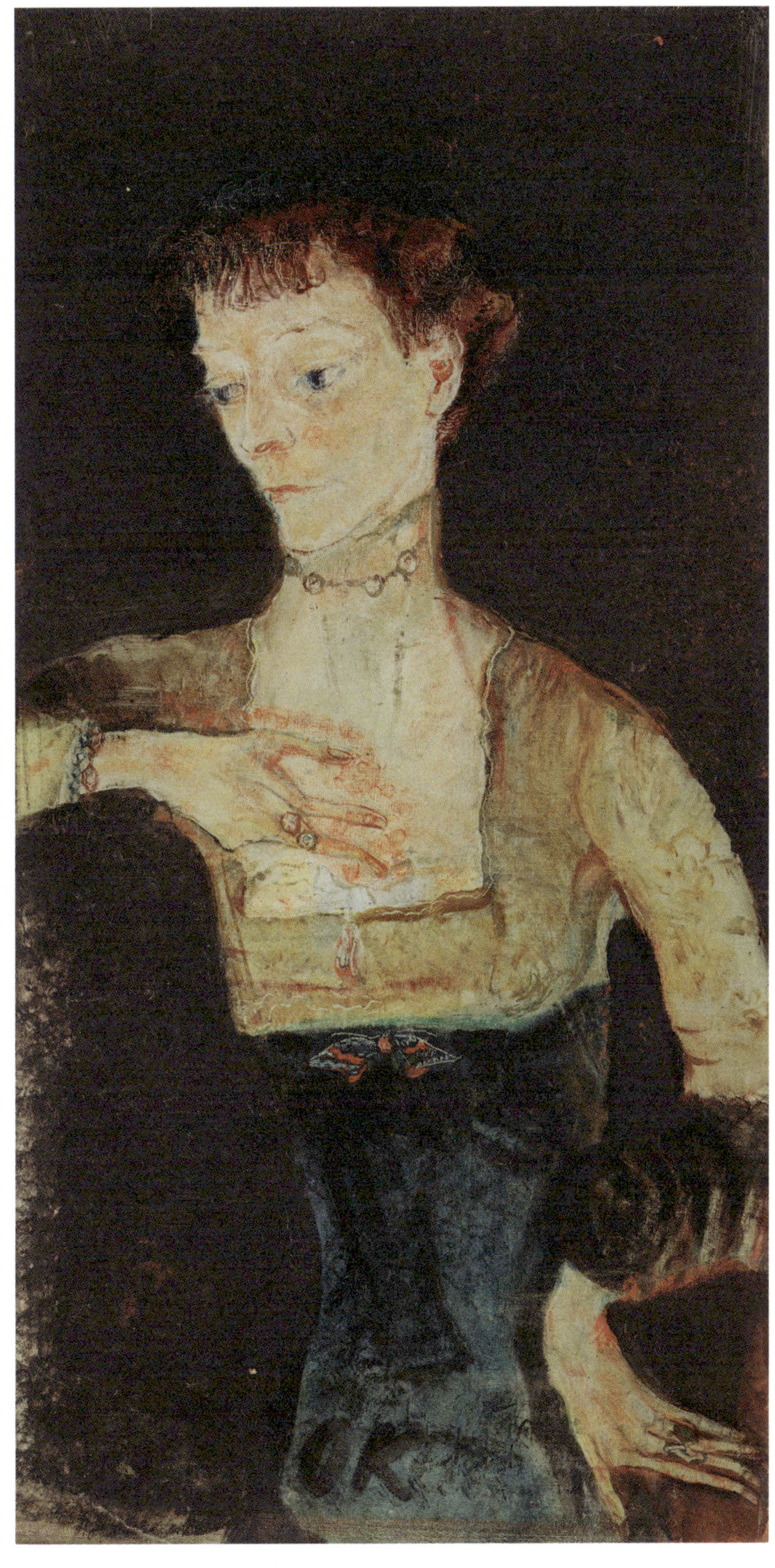

## 2

# Alexej von Jawlensky (1864–1941)

### Seated Woman, 1911

oil on composition board, 28⅛ × 19¾ in. (71.4 × 50.2 cm)
Cincinnati Art Museum, Fanny Bryce Lehmer Endowment, 1975.73

Alexej von Jawlensky trained in Moscow and St. Petersburg. He moved to Munich with several other Russian artists in 1896 to expand his style beyond the realist tradition of painting current in Russia. He began experimenting with subversions of pictorial convention, expressing himself using free lines and bright, non-realist colors. From Munich, Jawlensky explored much of Europe until the outbreak of World War I. He exhibited in Paris at the Salon d'Automne in 1905 alongside the Fauves, drank in the influence of the works of Vincent van Gogh and Paul Gauguin, and worked in the company of artist-friends like Ferdinand Hodler, Emil Nolde, Wassily Kandinsky, and Henri Matisse. Jawlensky has been called a leader of the German expressionist movement. His art resonates with that of other influential artist groups and movements of the period, like Der Blaue Reiter and the Fauves, and he was strongly influenced by the mysticism of the Nabis.

For much of his career, two subjects—landscapes and portraits—preoccupied Jawlensky. *Seated Woman* treats one of his most frequent and enduring subjects, the female head. The figure is based on Jawlensky's wife, Helene Nesnakomoff.

As with Ernst Barlach and Käthe Kollwitz (cat. 3–4), Jawlensky and his art were affected by both World Wars. He was expelled from Germany in 1914 as an enemy alien, forced to leave everything in his studio in Munich and resettle in Switzerland. *Seated Woman* may have been among the paintings Jawlensky left in Munich, which were recovered in 1919 by the artist and his advocate and representative Galka Scheyer. The last phase of Jawlensky's life took place in Wiesbaden, where he moved in 1921. There, a group of artists and collectors, including Alo Altripp and Hanna Bekker vom Rath, founded the Jawlensky Gesellschaft in 1933, which provided a stipend to sustain the artist through his crippling arthritis and persecution by the state. In that year, the Nazis banned the exhibition of his art and forbade its export from Germany. His work was labeled "degenerate," and seventy-two works were seized from public collections in Germany, destroyed, or sold abroad; six lithographs and two paintings were included in the 1937 "Degenerate Art" exhibition. Jawlensky died in 1941, and hundreds of his works were destroyed in a bombing raid of Wiesbaden four years later, shortly before the end of the Second World War. –PJB

FURTHER READING

Mochon 1991; Barron 1991a; Jawlensky et al. 1998

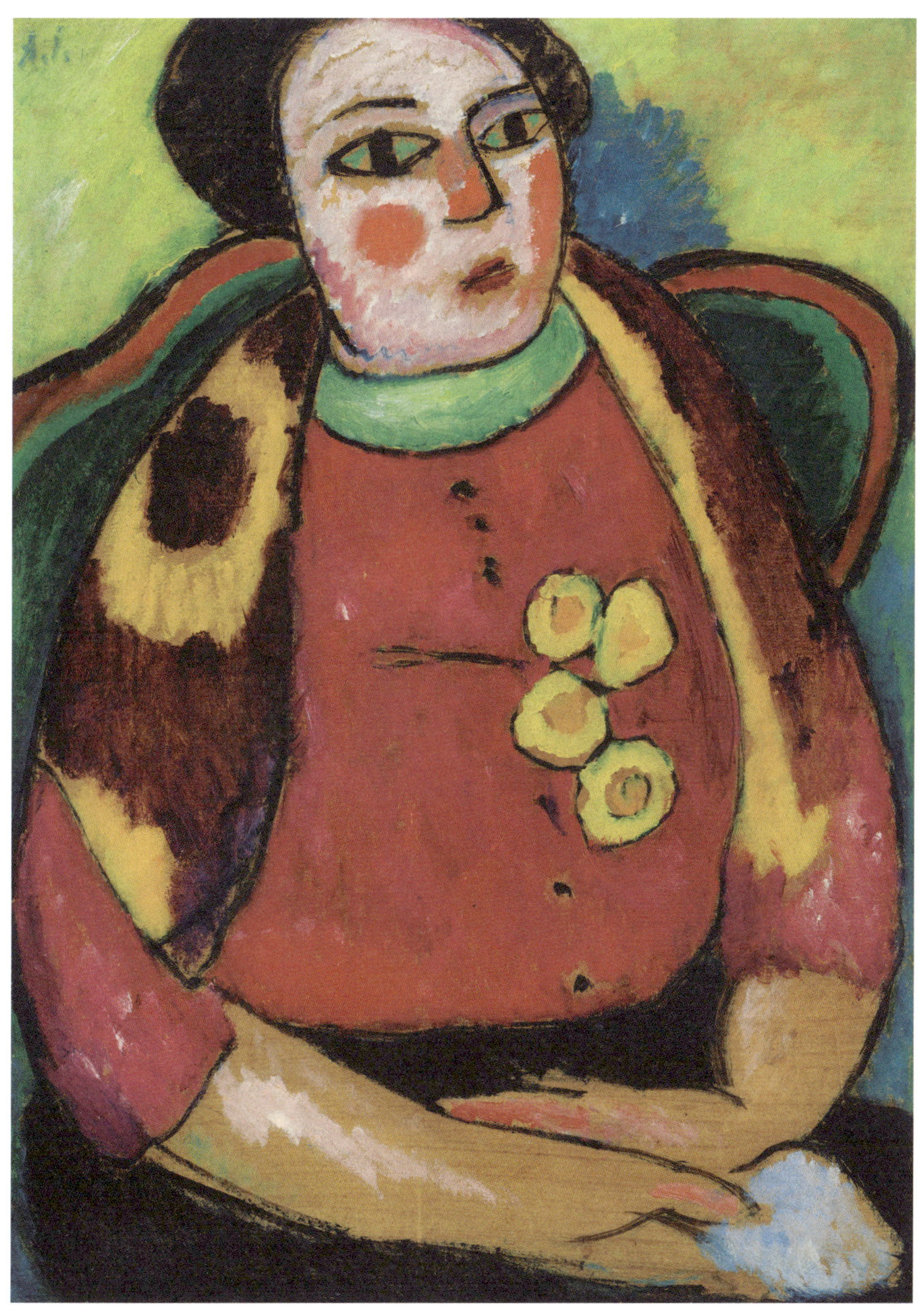

3

## Ernst Barlach (1870–1938)

### Christ at Gethsemane, 1919

woodcut, 7⅞ × 9⅞ in. (20 × 25.1 cm)
Cincinnati Art Museum, Gift of Mr. and Mrs. Walter I. Farmer, 1952.327

Ernst Barlach was one of the most original artistic personalities of prewar Germany. Renowned above all as a sculptor and printmaker, Barlach was also an accomplished playwright. He studied in Hamburg and Dresden and, briefly, in Paris. Throughout his work he interpreted and reinterpreted the human figure and human condition, often taking peasants, pilgrims, and beggars as his subjects. A visit to Russia in the summer of 1906 was particularly influential in this regard. Beginning in 1907 the art collector, dealer, and publisher Paul Cassirer supported the artist, allowing him freedom to experiment, and published most of his print series. 1917 saw Barlach's first major exhibition at Cassirer's gallery in Berlin. Barlach served in the First World War, after which the mystical tone of his work came to embrace haunting, plaintive qualities of loss. He was commissioned to create war memorials and religious sculptures across northern Germany.

1919 was a signal year for Barlach in many regards. He was offered professorships in Berlin and Dresden, became a full member of the Prussian Academy of Arts, and premiered two of his plays. In the war years, Barlach turned to the woodcut technique, drawn to its "obligation to be hard and simple." He produced prints in series, and, especially in 1919, a number of large single woodcuts, including *Christ at Gethsemane.* Woodcut has a deep history in German art and experienced a revival in the early twentieth century in the hands of artists including Barlach and Käthe Kollwitz.

Barlach reveals Christ's inner torment as he reflects on his fate and prays. The spare figure of Christ on hands and knees looms in the foreground. He is wringing his hands, even as they support the weight of his body. A fixed gaze smolders from hunched shoulders and a haggard face. The blasted landscape and Christ's disciples, asleep in the background, evoke the Great War's horrendous battlefields, with trees stripped bare and bodies strewn about.

Soon after the Nazis took power in 1933, Barlach's work came under attack. Commissions dried up quickly. A volume of his drawings published in 1936 was confiscated by the Gestapo before it could be distributed, on the basis that it "endangered public safety, peace and order."

In 1937 Barlach's work was seized from museums, and one of his sculptures was included in the "Degenerate Art" exhibition in Munich. His great work, the war memorial for the cathedral in Güstrow, the north German town where he had lived for twenty-seven years, was removed and destroyed later that summer, along with most of his public sculptures across Germany. He was threatened with a total ban on his art, and in December he wrote that "no exhibitions of my works are possible. In Spain this is called garroting, asphyxiation. What can one say?" The artist died a few months later. –PJB

FURTHER READING

Carls 1969; Just and Lohmann-Siems 1971; Groves 1972

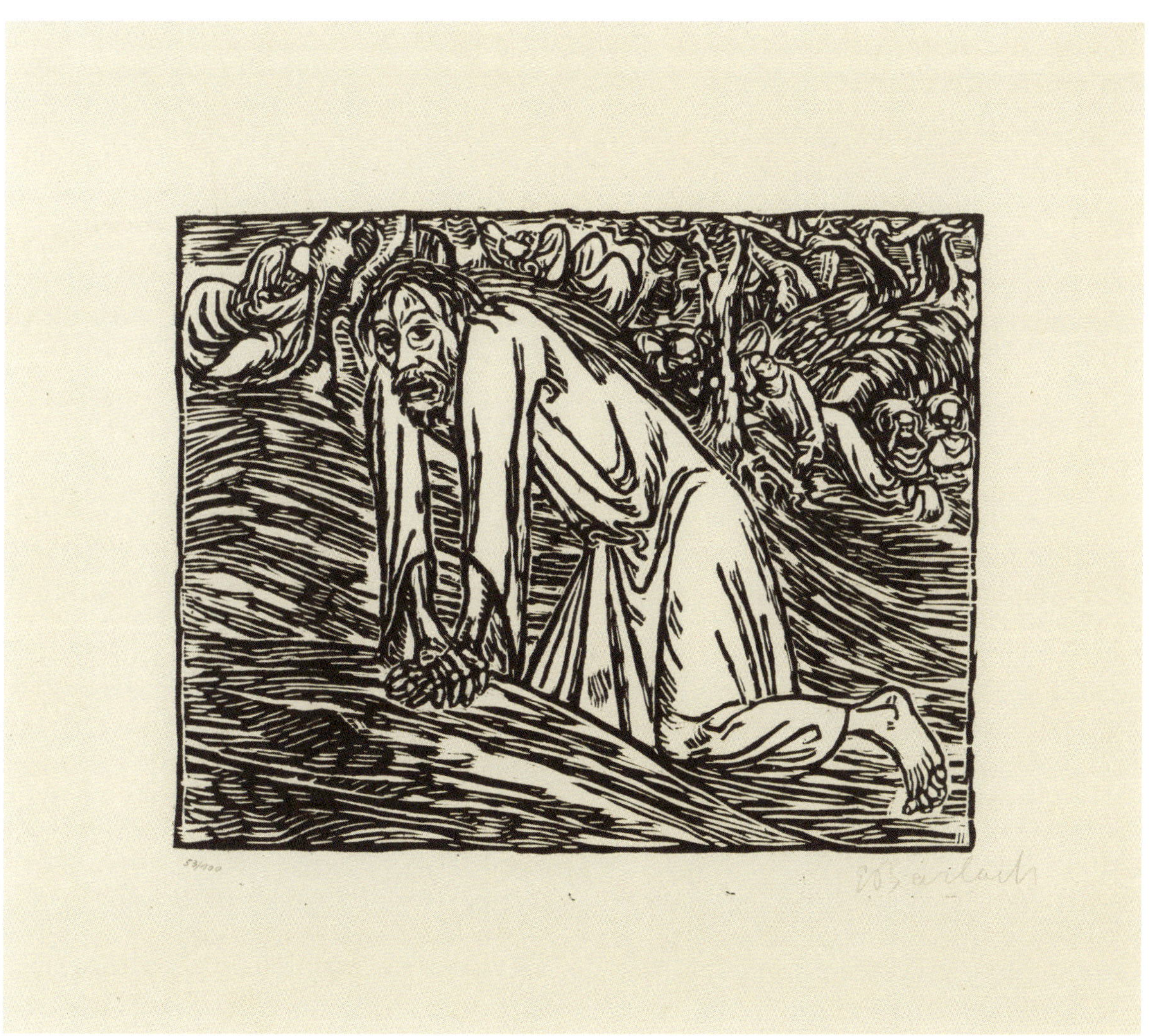

## 4

# Käthe Kollwitz (1867–1945)

### Death Grasps at a Group of Children, 1934

lithograph, sheet 26¼ × 19⅞ in. (66.7 × 50.5 cm)
Cincinnati Art Museum, Gift of Robert and Elaine Blatt, 1985.128

Käthe Kollwitz trained in Munich and Berlin in the late 1880s and early 1890s. From early on, her art was often devoted to socially aware themes, and she became well known for poster art advocating improved conditions for the peasantry and working class. She channeled a masterful command of her media, whether in drawing, printmaking or, later, sculpture, to communicate powerful emotions, often with a close connection to events in her life. These qualities, along with her deep study of the human figure in all its states, gave her great success in her day, and created enduring images. One of her sons was killed in World War I, one of her grandsons in World War II. Themes of war, death, desperation, and grief are common in her work, although she often manages to convey a sense of hope and love through her subjects.

Kollwitz published a suite of eight lithographs entitled "Death" in 1934 and 1935, each depicting a different encounter with death. The series has been interpreted as belonging to the Dance of Death allegorical tradition that stretches back to the Middle Ages. The artist referred to it simply as a series "on the theme of death." This, the last print series she would produce, demonstrates her mastery of composition, emotive communication, and use of the lithographic crayon. *Death Grasps at a Group of Children* is the most violent in the series. Others show their subject tranquil, accepting, or even welcoming of death. Half of the prints in the series include children. The Cincinnati Art Museum also owns *The Call of Death*, in which a man with closed eyes turns his head to acknowledge a hand (of Death) on his shoulder, one of Kollwitz's most iconic images. Made in the first years of the Nazi regime, *Death Grasps at a Group of Children* seems to foreshadow the mass displacement and death that were to come.

The prominent themes of social protest in Kollwitz's art had brought censure from the earliest days of National Socialist rule. She, along with her friend Ernst Barlach, was expelled from the Prussian Academy of Arts in 1933. Kollwitz seems to have had an ambiguous status under the Nazi regime. She was a popular artist whose work steered clear of abstraction and expressionism—those artistic manifestations that drew the most ire from Nazi authorities—and yet the clear political stance of much of her earlier art put her in question. She was not politically active in the 1930s and so escaped the worst repercussions of censorship. Her work was included in the 1937 Munich "Degenerate Art" exhibition, but withdrawn from its subsequent venues, reflecting this continued uncertainty on the part of the authorities. Many of her works, stored in the basement of her house in Berlin, were destroyed along with the house in 1943, during war actions. –PJB

FURTHER READING

Klipstein 1955; Prelinger 1992

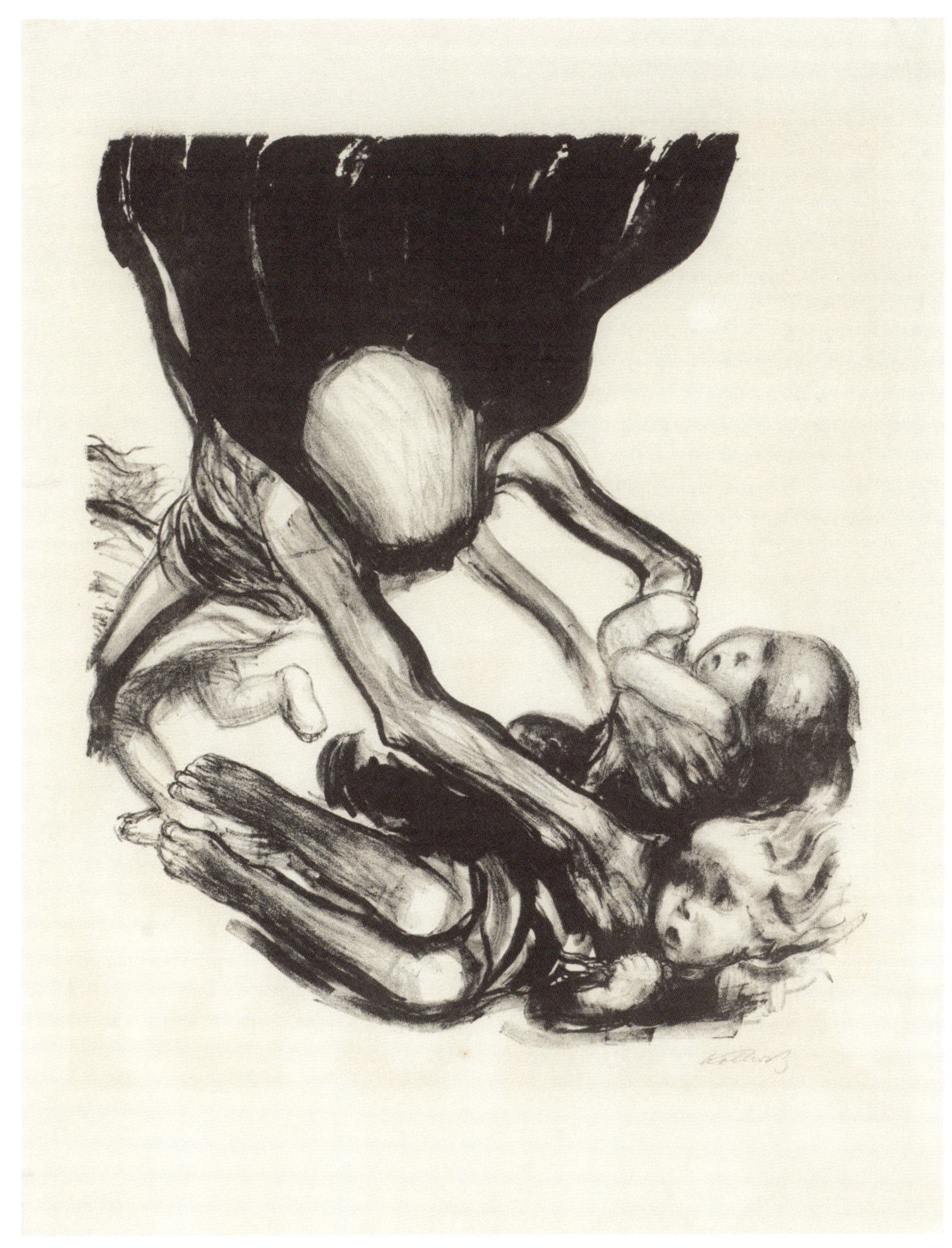

## 5

# Follower of Fra Angelico (circa 1395–1455)

### Madonna and Child, circa 1450s

tempera and gold leaf on panel, diam. 8⅞ in. (22.5 cm)
Cincinnati Art Museum, Fanny Bryce Lehmer Fund, 1966.267

The style and composition of this small devotional painting place its production firmly in Florence of the mid-1400s, by an artist much influenced by Masolino and Fra Angelico, both among the foremost proponents of a newly realistic depiction of depth, volume, and emotion in Renaissance painting. In this early example of the round format in Florentine painting, the Madonna fills the picture, seated before a low wall. The Christ Child stands on her left thigh, reaching across her toward a bird she holds in her raised right hand. Her pensive gaze at the child foreshadows his fate of self-sacrifice.

The painting was unknown before Jacques Goudstikker acquired it in the early twentieth century from a noble family in Siena, the Palmieri-Nuti. Goudstikker was among the most prominent art dealers in Amsterdam in the decades between the World Wars, and the fate of his stock has become among the best-known case studies of the Nazi art trade. In May 1940, he was killed in an accident while fleeing the Netherlands during the German invasion. Two months later, under pressure and subterfuge, his firm was sold to Alois Miedl, an agent for Hermann Göring, then the second most powerful person in the Nazi state, and its stock—some 1,400 paintings—was sold to Göring himself. Miedl bought back about half the paintings and continued to operate the business under Goudstikker's name, selling works to Göring and other Germans and enriching himself considerably.

Goudstikker had owned the *Madonna and Child* since at least December 1927. An entry for it appears in his "black book," the inventory of his collection that Goudstikker was carrying in his pocket when he died. It was also listed in an inventory prepared during Miedl's acquisition of the gallery. Coded annotations on both lists, and the fact that notice of the painting does not appear subsequently in the archives of the Miedl-Goudstikker firm, suggest it was among a group of works that Goudstikker shipped to the United States ahead of his departure from Holland. This hypothesis is strengthened by the fact that the Cincinnati Art Museum acquired the painting through Piero Tozzi Galleries, the New York firm that handled the sale of paintings owned by Goudstikker's heirs in America.

The Goudstikker collection remains dispersed. About two hundred of the paintings that Göring took to Germany were transferred back to the Netherlands at the end of the war, but remained in state collections until 2006, when they were restituted to Goudstikker's heirs after a lengthy legal process. Many more have been identified in public collections and private hands by a team of provenance researchers and lawyers engaged by Goudstikker's heirs in the years since. However, over a thousand paintings owned by the legendary dealer at the time of his death remain untraced. —PJB

FURTHER READING

Spike 1993; Sutton 2008; Ahl 2008

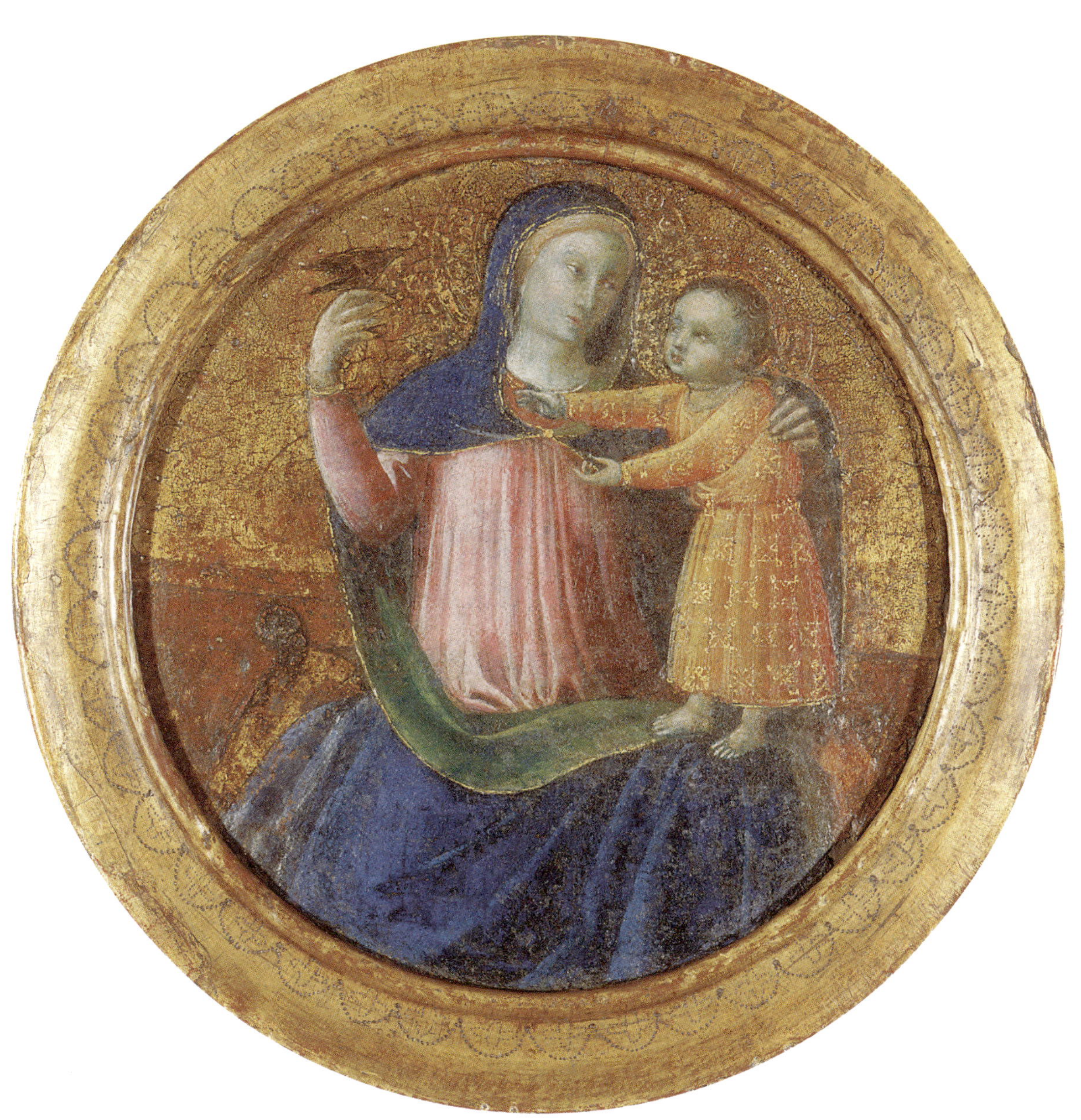

## 6

# Jacob Duck (1600–1667)

**Interior with Soldiers and Women**, circa 1650

oil on panel, 16⅞ × 24¼ in. (42.9 × 61.6 cm)
The J. Paul Getty Museum, Los Angeles, Gift of J. Paul Getty, 70.PB.19

Jacob Duck, based in Utrecht, was one of many Dutch artists in the middle decades of the seventeenth century to specialize in genre scenes—domestic interiors, merry companies—in which detailed depictions of everyday life provide engaging subject matter while often harboring deeper symbolic and moral meanings. The scene unfolds in a kitchen through an arched doorway. Two soldiers sit, smoking and drinking while conversing with a young woman seated on the stairs. The painter has incorporated several still lifes into the scene—the soldier's armor and weapons piled on a chair behind them, a stringed instrument leaning on a cupboard in the foreground with books of music and dice.

This painting was in French noble collections from the late eighteenth to the mid-nineteenth century. It was acquired by the successful commodities broker Adolphe Schloss (1842–1910), who assembled the greatest collection of Dutch and Flemish art of his day in his Parisian townhouse: over three hundred paintings of the highest quality, with a particular focus on seventeenth-century masters. The Schloss collection stayed together after Adolphe's death, cared for by his wife and their five children. The collection's renown, and the fact that its owners were Jewish, made it a prime target for official and unofficial art-acquisition elements within and around the Nazi administration during World War II.

In 1939, as France became threatened by war, the collection was quietly moved from Paris to a family friend's chateau, Chambon, in central France. It remained hidden there, along with a collection of modern art of another Jewish collector, Prosper-Émile Weil, until the spring of 1943, when a series of paid informants led German and collaborationist French agencies to one of the Schloss sons, from whom the location of the paintings was extracted. The collection was taken to Paris and catalogued. Louvre officials found out and intervened, purchasing forty-nine of the Schloss paintings for the state. The majority of the collection, however, some 260 paintings, was earmarked for the art museum Hitler had planned for his hometown of Linz. Most of these were sent to Germany in the fall of that year.

Jacob Duck's *Interior with Soldiers and Women* was one of the paintings acquired by the Louvre, all of which were returned to the Schloss family after the war. Sales of the Schloss collection in the 1950s brought many paintings legitimately onto the market, including the Duck, which was acquired along with four other works by J. Paul Getty in 1951. He donated them to his museum in the 1970s. Two other of the Schloss-Louvre paintings were acquired by the Getty in the 1980s.

Other paintings were dispersed across the art market through various avenues to museums and private collectors. Today, about half of the 333 Schloss paintings remain to be returned to their rightful owners, the heirs of Adolphe Schloss. –PJB

FURTHER READING

Feliciano 1997; Karlsgodt 2011; Schloss collection website

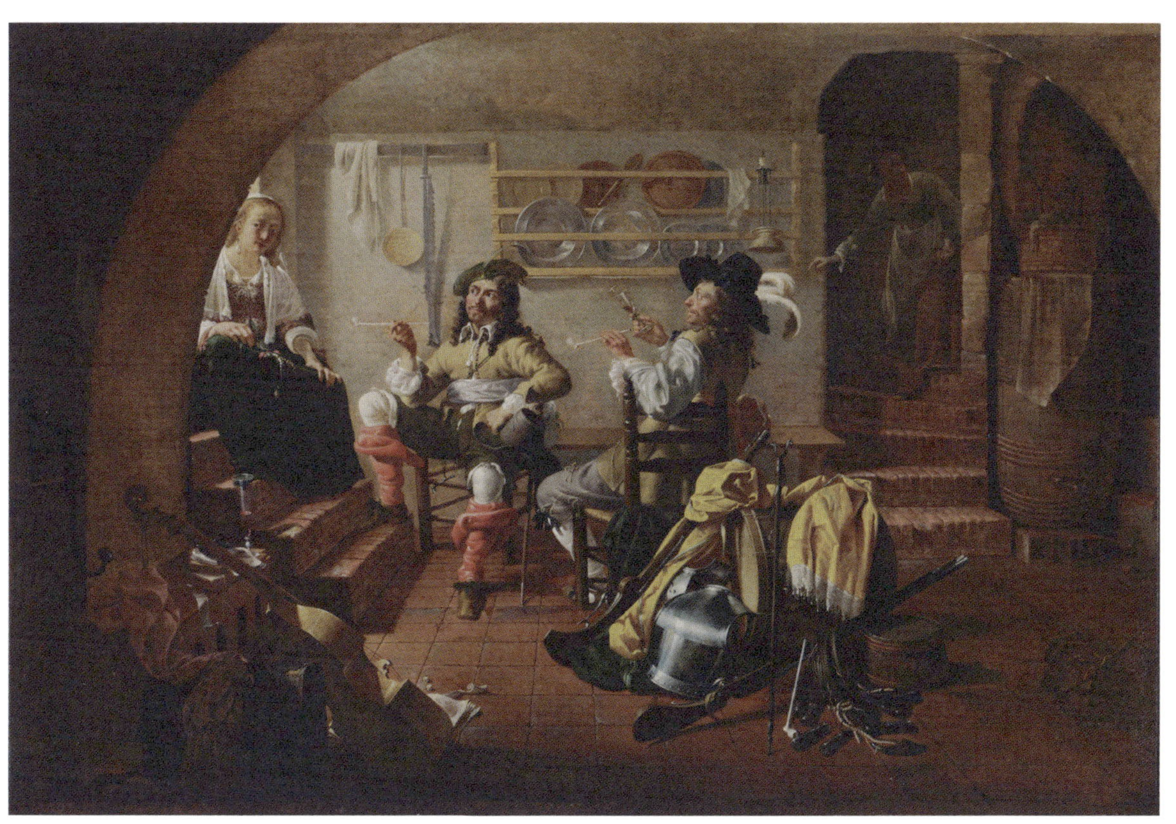

## 7

# Fra Filippo Lippi (circa 1406–1469)

### Madonna and Child, circa 1440

tempera on poplar panel, 31⅛ × 20⅛ in. (79 × 51.1 cm)
National Gallery of Art, Washington, DC, Samuel H. Kress Collection, 1939.1.290

In his 1568 *Lives of the Artists*, Giorgio Vasari wrote that "if Fra Filippo was outstanding in all of his pictures, in his small ones he surpassed even himself, because he made them so gracious and beautiful that they could not be done better." Vasari's high praise is borne out in this sensitive work, a highly expressive devotional painting of a compositional type common in Florence in the fourteenth and fifteenth centuries. Filippo Lippi was among the most important artists in Florence in the middle decades of the fifteenth century, and a crucial link between the generation of Fra Angelico and Masaccio and that of Botticelli. Lippi worked for the Medici family, executed major fresco cycles, and was among the first Italians to respond to and adapt the realism of northern artists like Jan van Eyck. The Christ Child draws the Madonna's hand to his chest and throat, a playful gesture that also foreshadows Christ's sacrifice; the latter is also hinted at by the figures' melancholic expressions. Lippi set the pair in an elaborate architectural structure, typical of his works from the 1430s and 1440s. This classicizing invention, made of multicolored stones with scalloped niche and layers of moldings, anchors the monumental Virgin and pushes the figures toward the viewer.

This painting was purchased for the Königliches Museum, Berlin, from the great collector Edward Solly in 1821. It remained there until 1937 when it was traded, along with a predella panel from Duccio's *Maestà*, the monumental high altarpiece installed in Siena Cathedral in 1311, for a portrait by Hans Holbein, the Younger believed to represent Jean de Dinteville (the French diplomat famously portrayed in Holbein's masterpiece *The Ambassadors* in the National Gallery, London) and now called *Portrait of a Man with a Lute* (Bell, fig. 3). This exchange was accomplished through the preeminent old master art dealer Joseph Duveen, following an existing practice of German museums. In the economic difficulties of the Weimar Republic, acquiring by purchase was beyond the means of many museums, so they exchanged works of art to refine and enhance their collections. In the late 1930s, this practice had the potential of drawing museum directors into the ethically corrupt worldview of the Nazi regime, entangling collection stewardship with nationalistic beliefs stemming from Aryanism. Some directors sought to 'repatriate' works by important historical German artists, either implicitly or explicitly invoking Adolf Hitler's approbation.

The two works that left Berlin under these circumstances quickly found their way to another major public collection, the nascent National Gallery of Art. Duccio's *Nativity with the Prophets Isaiah and Ezekiel* (NGA 1937.1.8) was purchased by Andrew W. Mellon's trust from Duveen for the National Gallery as soon as it left Germany in April 1937. The following year, Duveen sold the Lippi *Madonna* to Samuel H. Kress, who had it restored before giving it to the National Gallery in 1939. –PJB

FURTHER READING

Boskovits and Brown 2003; Ruda 1993

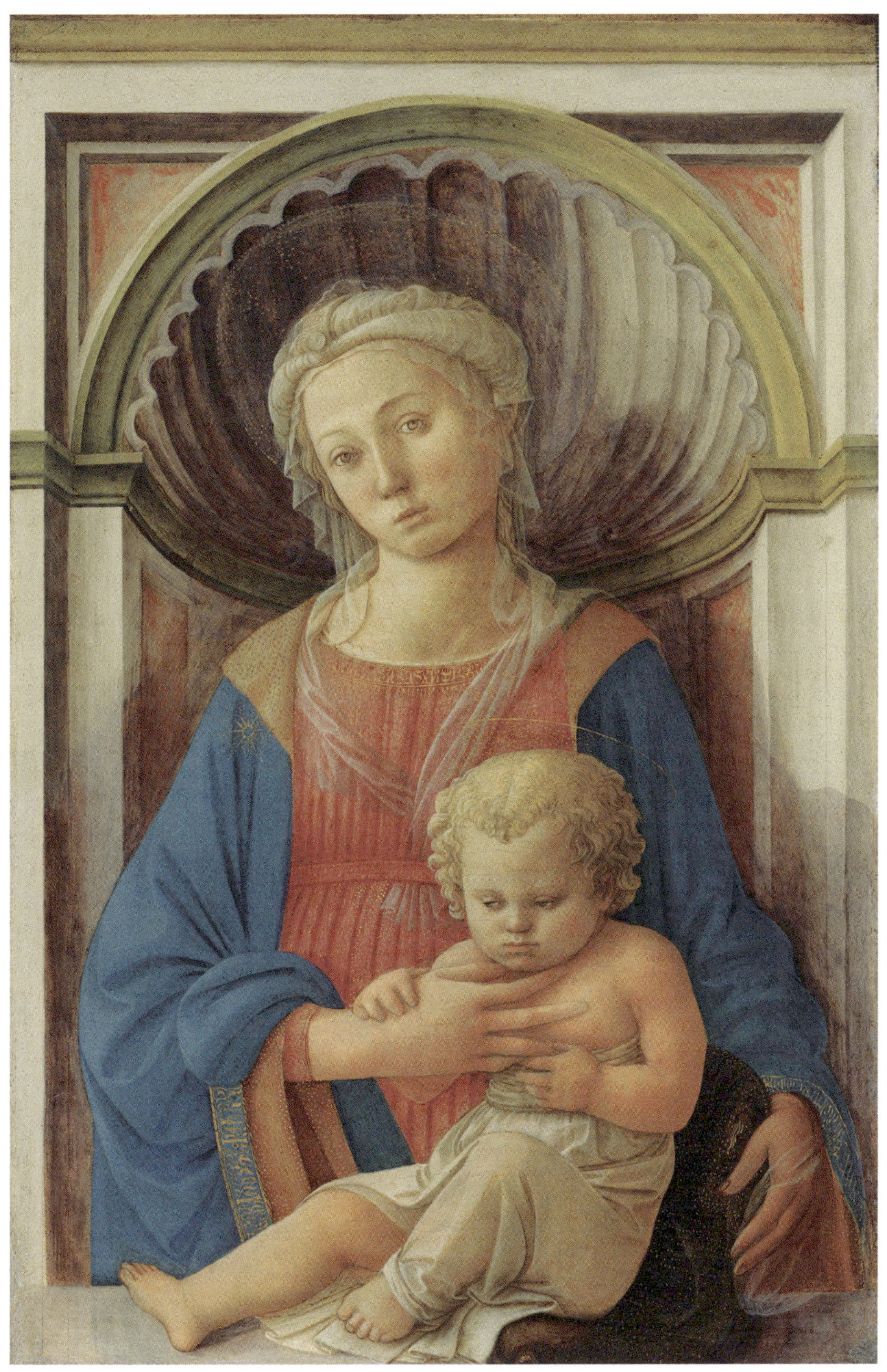

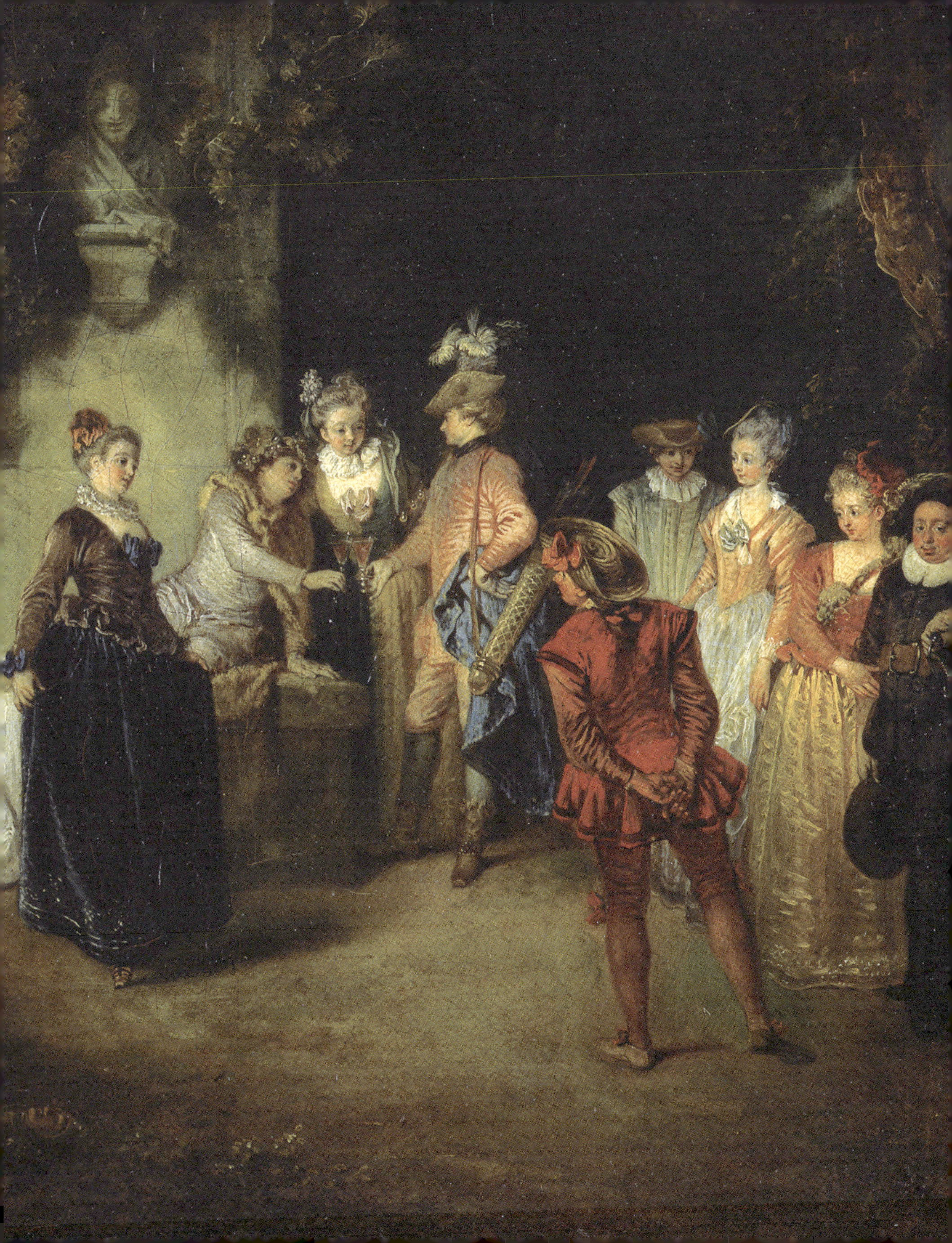

# THE "BERLIN 202"

## 8

# Attributed to Konrad Witz (1400/10–1444/46)

### The Crucifixion, circa 1440–50

oil on panel transferred to canvas, 13⅜ × 10¼ in. (35.5 × 27.4 cm)
Gemäldegalerie, Berlin, 1656

Konrad Witz was born in Germany, but moved to Basel in present-day Switzerland in 1434. He produced most of his work, of which few paintings survive today, in Basel and Geneva. *The Crucifixion* is set in a verdant landscape with a view to a city on the right and a lake bordered by mountains in the distance. Mary, in blue, stands to the left of the cross supported by two companions robed in red and yellow, while John, to the right, clasps his hands in agony. Of particular stylistic note is the attention to detail in the rendering of the folds and creases in the draperies of the somewhat stocky figures, and the intense emotion on the faces of the mourners. In the left foreground the painting's donor is portrayed in a red robe, kneeling in prayer with head raised upward, his eyes averted from the religious scene itself. This pious man is engrossed in private and personal prayer and does not really interact with Jesus or the other figures. Rather, it is through the intensity of his prayer that Christ's sacrifice on the cross is made present in the painting. *The Crucifixion* thus presents an ambiguity between the realistic elements in the painting and the visionary aspects of the donor's piety.

The attribution to Witz is based on the handling of light across the landscape and the clear organization of deep space that gradually moves from foreground to horizon. These characteristics can be found in Witz's most famous work, *The Miraculous Draft of Fishes*, one of the wing panels from the *Altarpiece of Saint Peter*, painted in 1444 for the cathedral in Geneva and now in the city's Musée d'Art et d'Histoire. In that panel, the landscape setting is remarkable for the naturalistic representation of the lake and the reflection of light in the water.

Witz's work further shows the influence of Flemish artists working at this time, in particular Jan van Eyck, who is also represented among the "202" (BR 63–67). Van Eyck's work is especially noted for its incredible attention to detail, handling of reflective light, and the contrast between naturalism and spirituality, especially in paintings with religious subject matter. *The Crucifixion* (BR 200) was among the paintings transferred to the US in 1945; it was shown in part of the exhibition tour, and returned to Germany with the second group of paintings. Also included in the American tour was Witz's *The Counsel of Salvation* (formerly titled *The Decision on the Redemption of Man*) (BR 199). –KN

FURTHER READING

Röttgen 1961; Gemäldegalerie 1978; Brinkmann et al. 2011

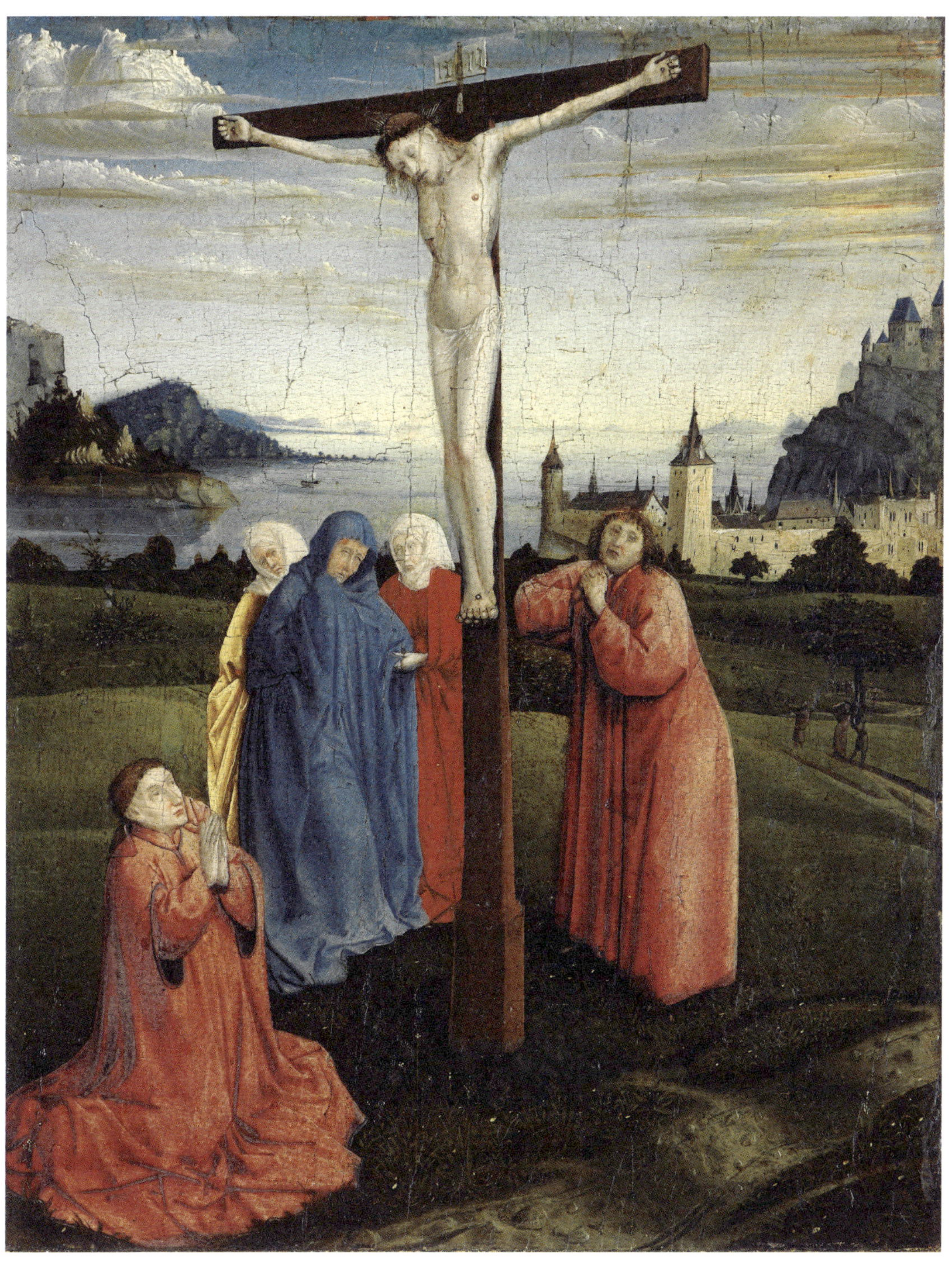

## 9

# Sandro Botticelli (1445–1510)

### Ideal Portrait of a Lady ("Simonetta Vespucci"), 1475–80

tempera on poplar panel, 18¾ × 13¾ in. (47.5 × 35 cm)
Gemäldegalerie, Berlin, 106 A

Sandro Botticelli was one of the most highly regarded Florentine painters of his age. A pupil of Filippo Lippi (see cat. 7), by the mid-1480s he was working for the leading patrons and at important sites across Italy, including the Sistine Chapel. His famed mythological and allegorical paintings, such as the *Primavera* and *Birth of Venus*, were made for the ruling Medici family of Florence. The elegant figure style, iconographical richness, and decorative splendor of these compositions have elicited praise and inspired reinterpretation continuously since their creation. In his religious paintings sacred figures often appeal directly to the viewer while embodying otherworldly, idealized beauty.

The present painting is one of several idealized portraits in painting and sculpture made in the 1460s and 1470s by Botticelli and other artists in Florence that have much to do with the influential literary tradition of idealized beauty begun by the fourteenth-century poet Petrarch. These painted and sculpted figures walk the line between individualized portrait and idealized beauty. This woman's elaborate coiffure—braided, tied, and studded with pearls—would have been inconceivable on the streets of fifteenth-century Florence, where sumptuary laws strictly limited such ostentatious displays of wealth. Instead, the subject here becomes an embodiment of Florence, the birthplace of eternal beauty.

The patrician Simonetta Vespucci was lauded for her beauty in poetry and at the highest levels of Florentine society. She was anointed the "queen of beauty" by Giuliano de' Medici in chivalric games put on by the Medici in 1475. Although Simonetta was married to another leading citizen, Marco Vespucci, Giuliano's devotion to her, figured as platonic love, was widely remarked upon. After her untimely death in 1476, and Giuliano's murder two years later, her beauty and their love became civic myth. Several paintings of idealized beauties made at the time have been associated with Simonetta, although it is likely that none of them present an objective likeness. Elements of the female archetype Botticelli portrays here also appear in his mythological figures and even his depictions of the Madonna where, arguably, they continue to promote Florentine civic identity and refinement.

Five paintings by Botticelli or his workshop were included among the "202" sent to the US in 1945, but only the present portrait (BR 18) and the large standing, nude *Venus* (BR 22), made the complete tour of thirteen venues in 1948–49. A photograph of the portrait being examined upon uncrating at the Saint Louis Art Museum is printed above the headline "$50,000,000 Berlin Art Exhibit Will Open at Museum Tomorrow" in the *St. Louis Post-Dispatch*, January 29, 1949. –PJB

FURTHER READING

Schumacher 2009; Christiansen and Weppelmann 2011

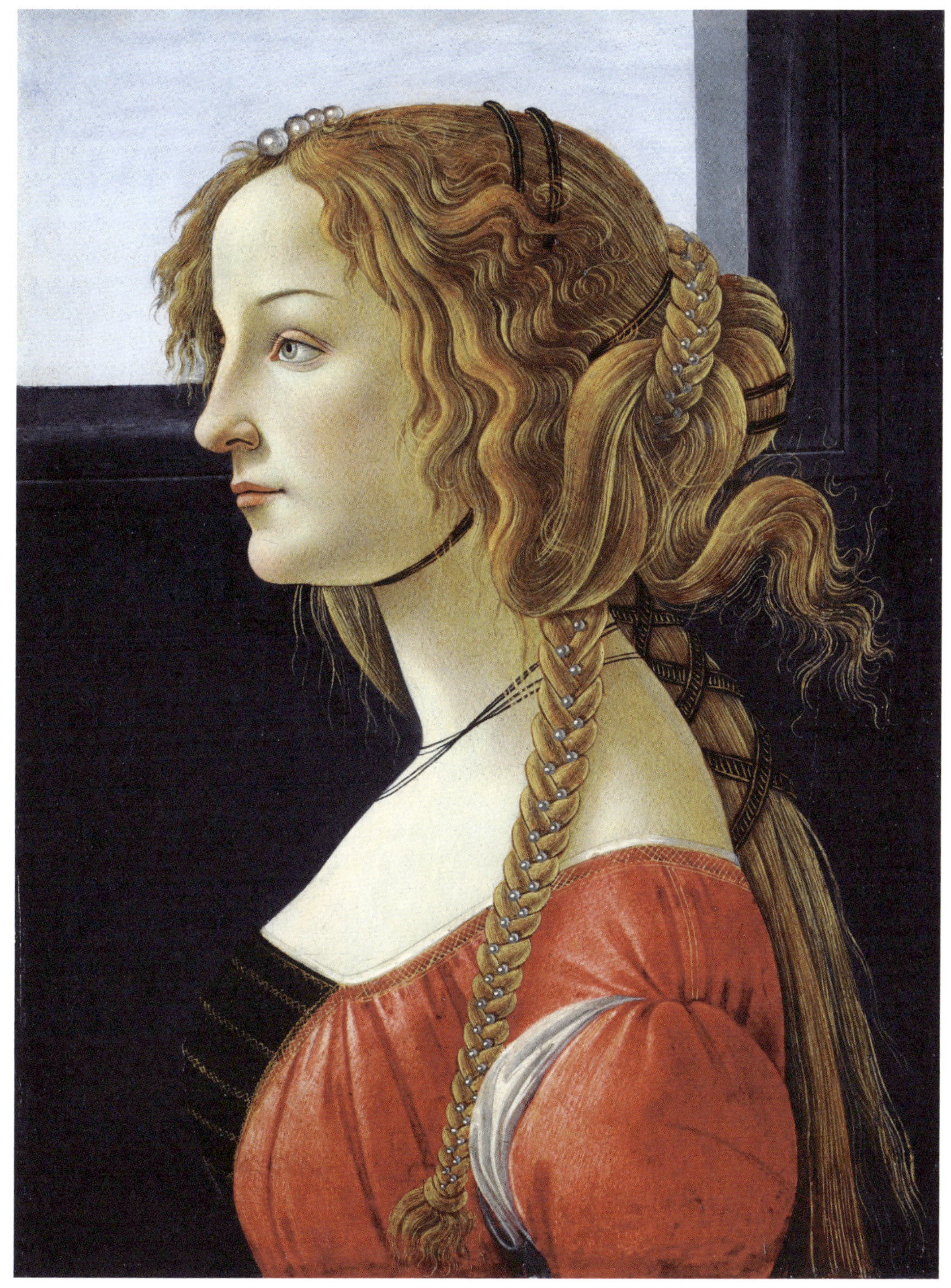

## 10

# Philips Koninck (1619–1688)

**Panorama of Holland**, circa 1655–60

oil on canvas, 36⅝ × 66³⁄₁₆ in. (93 × 168.1 cm)
Gemäldegalerie, Berlin, 821 A

During the seventeenth century Dutch artists invented the genre of naturalistic landscape, recording their modest land—its fields, dunes, forests, and rivers—with equal measures of veracity and thoroughness in their paintings and prints. Despite the similarity of these images to nature, most of these works were not executed from life, but were produced in the studio where the artists, informed by observation recorded in drawings, creatively rearranged the parts of nature to produce a convincing representation of the land. Philips Koninck's *Panorama of Holland* is an excellent example of this approach. From a brightly illuminated foreground plateau the land recedes in horizontal bands of alternating dark and light that stretch toward a river and eventually the horizon. Tiny figures on horseback, field animals, and a winding road between red-roofed cottages populate the view. Typical of Koninck's panoramas, the space seems to extend for a great distance, with the land and sky occupying equal parts of the composition. Koninck was especially adept with this subject matter. His panoramas, with their loose brushwork and palette of yellow and brown hues, are noteworthy for their vastness and majestic beauty, making these works some of the most creative among Dutch landscapes.

Koninck may have studied with Rembrandt, and his panoramas share a kindred spirit with Rembrandt's landscapes, and those of his school. The brown tones and rich brushwork in *Landscape with an Arched Bridge*, which was included in the "202" as by Rembrandt, but is now attributed to Govaert Flinck (BR 136), are similar to those of the present work. Koninck's panoramas are also reminiscent of the work of Hercules Seghers, who was active at the beginning of the seventeenth century and was represented among the "202" with *View of Rhenen* (BR 162). Seghers's panorama is realistically conceived and includes a view of the city and the surrounding land, in a deep perspective under an expansive sky.

*Panorama of Holland* (BR 97) was shown in all venues of the US exhibition tour. Other landscapes among the Berlin masterpieces that, like Koninck's, hymn the Dutch countryside, include Hobbema's *Village Street under Trees* (BR 89) and Jacob van Ruisdael's *Landscape with a View of Haarlem* (BR 155). We might also add Rubens's *Landscape with the Shipwreck of Paul* (BR 151, then entitled *Landscape with the Shipwreck of Aeneas*) to this group since it, too, includes a panoramic view suggestive of the landscape of Flanders in the southern Netherlands. –KN

FURTHER READING

Stechow 1966; Gemäldegalerie 1978; Sutton 1987

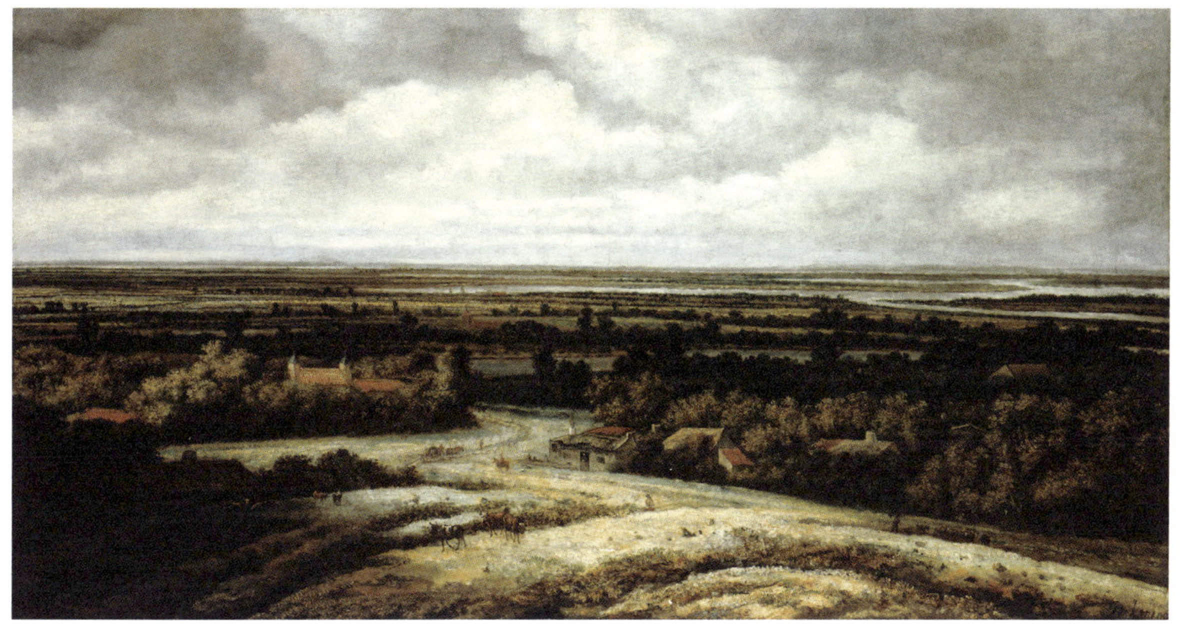

## 11

# Antoine Watteau (1684–1721)

### The French Comedians, 1715–17

oil on canvas, 15¼ × 19⁹⁄₁₆ in. (38.8 × 49.4 cm)
Gemäldegalerie, Berlin, 468

In an imaginary garden two actors perform a *dance à deux* in the company of revelers who form a semicircle around them. Many of the figures are stock characters, revealed by their costumes and roles, demonstrating Watteau's interest in the contemporary Parisian theater. The female dancer wears a black skirt with lilac bodice and a ruff, while the male figure is clad in red with a straw hat trimmed with bows. Behind them, Bacchus, dressed in lavender with a wreath on his head and animal pelt draped over his shoulder, reclines on a stone bench. He toasts with a huntsman wearing a plumed hat and carrying a quiver with arrows, which may indicate he is playing the part of Cupid. On the left, musicians play a musette, oboe, and violin, while a tambourine rests on the ground in front of them. Behind them, a Pierrot-like character holding a staff decorated with vine leaves stands with other onlookers. The figure on the far right who has removed his hat and looks out to the viewer has been identified as the actor Paul Poisson, in the guise of Crispin, a symbol of French comedy. Watteau took great care with the individualization of his face and the depiction of his costume, which is Spanish in origin, and includes the black cap, stiff white collar, wide leather belt, and sword. On the stone bracket above Bacchus is the bust of a hooded figure, perhaps Momus, personification of satire, and another reference to the theater.

Although no specific subject has been identified with certainty, an intermezzo in the *Festes de l'Amour et de Bacchus*, a comic opera by Jean-Baptiste Lully (1672), is frequently cited as a possible source of inspiration for this delightful picture. It was performed twice in Watteau's lifetime and tells of the reconciliation between Bacchus and Cupid, who figure prominently here.

The shimmering colors and bright light reflect Watteau's knowledge of Renaissance and Baroque masters and lend the painting a feeling of luxury and elegance. Watteau produced a number of chalk preparatory drawings for the figures used in this painting. They were reused in several of his other paintings and demonstrate the care he took in working up his figures in order to get the pose and stance exactly right.

*The French Comedians* (BR 190) and *The Italian Comedians* (BR 191) are among the most famous pictures by Watteau. They were probably not conceived as a pair, given the differing scale and arrangement of the figures, but they have functioned as pendants since 1769 when they entered the collection of Frederick the Great of Prussia. A third canvas by Watteau, *Company Outdoors* (or *Outdoor Festival*) (BR 192), was also among the "202." The three were exhibited at every venue on the American tour. –KN

FURTHER READING

Grasselli and Rosenberg 1984; Sheriff 2006; Baetjer, Rosenberg, and Cowart 2009

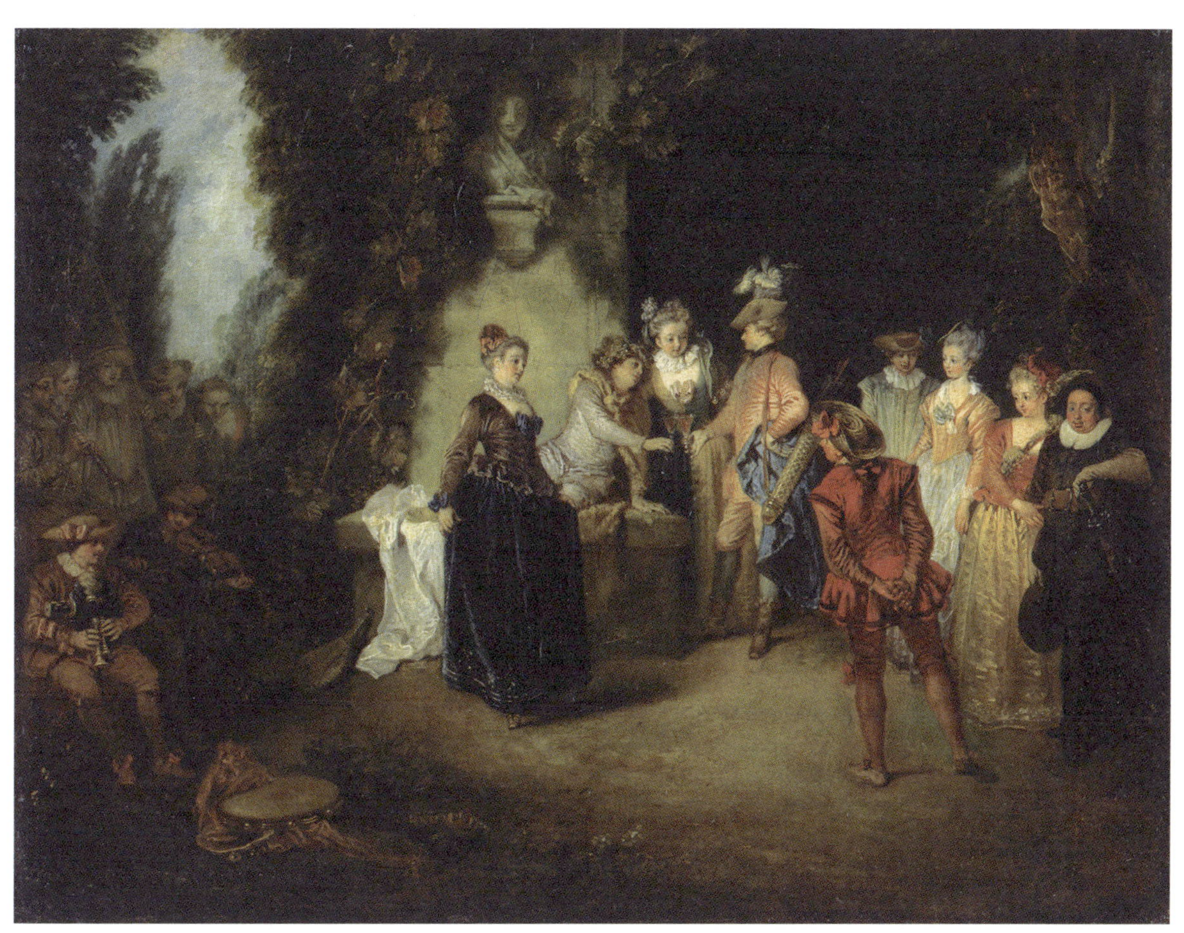

## 12

# Andrea Mantegna (circa 1431–1506)

### A Sibyl and a Prophet, circa 1495

distemper and gold on canvas, 22½ × 19⅛ in. (56.2 × 48.6 cm)
Cincinnati Art Museum, Bequest of Mary M. Emery, 1927.406

Among the most important artists of the Italian Renaissance, Andrea Mantegna regularly adapted the styles and motifs of ancient Roman art in his own work. He was immersed in humanist culture, in which scholars, artists, and patrons fostered the study and imitation of antique literature, art, and values. He was well-acquainted with scholars from the university in his native Padua and painters in nearby Venice; he married into that city's leading family of artists, the Bellini. In 1460, Mantegna took up the position of court painter to the ruling Gonzaga family in Mantua. Apart from two years spent in Rome, he remained in their employ for the rest of his life, producing such celebrated works as the frescoed chamber (*camera picta*) in Mantua's ducal palace and paintings for the *studiolo* of Isabella d'Este.

Late in his career, Mantegna painted a number of works imitating sculptural media in paint: in the National Gallery in London, Mantegna's *Vestal Virgin Tuccia with a Sieve* and *A Woman Drinking* simulate bronze figures against colored marbles. In other works, Mantegna worked in *grisaille*, imitating the appearance of marble and other semi-precious stones in his paintings. Mantegna's extensive knowledge of ancient art, particularly sculptural relief, is evident in this painting. Here he limited his color palette to warm, golden tones, lending his figures the appearance of gilt bronze. The traces of actual gold he used enhance these metallic and sculptural effects.

The subject of the Cincinnati painting remains enigmatic, and the artist may have intended a certain amount of ambiguity. The crowned woman on the right may represent a sibyl or the Old Testament queen Esther, while the bearded man may be a prophet, a philosopher, the biblical patriarch Mordecai, or the ill-fated Roman king Tarquin. The two figures are discussing the scroll held between them. The woman points to a particular passage with her right hand, while her interlocutor, with a furrowed brow, raises his hand to express his disagreement. They meet in front of an open doorway framed by an acanthus pilaster, a Roman ornamental motif often incorporated into Renaissance architecture. Mantegna borrowed the *contrapposto* pose of the sibyl, as well as the style of her garments, from an ancient Roman relief. At some point in its history, the painting was cut down on the right. In its original dimensions, it may have fit above the entryway to Isabella d'Este's *studiolo*.

Included among the 202 Berlin paintings that came to America were two paintings by Mantegna, both from much earlier in his career: a portrait, *Cardinal Ludovico Trevisan* (BR 108), circa 1459, on panel, and the *Presentation of Christ in the Temple* (BR 109), circa 1465–66. Due to their fragile condition, neither painting made the full US tour. The *Presentation* was only exhibited in Washington, while *Cardinal Trevisan* returned to Germany after the Boston exhibition.
—PJB+KG

FURTHER READING

Martineau 1992; Spike 1993; Campbell et al. 2019

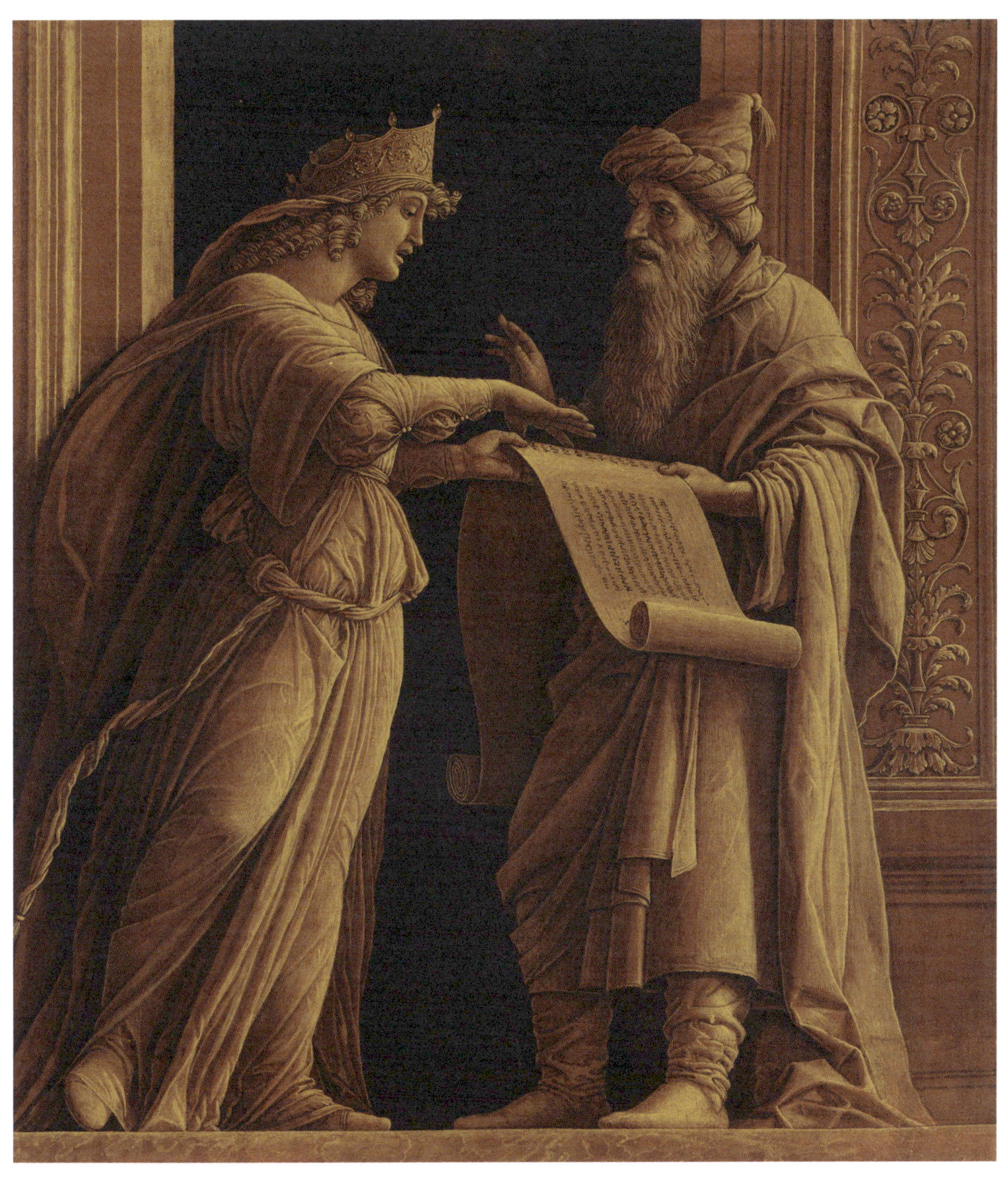

## 13

# Titian (circa 1488–1576)

### King Philip II of Spain, circa 1550–51

oil on canvas, 42³⁄₁₆ × 36½ in. (107.2 × 92.7 cm)
Cincinnati Art Museum, Bequest of Mary M. Emery, 1927.402

Tiziano Vecellio, known as Titian in English, was the preeminent Venetian painter of the sixteenth century. At the peak of his career, his constructive use of coloring and loose brushwork set the terms of debates on the nature of art itself and won him an international reputation and patronage. Of particular relevance here is the painter's long association with the Spanish House of Habsburg. He first met Charles V, Holy Roman emperor and king of Spain, in 1530; over the subsequent two decades, the emperor ennobled the painter, patronized him, and in the late 1540s sent him to paint his son, the future Philip II, who would become Titian's principal patron until the artist's death in 1576.

Titian probably painted this portrait from life sometime between 1549, when Charles arranged for Philip to inherit Spain and Spanish holdings in the Netherlands and the Americas, and 1556, when Charles abdicated, and Philip was crowned ruler of the Spanish Empire.

Although this portrait remained unfinished, the elements of Titian's mature style are apparent. His suggestive approach to depiction eschews precise definition of forms, and is enabled by free and insistent brushwork. Titian manifests the might and majesty of the new sovereign. The king's arresting gaze and straight-backed posture underscore his royal authority. Even in its unfinished state, the portrait evinces Titian's masterful ability to suggest the sitter's psychological presence, as well as to represent the play of light across various surfaces and textures. The loose handling of paint and blurring of contours to create a sense of atmosphere are hallmarks of Titian's style in the last two decades of his career. Extraneous elements of the painting, like the sharply detailed crown, the chain of the Order of the Golden Fleece, and the chair were likely added soon after Titian's death to "finish" the painting and thus make it more appealing to tastes of the time.

Five works by Titian were among the 202 paintings from the Berlin Museums that came to the United States in 1945 (BR 176–180). Four of the paintings were portraits, including one of two surviving self-portraits. That painting (BR 178), contemporary with, or slightly later than *Philip II*, is also unfinished. It exhibits a similarly sketchy approach to the body and hands, and a loose handling of paint. Like the Cincinnati picture, it remained in the artist's studio until his death in 1576. –PJB+KG

FURTHER READING

Spike 1993; Hope 2003; Humfrey 2007

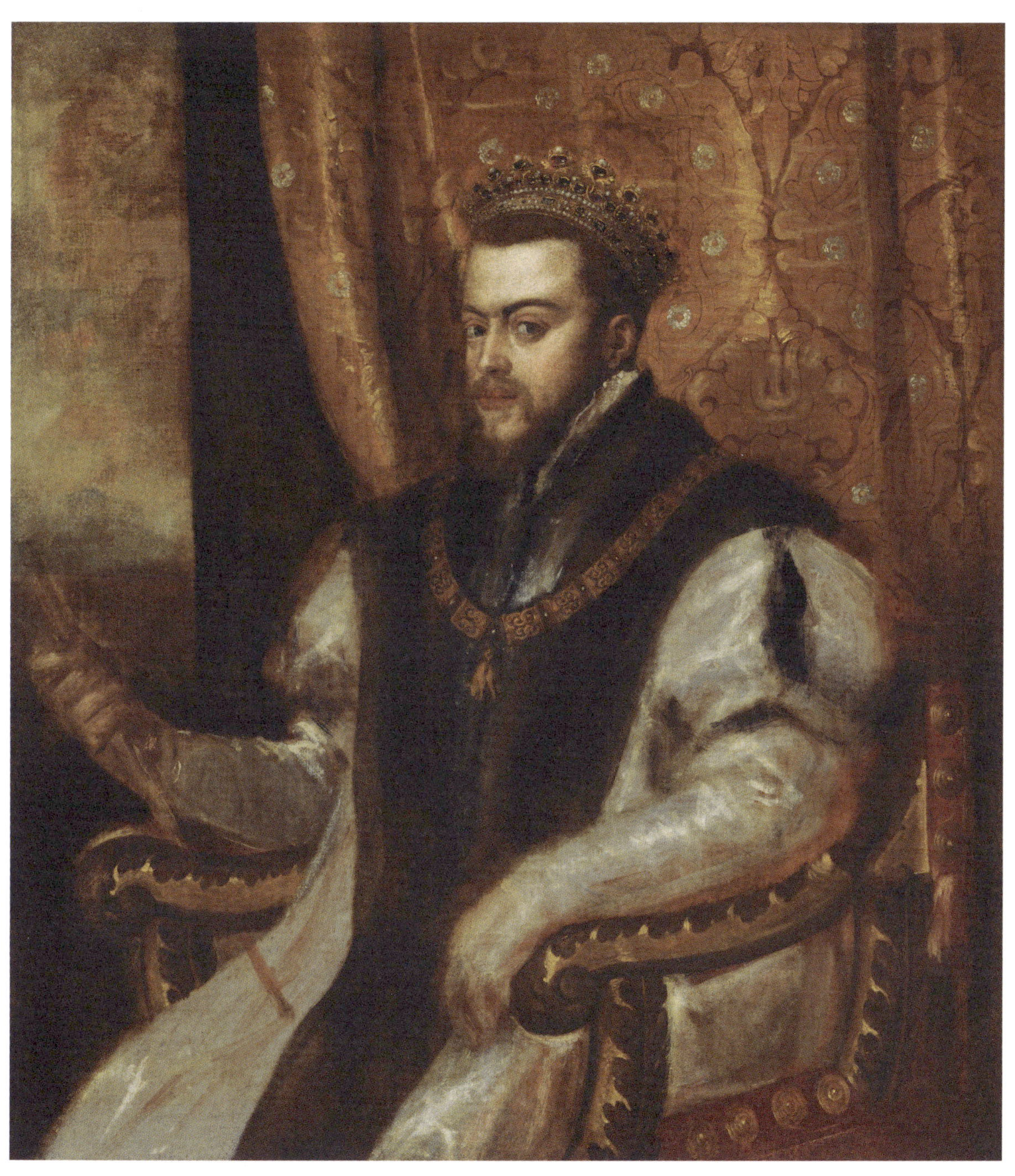

## 14

# Peter Paul Rubens (1577–1640)

### Samson and Delilah, circa 1609

oil on panel, 20½ × 19⅞ in. (52.1 × 50.5 cm)
Cincinnati Art Museum, Mr. and Mrs. Harry S. Leyman Endowment, 1972.459

Peter Paul Rubens probably created this beautiful oil sketch in 1609, soon after his return to Antwerp from Italy where he had spent eight years studying the works of classical antiquity and those of Renaissance and contemporary masters. It was produced as a preliminary study for a larger work commissioned by the Antwerp burgomaster Nicholas Rockox (1560–1640), who hung the finished painting above the mantelpiece in the great hall of his home in the Flemish city. That painting is today in the National Gallery in London, while an earlier pen-and-wash drawing (private collection, Amsterdam) probably records Rubens's early thoughts on this subject. The oil sketch shows Rubens's skill in working with this medium, in which he could map out his ideas from the beginning in color, allowing the brush to move easily and fluidly over the wood panel. It was an approach that especially appealed to Rubens and enabled him to display his narrative talents to best advantage, intuitively linking thought process and technical skill.

The sketch is based on the Old Testament biblical story (Judges 16) in which Delilah entices Samson into her bedchamber and cannily convinces him to reveal the source of his special power. Rubens chose to represent the critical moment when Samson, asleep in Delilah's lap and unaware of her betrayal, loses his strength as the young Philistine cuts his hair. Her state of partial undress clearly shows that Delilah used seduction as a means to unravel the powerful Samson, confirmed by the presence of the old hag behind her, a common feature in procuress scenes in Netherlandish art of the sixteenth and seventeenth centuries. A group of Philistines seen through the open door in the background will soon complete the deed and blind the helpless Samson.

Rubens's fully developed Baroque style, characterized by dynamic composition, aqueous brushwork, and the use of strong colors, is vividly present in the Cincinnati sketch. His interest in Michelangelo is evident in Samson's muscular torso, while the chiaroscuro effects and interior sources of light reflect the influence of the Italian artist Caravaggio and the German painter Adam Elsheimer, both represented among the 202 masterpieces: *Amor Victorious* (or *Conquering Love*) (BR 34) and *The Holy Family with Angels and Infant Saint John* (BR 60).

Another oil sketch was one of the six paintings by Rubens in the "202." Like the Cincinnati work, *Madonna and Child Enthroned with Saints* (BR 152) was made as a *modello* for a larger painting, in this case an altarpiece for the church of Saint Augustine, Antwerp. The other five Rubens pictures among the Berlin paintings reflect the breadth and depth of the artist's oeuvre and include portraiture, landscape, and biblical and mythological paintings (see BR 149, 150, 151, 153, 154). –KN

FURTHER READING

Held 1980; Sutton, Wieseman, and Van Hout 2004; Jaffé et al 2007–08; Suda and Nickel 2019

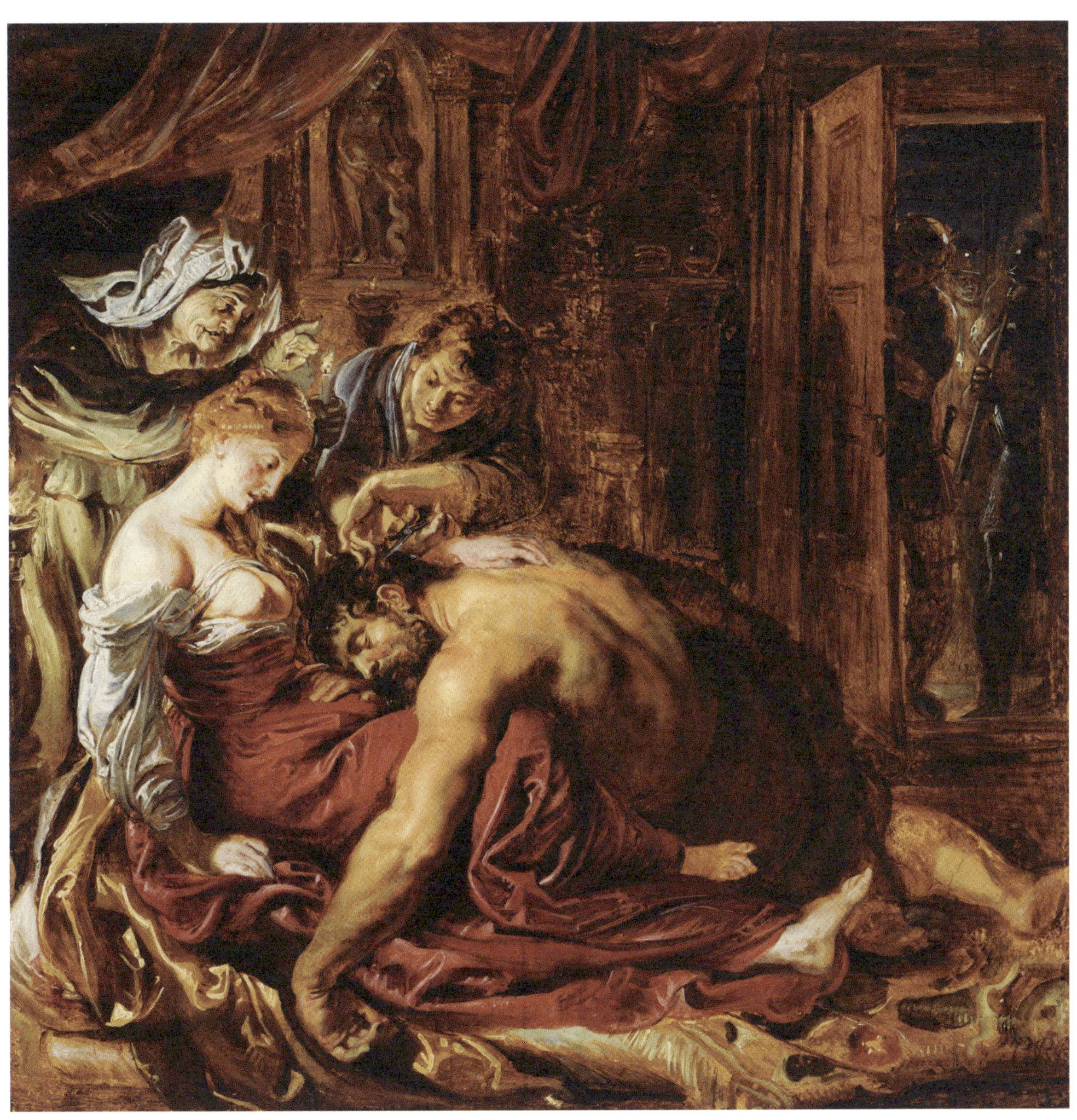

## 15

# Gerard ter Borch (1617–1681)

### The Music Party, circa 1670

oil on oak panel, 22⅞ × 18⅝ in. (58.1 × 47.3 cm)
Cincinnati Art Museum, Bequest of Mary M. Emery, 1927.421

Gerard ter Borch was one of the most talented painters of small-scale genre and portrait pictures in the Netherlands during the seventeenth century. Born in Zwolle, he worked in a number of Dutch cities, traveled widely in Europe, and eventually settled in Deventer. His *Music Party* is an excellent example of one of the most popular subjects among genre painters at this time and centers on the theme of music. A beautiful young woman holds an expensive, thirty-two string theorbo on her knees while turning the pages of a music book. She appears to pay little attention to the lounging gentleman holding an open songbook across the table from her, nor the other male standing figure, whose presence is unclear. Despite this, a quietly veiled flirtation links the figures through posture and gaze, while time seems to be suspended. This tension is counterbalanced by the exquisitely rendered white satin skirt with its shimmering surface and the yellow fur-trimmed jacket worn by the woman. Her hair is fashionably curled and decorated with ribbons and pearls. Equally smart is the gentleman suitor whose elegantly appointed outfit and sword indicate his social status.

Music was a highly respected and socially acceptable pastime in all levels of Dutch society during the seventeenth century. Many paintings were produced that represent the pleasure of music-making among couples, family members, and friends. Indeed, it was during this century that instrumental music came into its own, and literary and emblematic references linking music and love are diverse and widespread. They allude frequently to balance and harmony in family units and to love and sexual desire among romantic couples. Equally significant, however, and substantiated by seventeenth-century writers, is that Dutch painting at this time was appreciated by collectors and others not only for its symbolism, but even more so for its ability to visually delight the viewer through its precise imitation of nature. This is made eminently clear in this work, with Ter Borch's beautifully rendered textures, contemporary setting, and overall quiet elegance.

There were two Ter Borch paintings among the "202": *The Concert* (BR 169) and *Gallant Conversation* (formerly titled *Fatherly Advice*) (BR 170). The former was produced about the same time as the Cincinnati work and shows a woman from behind playing the cello, while the latter testifies to Ter Borch's great artistic skill in rendering textures and amorously tinged social scenes where the outcome remains unclear. –KN

FURTHER READING

Sutton et al. 1984; Wheelock et al. 2004; Franits 2004

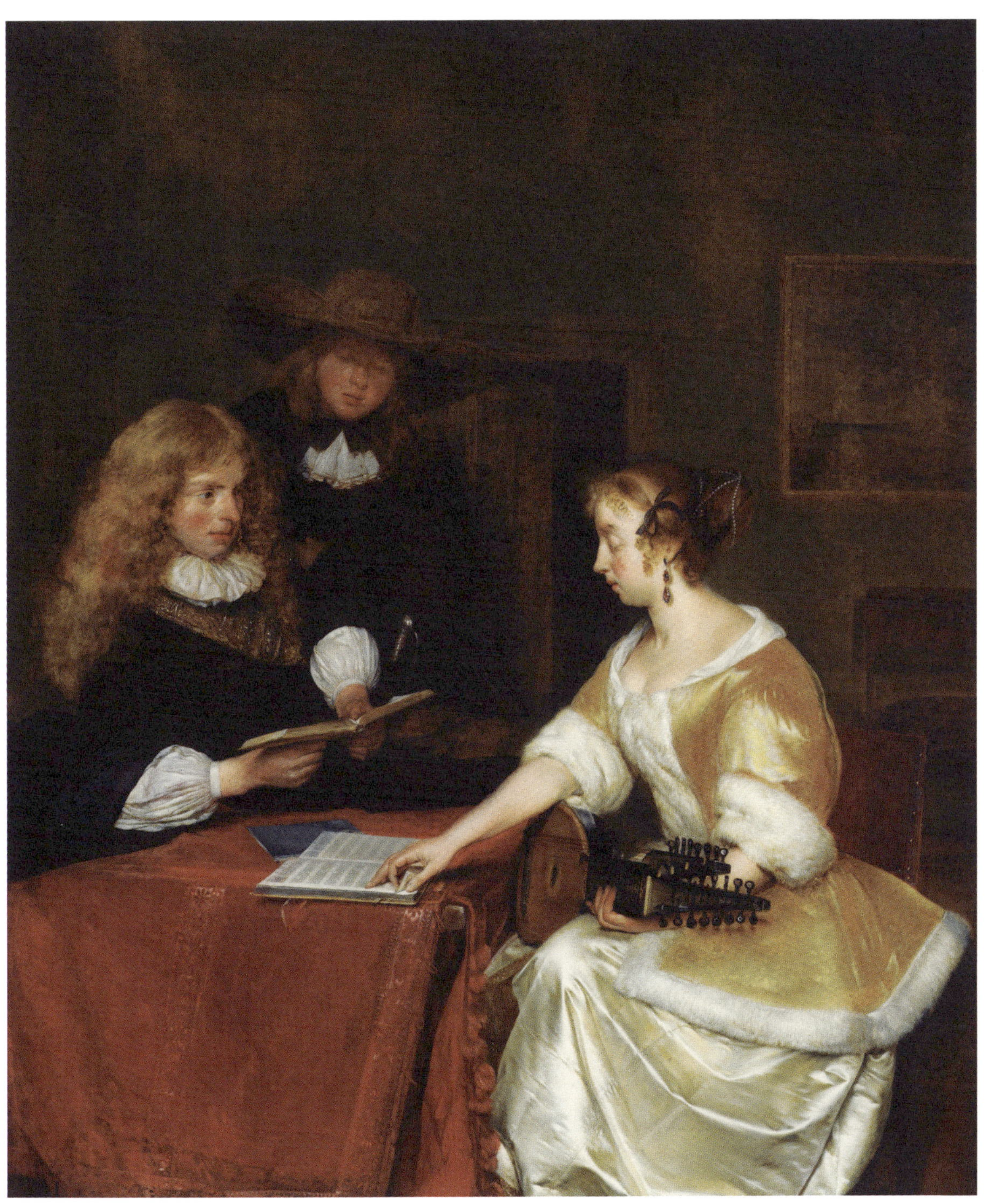

## 16

# Hans Memling (1430/40–1494)

### Saint Stephen, circa 1479–80

oil on panel, 18¾ × 6⅜ in. (47.5 × 16.2 cm)
Cincinnati Art Museum, Gift of Mrs. E. W. Edwards, 1956.11

### Saint Christopher, circa 1479–80

oil on panel, 18¹³⁄₁₆ × 6³⁄₁₆ in. (47.8 × 15.6 cm)
Cincinnati Art Museum, Gift of Mrs. E. W. Edwards, 1955.793

Born in the German city of Seligenstadt in the 1430s, Hans Memling spent the majority of his career in Flanders (a region of modern Belgium). He may have trained in Brussels in the workshop of the renowned Netherlandish painter Rogier van der Weyden (1399/1400–1464). Memling settled in Bruges in the 1460s, where he executed portraits, devotional panels, and altarpieces for prominent patrons and churches, becoming one of the city's most important painters. He also enjoyed commissions from international patrons such as Florentine bankers stationed in Bruges. In his use of the relatively new medium of oil paint and his rendering of subjects with exquisite attention to detail, Memling built upon the innovations of Netherlandish artists such as Van der Weyden and Jan van Eyck.

These narrow panels present sensitive devotional images of Saint Stephen, the first Christian martyr, and Saint Christopher, whose charity was tested and honored when he carried the Christ Child across a river. In the background, Memling painted scenes from the saints' lives, including their deaths, setting them in a fifteenth-century Flemish town. Particularly notable are the incredible precision and delicacy with which Memling painted the flowering plants in the foreground, identifiable as nettles, buttercups, and English daisies, as well as the miniature figures populating the narrative in the background.

*Saint Stephen* and *Saint Christopher* originally decorated the outside of the wings of a portable triptych altarpiece that was disassembled in the nineteenth century. The wings were split to create five individual paintings, an all-too-common fate for fifteenth-century works in the nineteenth-century art market. When the original triptych was closed, the continuous landscape behind the saints created a unified composition. The wings would have opened to reveal *Saint John the Baptist* and *Saint Mary Magdalene* framing a *Rest on the Flight to Egypt*, paintings now in the Louvre.

Three works by Memling were included among the 202 paintings from the Berlin Museums shipped to Washington in 1945, each a representation of the Madonna and Child. One of those (BR 116) was originally the central panel of a triptych of a similar size to the Cincinnati/Louvre work, the wings of which are now in the Uffizi. —PJB+KG

FURTHER READING

Scott 1987; Lane 2009

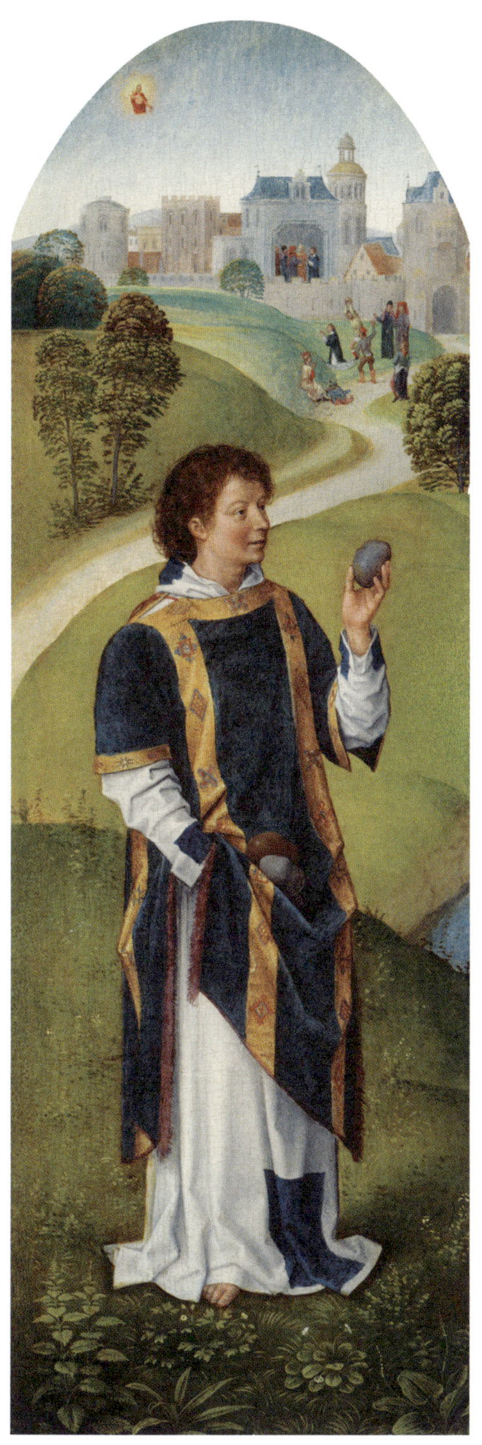

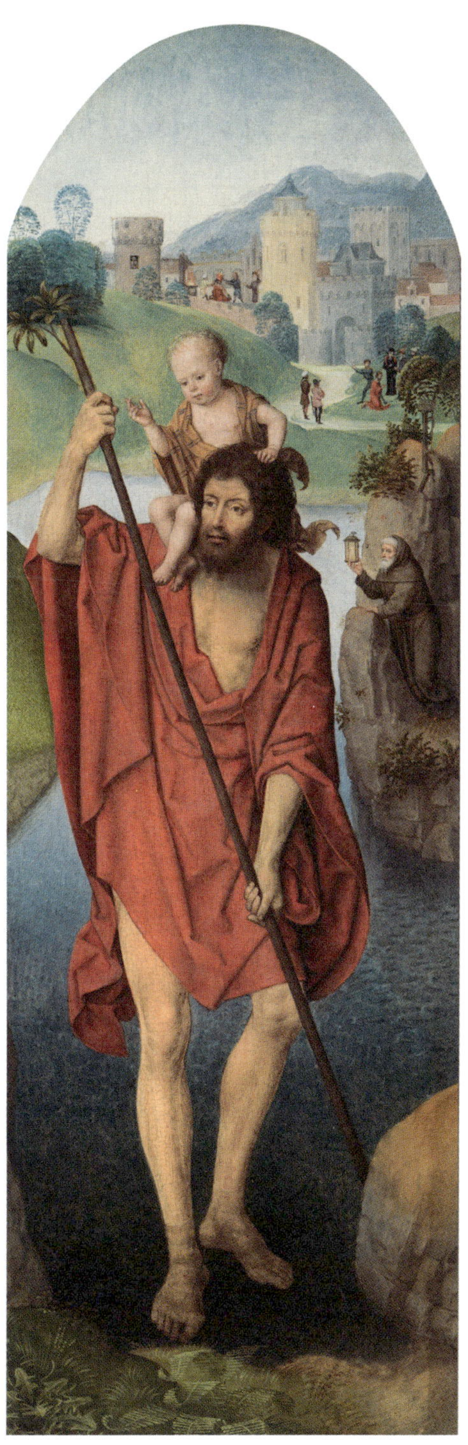

## 17

# Lucas Cranach, the Elder (1472–1553)

### Saint Helena with the Cross, 1525

oil on panel, 16⅛ × 10⅝ in. (41 × 27 cm)
Cincinnati Art Museum, Bequest of Mary M. Emery, 1927.387

Alongside Albrecht Dürer (1471–1528) and Matthias Grünewald (1470/75–1528), Lucas Cranach was one of the major artists of the German High Renaissance. Over the course of his long career, Cranach served as a royal portraitist to the Electors of Saxony at their court in Wittenberg, and was also a prolific draftsman and printmaker, employing a large workshop of assistants to execute his designs. He was a close friend of Martin Luther and staunch supporter of the Protestant Reformation.

Cranach developed a highly distinctive style of painting, often characterized by bold, intense colors, flattened forms, and meticulously detailed costumes, whether his subjects were Saxon royalty and aristocrats or drawn from the Bible or the history of the Church.

In this small panel, Cranach depicted Saint Helena (circa 255–330), mother of the Roman emperor Constantine, who was celebrated as the emperor who established Christianity as an official religion in the Roman Empire. Renowned for her piety, Helena went on pilgrimage to Jerusalem in 327, intending to restore important holy sites. There she ordered the excavation of the hill at Golgotha and allegedly discovered the True Cross of Christ. In many artistic depictions, as here, Saint Helena is identified by a royal crown and the cross.

Cranach depicts Saint Helena not as a Roman woman, but in the sumptuous dress of a sixteenth-century Saxon noblewoman. The emphasis on her costume is particularly dramatic against the dark background of the panel. She is dressed in a deep red velvet gown with slashed sleeves, trimmed with gold brocade with floral patterns. Laden with jewelry, she wears a gold hairnet, from which a few delicate curls of hair escape. Cranach depicted very similar costumes and jewelry in his portraits of women of the Saxon court, and it is possible that Cranach portrayed a contemporary woman in the guise of the saint.

Cranach painted his distinctive emblem—a crowned winged serpent with a ring in its mouth—along with the date in the upper right corner of the panel. This crest was given to Cranach by Frederick the Wise, Elector of Saxony, in 1508, and relates to Chronos, god of time, whose name plays on that of the artist and his birthplace.

Three works by Cranach were among the paintings sent to Washington in 1945: *Portrait of a Lawyer's Wife* (BR 48, then identified as Frau Reuss), *Rest on the Flight into Egypt* (BR 47), and *Lucretia* (BR 46), which represent the range of subjects in Cranach's body of work. The full-length, nude *Lucretia*, dated 1533, is, like Cincinnati's *Saint Helena*, an idealized beauty silhouetted against a dark background. –PJB+KG

FURTHER READING

Scott 1987; Brinkmann et al. 2007–08

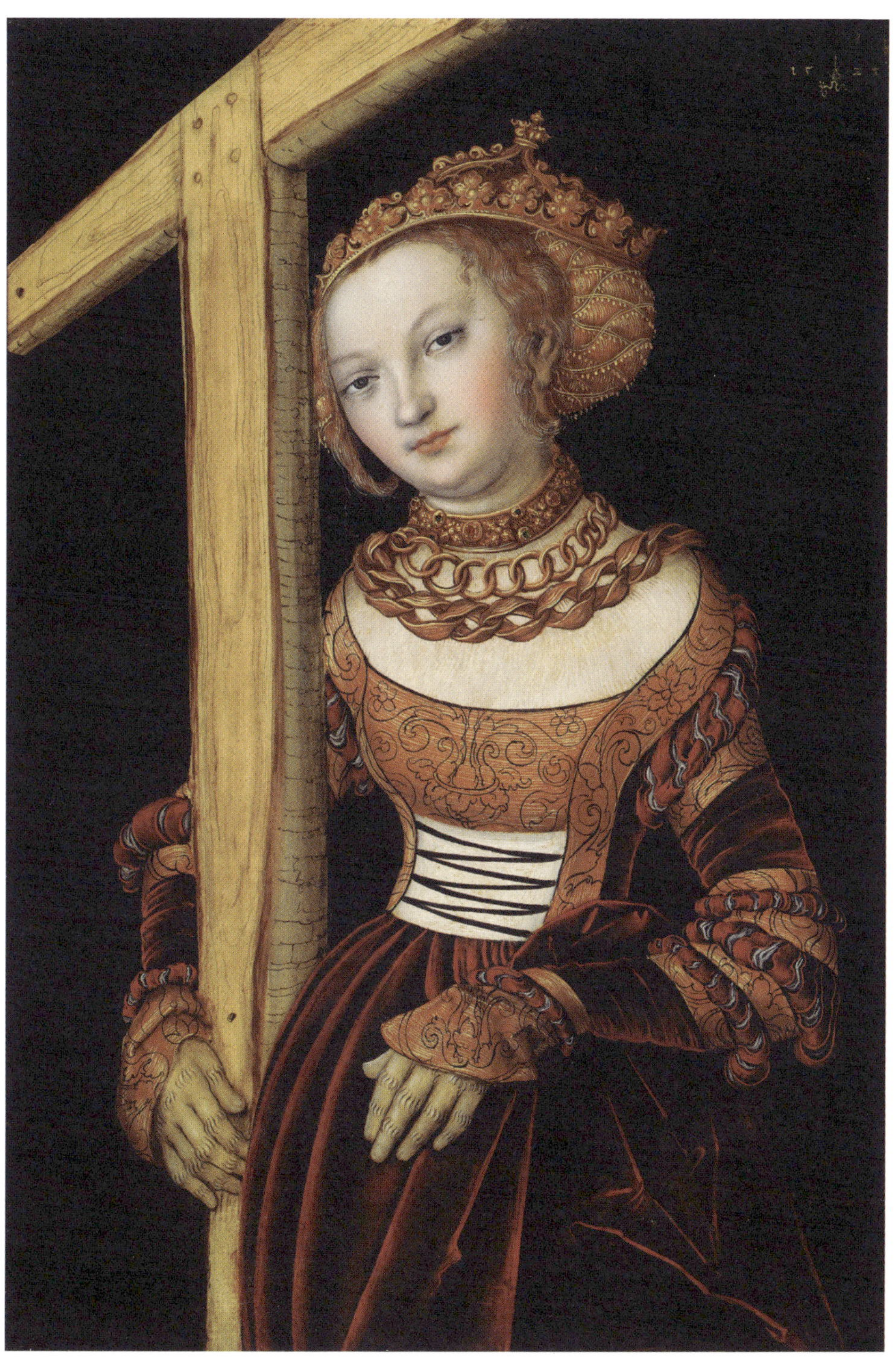

## 18

# Claude Lorrain (1604–1682)

### An Artist Studying from Nature, 1639

oil on canvas, 30¾ × 39¾ in. (78.1 × 101 cm)
Cincinnati Art Museum, Gift of Mary Hanna, 1946.102

Born in France, Claude Lorrain spent most of his life in Italy where he achieved renown for his landscapes—river and coastal scenes populated with classical architectural elements and suffused with the gentle luminosity of sunrise or sunset. A draftsman, etcher, and painter, Claude specialized in the genre of imaginary landscape, in contrast to Dutch artists of this era who created naturalistic renderings of their native land (see Philips Koninck, *Panorama of Holland*; cat. 10). The Cincinnati painting, *An Artist Studying from Nature*, is an excellent example of Claude's idealizing approach to the beauty and mystery of nature. An artist, seated near classical ruins and logs, sketches in the company of country folk and figures on horseback. The scene is divided by a large tree in the center middleground and bathed in a pink-red afternoon light. An imaginary harbor and the towers of a fortress or walled town appear on the right, and the vista opens on the left with boats and a mountainous coast leading toward the horizon. Claude frequently referenced the architecture of ancient and Renaissance Rome, and the building here is often compared to Palo Castle, a fortified structure on the Mediterranean coast west of Rome, which Claude depicted in several drawings. Together, these elements lend a feeling of stately beauty and grandeur to the painting, the compositional elements of which are partly drawn from nature and partly fanciful. Meanwhile, the vignette of an artist drawing out-of-doors appears in a number of Claude's works (early biographers including Joachim von Sandrart recorded that he frequently drew *en plein air*).

Claude included a drawing of this painting in his *Liber Veritatis* (Book of Truth; British Museum, London), where he methodically recorded all his paintings to document their authorship. An etching, which depicts the Cincinnati painting (in reverse) and exists in several states, was probably produced in the same year, 1639.

Claude's *Italian Coastal Landscape in Early Morning Light* (BR 105), included in the "202," was painted in 1642, a few years after the Cincinnati picture. In that work, under an early morning haze, figures roam among the ruins of a Roman temple with a distant view of a harbor. Although some writers have suggested a mythological interpretation, it is now generally understood that the figures are shepherds, of which there are many examples in Claude's oeuvre, enhancing the pastoral quality of the picture. –KN

FURTHER READING

Roethlisberger 1961; Russell 1982; Rand 2006

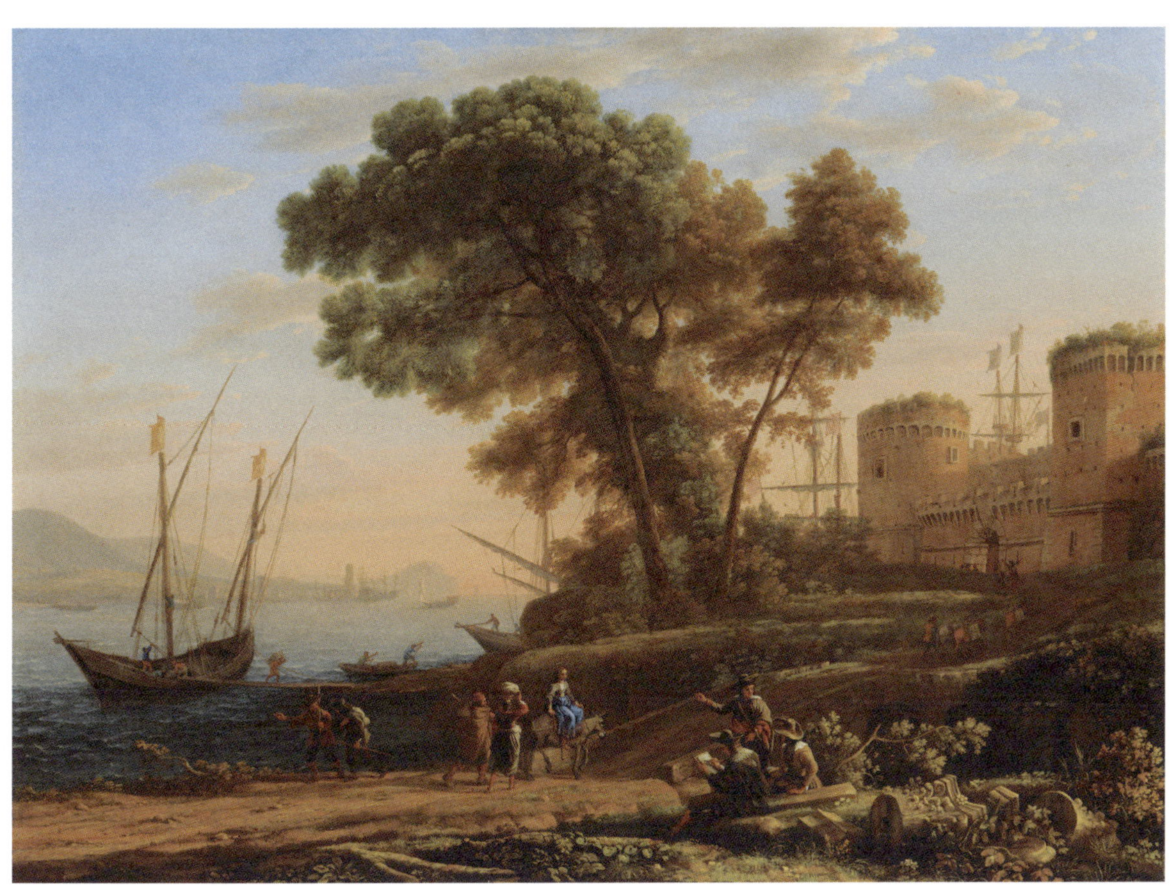

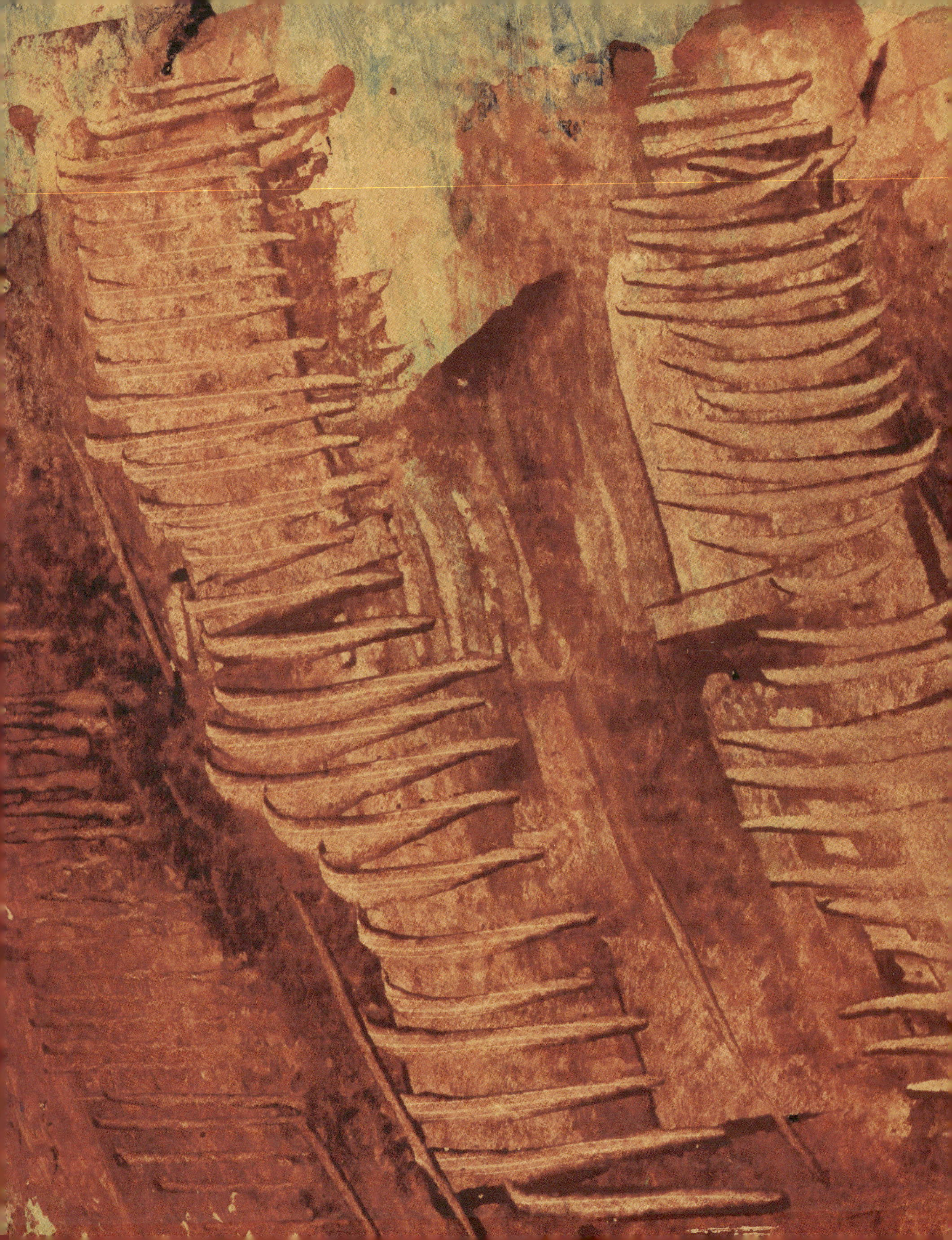

# WALTER INGS FARMER AND THE CINCINNATI ART MUSEUM

## 19

# Orazio de Santis (active 1568–84), after Pompeo Cesura called Aquilano (d. 1571)

### Saint George, circa 1570

engraving, 10⅞ × 8 9/16 in. (27.6 × 21.7 cm)
Cincinnati Art Museum, Gift of Mr. and Mrs. Walter I. Farmer, 1952.339

This engraving is one of twenty-two prints that Walter and Renate Hobirk Farmer presented to the Cincinnati Art Museum in 1952. Mostly Dutch seventeenth-century works, the group also includes a few French, British, and Italian pieces, and three from the twentieth century. This representation of Saint George was engraved by Orazio de Santis after a design by Pompeo Cesura, generally referred to as Pompeo dall'Aquila or Aquilano. The latter arrived in Rome early in his career, may have studied under Raphael, and died in Rome in 1571. Orazio was active 1568–84, and signed other plates by Pompeo, seventeen of which were identified by Adam Bartsch. This print should be dated around 1570.

At the left, Saint George on horseback uses his lance to slay a dragon crouched beneath him. With this action he frees the princess who is seen from behind on the right supporting herself with two outstretched arms against the rocky cliff and one foot resting on tiptoes. It is a time-honored tale of good versus evil. Here, the intensity of the drama is heightened through the dense composition, the swirling draperies that wrap around the princess, and the muscular dragon who does battle with the saint. The skeletal remains in the lower right corner probably reference earlier sacrifices made to the dragon.

The story of Saint George is based on the life of George of Lydda, who died in 303, and became the object of great devotion throughout Europe and beyond. He was popularized during the Renaissance through the *Golden Legend*, a compendium of saints' lives compiled by Jacobus da Voragine. The dramatic possibilities inherent in the tale were adapted by artists in all media—paintings, prints, and sculpture. The narrative has pre-Christian origins in the myth of Perseus and Andromeda, of which there were two representations by Rubens in the "202" (BR 149, 153). Saint George is often included in the company of other saints, or in the wings of an altarpiece, as in the left panel of Hans Baldung Grien's *Three Kings Altarpiece*, another of the paintings in the "202" (BR 14). –KN

FURTHER READING

Bartsch 1870

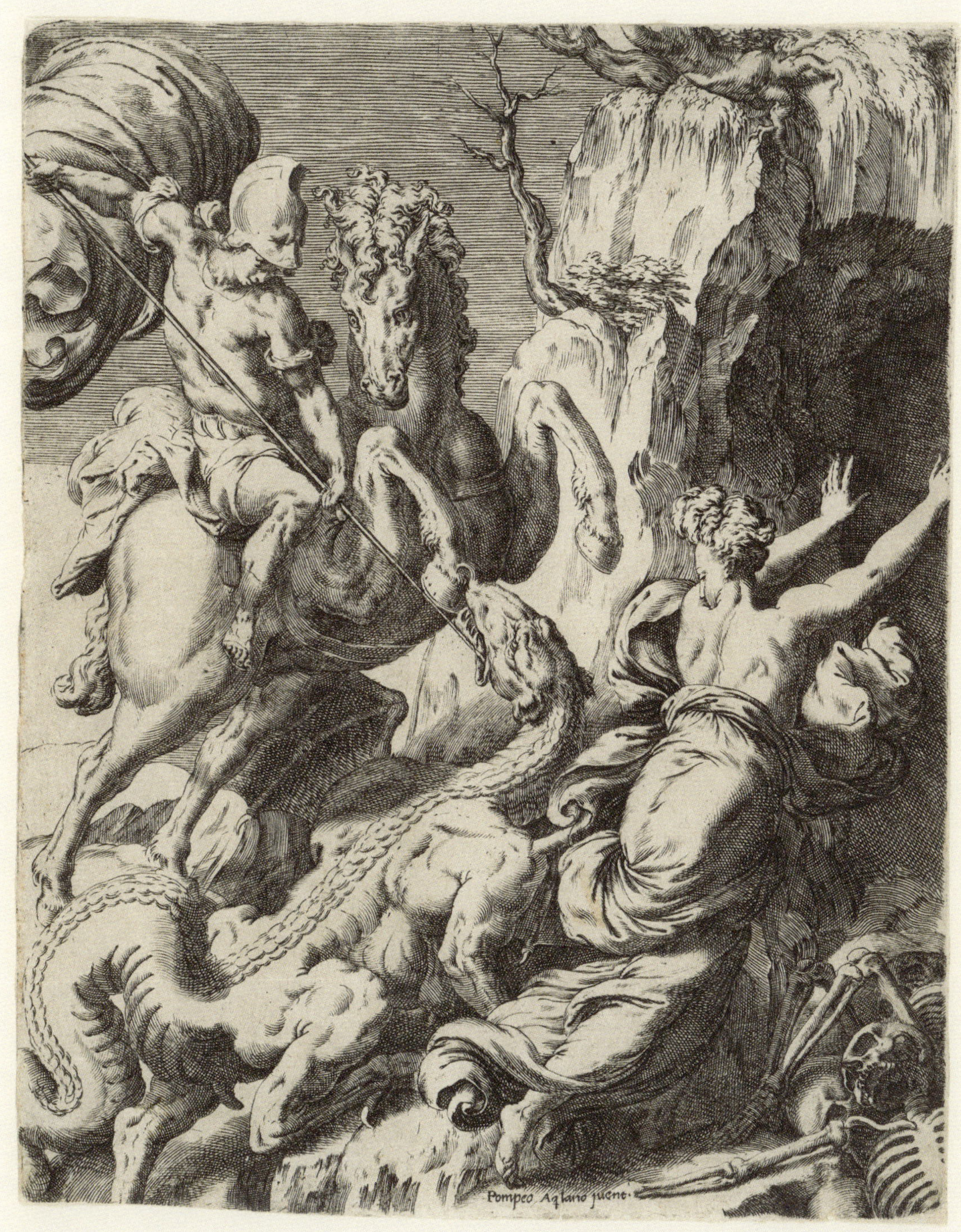
Pompeo Aqlano iuent·

## 20

# European Artist

### **Male Nude**, 18th century

red, brown, and white chalk on tan laid paper, 17¾ × 14 in. (45.1 × 35.6 cm)
Cincinnati Art Museum, Gift of Walter Ings Farmer, 1952.364

In 1952, soon after he returned to Cincinnati, Walter Farmer donated fifteen old master drawings to the Cincinnati Art Museum. Most of these works are unidentified with regard to artist and provenance, but represent Farmer's collecting tastes and his interest in beauty. He writes in his memoir *The Safekeepers* that he was an architect by training, "but in spirit I was a collector and a student of beautiful objects." Although not documented, it is possible many of these pieces were acquired while Farmer was in Great Britain and Europe during and immediately following World War II.

This handsome red-and-white chalk drawing of a seated male nude reflects a well-established practice of drawing from a live model. Such exercises were often the starting point for a larger work, since the figures could be used in many types of paintings including biblical, mythological, or genre scenes. The drawing's subject relates to two of the most famous antique sculptures in Rome. The pose of the figure with one leg crossed over the other is somewhat reminiscent of the *Spinario*, a Hellenistic sculpture of a boy withdrawing a thorn from the sole of his foot (Capitoline Museums). The muscular torso and animal skin on which the figure is seated evoke the *Belvedere Torso*, a fragmentary marble statue of a nude male, probably from the second–first century BCE (Vatican Museums). This piece influenced many Renaissance and Baroque artists, including Michelangelo and Rubens, the latter represented by six paintings in the "202" (BR 149–154). Of particular interest in this drawing are the lively touches of white chalk on the legs and torso and the animated expression on the face of the figure. –KN

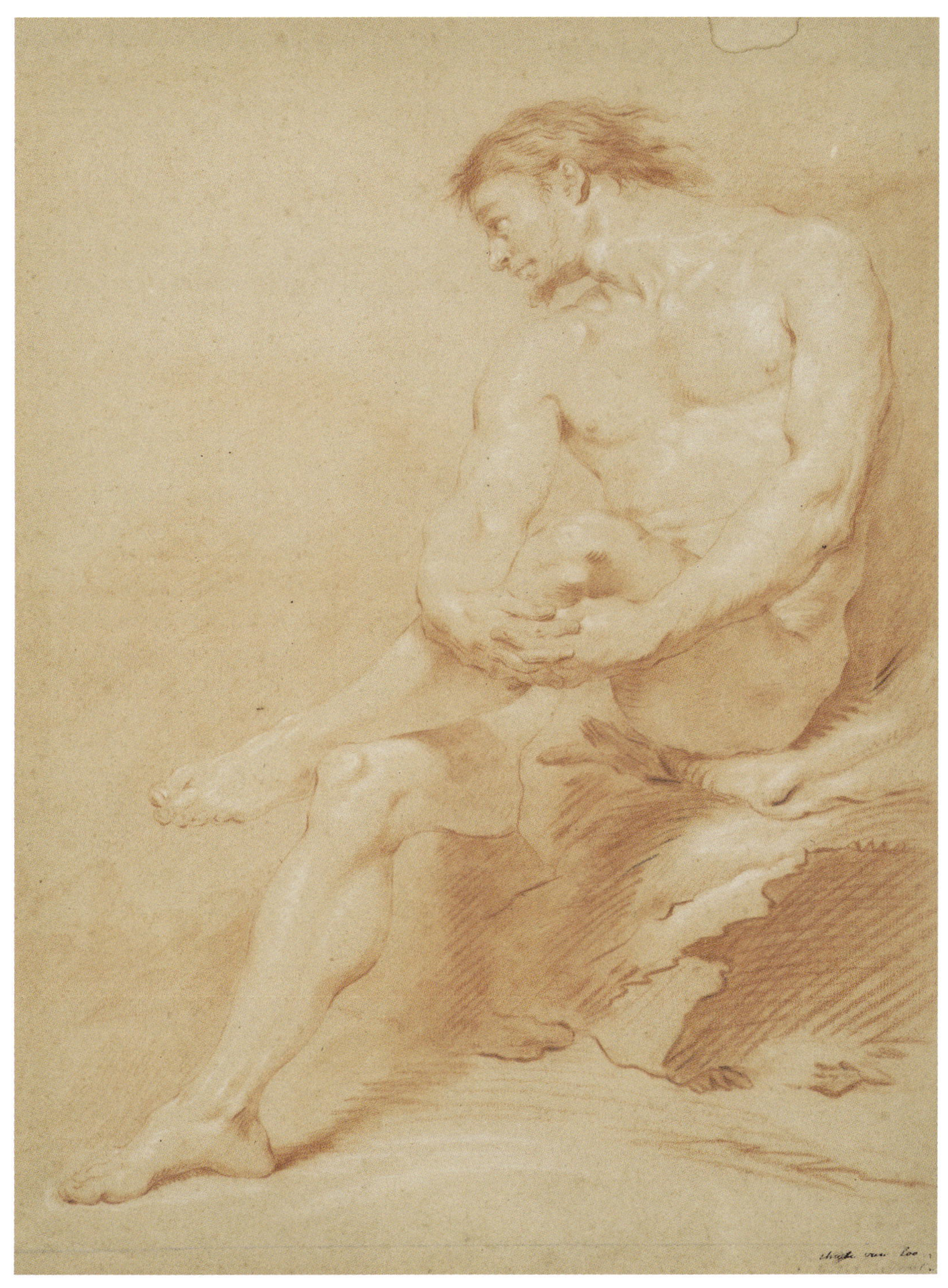

## 21

# Martin Quadal (1736–1808)

### Self-Portrait, 1788

oil on canvas, 40¾ × 33¼ in. (103.5 × 84.5 cm)
Cincinnati Art Museum, Bequest of Walter I. Farmer, 1997.118

Born in Moravia (modern Czech Republic), the artist Martin Quadal traveled widely in Europe from a young age, painting for patrons across the continent. He studied first in Vienna and, from 1767, in Paris. In the 1770s he worked in England and Ireland; in the 1780s in Italy; and in the 1790s in the Netherlands and Germany. He spent the last decade of his life in St. Petersburg, Russia.

Quadal painted portraits throughout his career and was especially known for his paintings and prints of animal subjects. This self-portrait combines these two strengths. It is among a series of self-portraits he seems to have begun while in Italy in the mid-1780s, in which the seated artist, facing right, turns his head to meet the viewer's gaze. He has a palette in his left hand resting on a tabletop, a brush in his right, and a solicitous dog on his lap. An unfinished canvas on an easel behind him completes the composition.

The Cincinnati painting is very close to the version Quadal made for the famed collection of self-portraits at the Uffizi, Florence, kept in the Vasari Corridor, and which entered that collection in July 1785. It was likely made in preparation for the latter or very soon after it. It is signed and dated on the edge of the table at right, along with an indecipherable monogram, which seems to read "mmβ." A related, bust-length oil sketch is in the Rhode Island School of Design Museum, Providence. An adaptation of the composition, dated 1787, is in the Pushkin Museum, Moscow. Quadal seems to have revisited the basic elements at least once more before 1789, the date of a mezzotint made in Vienna by Vincenz Georg Kininger after a related, but untraced, painting. In this print, an impression of which is in the British Museum, the artist stands, leaning over the chair, and the dog is seated on the tabletop.

Walter Farmer acquired the painting in 1976 in Bologna, and displayed it prominently in his home for the following twenty years. –PJB

FURTHER READING

Garas 2003

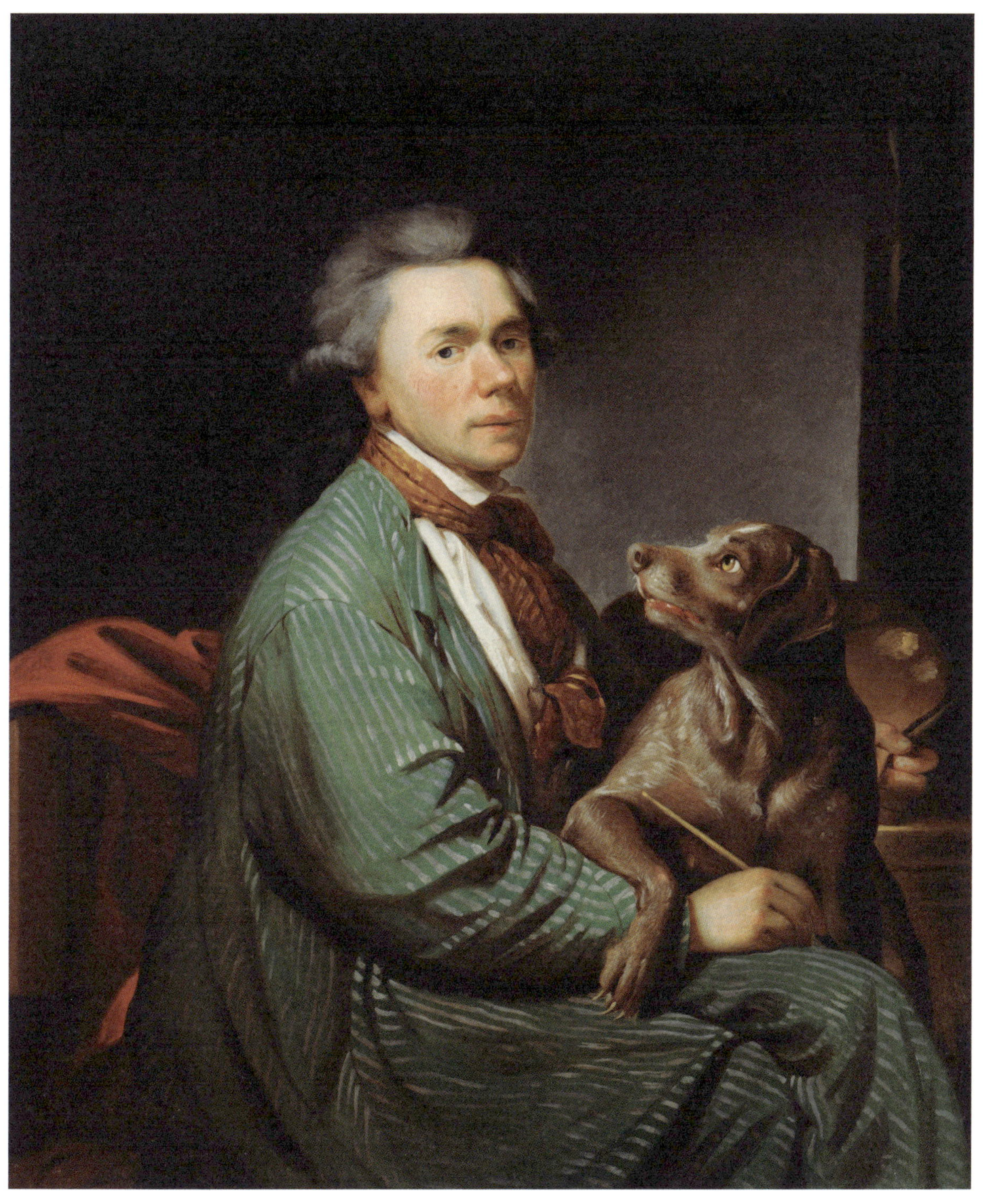

## 22

# Alo Altripp (1906–1991)

### Composition in Red, 1938

oil on paper, 13 × 19¼ in. (33 × 48.9 cm)
Cincinnati Art Museum, Bequest of Walter I. Farmer, 1997.195

Painter and draftsman Alo Altripp was active in German avant-garde circles in the interwar period. He studied in Mainz and Dresden in the mid-1920s. Early in his career he participated in the New Objectivity (Neue Sachlichkeit) movement, when German artists working after World War I rejected expressionism in favor of exaggerated realism. Altripp was prohibited from painting by the Nazis in the 1930s, but he continued to work in secret in his home in Wiesbaden. In that decade he maintained friendships with Alexej von Jawlensky (1864–1941), who also lived in Wiesbaden, and Paul Klee (1879–1940), whom he visited regularly in Bern, Switzerland. During World War II, Altripp was called up for military service and stationed as a guard at a prisoner-of-war camp before being employed as a draftsman at the Opel automobile plant from 1943 until the end of the war.

According to Walter Farmer, at the end of the war Altripp asked the American military government at the Wiesbaden Central Collecting Point for permission to work publicly again. The two men struck up a lasting friendship, which Farmer fondly described in his memoir. Farmer wrote to his wife in America to ship art supplies to Germany for Altripp and other artists in Wiesbaden. He purchased a number of Altripp's paintings, five of which he bequeathed to the Cincinnati Art Museum. He promoted his friend's career in America, contacting dealers and helping Altripp secure a fellowship at the Barnes Foundation in Pennsylvania in 1949. Albert Barnes, one of the early twentieth-century's foremost collectors of impressionist and postimpressionist art, championed Altripp's work, writing an essay for an exhibition of his work at a New York gallery in June of that year.

*Composition in Red* is one of the works the artist produced in secret before the outbreak of World War II. The prohibition to paint restricted his access to materials: Farmer describes how Altripp gave him a tour of his studio, showing him "the paintings he had made with common house paint and brushes fashioned from rubber hose." In this painting, Altripp began with a blue background, over which he layered wide swathes of red paint. With a blunt implement or the end of his brush, he added sharp horizontal strokes in the still-wet paint, creating the distinctive marks that dominate the composition. Grouped together, these marks are also suggestive of organic forms, which may have inspired an alternate title for the painting recorded in the museum's files: *Red Ferns*. An undated photograph of Farmer's home in Cincinnati shows that he once displayed this painting and three others by the artist around *Self-Portrait* by Martin Quadal (see cat. 21).
—PJB+KG

FURTHER READING
Museum Wiesbaden 1988; Farmer 2000; Curatorial file, Cincinnati Art Museum

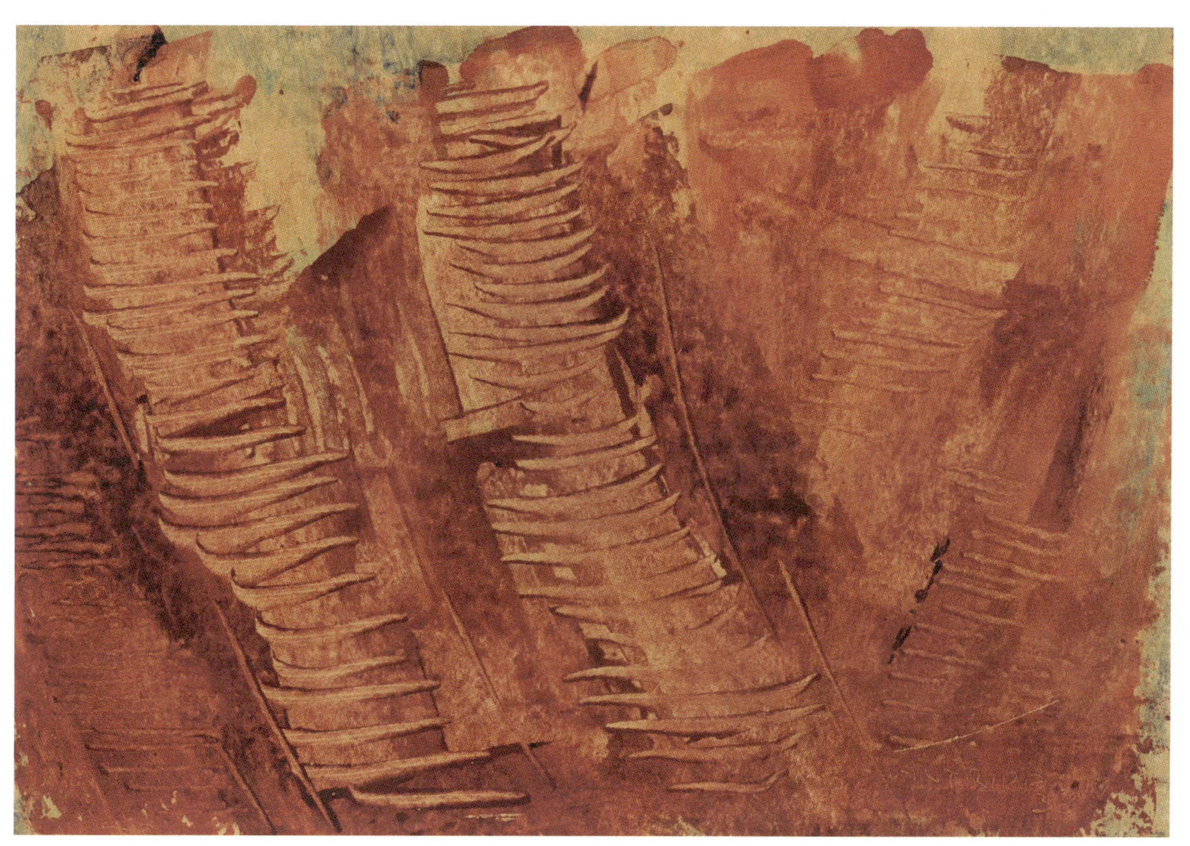

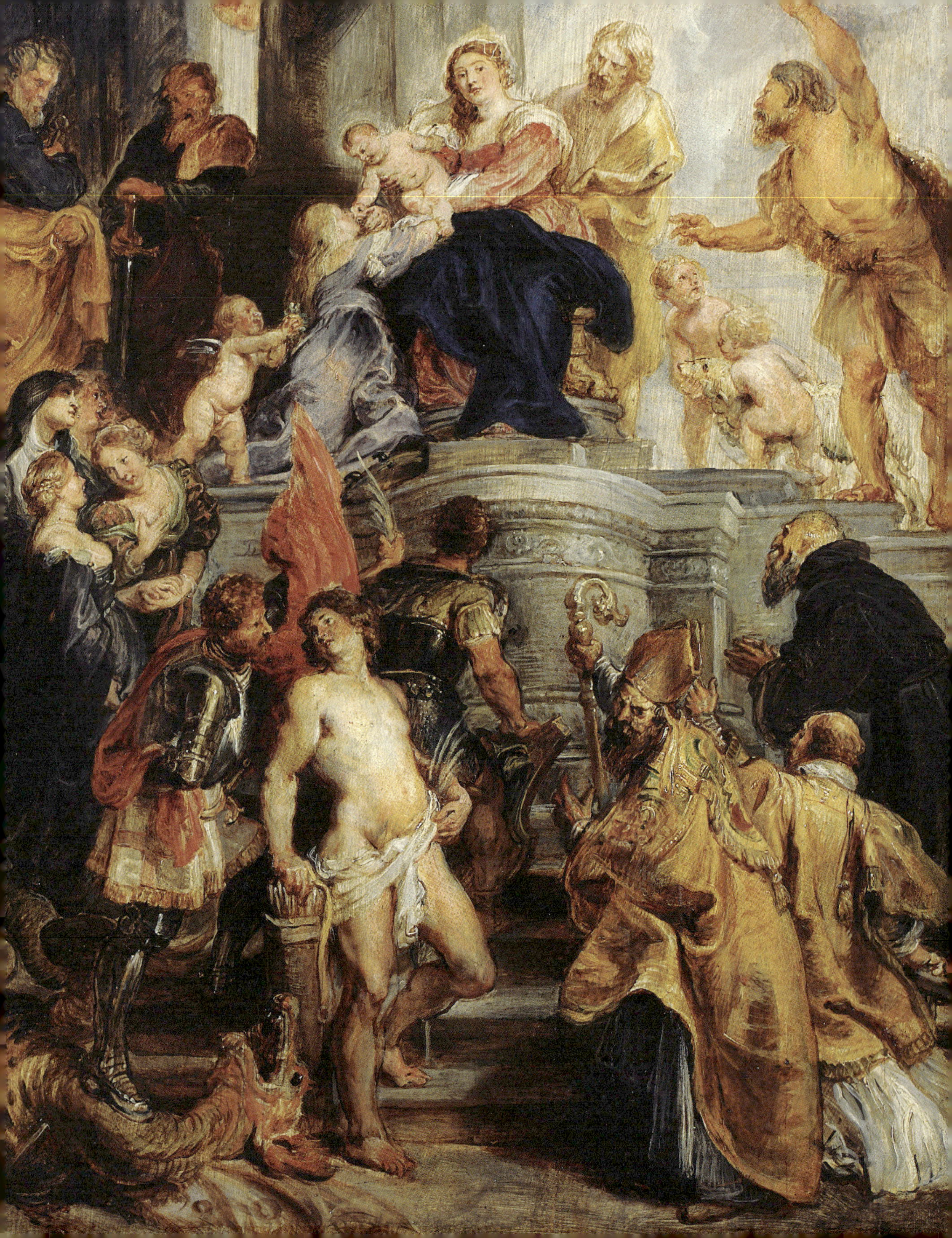

APPENDIX

# PAINTINGS FROM THE BERLIN MUSEUMS

## EXHIBITION TITLES

The title of the exhibition changed over the course of the tour.

Paintings from the Berlin Museums (★)
Masterpieces of Painting Saved from the German Salt Mines (✱)
Masterpieces from the Berlin Museums (⁜)

## TRAVEL SCHEDULE

★ National Gallery of Art, Washington, DC
March 17–April 25, 1948

★ The Metropolitan Museum of Art, New York, New York
May 17–June 11, 1948

★ Philadelphia Museum of Art, Philadelphia, Pennsylvania
June 19–July 7, 1948

✱ Art Institute of Chicago, Chicago, Illinois
July 17–August 3, 1948

★ Museum of Fine Arts, Boston, Massachusetts
August 14–31, 1948

⁜ Detroit Institute of Arts, Detroit, Michigan
September 10–26, 1948

⁜ Cleveland Museum of Art, Cleveland, Ohio
October 6–24, 1948

⁜ Minneapolis Institute of Arts, Minneapolis, Minnesota
November 2–17, 1948

⁜ Portland Art Museum, Portland, Oregon
November 26–December 3, 1948

⁜ M.H. de Young Memorial Museum, San Francisco, California
December 11–28, 1948

⁜ Los Angeles County Museum of Art, Los Angeles, California
January 4–22, 1949

⁜ City Art Museum (later the Saint Louis Art Museum), St. Louis, Missouri
January 30–February 17, 1949

⁜ Carnegie Institute, Pittsburgh, Pennsylvania
February 27–March 14, 1949

⁜ Toledo Museum of Art, Toledo, Ohio
March 22–31, 1949

## EXHIBITION CHECKLIST

Several checklists of the Berlin paintings that traveled to the US were made in the 1940s for different purposes—selection, crating and shipping, exhibition, etc. This illustrated checklist follows the numbering system of the "Report on 202 Paintings from the Berlin Museums in the United States of America," dated April 22, 1949 and prepared by the German curator Karl M. Birkmeyer, chief advisor to the MFAA, who accompanied the paintings around the US (see Nelson, pp. 52–71).

Birkmeyer organized the list alphabetically by artist. However, some attributions as well as titles have changed since 1949. The following checklist reflects current research, and includes historical attributions and titles where neccessary.

The paintings were returned to Germany in three shipments: after the exhibition closed in Washington, DC, after the exhibition closed in Boston, and after the exhibition closed in Toledo.

**Key**
BR = Birkmeyer Report number
Kat. = Gemäldegalerie catalogue number

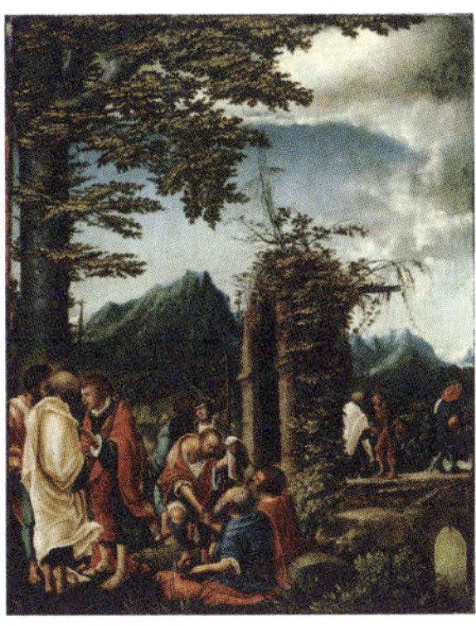

BR 1
**Albrecht Altdorfer (German, circa 1480–1538)**
*Departure of the Apostles*, circa 1523
oil on panel, 16¹¹⁄₁₆ × 12¹³⁄₁₆ in.
(42.4 × 32.5 cm), Kat. 1883
Returned after Boston

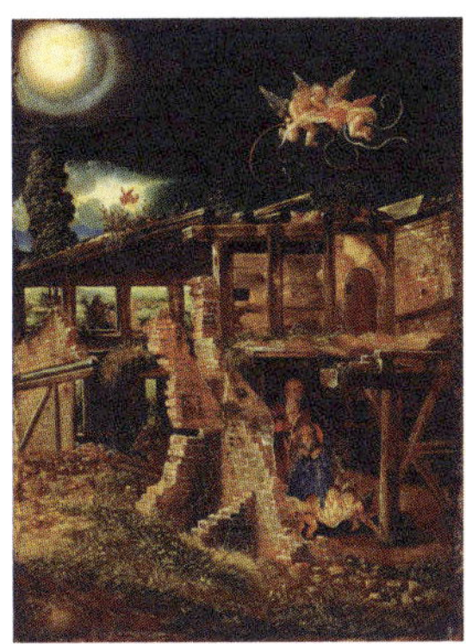

BR 2
**Albrecht Altdorfer (German, circa 1480–1538)**
*The Nativity*, circa 1513
oil on linden panel, 14¼ × 10³⁄₁₆ in.
(36.2 × 25.8 cm), Kat. 638 E
Returned after Boston

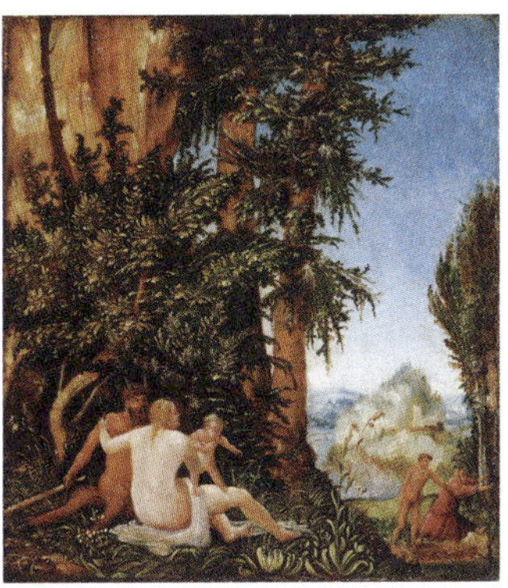

BR 3
**Albrecht Altdorfer (German, circa 1480–1538)**
*Landscape with a Satyr Family*, 1507
oil on linden panel, 9⅛ × 8¹⁄₁₆ in.
(23.1 × 20.4 cm), Kat. 638 A
Returned after Washington, DC

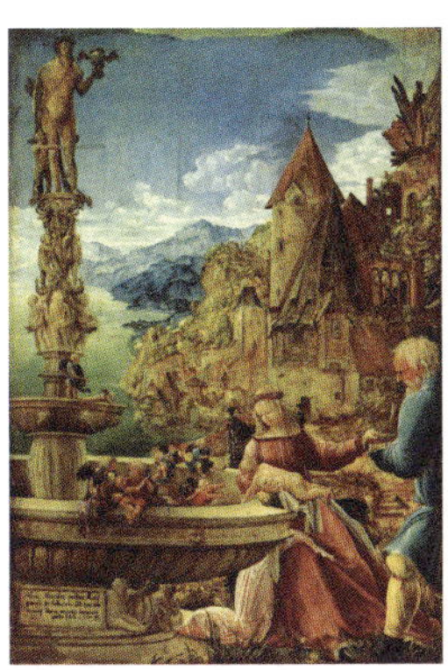

BR 4
**Albrecht Altdorfer (German, circa 1480–1538)**
*Rest on the Flight to Egypt*, 1510
oil on linden panel, 22¹⁵⁄₁₆ × 15½ in.
(58.2 × 39.3 cm), Kat. 638 B
Returned after Boston

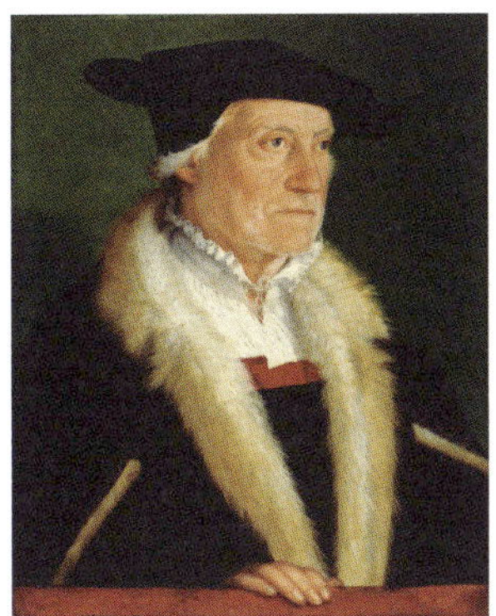

BR 5
**Christoph Amberger (German, circa 1500–1561/62)**
*The Cosmographer Sebastian Münster*, circa 1552
oil on panel, 21¹⁵⁄₁₆ × 17¹⁄₁₆ in.
(55.8 × 43.3 cm), Kat. 583
Shown in all cities

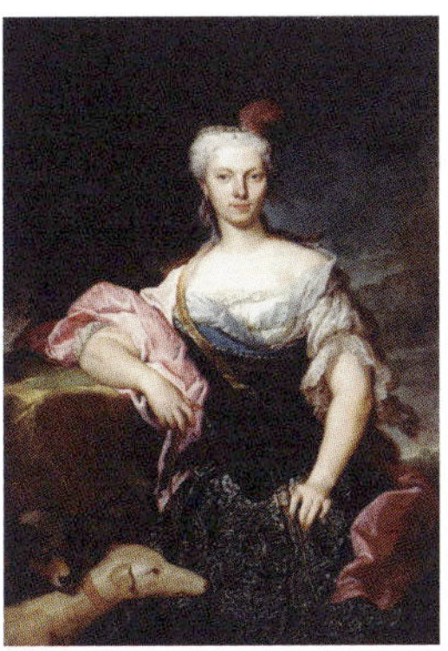

BR 6
**Jacopo Amigoni (Italian, circa 1675–1752)**
*Portrait of a Lady as Diana*, 1739–47
oil on canvas, 50⅜ × 37 in.
(128 × 94 cm), Kat. 1659
Shown in all cities

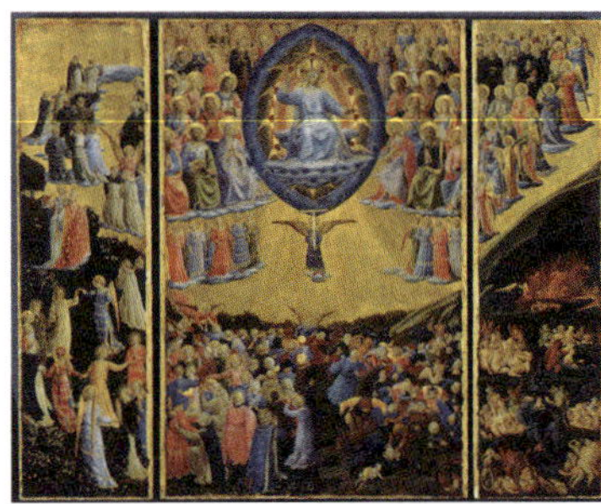

**BR 7**
**Fra Angelico (Italian, circa 1395–1455)**
*The Last Judgement*, 1435–40
tempera on poplar panel, central panel $40\frac{9}{16} \times 25\frac{11}{16}$ in. (103 × 65.3 cm), wings each $40\frac{9}{16} \times 11\frac{1}{8}$ in. (103 × 28.2 cm), Kat. 60 A
Returned after Washington, DC

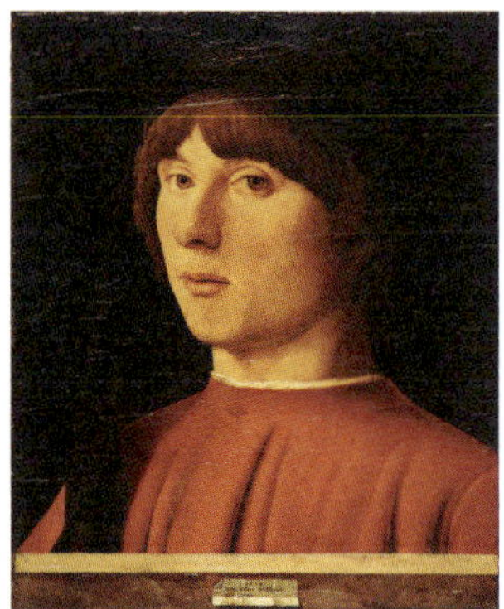

**BR 8**
**Antonello da Messina (Venetian, circa 1430–1479)**
*Portrait of a Young Man*, 1474
oil on poplar panel, $13\frac{7}{16} \times 10\frac{11}{16}$ in. (34.1 × 27.1 cm), Kat. 18 A
Returned after Washington, DC

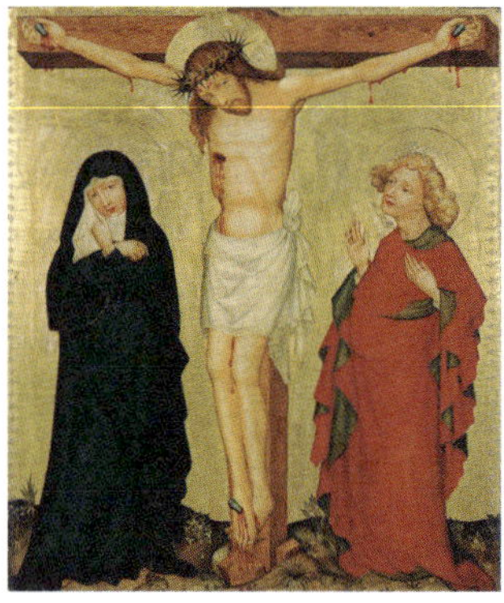

**BR 9**
**Austrian School**
*The Crucified Christ Mourned by Mary and Saint John*, circa 1430
oil on fir panel, $33\frac{7}{16} \times 31\frac{7}{8}$ in. (85 × 81 cm), Kat. 1662
Shown in all cities

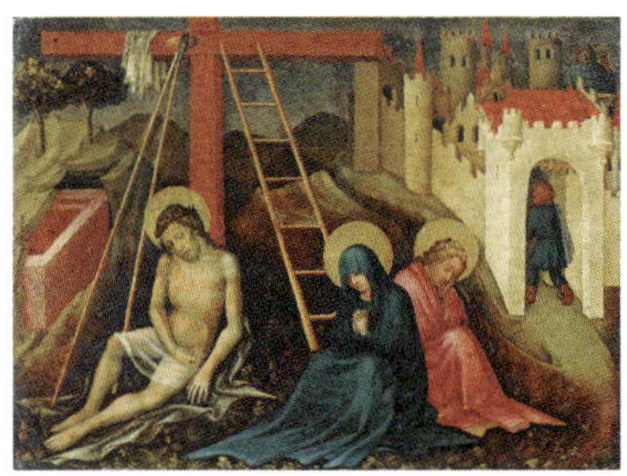

**BR 10**
**Austrian (Vienna?) Master**
*Christ as the Man of Sorrows with Mary and Saint John*, circa 1420
oil on fir panel, $9\frac{7}{8} \times 13\frac{5}{8}$ in. (25.1 × 34.6 cm), Kat. 1837
Shown in all cities

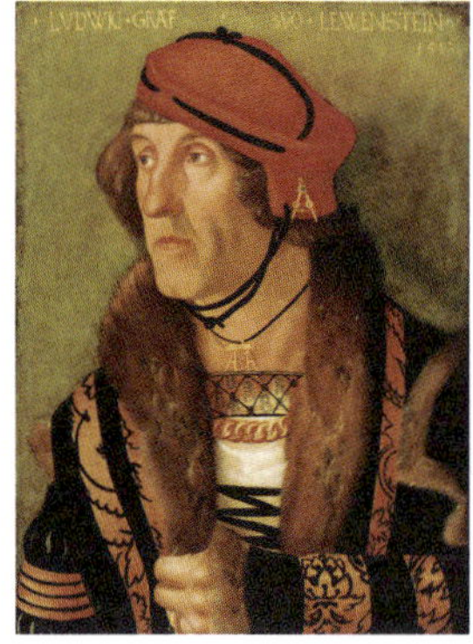

**BR 11**
**Hans Baldung Grien (German, 1480/85–1545)**
*Ludwig, Count of Löwenstein*, 1513
oil on linden panel, $18\frac{1}{8} \times 13$ in. (46 × 33 cm), Kat. 1842
Shown in all cities

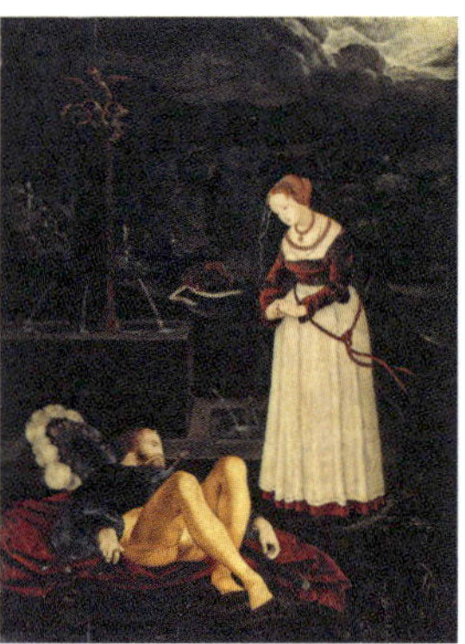

**BR 12**
**Hans Baldung Grien (German, 1480/85–1545)**
*Pyramus and Thisbe*, circa 1530
oil on linden panel, $36\frac{5}{8} \times 26\frac{5}{16}$ in. (93.1 × 66.9 cm), Kat. 1875
Returned after Washington, DC

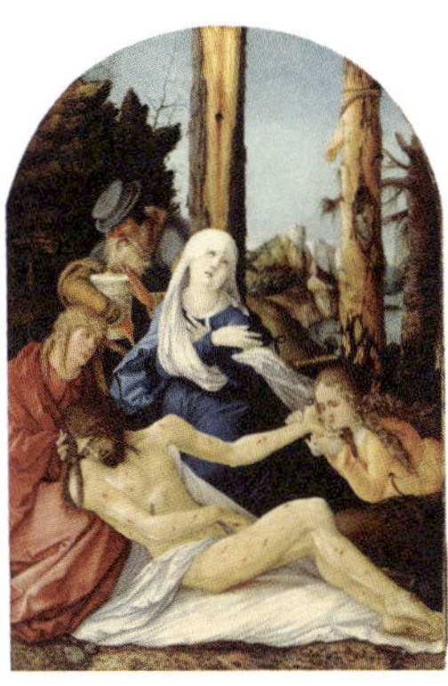

**BR 13**
**Hans Baldung Grien (German, 1480/85–1545)**
*Mourning over the Body of Christ*, circa 1517
oil on linden panel, 55⁹⁄₁₆ × 37⁵⁄₁₆ in. (141.1 × 94.7 cm), Kat. 603 B
Returned after Washington, DC

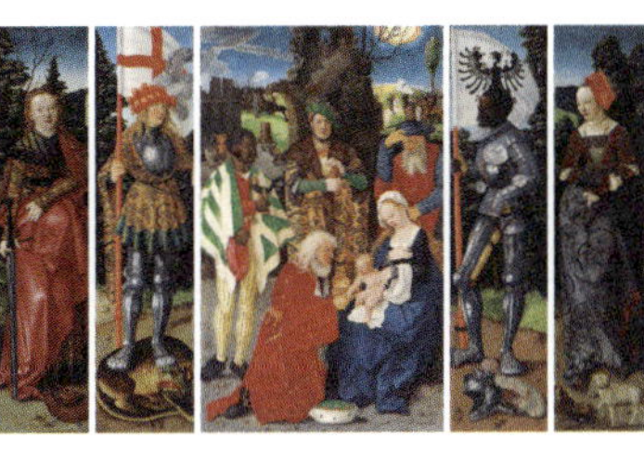

**BR 14**
**Hans Baldung Grien (German, 1480/85–1545)**
*Three Kings Altarpiece: Saint Catherine* (left wing exterior), *Saint George* (left wing interior), *The Adoration of the Magi* (central panel), *Saint Maurice* (right wing interior), *Saint Agnes* (right wing exterior), 1507
oil on linden panel, central panel 47⅝ × 27⅝ in. (121 × 70 cm), wings each 47⅝ × 11 in. (121 × 28 cm), Kat. 603 A
Returned after Washington, DC

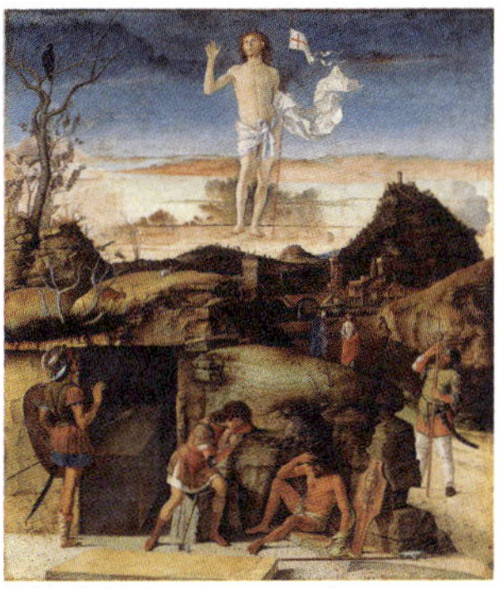

**BR 15**
**Giovanni Bellini (Italian, 1435–1516)**
*The Resurrection of Christ*, 1475–79
oil on poplar transferred to canvas, 58¼ × 50⅜ in. (148 × 128 cm), Kat. 1177 A
Returned after Boston

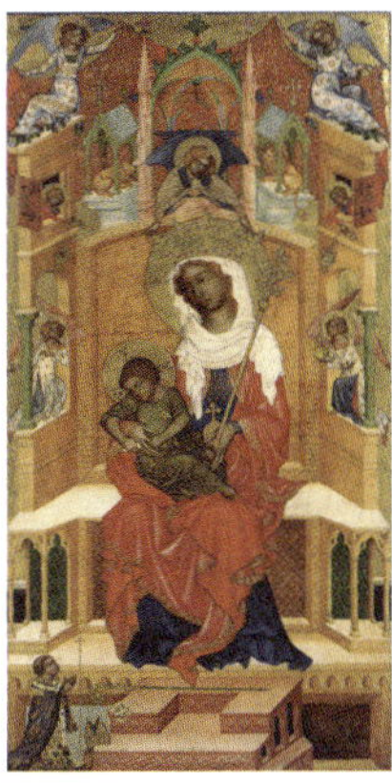

**BR 16**
**Bohemian School**
*Enthroned Madonna and Child with Donor (Glatz Madonna)*, circa 1350
oil on poplar panel, 73¼ × 37⅜ in. (186 × 95 cm), Kat. 1624
Returned after Washington, DC

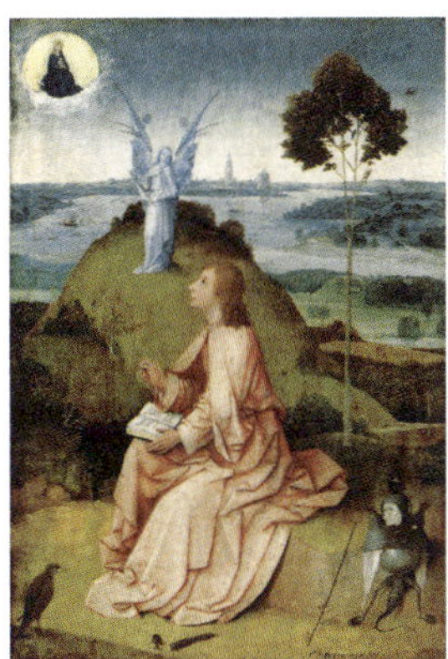

**BR 17**
**Hieronymus Bosch (Dutch, circa 1460–1516)**
*Saint John on Mount Patmos*, 1485–1500
oil on oak panel, 24¹³⁄₁₆ × 17¹⁄₁₆ in. (63 × 43.3 cm), Kat. 1647 A
Returned after Washington, DC

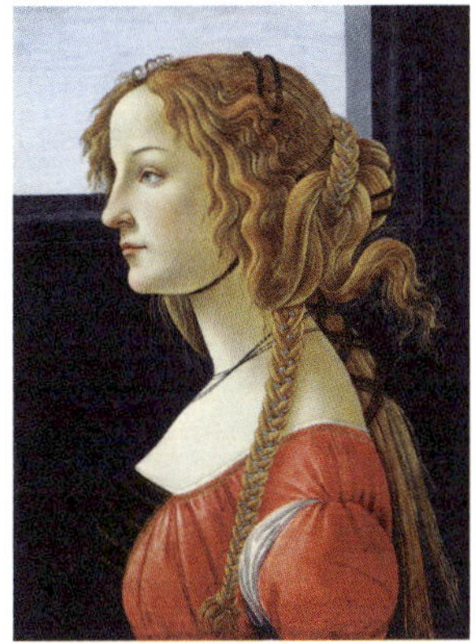

**BR 18**
**Sandro Botticelli (Italian, 1445–1510)**
*Ideal Portrait of a Lady ("Simonetta Vespucci")*, 1475–80
tempera on poplar panel, 21¹³⁄₁₆ × 16¹⁵⁄₁₆ in. (55.4 × 43 cm), Kat. 106 A
Shown in all cities

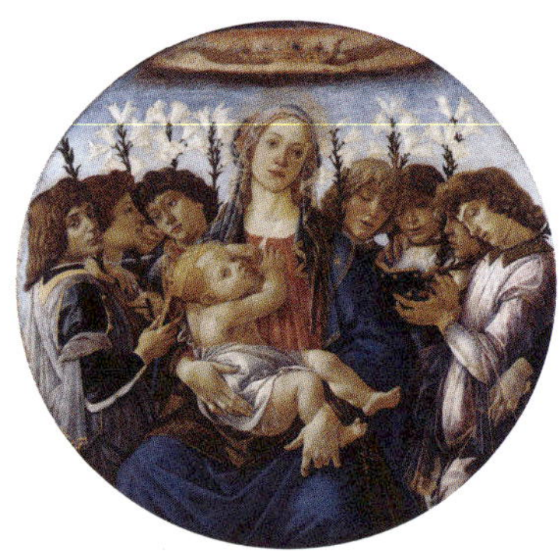

BR 19
**Sandro Botticelli (Italian, 1445–1510)**
*Madonna and Child with Singing Angels (Raczynski tondo)*, circa 1477
tempera on poplar panel,
diam. 53¾ in. (136.5 cm), Kat. 102 A
Returned after Washington, DC

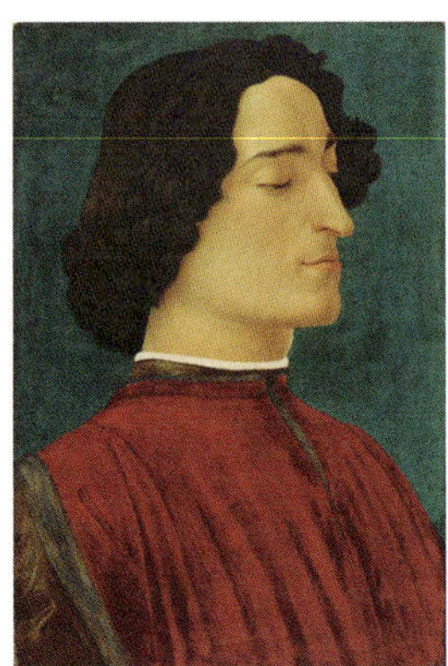

BR 20
**Workshop of Sandro Botticelli (Italian, 1445–1510), formerly attributed to Sandro Botticelli**
*Giuliano de' Medici*, circa 1478
tempera on poplar panel, 22½ × 15 in. (57.1 × 38.4 cm), Kat. 106 B
Returned after Boston

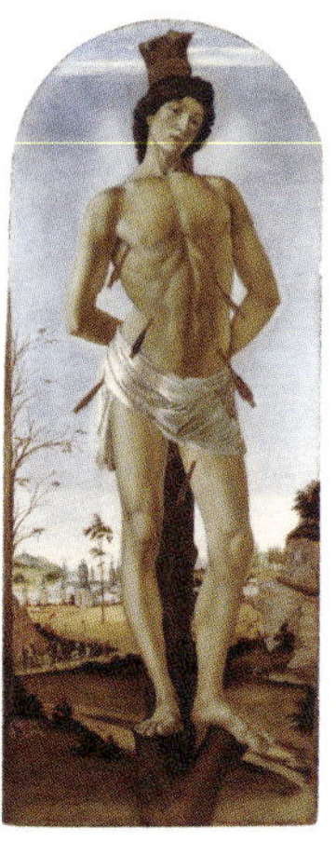

BR 21
**Sandro Botticelli (Italian, 1445–1510)**
*Saint Sebastian*, 1474
tempera on poplar panel, 76¾ × 29½ in. (195 × 75 cm), Kat. 1128
Returned after Boston

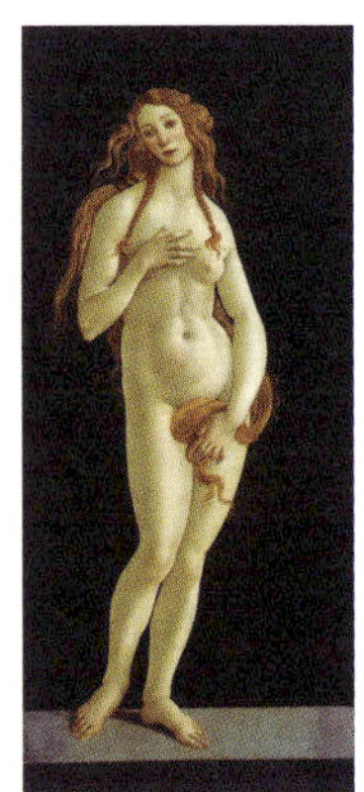

BR 22
**Workshop of Sandro Botticelli (Italian, 1445–1510), formerly attributed to Sandro Botticelli**
*Venus*, circa 1490
oil on canvas, 62¼ × 26<sup>15</sup>⁄16 in.
(158.1 × 68.5 cm), Kat. 1124
Shown in all cities

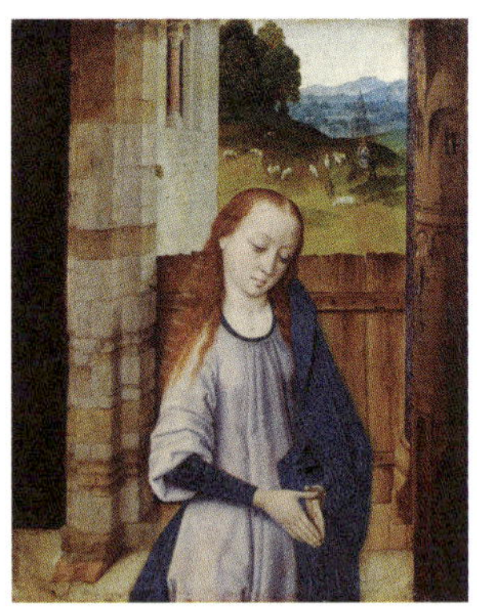

BR 23
**Dieric Bouts (Flemish, 1410/20–1475)**
*The Virgin Mary, fragment of a Nativity*, circa 1470
oil on oak panel, 9 13/16 × 7 11/16 in.
(24.9 × 19.6 cm), Kat. 545 B
Shown in all cities

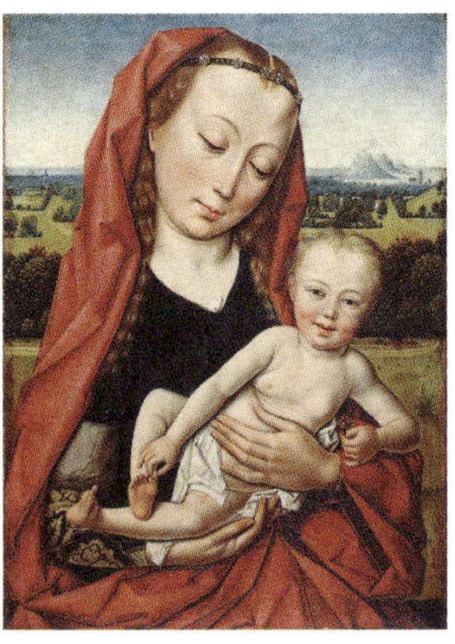

BR 24
**Circle of Dieric Bouts (Flemish, 1410/20–1475), formerly attributed to Dieric Bouts**
*Madonna and Child*, circa 1480–1500
oil on panel, 11 × 7 11/16 in.
(28 × 19.5 cm), Kat. 545 C
Shown in all cities

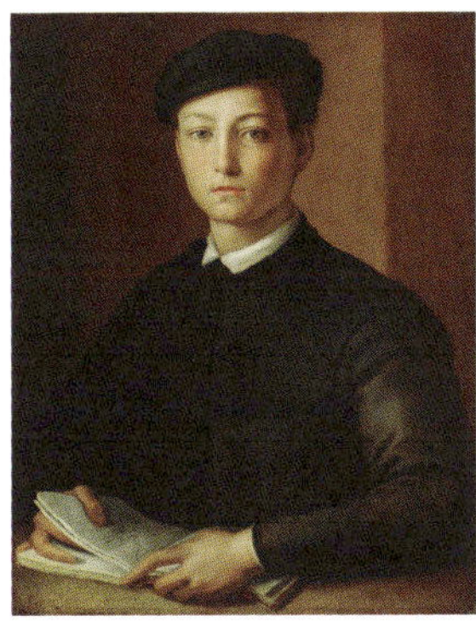

BR 25
**Attributed to Agnolo Bronzino (Italian, 1503–1572)**
*Portrait of a Youth*, circa 1560
oil on poplar panel, $29\frac{5}{16} \times 23\frac{13}{16}$ in.
(74.4 × 58 cm), Kat. S 2
Shown in all cities

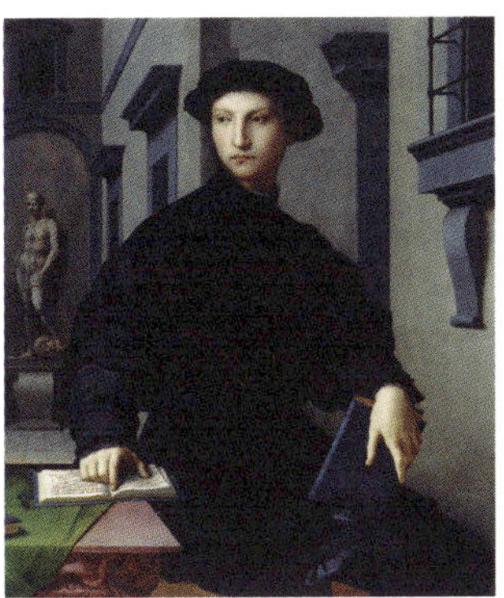

BR 26
**Agnolo Bronzino (Italian, 1503–1572)**
*Ugolino Martelli*, circa 1535–38
oil on poplar panel, $40\frac{3}{16} \times 33\frac{7}{16}$ in.
(102 × 85 cm), Kat. 338 A
Returned after Boston

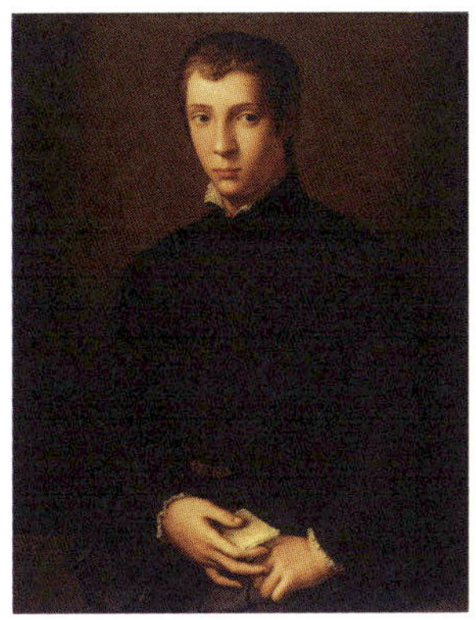

BR 27
**Alessandro Allori (Italian, 1535–1607), formerly attributed to Agnolo Bronzino (Italian, 1503–1572)**
*Portrait of a Young Man*, circa 1550
oil on panel, $33\frac{7}{8} \times 26\frac{3}{8}$ in.
(86 × 67 cm), Kat. 338
Shown in all cities

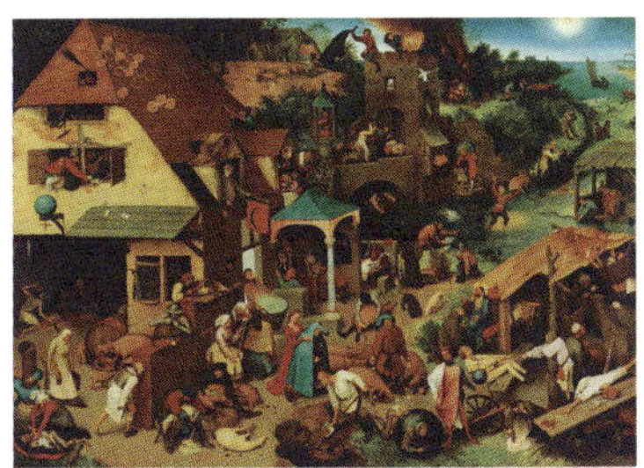

BR 28
**Pieter Bruegel, the Elder (Flemish, 1526/30–1569)**
*Netherlandish Proverbs*, 1559
oil on oak panel, $46 \times 64\frac{1}{2}$ in.
(117.2 × 163.8 cm), Kat. 1720
Returned after Washington, DC

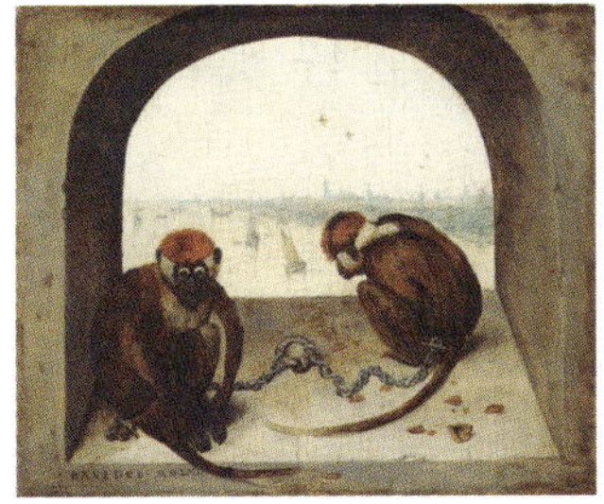

BR 29
**Pieter Bruegel, the Elder (Flemish, 1526/30–1569)**
*Two Chained Monkeys*, 1562
oil on oak panel, $7\frac{13}{16} \times 9\frac{3}{16}$ in.
(19.9 × 23.3 cm), Kat. 2077
Shown in all cities

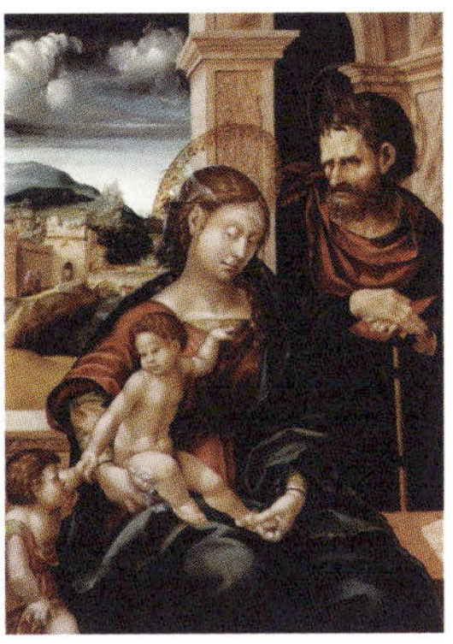

BR 30
**Hans Burgkmair (German, 1473–1531)**
*The Holy Family with Young Saint John*, circa 1525
oil on panel, $29\frac{3}{16} \times 21\frac{1}{16}$ in.
(74.2 × 53.5 cm), Kat. 1732
Shown in all cities

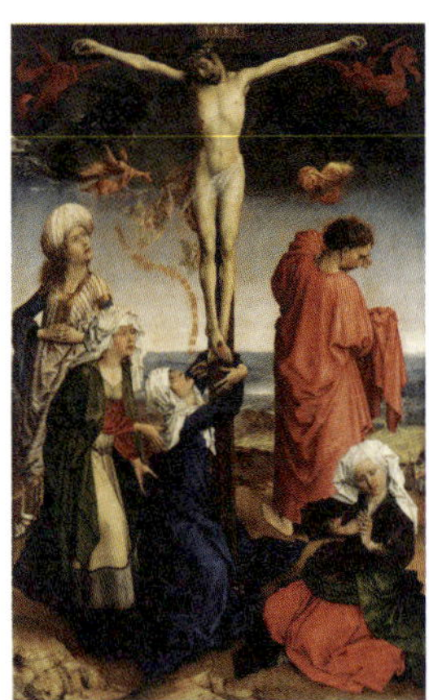

BR 31
**Workshop of Rogier van der Weyden (Flemish, 1399–1464), formerly attributed to Robert Campin (Flemish, 1375–1444)**
*The Crucifixion*, circa 1440
oil on oak panel, 31¼ × 19⅝ in. (79.3 × 49.9 cm), Kat. 538 A
Returned after Boston

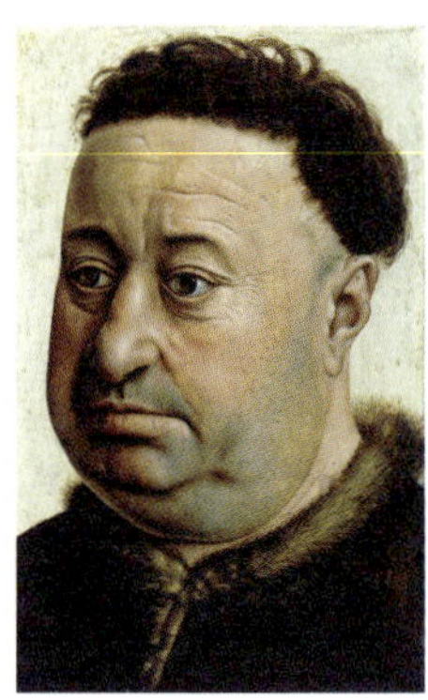

BR 32
**Master of Flémalle (Rogier van der Weyden?), formerly attributed to Robert Campin (Flemish, 1375–1444)**
*Portrait of a Man*, circa 1430–40
oil on oak panel, 12⅜ × 8 in. (31.5 × 20.3 cm), Kat. KFMV 537 A
Returned after Washington, DC

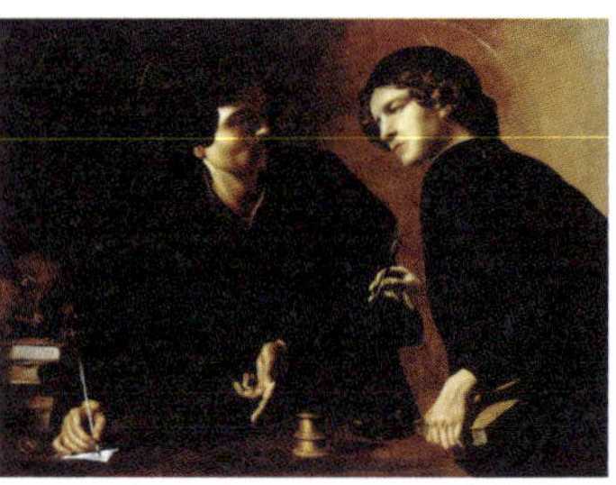

BR 33
**Giovanni Battista Caracciolo (Italian, 1578–1635)**
*Saint Cosmas and Saint Damian* (formerly titled *Two Physicians in the Roles of Saint Cosmas and Saint Damian*), circa 1615–20
oil on canvas, 38⁷⁄₁₆ × 50 in. (97.7 × 127 cm), Kat. 1981
Shown in all cities

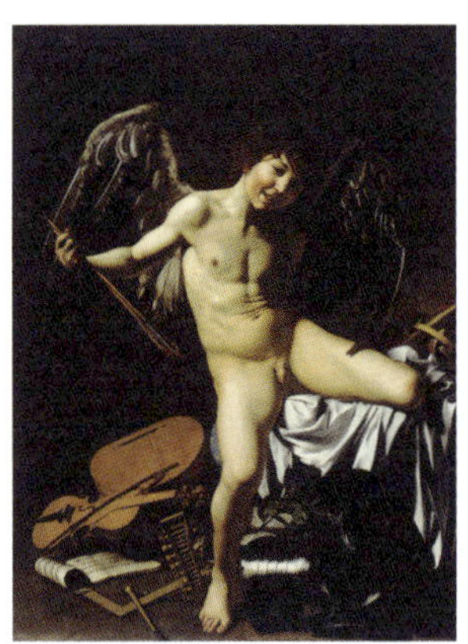

BR 34
**Michelangelo Merisi da Caravaggio (Italian, 1571–1610)**
*Amor Victorious* (or *Conquering Love*), 1601–2
oil on canvas, 61⅝ × 44⅝ in. (156.5 × 113.3 cm), Kat. 369
Retuned after Boston

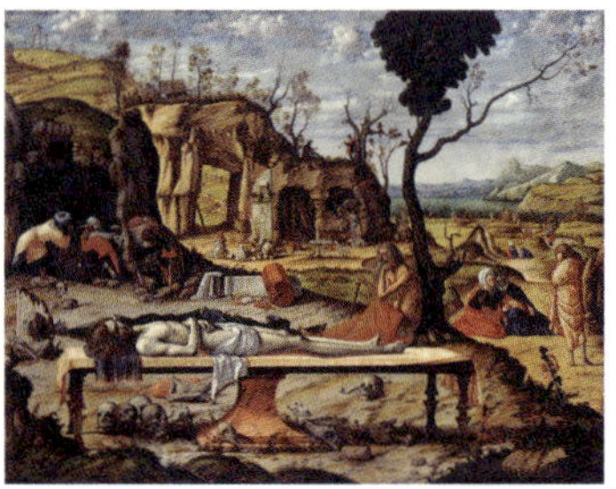

BR 35
**Vittore Carpaccio (Italian, 1465–1525)**
*The Preparation of Christ's Tomb*, circa 1505
tempera on canvas, 57¹⁄₁₆ × 71¹⁄₁₆ in. (145 × 180.5 cm), Kat. 23 A
Returned after Boston

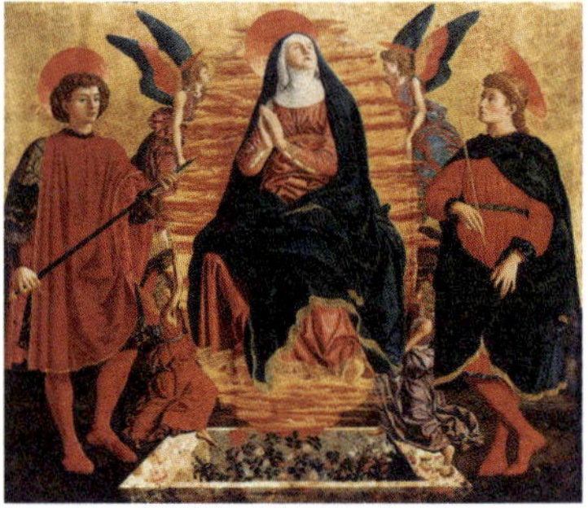

BR 36
**Andrea del Castagno (Italian, 1410–1457)**
*The Assumption of the Virgin*, 1449–50
tempera and gold on poplar panel, 51¹¹⁄₁₆ × 59³⁄₁₆ in. (131.3 × 150.3 cm), Kat. 47 A
Returned after Boston

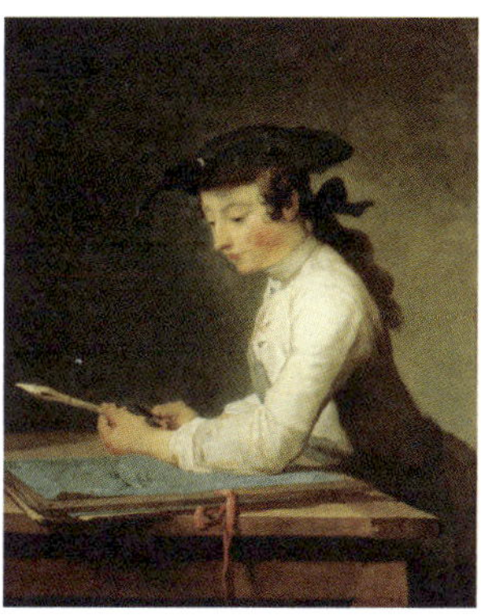

BR 37
**Jean-Baptiste-Siméon Chardin (French, 1699–1779)**
*The Draftsman*, 1737
oil on canvas, 32 × $25\frac{9}{16}$ in.
(81.3 × 65 cm), Kat. 2076
Shown in all cities

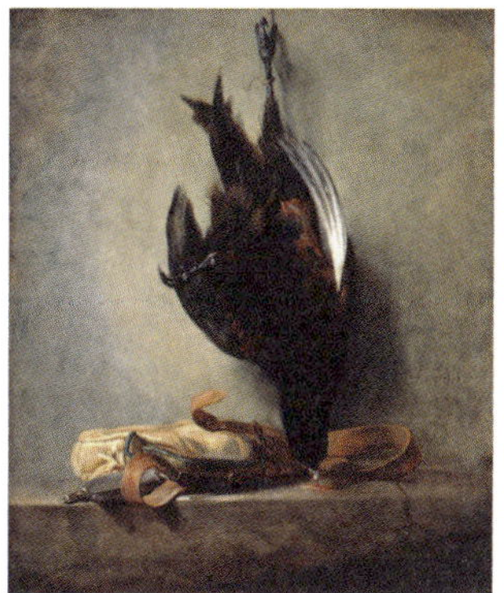

BR 38
**Jean-Baptiste-Siméon Chardin (French, 1699–1779)**
*Still Life with Pheasant and Game Bag*, 1760
oil on canvas, $28\frac{11}{16}$ × $23\frac{3}{4}$ in.
(72.8 × 60.4 cm), Kat. 1944
Shown in all cities

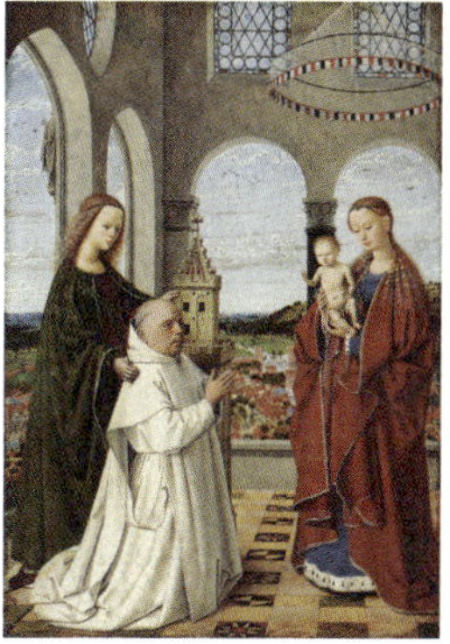

BR 39
**Petrus Christus** (**Flemish, circa 1420–1476**)
*Madonna and Child with Saint Barbara and the Carthusian Jan Vos (Exeter Madonna)*, circa 1450
oil on oak panel, $7\frac{1}{2}$ × $5\frac{1}{2}$ in.
(19 × 14 cm), Kat. 523 B
Returned after Washington, DC

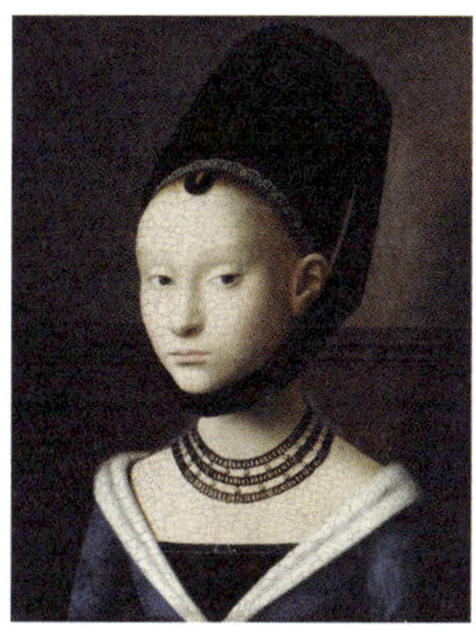

BR 40
**Petrus Christus (Flemish, circa 1425–1475)**
*Portrait of a Young Woman* (formerly titled *Lady Talbot*), circa 1460–73
oil on oak panel, $11\frac{7}{16}$ × $8\frac{7}{8}$ in.
(29 × 22.5 cm), Kat. 532
Returned after Washington, DC

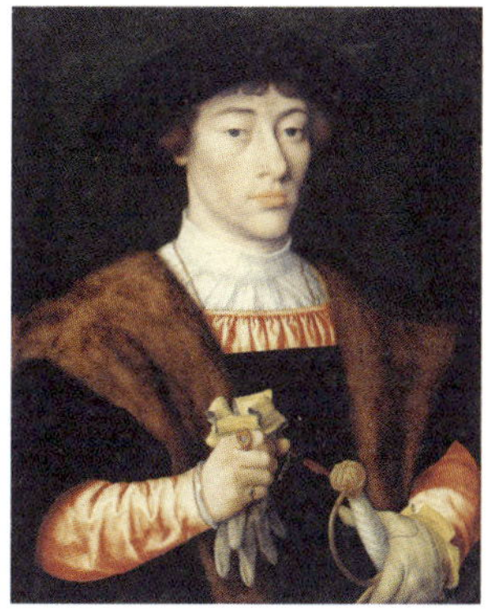

BR 41
**Joos van Cleve, the Elder (Flemish, 1485–1540)**
*Portrait of a Young Man* (formerly titled *Young Man with a Glove*), circa 1528
oil on panel, $24\frac{7}{16}$ × $18\frac{1}{2}$ in.
(62 × 47 cm), Kat. 615
Shown in all cities

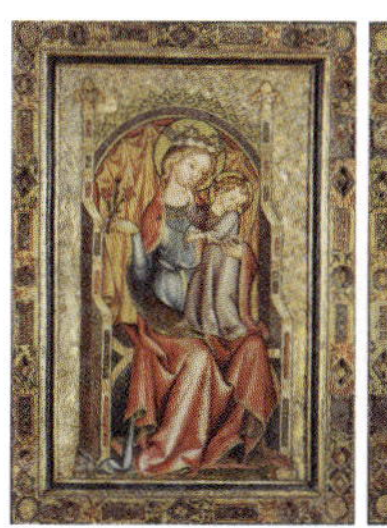
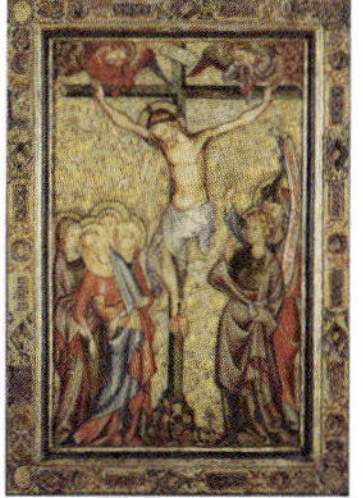

BR 42
**Cologne Master (German, 14th century)**
*Diptych with Madonna and Child Enthroned and Crucifixion*, circa 1300–20
oil on oak panel, each panel $19\frac{1}{2}$ × $13\frac{7}{16}$ in. (49.6 × 34.2 cm), Kat. 1627
Returned after Boston

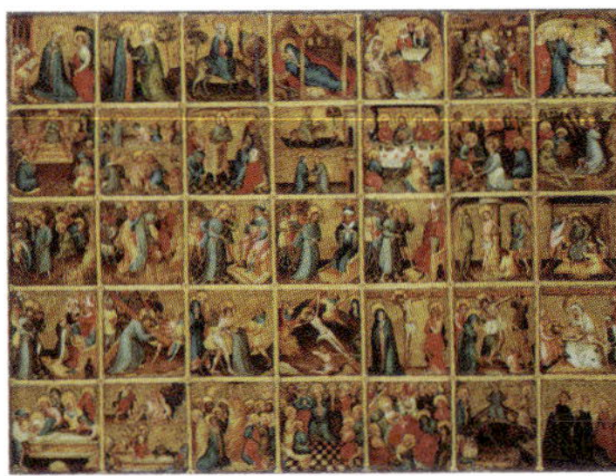

BR 43
**Cologne Master (German, 15th century)**
*The Life of Christ and Mary,* circa 1410–20
oil on oak panel, 33³⁄₁₆ × 44½ in. (84.3 × 113 cm), Kat. 1224
Returned after Washington, DC

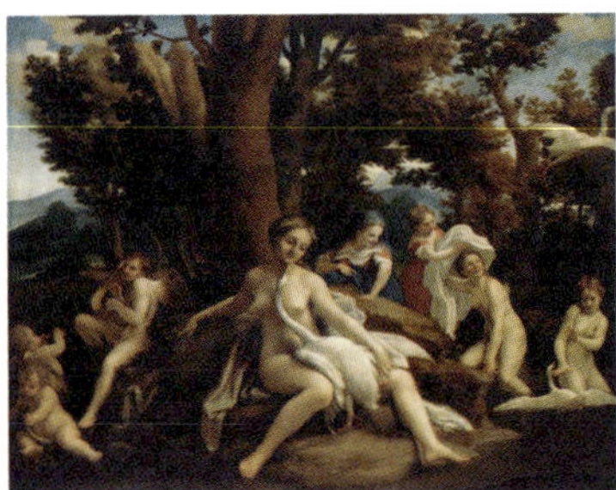

BR 44
**Antonio Allegri da Correggio (Italian, 1489–1534)**
*Leda and the Swan,* circa 1532
oil on canvas, 61½ × 76⅞ in. (156.2 × 195.3 cm), Kat. 218
Shown in all cities

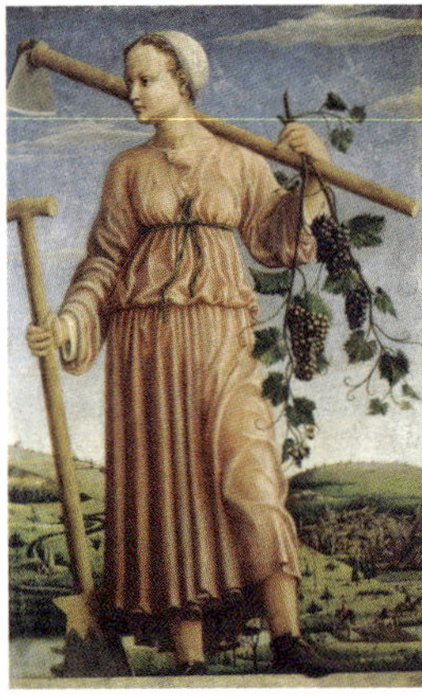

BR 45
**Ferrarese Master, formerly attributed to Francesco del Cossa (Italian, 1436–1477)**
*The Muse Polyhymnia* (formerly titled *Allegory of the Harvest*), circa 1455–60
oil on poplar panel, 46¹⁄₁₆ × 28¹³⁄₁₆ in. (117 × 73.2 cm), Kat. 115 A
Returned after Boston

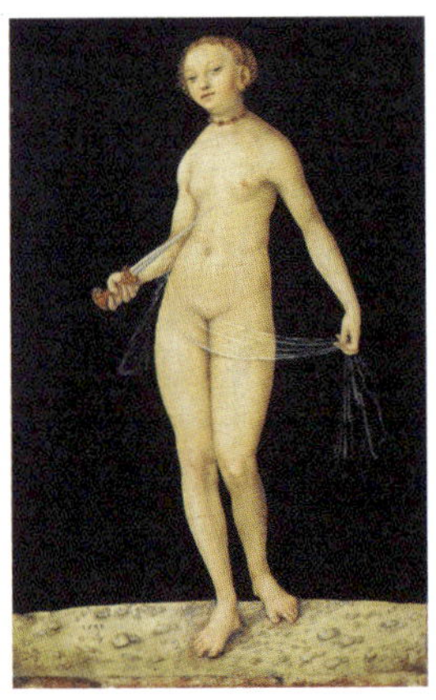

BR 46
**Lucas Cranach, the Elder (German, 1472–1553)**
*Lucretia,* 1533
oil on beech panel, 14¾ × 9⁷⁄₁₆ in. (37.4 × 23.9 cm), Kat. 1832
Shown in all cities

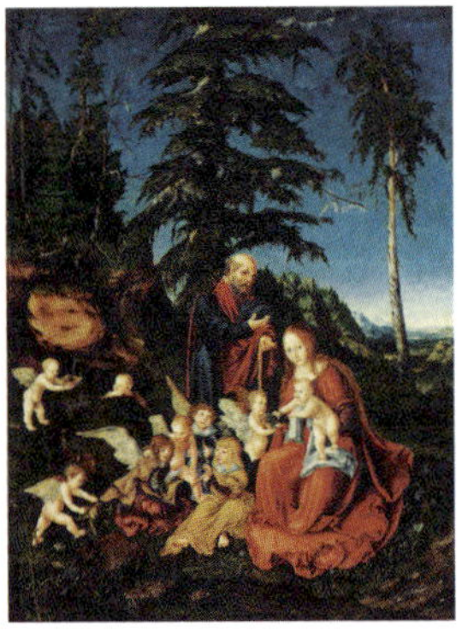

BR 47
**Lucas Cranach, the Elder (German, 1472–1553)**
*Rest on the Flight into Egypt,* 1504
oil on linden panel, 27¹⁵⁄₁₆ × 20⅞ in. (70.9 × 53 cm), Kat. 564 A
Returned after Boston

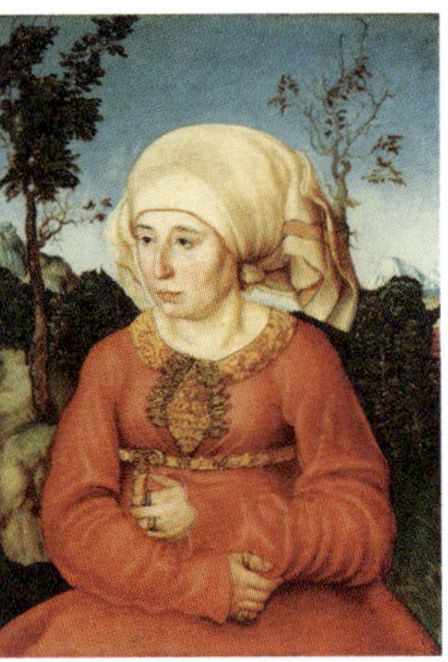

BR 48
**Lucas Cranach, the Elder (German, 1472–1553)**
*Portrait of a Lawyer's Wife* (formerly titled *Frau Reuss*), 1503
oil on spruce panel, 20¹¹⁄₁₆ × 14⁷⁄₁₆ in. (52.6 × 36.7 cm), Kat. 1907
Shown in all cities

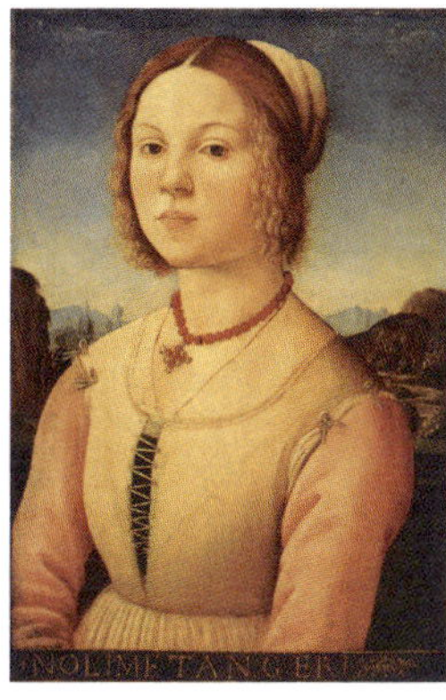

BR 49
**Agnolo di Donnino del Mazziere (Italian, 1466–1513), formerly attributed to Lorenzo di Credi (Italian, 1456/59–1536)**
*Portrait of a Young Woman*, circa 1490
oil on poplar panel, 18 15/16 × 12 5/8 in. (48.1 × 32.1 cm), Kat. 80
Shown in all cities

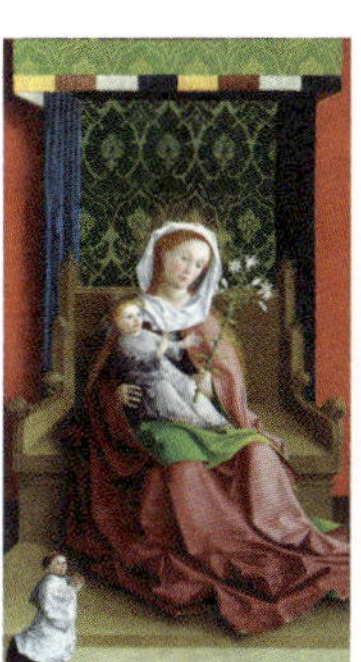

BR 50
**Master of the Darmstadt Passion**
*Wing of an Altarpiece: The Madonna Enthroned* (left wing exterior) and *Adoration of the Magi* (left wing interior), circa 1450–60
oil on pine panel, each panel 81 1/2 × 42 15/16 in. (207 × 109 cm), Kat. 1205
Returned after Washington, DC

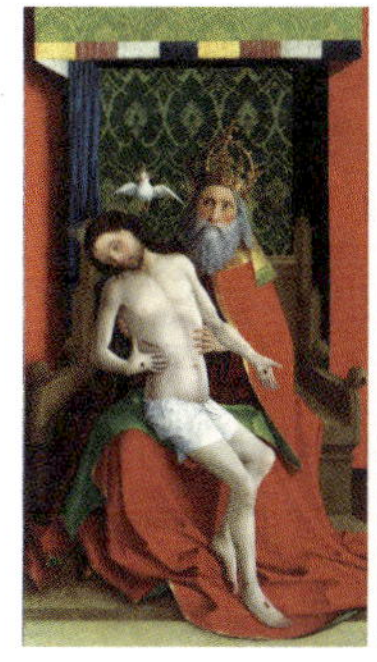

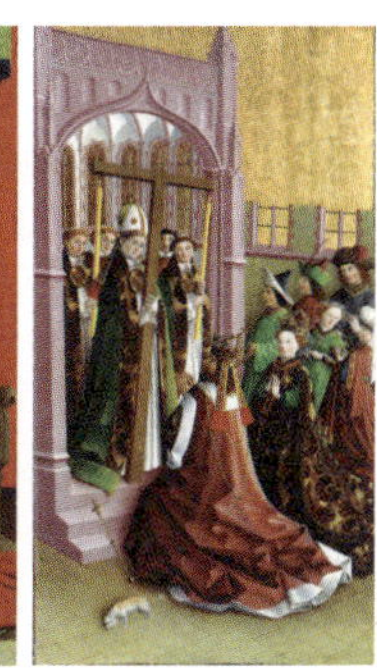

BR 51
**Master of the Darmstadt Passion**
*Wing of an Altarpiece: The Holy Trinity* (right wing exterior) and *The Worship of the Cross* (right wing interior), circa 1450–60
oil on pine panel, each panel 81 1/2 × 42 15/16 in. (207 × 109 cm), Kat. 1206
Returned after Washington, DC

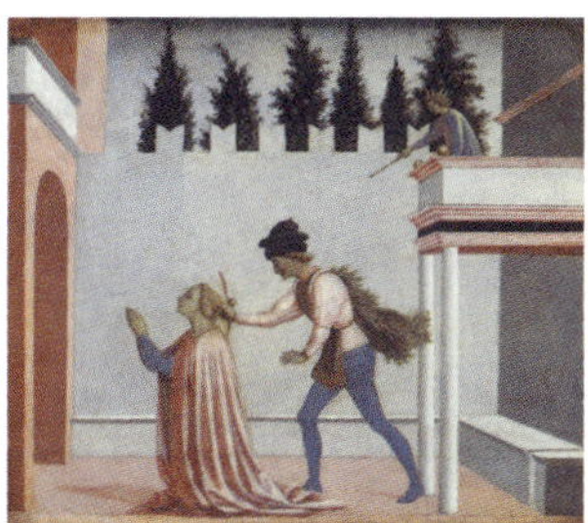

BR 52
**Domenico Veneziano (Italian, 1410–1461)**
*Martyrdom of Saint Lucy*, circa 1445
tempera on poplar panel, 10 3/8 × 11 3/4 in. (26.3 × 29.8 cm), Kat. 64
Shown in all cities

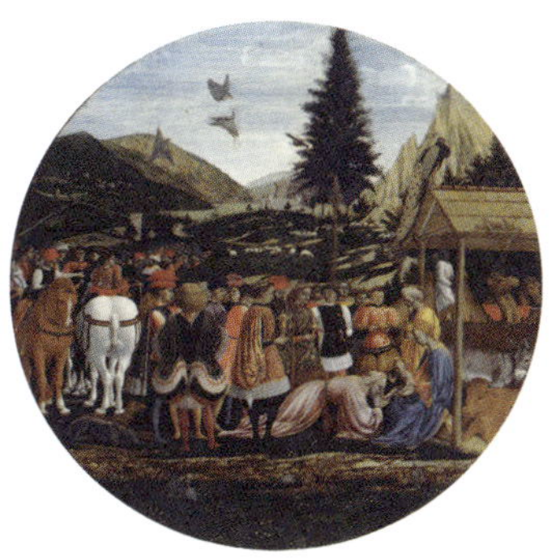

BR 53
**Domenico Veneziano (Italian, 1410–1461)**
*Adoration of the Magi*, circa 1435–40
tempera on panel, diam. 35 7/16 in. (90 cm), Kat. 95 A
Returned after Washington, DC

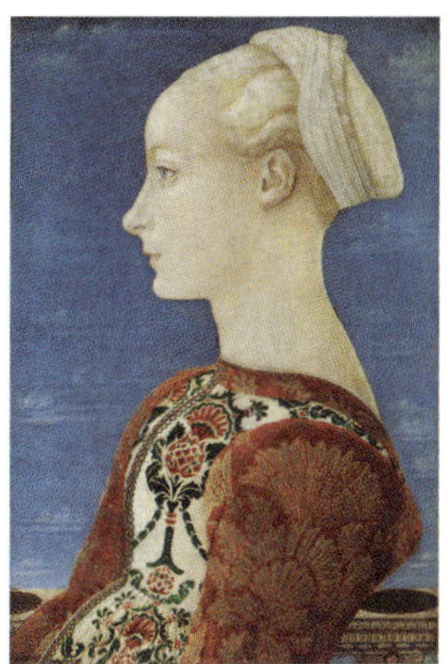

BR 54
**Piero del Pollaiuolo (Italian, 1443–1496), formerly attributed to Domenico Veneziano (Italian, 1410–1461)**
*Profile Portrait of a Young Woman*, circa 1465
oil on poplar panel, 20 9/16 × 14 1/4 in. (52.2 × 36.2 cm), Kat. 1614
Returned after Washington, DC

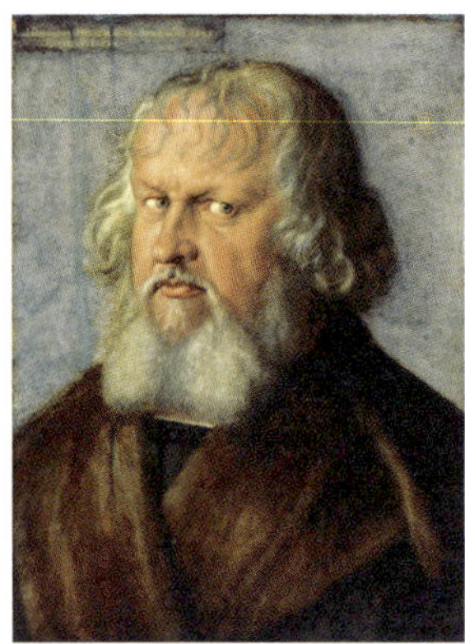

BR 55
**Albrecht Dürer (German, 1471–1528)**
*Hieronymus Holzschuher*, 1526
oil on linden panel, 20¹⁄₁₆ × 14⅝ in.
(54.1 × 37.1 cm), Kat. 557 E
Returned after Boston

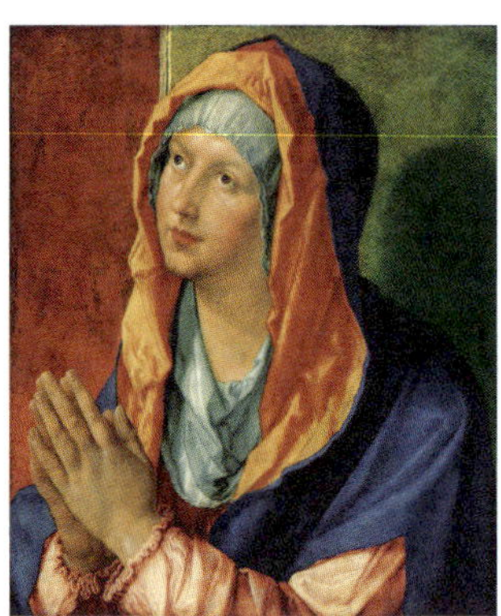

BR 56
**Albrecht Dürer (German, 1471–1528)**
*Madonna in Prayer*, 1518
oil on linden panel, 21⅝ × 17¹³⁄₁₆ in.
(54.9 × 45.3 cm), Kat. 557 H
Returned after Boston

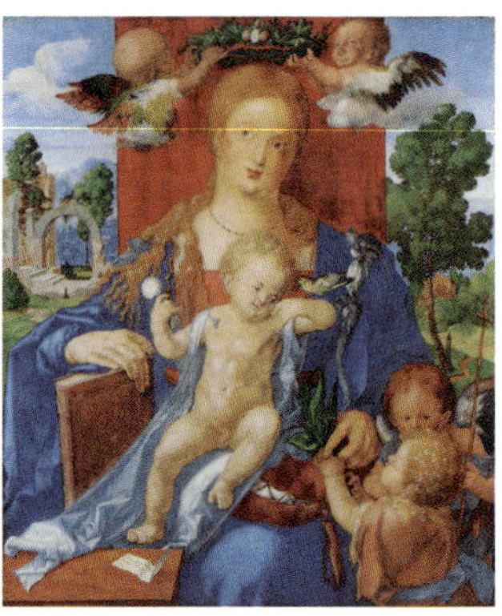

BR 57
**Albrecht Dürer (German, 1471–1528)**
*The Virgin and Child with the Siskin*, 1506
oil on poplar panel, 36¹³⁄₁₆ × 31¹⁄₁₆ in.
(93.5 × 78.9 cm), Kat. 557 F
Returned after Washington, DC

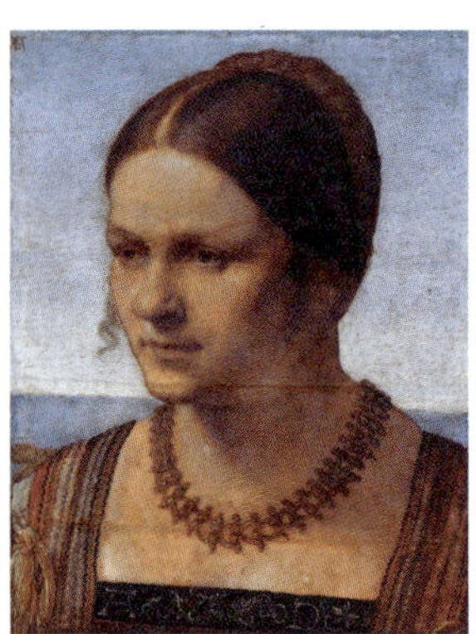

BR 58
**Albrecht Dürer (German, 1471–1528)**
*Portrait of a Young Venetian Woman*, circa 1506
oil on poplar panel, 11¼ × 8⁷⁄₁₆ in.
(28.5 × 21.5 cm), Kat. 557 G
Returned after Washington, DC

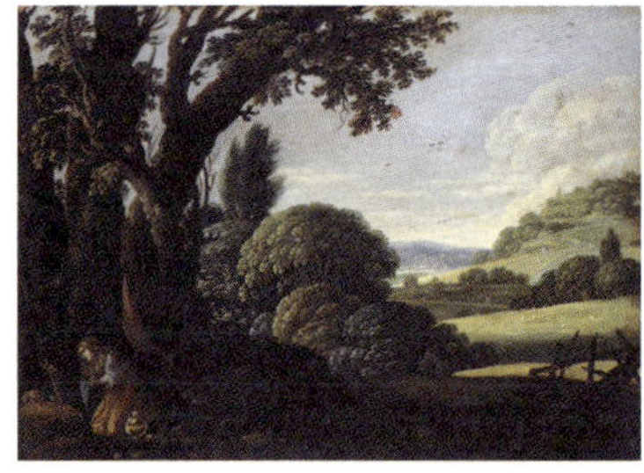

BR 59
**Jacob Pynas (Dutch, 1592/93–circa 1650), formerly attributed to Adam Elsheimer (German, 1578–1610)**
*Landscape with Penitent Magdalene*, 1640
oil on copper, 7⁵⁄₁₆ × 9⁹⁄₁₆ in.
(18.5 × 24.3 cm), Kat. 1973
Returned after Boston

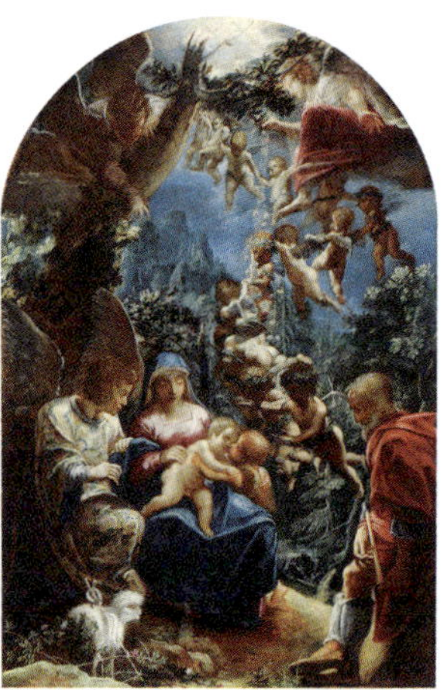

BR 60
**Adam Elsheimer (German, 1578–1610)**
*The Holy Family with Angels and Infant Saint John*, circa 1600
oil on copper, 14⅞ × 9⅝ in.
(37.8 × 24.4 cm), Kat. 2039
Returned after Washington, DC

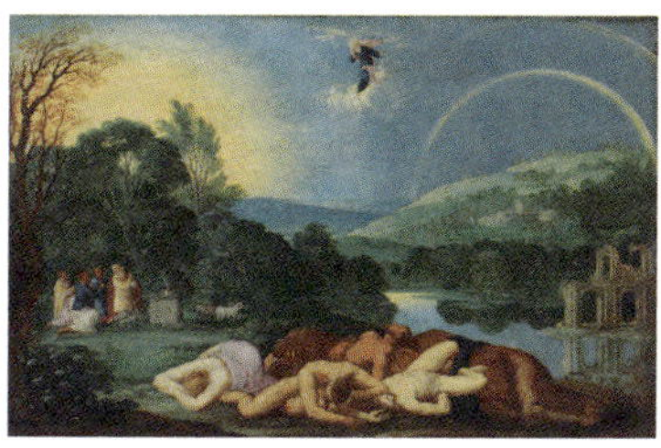

**BR 61**
**Johann König (German, 1586–1642), formerly attributed to Adam Elsheimer (German, 1578–1610)**
*The Sacrifice of Noah*, circa 1620–30
oil on copper, 6⅞ × 10⁷⁄₁₆ in.
(17.5 × 26.5 cm), Kat. 1843
Shown in all cities

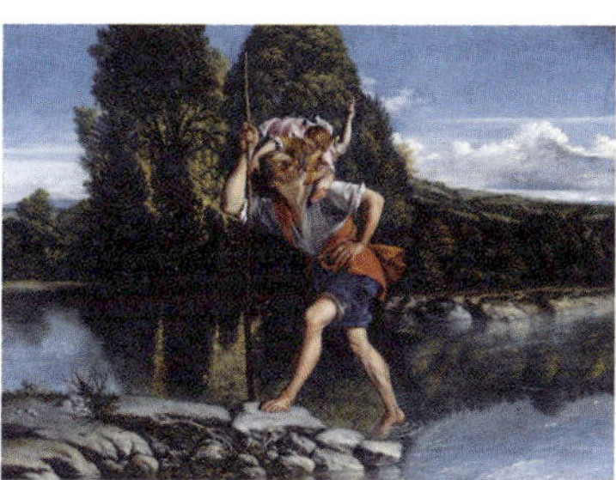

**BR 62**
**Orazio Gentileschi (Italian, 1562–1640), formerly attributed to Adam Elsheimer (German, 1578–1610)**
*Landscape with Saint Christopher*, 1635–38
oil on copper, 8¼ × 11¹⁄₁₆ in.
(20.5 × 26 cm), Kat. 1707
Shown in all cities

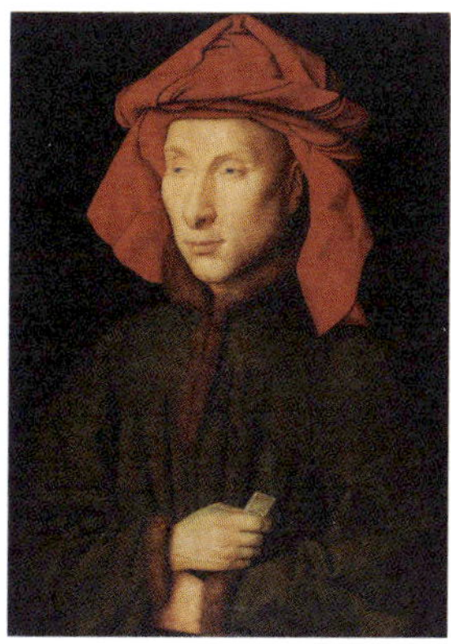

**BR 63**
**Jan van Eyck (Flemish, circa 1390–1441)**
*Portrait of a Man* (formerly titled *Giovanni Arnolfini*), circa 1438–40
oil on oak panel, 11⁷⁄₁₆ × 7⅞ in.
(29 × 20 cm), Kat. 523 A
Returned after Washington, DC

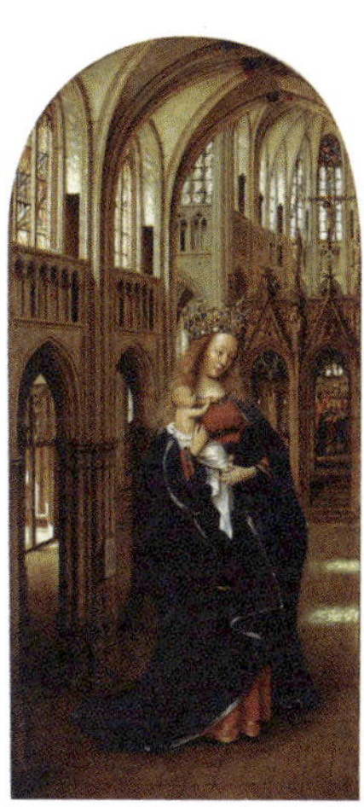

**BR 64**
**Jan van Eyck (Flemish, circa 1390–1441)**
*Madonna and Child in a Church*, circa 1440
oil on oak panel, 12¼ × 5½ in.
(31.1 × 13.9 cm), Kat. 525 C
Returned after Washington, DC

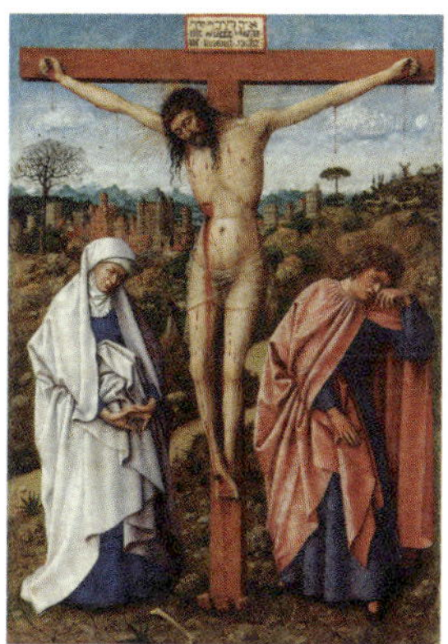

**BR 65**
**Jan van Eyck (Flemish, circa 1390–1441), or Workshop of Jan van Eyck**
*Christ Crucified*, circa 1430–40
oil on panel, 16¹⁵⁄₁₆ × 10¼ in.
(43 × 26 cm), Kat. 525 F
Returned after Boston

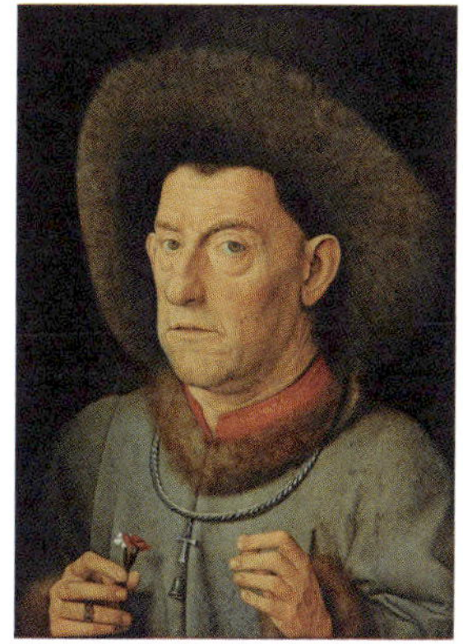

**BR 66**
**Copy after Jan van Eyck (Flemish, circa 1390–1441), formerly attributed to Jan van Eyck**
*The Man with the Pinks*, circa 1520
oil on oak panel, 16¹⁵⁄₁₆ × 12⅜ in.
(41.5 × 31.5 cm), Kat. 525 A
Returned after Washington, DC

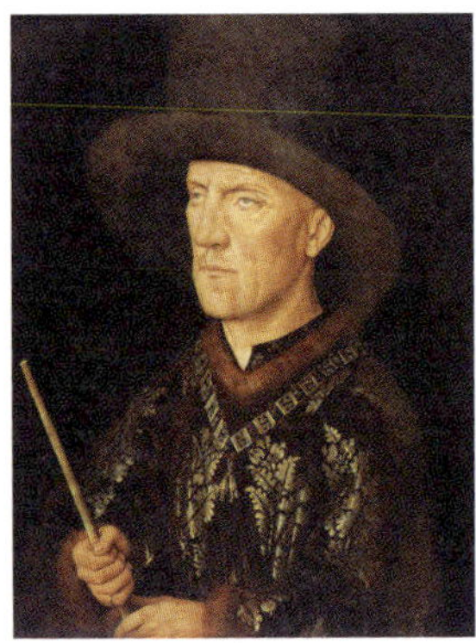

BR 67
**Jan van Eyck (Flemish, circa 1390–1441)**
*Baudouin de Lannoy*, circa 1435–40
oil on oak panel, 10¼ × 7¹¹⁄₁₆ in. (26 × 19.5 cm), Kat. 525 G
Returned after Washington, DC

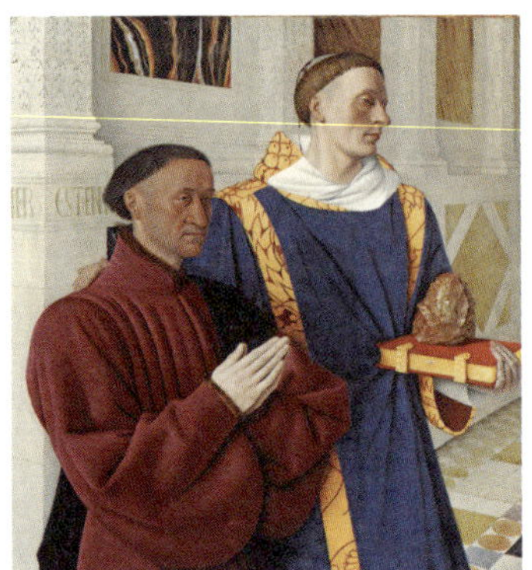

BR 68
**Jean Fouquet (French, circa 1420–1477/81)**
*Étienne Chevalier with Saint Stephen*, circa 1455
oil on oak panel, 37¾ × 34¾ in. (95.9 × 88.2 cm), Kat. 1617
Returned after Boston

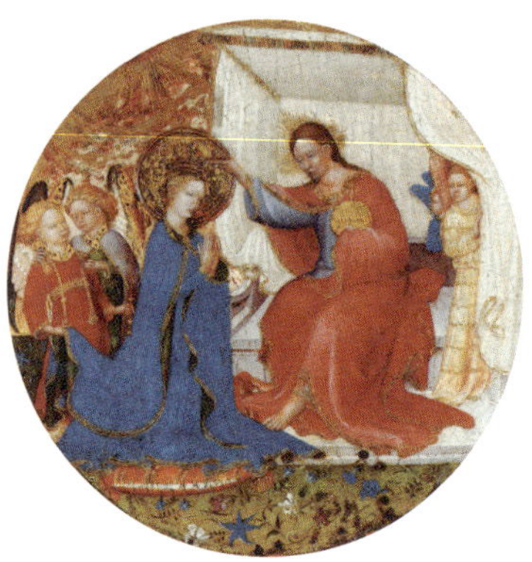

BR 69
**French School**
*Coronation of the Virgin*, circa 1400
oil on panel, diam. 8¹⁄₁₆ in. (20.5 cm), Kat. 1648
Returned after Washington, DC

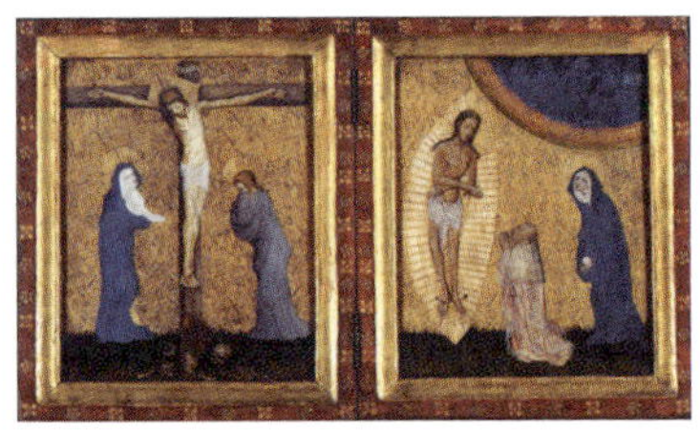

BR 70
**North German School, formerly attributed to French School**
*Christ on the Cross* and *The Man of Sorrows*, circa 1400
oil on panel, each panel 13⅜ × 10⁷⁄₁₆ in. (34 × 26.5 cm), Kat. 1620
Returned after Washington, DC

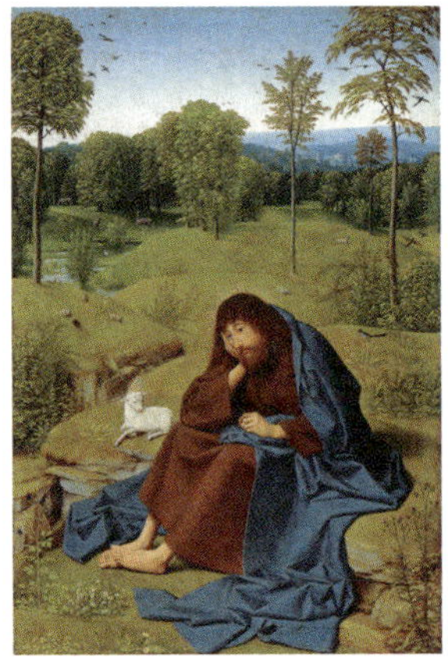

BR 71
**Geertgen tot Sint Jans (Dutch, circa 1460–1495)**
*John the Baptist in the Wilderness*, circa 1480–90
oil on oak panel, 16¹⁵⁄₁₆ × 11 in. (41.5 × 27.9 cm), Kat. 1631
Returned after Boston

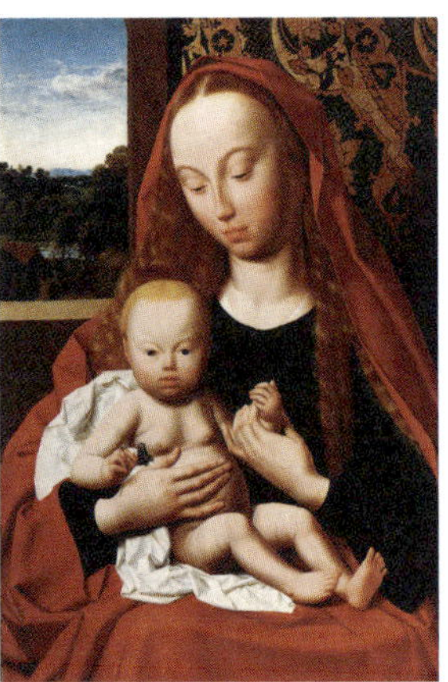

BR 72
**Geertgen tot Sint Jans (Dutch, circa 1460–1495)**
*Madonna and Child*, 1487
oil on oak panel, 31⅞ × 20½ in. (81 × 52 cm), Kat. 1853
Shown in all cities

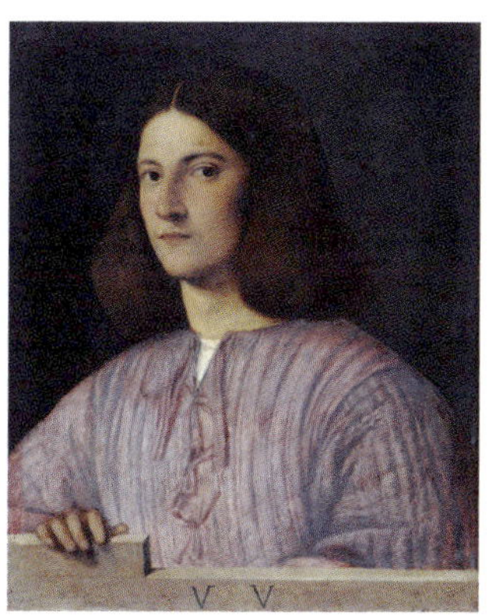

**BR 73**
**Giorgione (Italian, circa 1477/78–1500)**
*Portrait of a Young Man*, circa 1505–6
oil on canvas, 22 13/16 × 18 in. (58 × 46 cm), Kat. 12 A
Shown in all cities

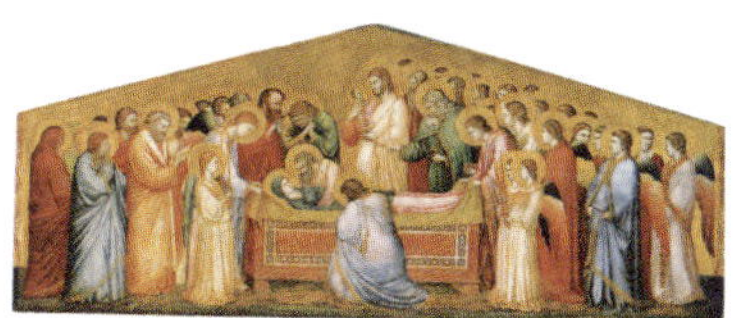

**BR 74**
**Giotto (Italian, 1266–1337)**
*Death of the Virgin*, circa 1310
tempera and gold on poplar panel, 29 13/16 × 70¾ in. (75.8 × 179.7 cm), Kat. 1884
Returned after Washington, DC

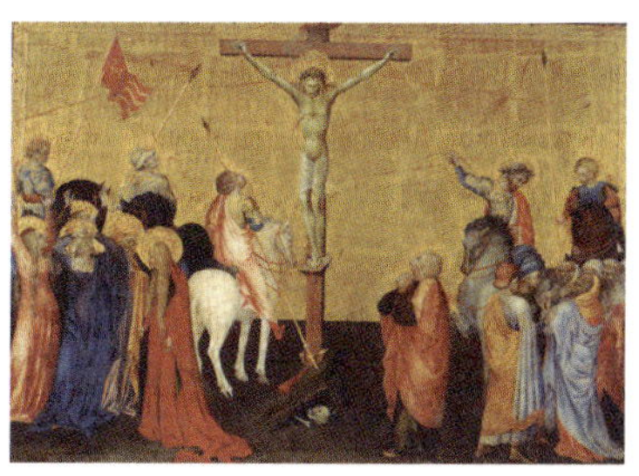

**BR 75**
**Giovanni di Paolo (Italian, 1399/1403–1482/83)**
*The Crucifixion*, 1440–45
tempera and gold on poplar panel, 15 13/16 × 22 3/16 in. (40.2 × 56.3 cm), Kat. KFMV 1112 C
Shown in all cities

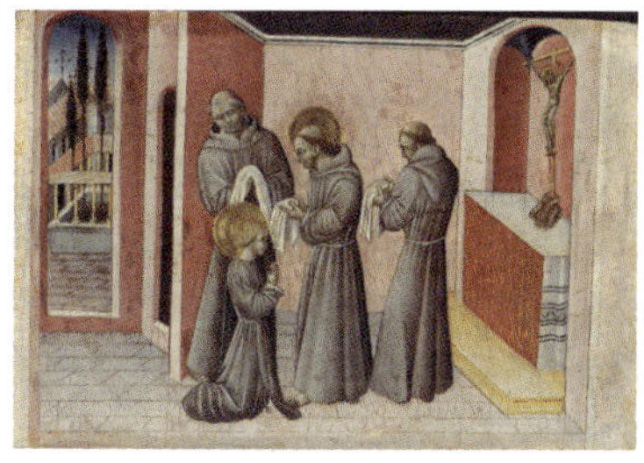

**BR 76**
**Giovanni di Paolo (Italian, 1399/1403–1482/83)**
*The Ordination of Saint Clara of Assisi*, circa 1455–60
oil on poplar panel, 8 1/16 × 11⅝ in. (20.5 × 29.5 cm), Kat. 2170
Returned after Boston

*Restituted in 2019 to the heirs of Harry Fuld, Sr. (see Rowley, p. 90)

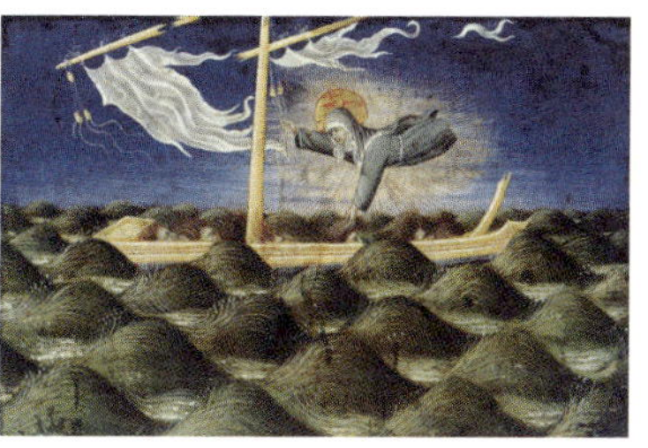

**BR 77**
**Giovanni di Paolo (Italian, 1399/1403–1482/83)**
*Saint Clara Aids the Shipwrecked*, circa 1455–60
poplar panel, 8 1/16 × 11⅝ in. (20.5 × 29.5 cm), Kat. 2171
Returned after Boston

*Restituted in 2019 to the heirs of Harry Fuld, Sr. (see Rowley, p. 90)

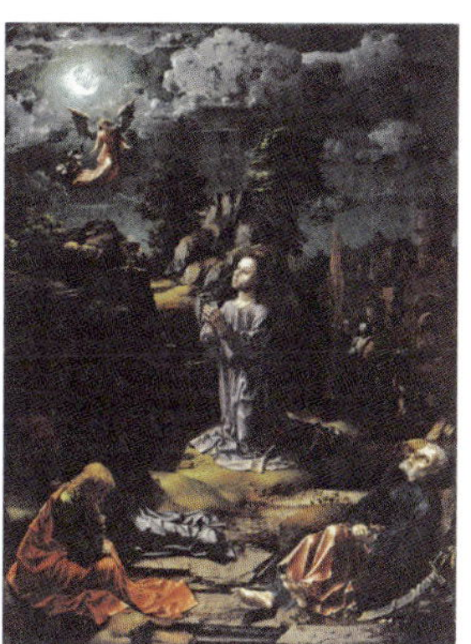

**BR 78**
**Jan Gossaert (Flemish, 1478–1532)**
*Christ in the Garden of Gethsemane*, circa 1510
oil on oak panel, 33 7/16 × 24 13/16 in. (85 × 63 cm), Kat. 551 A
Returned after Washington, DC

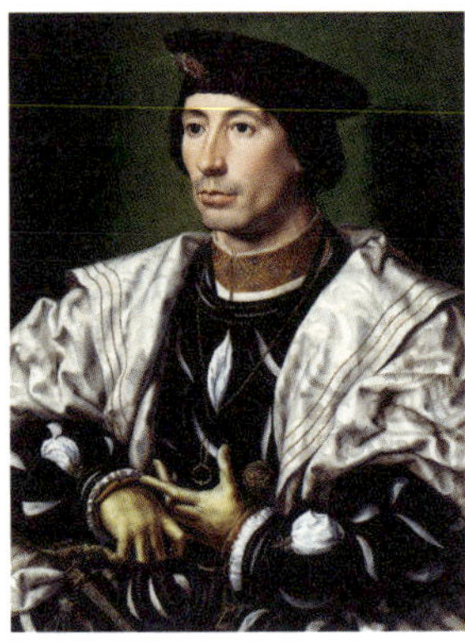

BR 79
**Jan Gossaert (Flemish, 1478–1532)**
*Portrait of a Nobleman* (formerly titled *Baudouin de Bourbon*), after 1530
oil on panel, 22¹⁄₁₆ × 16¾ in.
(56 × 42.5 cm), Kat. 586 A
Shown in all cities

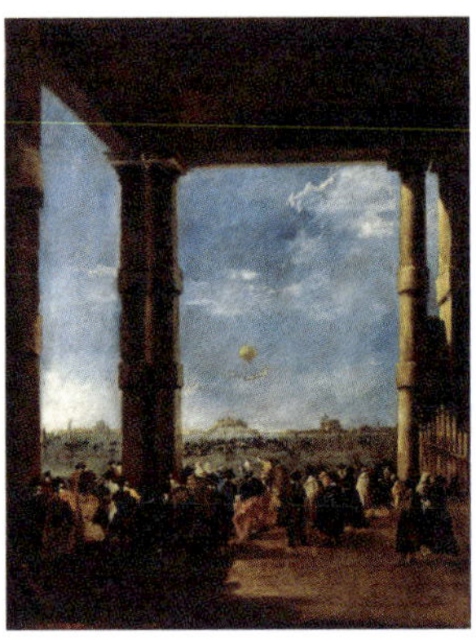

BR 80
**Francesco Guardi (Italian, 1712–1793)**
*The Balloon Flight of Count Zambeccari*, 1784
oil on canvas, 26 × 20¹⁄₁₆ in.
(66 × 51 cm), Kat. KFMV 501 F
Shown in all cities

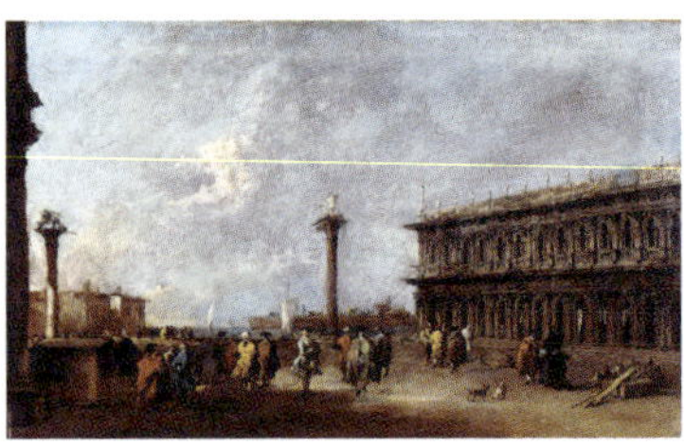

BR 81
**Francesco Guardi (Italian, 1712–1793)**
*The Piazzetta in Venice*, 18th century
oil on canvas, 12¹⁄₁₆ × 17¹⁵⁄₁₆ in.
(30.6 × 45.6 cm), Kat. 1836
Shown in all cities

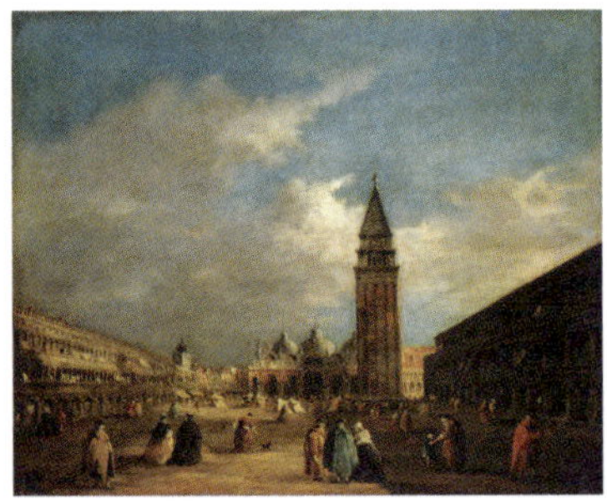

BR 82
**Follower of Francesco Guardi (Italian, 1712–1793), formerly attributed to Francesco Guardi**
*Piazza San Marco in Venice*, after 1760
oil on canvas, 21⁷⁄₁₆ × 26 in.
(54.5 × 66 cm), Kat. KFMV 501 G
Shown in all cities

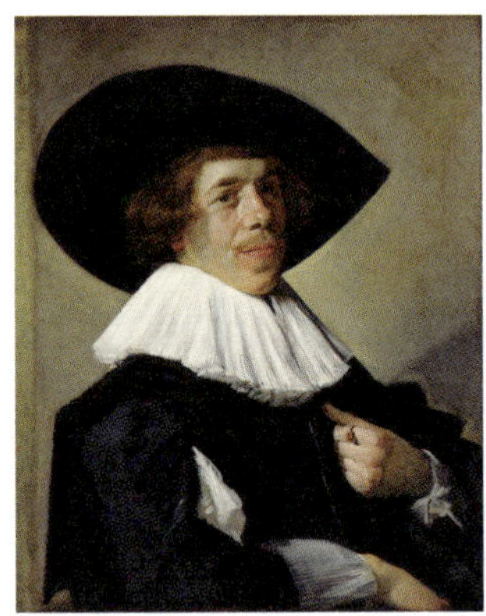

BR 83
**Frans Hals (Dutch, 1582/83–1666)**
*Portrait of a Man*, 1633–35
oil on canvas, 29½ × 22¹³⁄₁₆ in.
(75 × 58 cm), Kat. 800
Shown in all cities

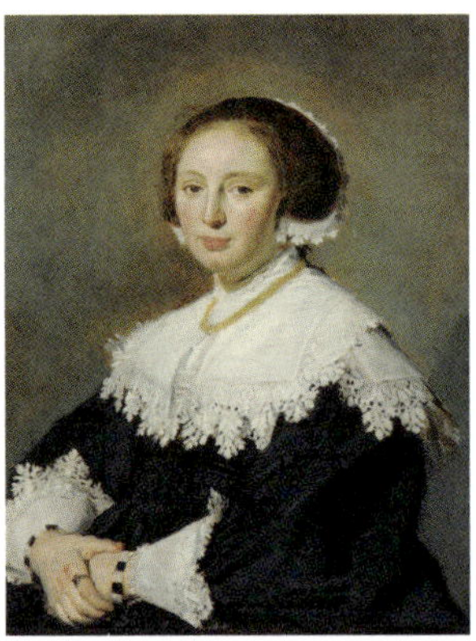

BR 84
**Frans Hals (Dutch, 1582/83–1666)**
*Portrait of a Woman*, 1632–35
oil on canvas, 29½ × 22¹³⁄₁₆ in.
(75 × 58 cm), Kat. 801
Shown in all cities

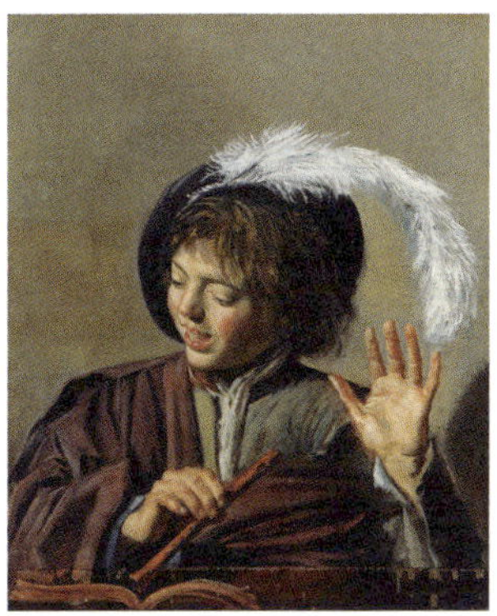

**BR 85**
**Frans Hals (Dutch, 1582/83–1666)**
*Singing Boy with a Flute*, circa 1627
oil on canvas, 27 1/16 × 21 3/4 in.
(68.8 × 55.2 cm), Kat. 801 A
Shown in all cities

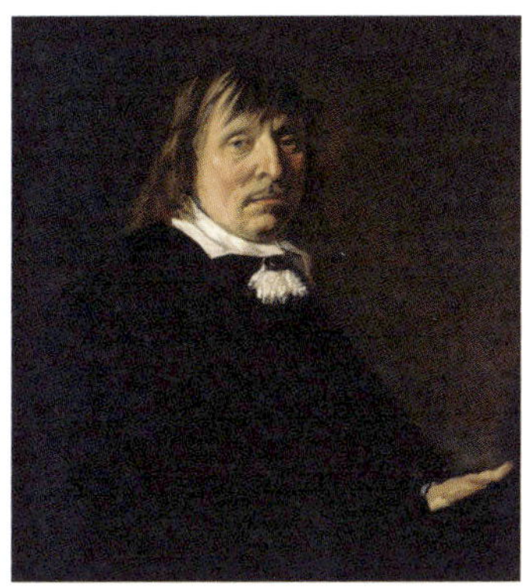

**BR 86**
**Frans Hals (Dutch, 1582/83–1666)**
*Tyman Oosdorp*, 1656
oil on canvas, 32 5/16 × 28 15/16 in.
(82 × 73.5 cm), Kat. 801 H
Shown in all cities

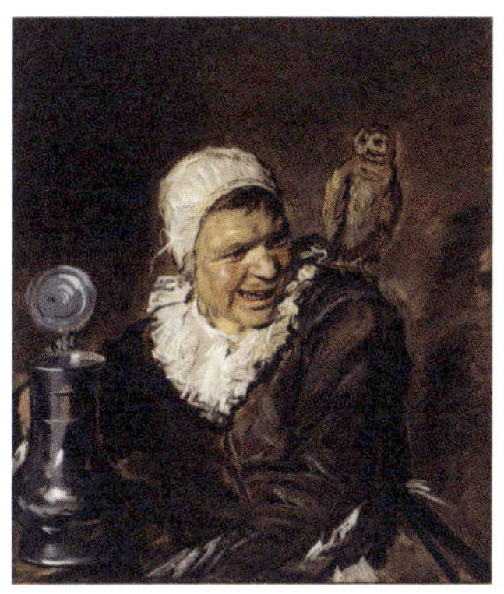

**BR 87**
**Frans Hals (Dutch, 1582/83–1666)**
*"Malle Babbe"*, 1629–30
oil on canvas, 30 7/8 × 26 1/16 in.
(78.5 × 66.2 cm), Kat. 801 C
Shown in all cities

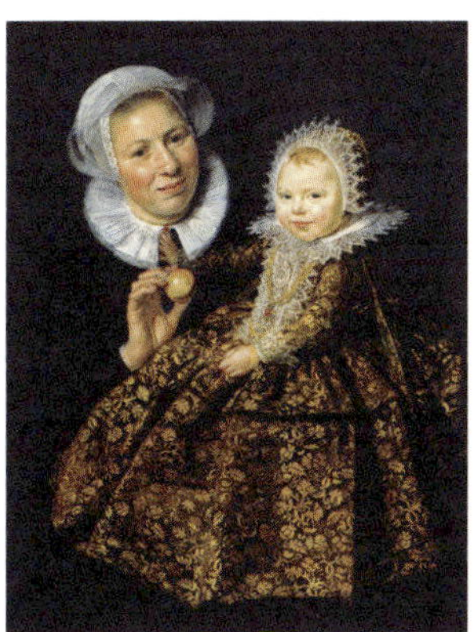

**BR 88**
**Frans Hals (Dutch, 1582/83–1666)**
*Catharina Hooft with her Nurse*,
circa 1619–20
oil on canvas, 36 × 26 7/8 in.
(91.8 × 68.3 cm), Kat. 801 G
Shown in all cities

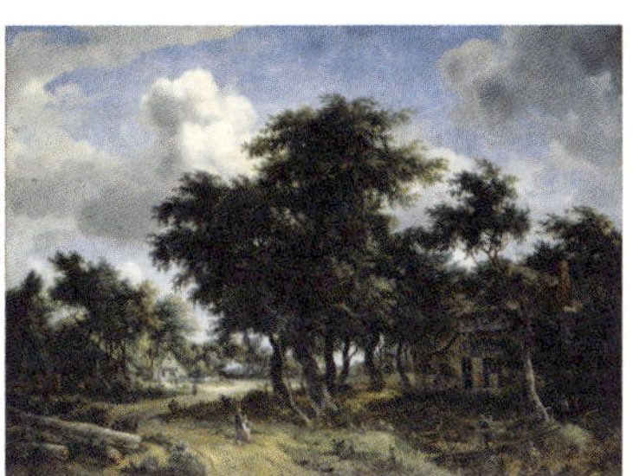

**BR 89**
**Meindert Hobbema**
**(Dutch, 1638–1709)**
*Village Street under Trees*, circa 1663
oil on canvas, 38 3/8 × 50 5/8 in.
(97.4 × 128.6 cm), Kat. 1984
Shown in all cities

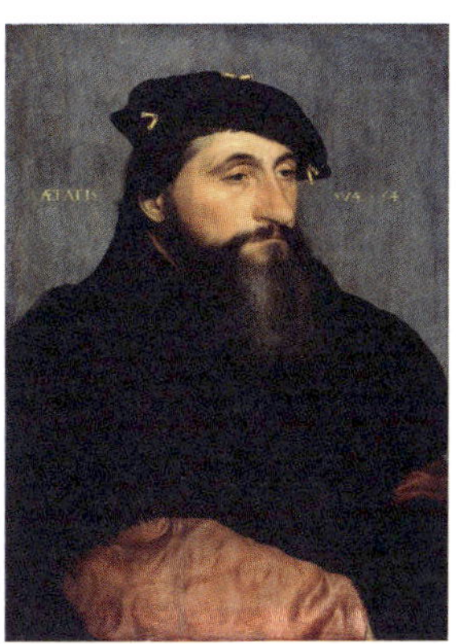

**BR 90**
**Hans Holbein, the Younger**
**(German, 1497/98–1543)**
*Antoine the Good, Duke of Lorraine*
(formerly titled *Portrait of an Elderly Man*), circa 1543
oil on oak panel, 20 1/16 × 14 9/16 in.
(51 × 37 cm), Kat. 586 D
Shown in all cities

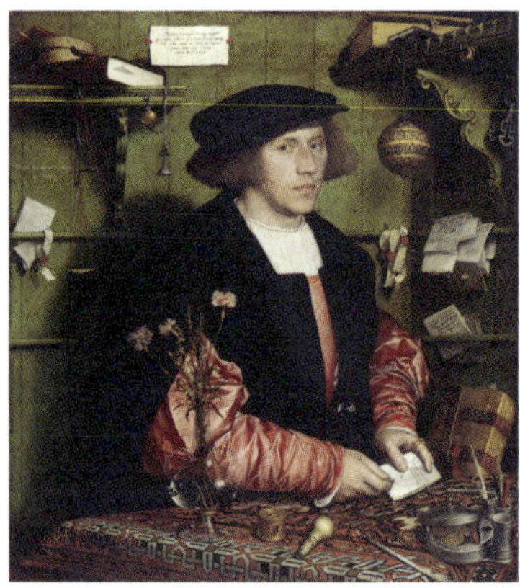

**BR 91**
**Hans Holbein, the Younger (German, 1497/98–1543)**
*Portrait of Georg Gisze*, 1532
oil on oak panel, 38⅜ × 33¹⁵⁄₁₆ in. (97.5 × 86.2 cm), Kat. 586
Returned after Washington, DC

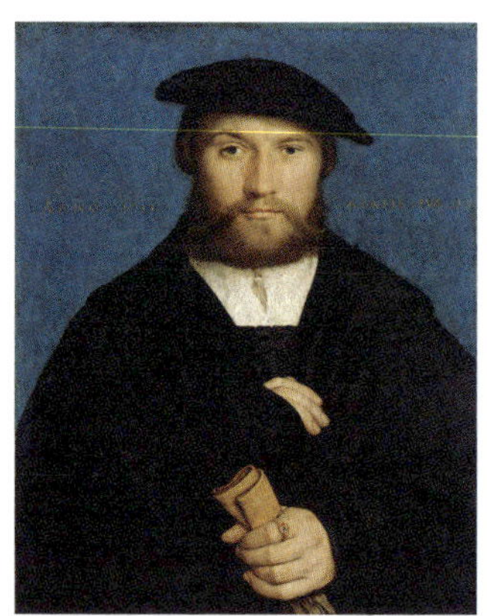

**BR 92**
**Hans Holbein, the Younger (German, 1497/98–1543)**
*A Member of the Wedigh Family from Cologne* (formerly titled *Hermann Hillebrandt von Wedigh*), 1533
oil and tempera on oak panel, 15⅜ × 11¹³⁄₁₆ in. (39 × 30 cm), Kat. 586 B
Returned after Washington, DC

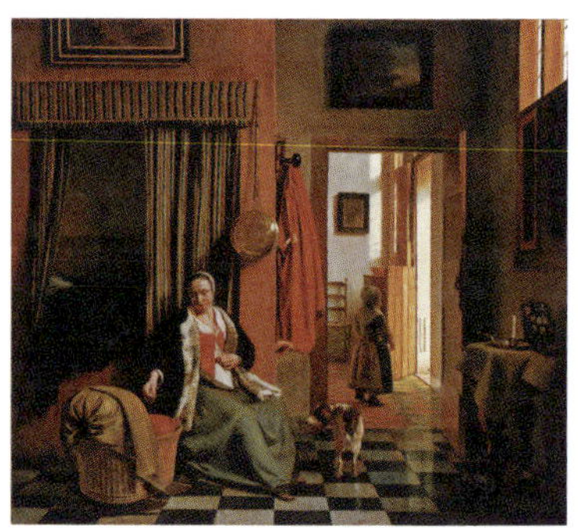

**BR 93**
**Pieter de Hooch (Dutch, 1629–circa 1694)**
*The Mother*, circa 1663
oil on canvas, 37½ × 40⅜ in. (95.2 × 102.5 cm), Kat. 820 B
Shown in all cities

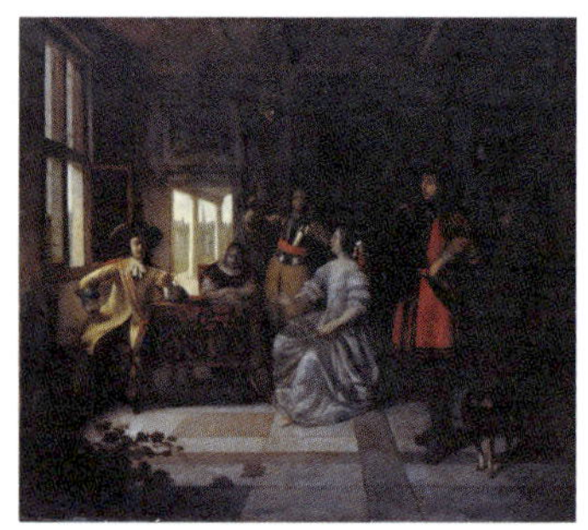

**BR 94**
**Pieter de Hooch (Dutch, 1629–circa 1694)**
*Merry Company with Bugler*, around 1675
oil on canvas, 33⁷⁄₁₆ × 36¼ in. (85 × 92 cm), Kat. 1401
Shown in all cities

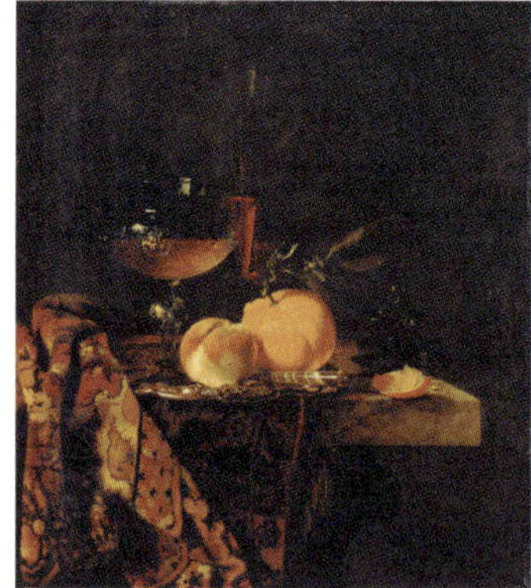

**BR 95**
**Willem Kalf (Dutch, 1619–1693)**
*Still Life with Glass Goblets and Fruit*, circa 1655
oil on canvas, 26¾ × 22¹¹⁄₁₆ in. (66.3 × 57.7 cm), Kat. 948 D
Shown in all cities

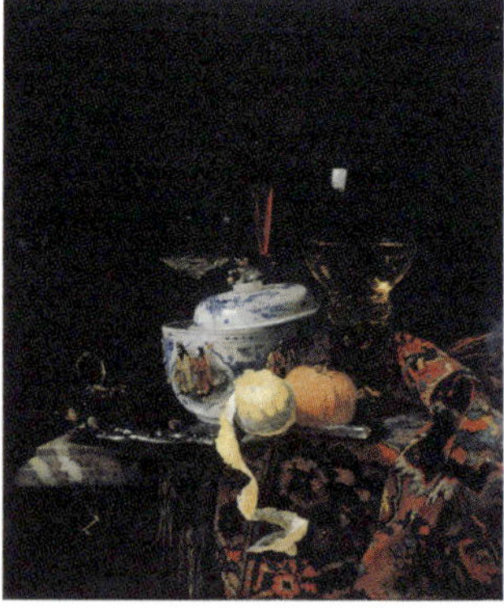

**BR 96**
**Willem Kalf (Dutch, 1619–1693)**
*Still Life with Chinese Porcelain Bowl*, 1662
oil on canvas, 26⅜ × 21⁹⁄₁₆ in. (67 × 54.7 cm), Kat. 948 F
Shown in all cities

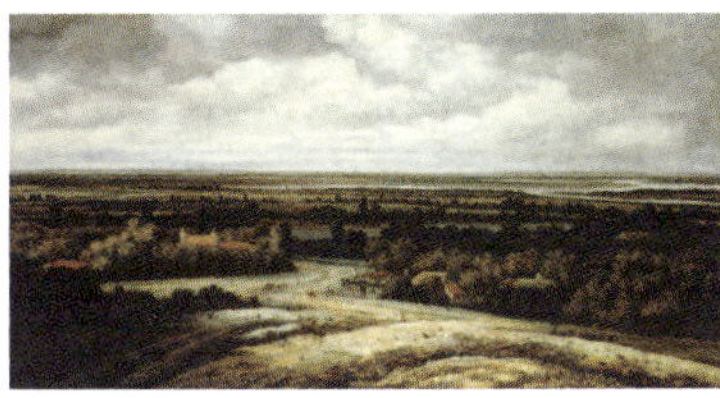

**BR 97**
**Philips Koninck (Dutch, 1619–1688)**
*Panorama of Holland*, circa 1655–60
oil on canvas, 36⅝ × 66³⁄₁₆ in.
(93 × 168.1 cm), Kat. 821 A
Shown in all cities

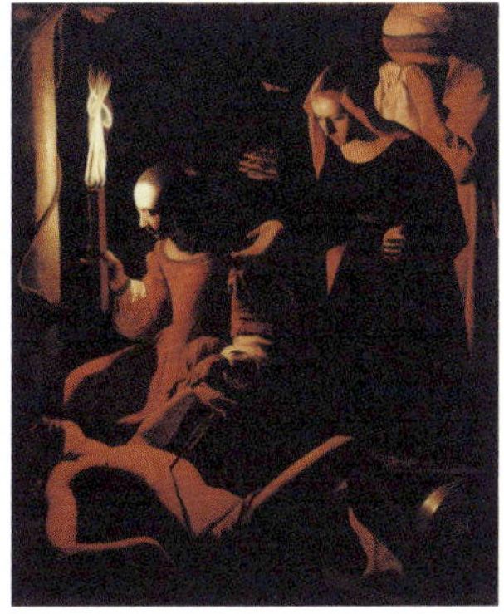

**BR 98**
**Copy of Georges de La Tour (French, 1593–1652), formerly attributed to Georges de La Tour**
*The Discovery of Saint Sebastian*, circa 1640
oil on canvas, 63¾ × 50¹³⁄₁₆ in.
(162 × 129 cm), Kat. 2046
Returned after Boston

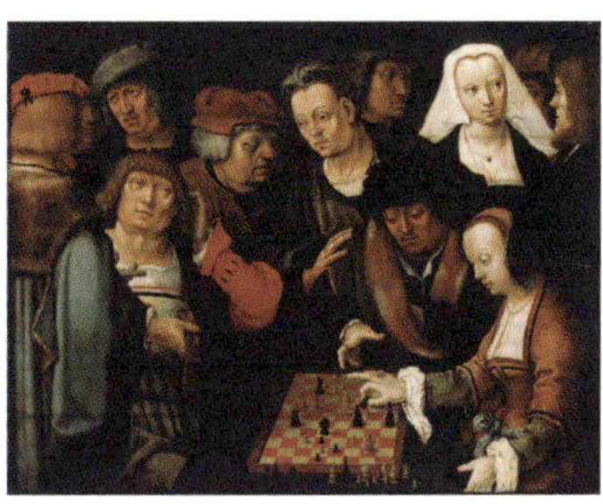

**BR 99**
**Lucas Hugensz. van Leyden (Dutch, 1494–1533)**
*The Chess Game*, circa 1508
oil on oak panel, 11¹⁄₁₆ × 14³⁄₁₆ in.
(28.1 × 36 cm), Kat. 574 A
Shown in all cities

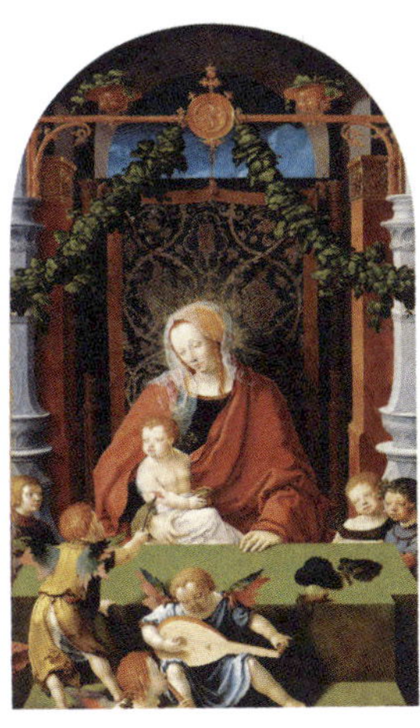

**BR 100**
**Lucas Hugensz. van Leyden (Dutch, 1494–1533)**
*Madonna and Child with Angels*, circa 1520
oil on oak panel, 30½ × 18¼ in.
(77.5 × 46.4 cm), Kat. 584 B
Returned after Washington, DC

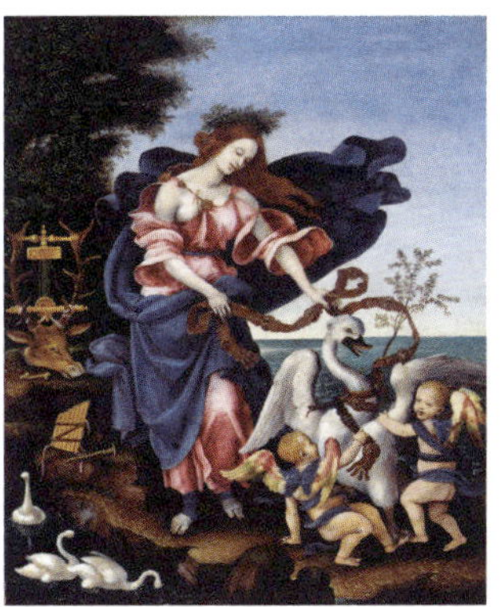

**BR 101**
**Filippino Lippi (Italian, 1457–1504)**
*The Muse Erato* (formerly titled *Allegory of Music*), circa 1500
tempera on poplar panel,
24⅝ × 20⅜ in. (62.5 × 51.8 cm),
Kat. 78 A
Shown in all cities

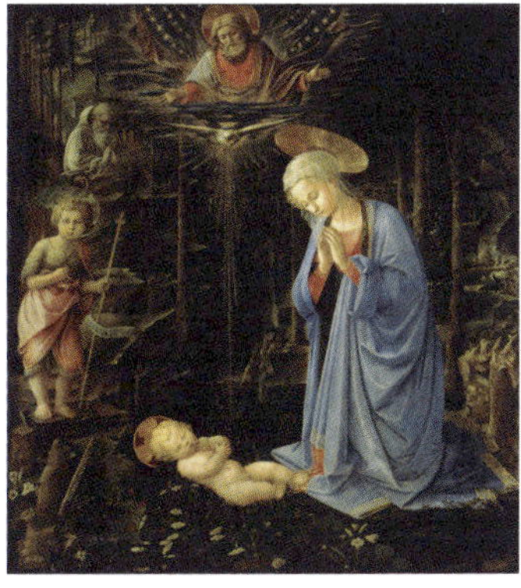

**BR 102**
**Fra Filippo Lippi (Italian, circa 1406–1469)**
*The Madonna Adoring the Christ Child*, circa 1459
tempera on poplar panel, 50¹⁵⁄₁₆ × 46¹¹⁄₁₆ in. (129.4 × 118.6 cm), Kat. 69
Returned after Washington, DC

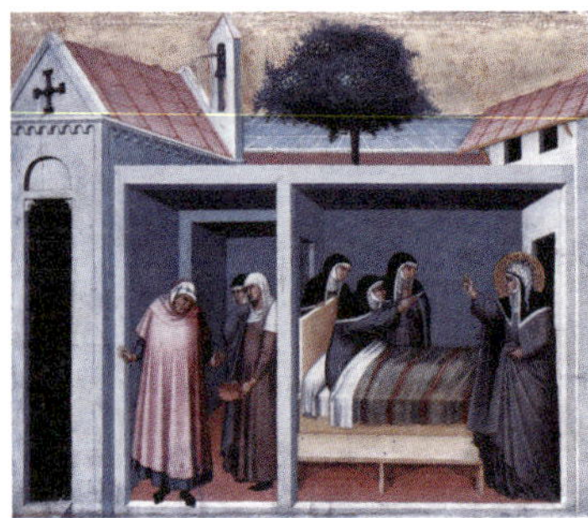

BR 103
**Pietro Lorenzetti (Italian, 1280–1348)**
*Saint Humilitas Heals a Sick Nun,* circa 1330–35
tempera on panel, 18³⁄₁₆ × 21¹³⁄₁₆ in. (46.2 × 55.4 cm), Kat. 1077
Returned after Washington, DC

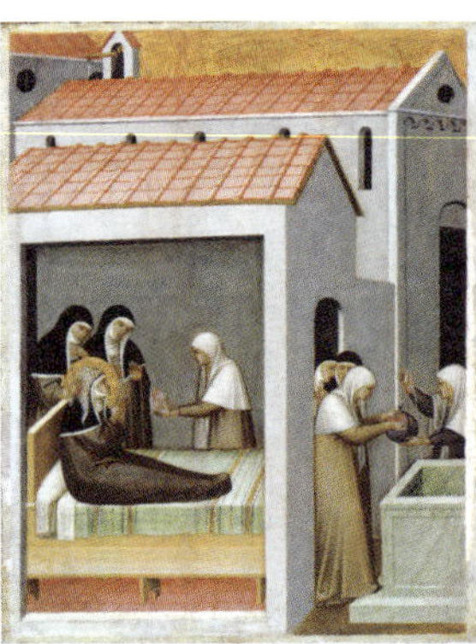

BR 104
**Pietro Lorenzetti (Italian, 1280–1348)**
*The Miracle of the Ice of Saint Humilitas* (formerly titled *Death of Saint Humilitas*), circa 1330–35
tempera on poplar panel, 17 × 13¼ in. (43.5 × 33.7 cm), Kat. 1077 A
Returned after Washington, DC

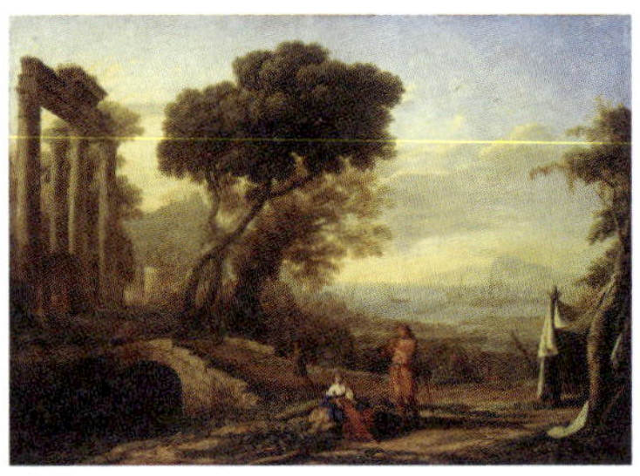

BR 105
**Claude Gellée, called Claude Lorrain (French, 1604–1682)**
*Italian Coastal Landscape in Early Morning Light,* 1642
oil on canvas, 38³⁄₁₆ × 51⁹⁄₁₆ in. (97 × 131 cm), Kat. 448 B
Shown in all cities

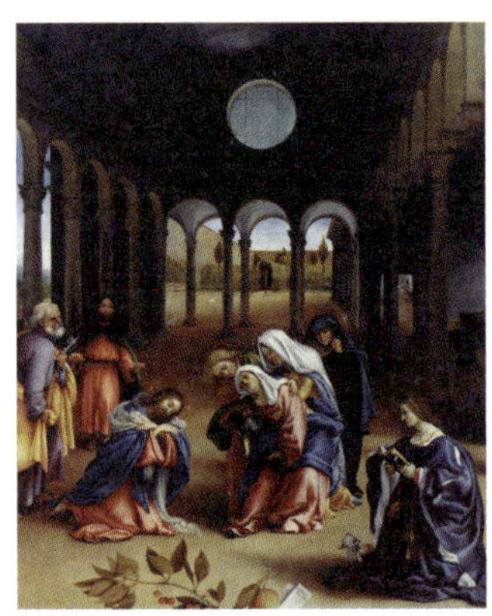

BR 106
**Lorenzo Lotto (Italian, 1480–1556)**
*Christ Takes Leave of His Mother,* 1521
oil on canvas, 49⅝ × 39 in. (126 × 99 cm), Kat. 325
Shown in all cities

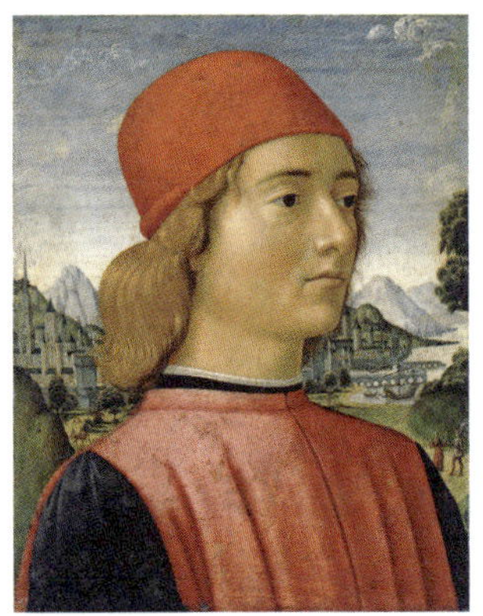

BR 107
**Davide Ghirlandaio (Italian, 1452–1525), formerly attributed to Sebastiano di Bartolo Mainardi (Italian, circa 1460–1513)**
*Portrait of a Young Man with a Red Cap,* circa 1490
tempera on poplar panel, 17⁹⁄₁₆ × 13½ in. (44.6 × 34.3 cm), Kat. 86
Shown in all cities

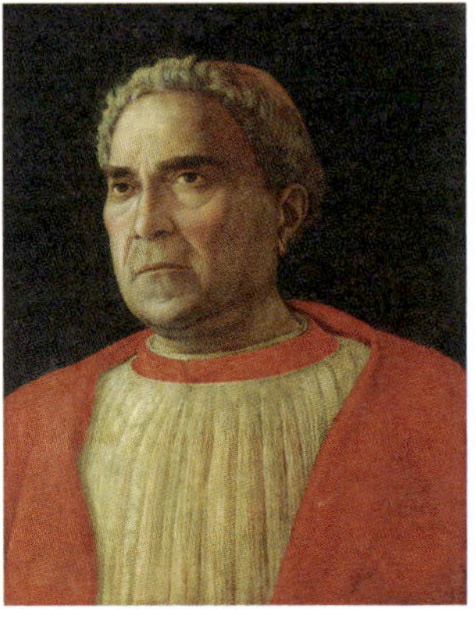

BR 108
**Andrea Mantegna (Italian, circa 1431–1506)**
*Cardinal Ludovico Trevisan,* circa 1459–60
tempera on poplar panel, 17¹⁵⁄₁₆ × 13¹¹⁄₁₆ in. (45.5 × 34.8 cm), Kat. 9
Returned after Boston

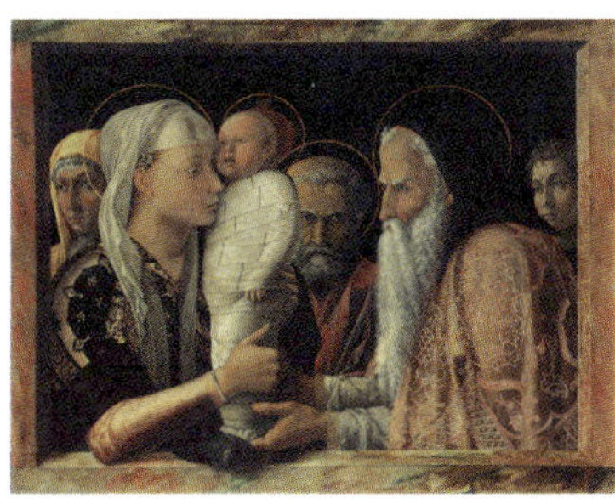

**BR 109**
**Andrea Mantegna (Italian, circa 1431–1506)**
*Presentation of Christ in the Temple*, circa 1454
tempera on canvas, 30⅜ × 37³⁄₁₆ in. (77.1 × 94.4 cm), Kat. 29
Returned after Washington, DC

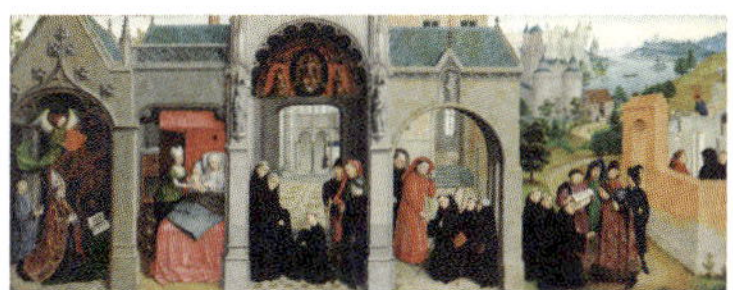

**BR 110**
**Simon Marmion (Flemish, 1420/25–1489)**
*Life of Saint Bertin (Altar of Saint-Omer)* (left wing), 1459
oil on oak panel, 22¹⁄₁₆ × 57⅞ in. (56 × 147 cm), Kat. 1645
Returned after Washington, DC

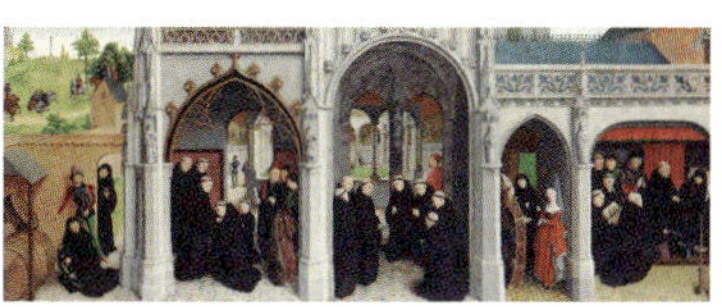

**BR 111**
**Simon Marmion (Flemish, 1420/25–1489)**
*Life of Saint Bertin (Altar of Saint-Omer)* (right wing), 1459
oil on oak panel, 22¹⁄₁₆ × 57⅞ in. (56 × 147 cm), Kat. 1645 A
Returned after Washington, DC

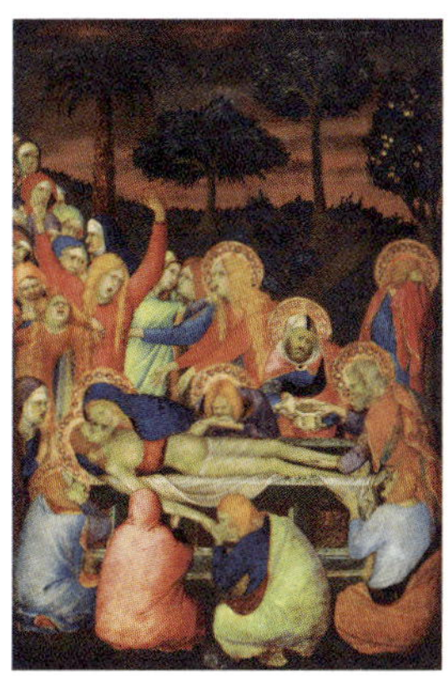

**BR 112**
**Simone Martini (Italian, 1284–1344)**
*The Burial of Christ*, 1335–40
tempera on poplar panel, 9⁵⁄₁₆ × 6⁹⁄₁₆ in. (23.7 × 16.7 cm), Kat. 1070 A
Returned after Boston

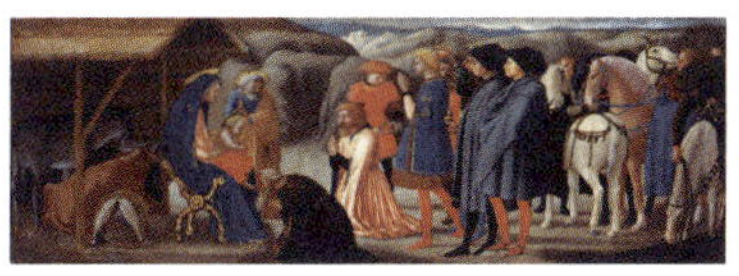

**BR 113 a**
**Masaccio (Italian, 1401–1428)**
*Pisa Altarpiece predella* (middle panel), *Adoration of the Magi*, 1426
tempera on poplar panel, 8¾ × 24⁵⁄₁₆ in. (22.3 × 61.7 cm), Kat. 58 A
Returned after Boston

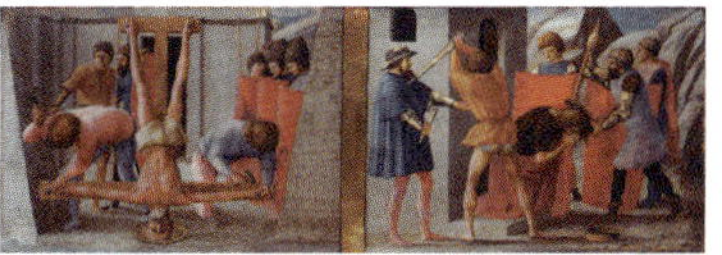

**BR 113 b**
**Masaccio (Italian, 1401–1428)**
*Pisa Altarpiece predella* (left panel), *Martyrdom of Saint Peter and Martyrdom of Saint Paul*, 1426
tempera on poplar panel, 8¾ × 24½ in. (22.3 × 62.2 cm), Kat. 58 B
Returned after Boston

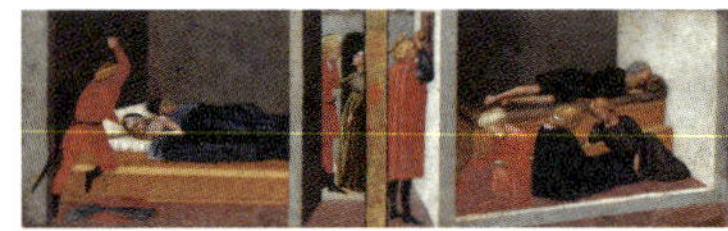

**BR 113 c**
**Masaccio (Italian, 1401–1428) and Workshop**
*Pisa Altarpiece predella* (right panel), *Saint Julian Slays his Parents and Saint Nicholas Endows Three Maidens*, 1426
tempera on poplar panel, 8¾ × 24¹¹⁄₁₆ in. (22.2 × 62.7 cm), Kat. 58 E
Returned after Boston

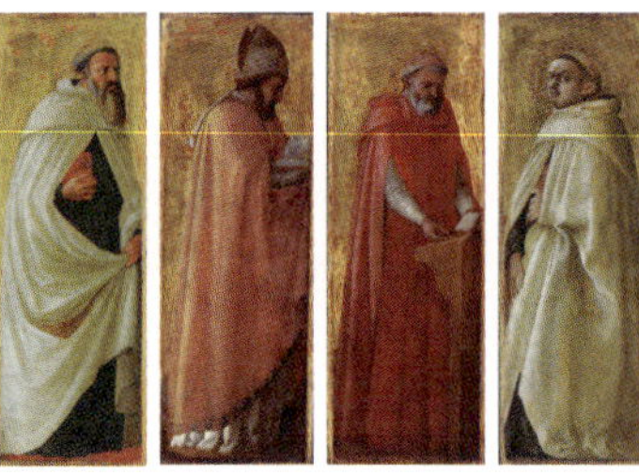

**BR 114**
**Masaccio (Italian, 1401–1428) and Fra Filippo Lippi (Italian, circa 1406–1469)**
*Pisa Altarpiece, Four Saints: An Elderly Carmelite, Saint Augustine, Saint Jerome, and a Young Carmelite*, 1426
tempera and gold on poplar panel, each panel 15⁹⁄₁₆ × 5½ in. (39.5 × 14 cm), Kat. 58 D
Returned after Washington, DC

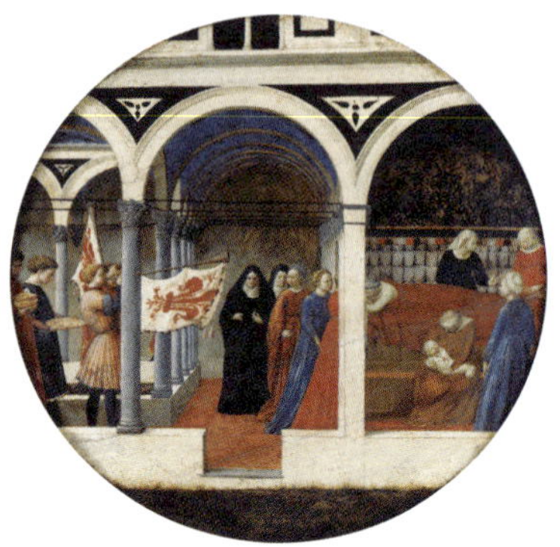

**BR 115**
**Masaccio (Italian, 1401–1428)**
*The Birth of a Florentine*, 1423
tempera on poplar panel, diam. 26 in. (66 cm), Kat. 58 C
Returned after Washington, DC

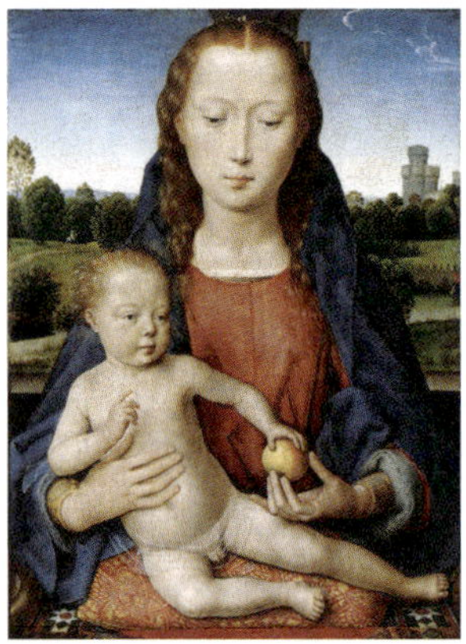

**BR 116**
**Hans Memling (Flemish, 1430/40–1494)**
*Madonna and Child*, 1487
oil on oak panel, 21½ × 17 in. (54.6 × 43.2 cm), Kat. 528 B
Returned after Boston

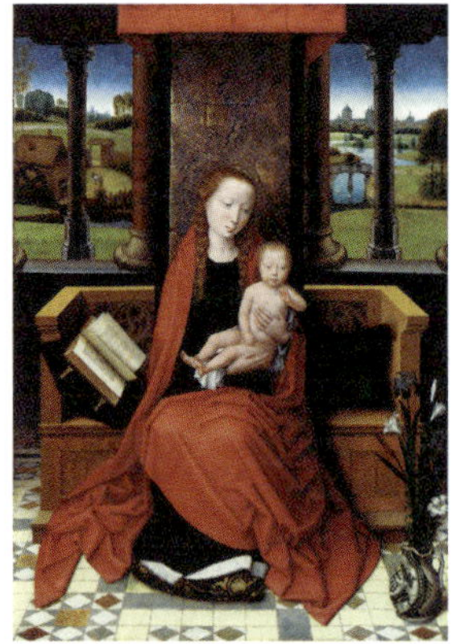

**BR 117**
**Hans Memling (Flemish, 1430/40–1494)**
*Madonna and Child*, circa 1480–90
oil on oak panel, 32¹¹⁄₁₆ × 22¹¹⁄₁₆ in. (83.1 × 57.7 cm), Kat. 529
Shown in all cities

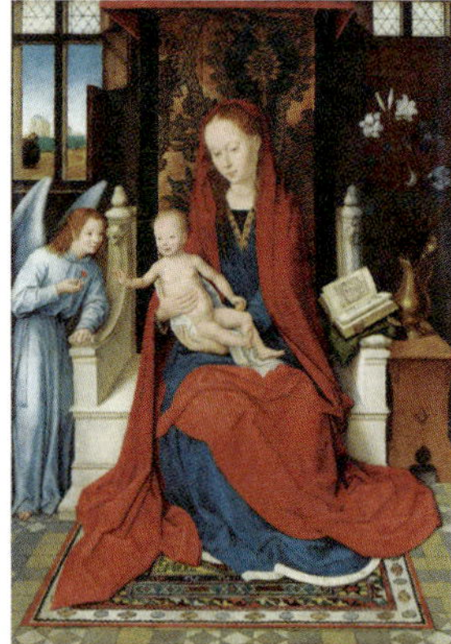

**BR 118**
**Hans Memling (Flemish, 1430/40–1494)**
*Madonna and Child*, circa 1485
oil on oak panel, 27⅜ × 18¹⁵⁄₁₆ in. (69.6 × 48.1 cm), Kat. 529 D
Shown in all cities

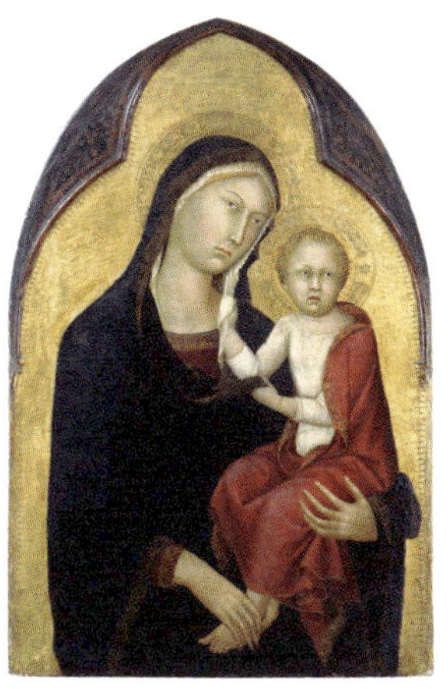

BR 119
**Lippo Memmi (Italian, circa 1291–1356)**
*Madonna and Child*, 14th century
tempera on poplar panel, $33\frac{7}{8}$ × $21\frac{13}{16}$ in. (86.1 × 55.4 cm), Kat. 1067
Returned after Boston

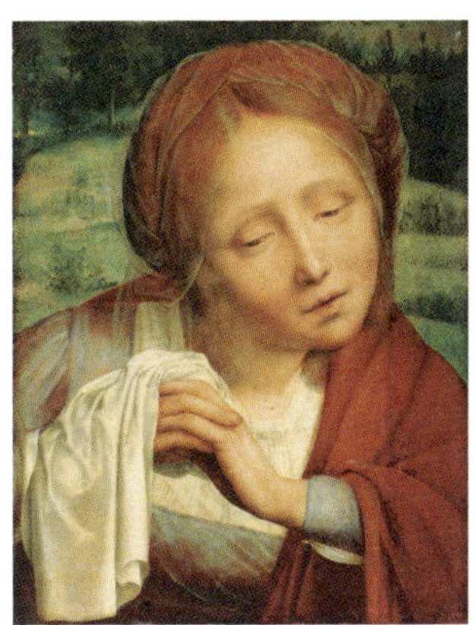

BR 120
**Quentin Massys (Flemish, 1465–1530)**
*The Mourning Magdalene*, circa 1525
oil on oak panel, $13\frac{3}{16}$ × $9\frac{5}{8}$ in. (33.5 × 24.5 cm), Kat. 574 C
Shown in all cities

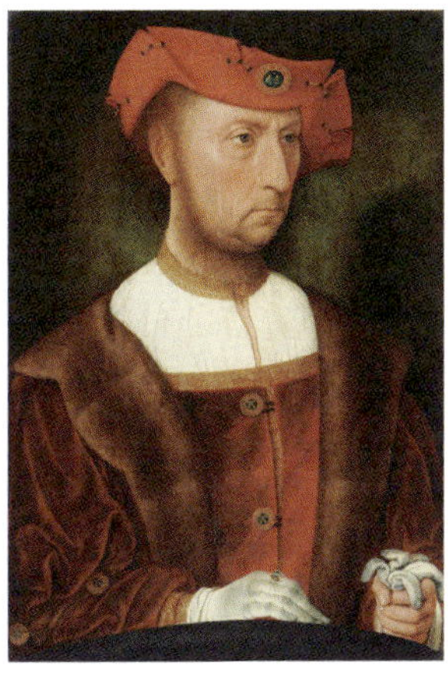

BR 121
**Jan Mostaert (Dutch, circa 1475–1552/53)**
*Portrait of a Man*, circa 1520
oil on oak panel, $16\frac{9}{16}$ × $11\frac{7}{16}$ in. (42 × 29 cm), Kat. 591
Shown in all cities

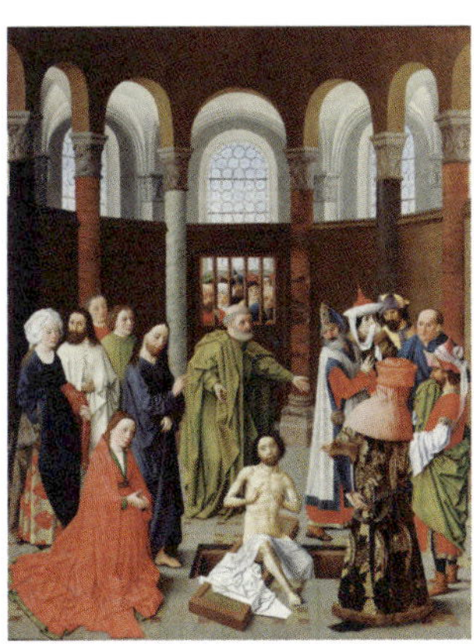

BR 122
**Albert van Ouwater (Dutch, circa 1410–after 1475)**
*The Raising of Lazarus*, circa 1465
oil on oak panel, $48\frac{13}{16}$ × $36\frac{1}{2}$ in. (124 × 92.7 cm), Kat. 532 A
Returned after Washington, DC

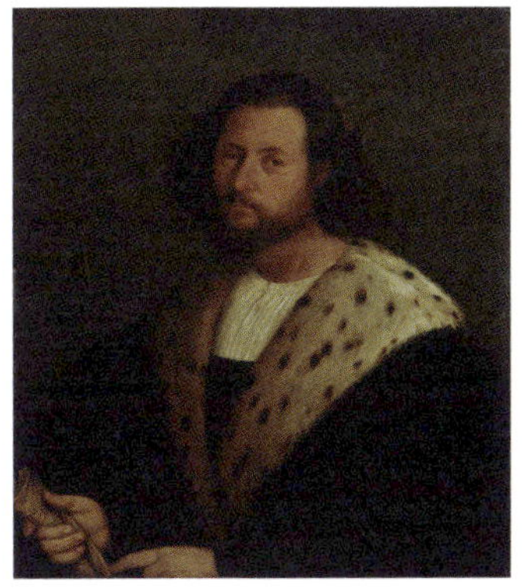

BR 123
**Palma il Vecchio (Italian, 1480–1528)**
*Portrait of a Man in Ermine Fur*, 1510–12
oil on poplar panel, 29 × 24 in. (74 × 61 cm), Kat. 174
Returned after Boston

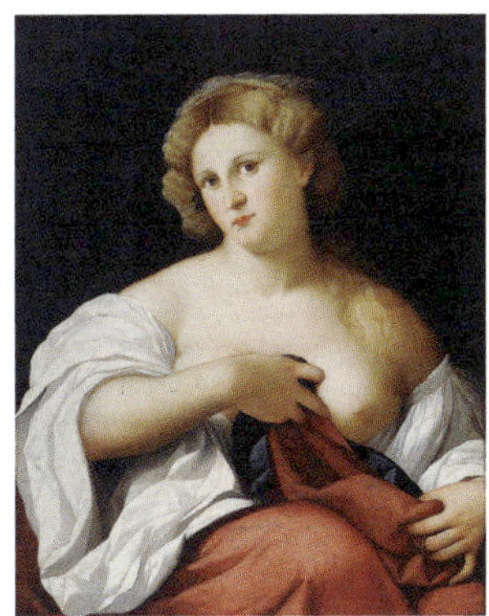

BR 124
**Palma il Vecchio (Italian, 1480–1528)**
*Portrait of a Woman*, 1525
oil on poplar panel, $28\frac{3}{4}$ × $22\frac{13}{16}$ in. (73 × 58 cm), Kat. 197 B
Shown in all cities

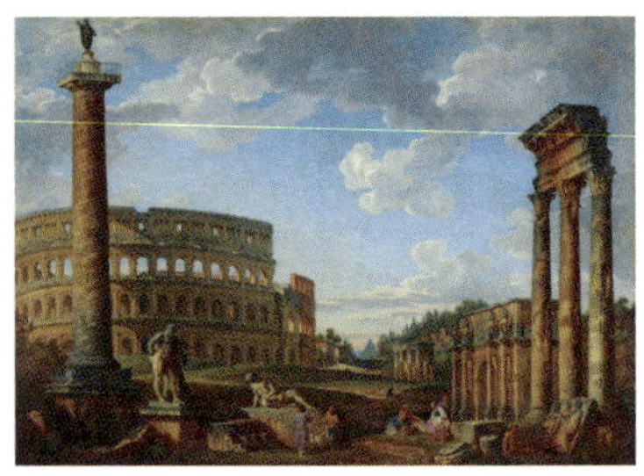

**BR 125**
**Giovanni Paolo Panini (Italian, 1691–1765)**
*Composite View of the Ruins of Rome*, 1735
oil on canvas, $38\frac{9}{16} \times 52\frac{3}{4}$ in.
(98 × 134 cm), Kat. 454 A
Returned after Boston

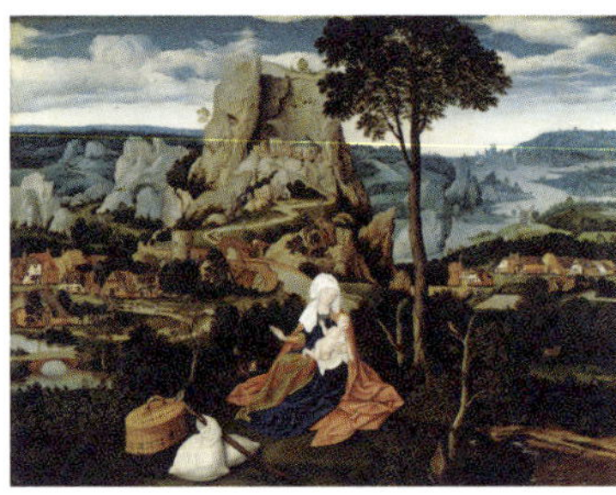

**BR 126**
**Joachim Patinir (Flemish, 1480–1524)**
*Rest on the Flight into Egypt*, circa 1520
oil on oak panel, $25\frac{11}{16} \times 31\frac{7}{8}$ in.
(65.3 × 81 cm), Kat. 608
Shown in all cities

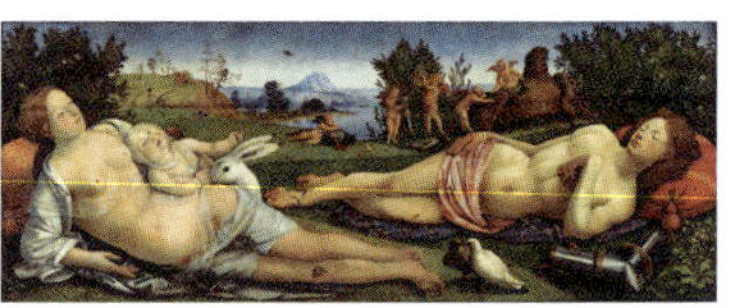

**BR 127**
**Piero di Cosimo (Italian, 1462–1521)**
*Venus, Mars, and Cupid*, circa 1505
oil on poplar panel, $29\frac{5}{16} \times 72\frac{5}{8}$ in.
(74.5 × 184.5 cm), Kat. 107
Returned after Washington, DC

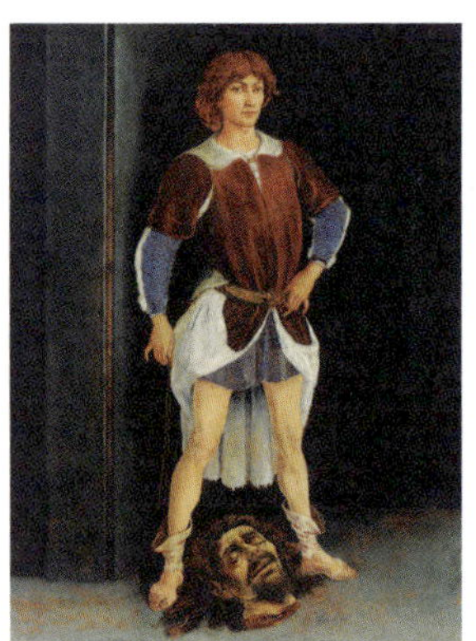

**BR 128**
**Antonio del Pollaiuolo (Italian, 1433–1498) and Piero del Pollaiuolo (Italian, 1443–1496)**
*David with the Head of Goliath*, 1465–70
oil on poplar panel, $19 \times 13\frac{11}{16}$ in.
(48.2 × 34.8 cm), Kat. 73 A
Returned after Washington, DC

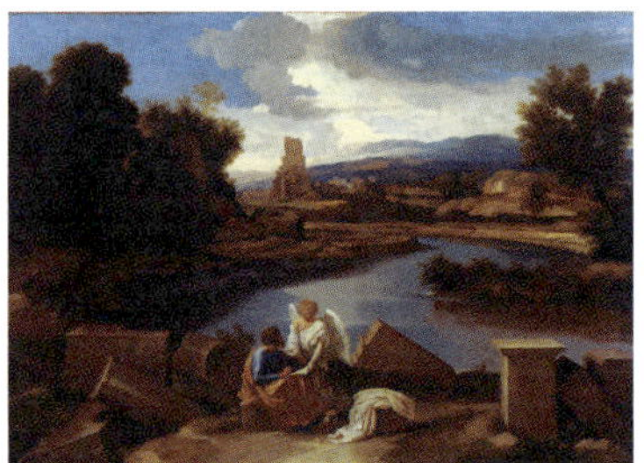

**BR 129**
**Nicolas Poussin (French, 1594–1665)**
*The Roman Campagna with Saint Matthew and the Angel*, 1640
oil on canvas, 39 × 53 in.
(99 × 135 cm), Kat. 478 A
Shown in all cities

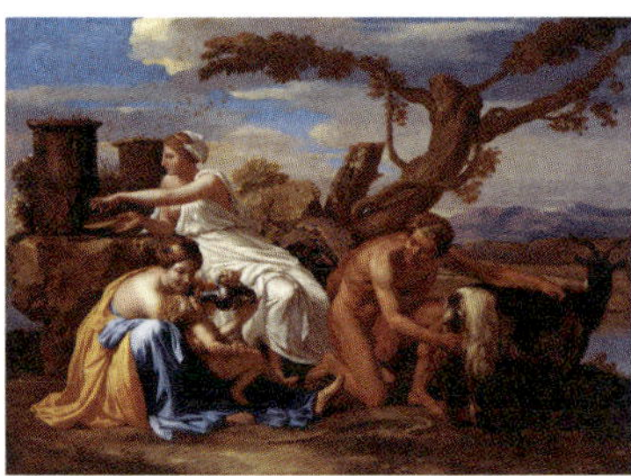

**BR 130**
**Nicolas Poussin (French, 1594–1665)**
*Jupiter as a Child Nourished by the Goat Amalthea*, circa 1639
oil on canvas, $38\frac{3}{16} \times 52\frac{3}{8}$ in.
(97 × 133 cm), Kat. 467
Shown in all cities

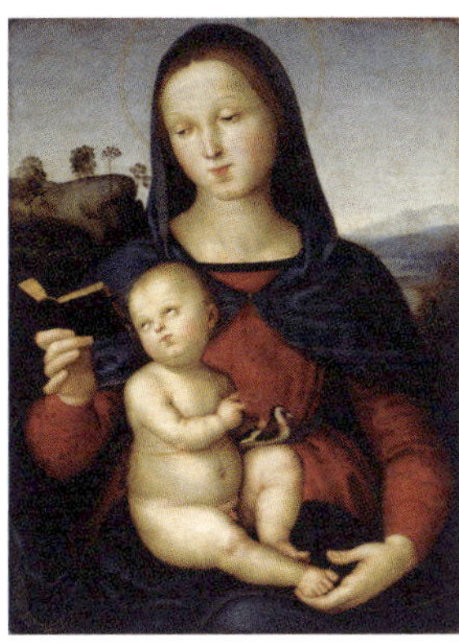

BR 131
**Raphael (Italian, 1483–1520)**
*Madonna and Child (Madonna Solly)*, 1500–1
oil on poplar panel, 20½ × 14¹⁵⁄₁₆ in. (52 × 38 cm), Kat. 141
Returned after Boston

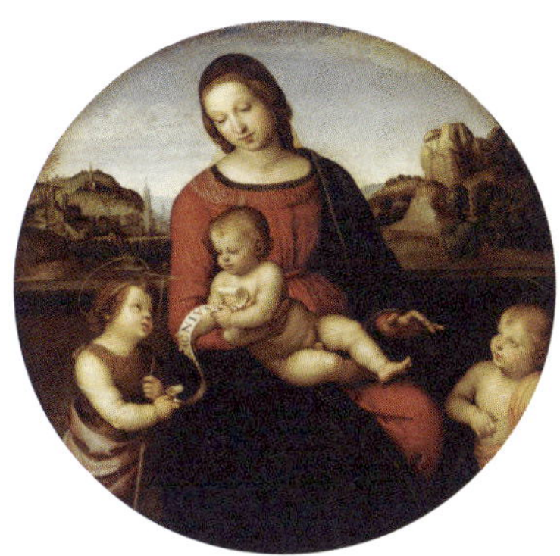

BR 132
**Raphael (Italian, 1483–1520)**
*Madonna and Child with Young Saint John and a Holy Youth (Madonna Terranuova)*, circa 1505
oil on poplar panel, diam. 33⅞ in. (86 cm), Kat. 247 A
Returned after Boston

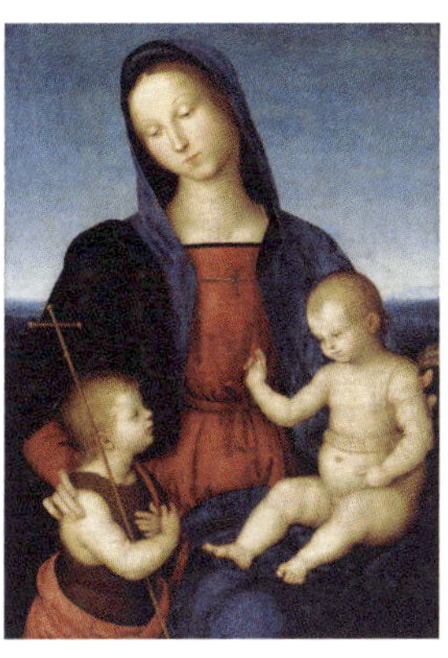

BR 133
**Raphael (Italian, 1483–1520)**
*Madonna and Child with Young Saint John (Madonna Diotallevi)*, circa 1503
oil on poplar panel, 27³⁄₁₆ × 19¹¹⁄₁₆ in. (69 × 50 cm), Kat. 147
Returned after Washington, DC

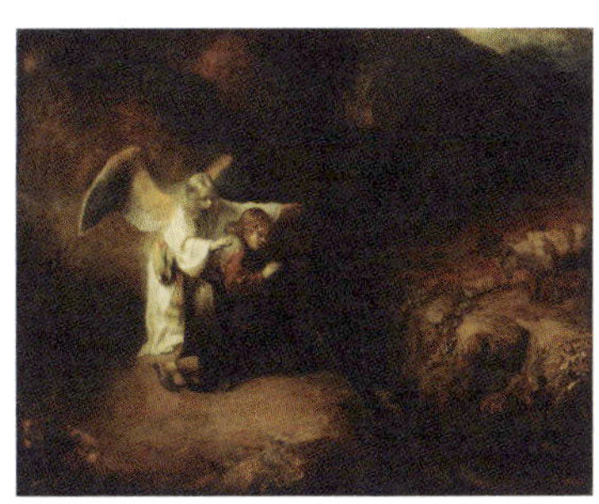

BR 134
**Sir Joshua Reynolds (English, 1723–1792) after Rembrandt, formerly attributed to Rembrandt Harmensz. van Rijn (Dutch, 1606–1669)**
*Daniel's Vision*, 18th century
oil on canvas, 38¾ × 46⅞ in. (98.5 × 119 cm), Kat. 828 F
Shown in all cities

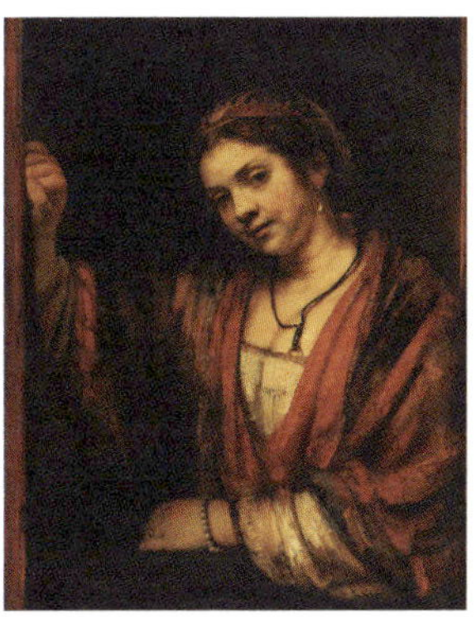

BR 135
**Rembrandt Harmensz. van Rijn (Dutch, 1606–1669)**
*Woman in a Doorway* (formerly titled *Hendrickje Stoffels*), 1654–57
oil on canvas, 34⅞ × 26⅜ in. (88.6 × 67 cm), Kat. 828 B
Shown in all cities

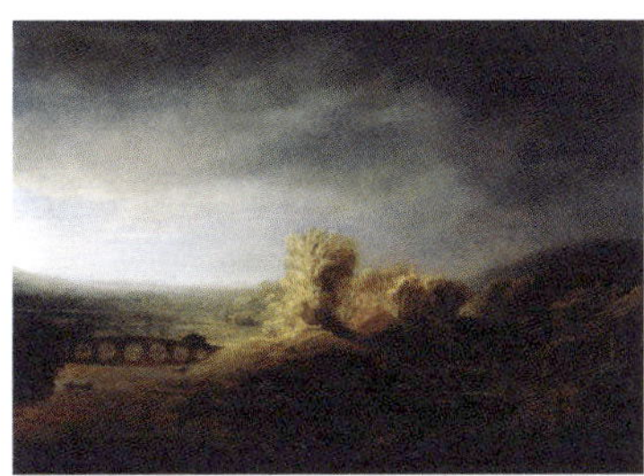

BR 136
**Attributed to Govaert Flinck (Dutch, 1615–1660), formerly attributed to Rembrandt Harmensz. van Rijn (Dutch, 1606–1669)**
*Landscape with an Arched Bridge*, circa 1640
oil on panel, 11¼ × 15⁹⁄₁₆ in. (28.5 × 39.5 cm), Kat. 1932
Returned after Boston

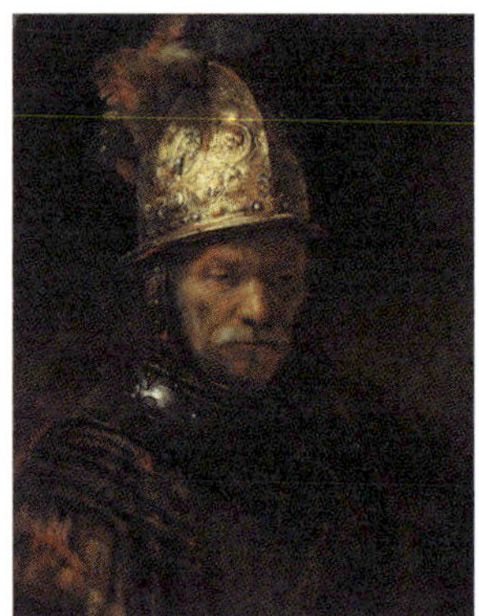

**BR 137**
**Circle of Rembrandt Harmensz. van Rijn (Dutch, 1606–1669), formerly attributed to Rembrandt Harmensz. van Rijn**
*Man with a Golden Helmet*, circa 1650
oil on canvas, 29⁹⁄₁₆ × 19¹⁵⁄₁₆ in.
(67.5 × 50.7 cm), Kat. 811 A
Shown in all cities

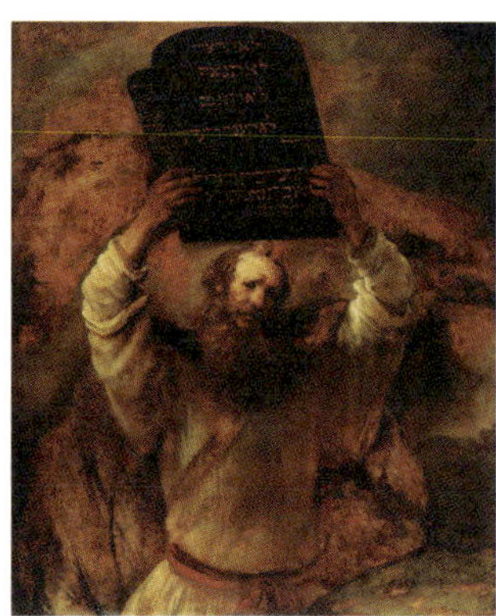

**BR 138**
**Rembrandt Harmensz. van Rijn (Dutch, 1606–1669)**
*Moses Breaking the Tablets of the Law*, 1659
oil on canvas, 66³⁄₁₆ × 53¾ in.
(168.1 × 136.5 cm), Kat. 811
Returned after Boston

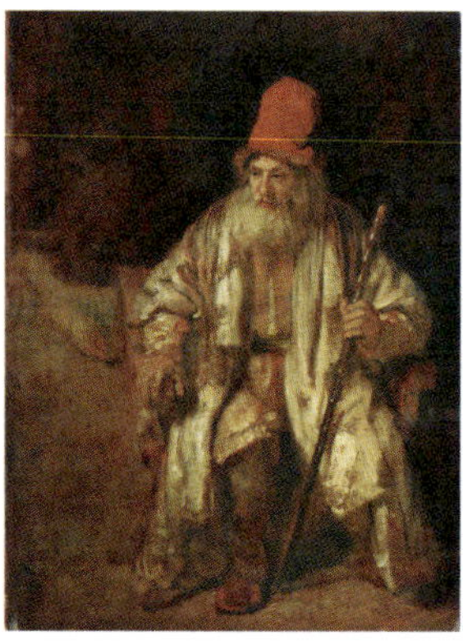

**BR 139**
**Rembrandt Harmensz. van Rijn (Dutch, 1606–1669)**
*Old Man with the Red Cap*, circa 1650
oil on canvas, 20⅝ × 14⁹⁄₁₆ in.
(52.4 × 37 cm), Kat. 828 I
Shown in all cities

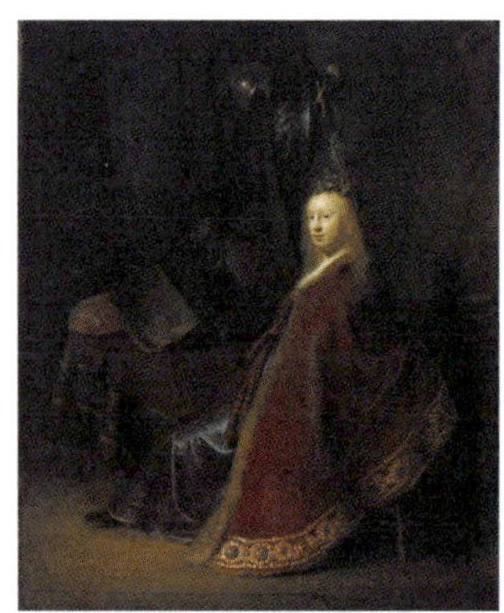

**BR 140**
**Rembrandt Harmensz. van Rijn (Dutch, 1606–1669)**
*Minerva*, circa 1631
oil on oak panel, 23¹³⁄₁₆ × 19⁵⁄₁₆ in.
(60.5 × 49 cm), Kat. 828 C
Returned after Boston

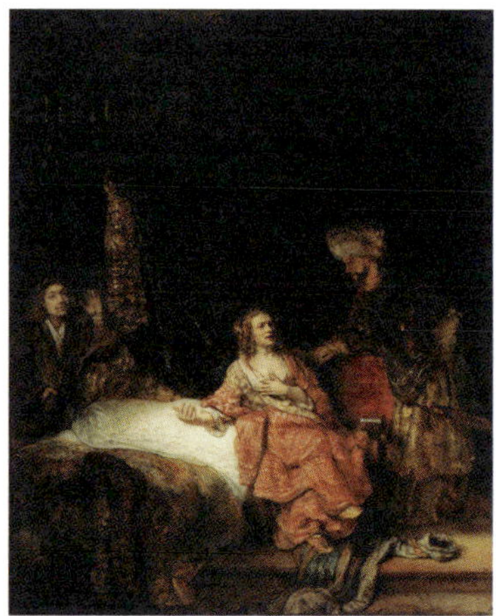

**BR 141**
**Rembrandt Harmensz. van Rijn (Dutch, 1606–1669)**
*Joseph Accused by Potiphar's Wife*, 1655
oil on canvas, 44¹¹⁄₁₆ × 35⅞ in.
(113.5 × 90 cm), Kat. 828 H
Shown in all cities

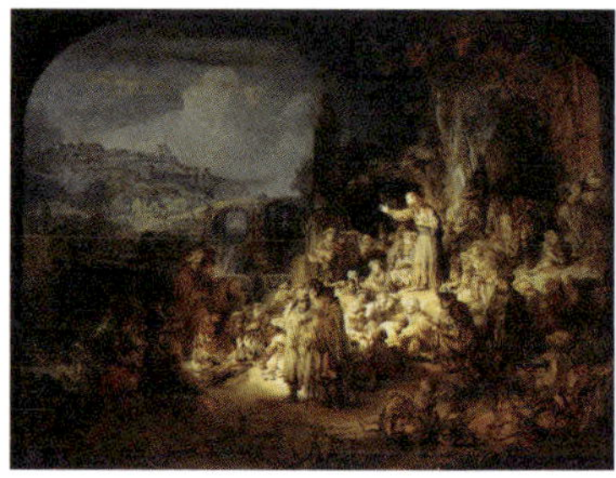

**BR 142**
**Rembrandt Harmensz. van Rijn (Dutch, 1606–1669)**
*The Preaching of John the Baptist*, 1634–36
oil on canvas, 24¹¹⁄₁₆ × 31¹⁵⁄₁₆ in.
(62.7 × 81.1 cm), Kat. 828 K
Shown in all cities

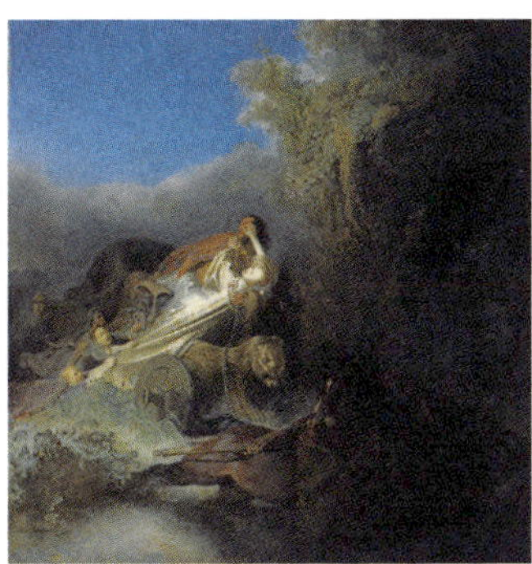

**BR 143**
**Rembrandt Harmensz. van Rijn (Dutch, 1606–1669)**
*Rape of Proserpina*, circa 1631
oil on oak panel, 33¼ × 31⁵⁄₁₆ in. (84.4 × 79.5 cm), Kat. 823
Returned after Washington, DC

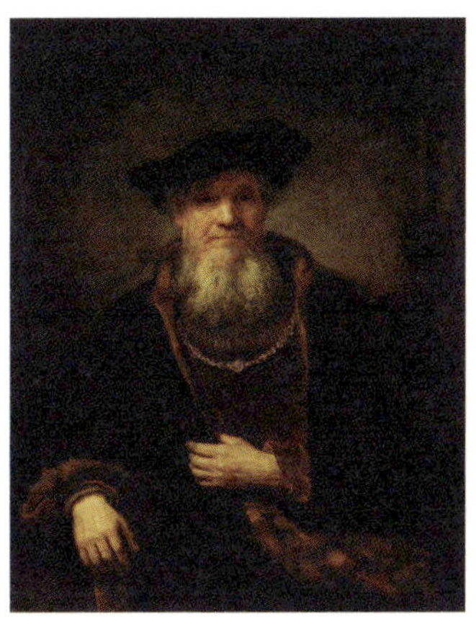

**BR 144**
**Rembrandt Harmensz. van Rijn (Dutch, 1606–1669)**
*Portrait of an Old Man* (formerly titled *A Rabbi*), 1645
oil on canvas, 43⁵⁄₁₆ × 32⁵⁄₁₆ in. (110 × 82 cm), Kat. 828 A
Shown in all cities

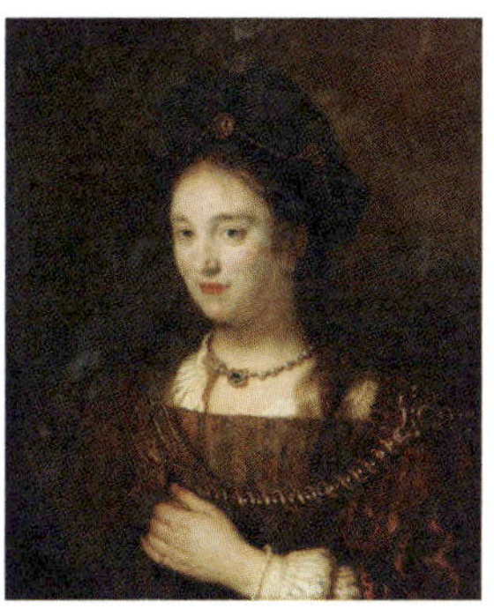

**BR 145**
**Studio of Rembrandt Harmensz. van Rijn (Dutch, 1606–1669), formerly attributed to Rembrandt Harmensz. van Rijn**
*Half-Figure of a Woman with a Beret* (formerly titled *Saskia*), 1643
oil on mahogany panel, 29 × 23⅝ in. (74 × 60 cm), Kat. 812
Returned after Washington, DC

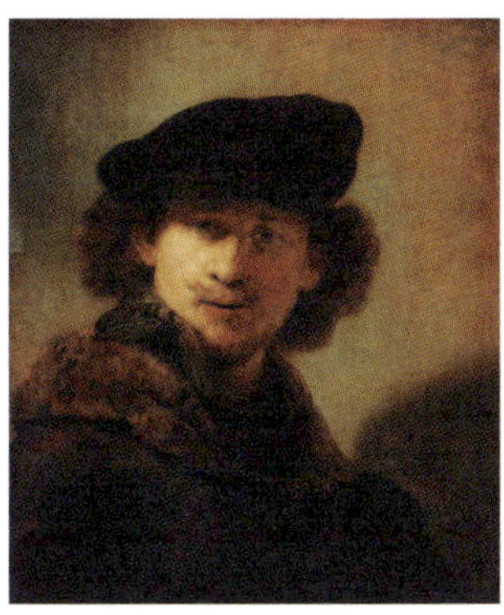

**BR 146**
**Rembrandt Harmensz. van Rijn (Dutch, 1606–1669)**
*Self-Portrait*, 1634
oil on oak panel, 23 × 18¾ in. (58.4 × 47.7 cm), Kat. 810
Shown in all cities

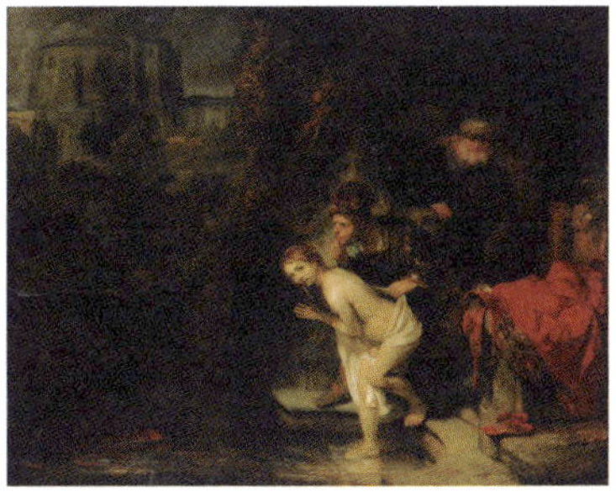

**BR 147**
**Rembrandt Harmensz. van Rijn (Dutch, 1606–1669)**
*Susanna and the Elders*, 1647
oil on tropical wood panel, 30³⁄₁₆ × 36⁹⁄₁₆ in. (76.7 × 92.9 cm), Kat. 828 E
Shown in all cities

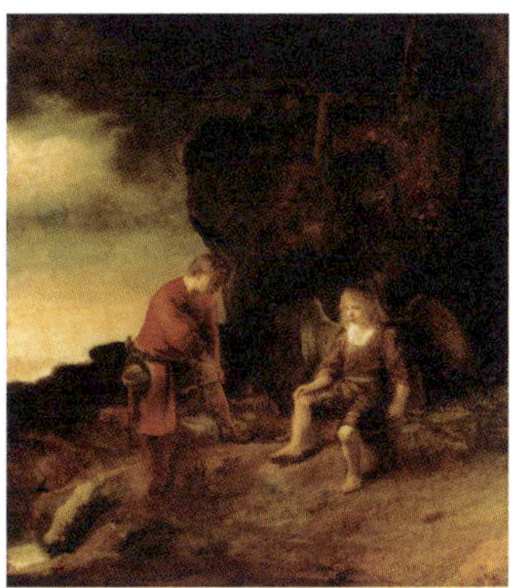

**BR 148**
**Attributed to Abraham van Dijck (Dutch, 1635–1680), formerly attributed to Rembrandt Harmensz. van Rijn (Dutch, 1606–1669)**
*Tobias and the Angel*, 1650
oil on canvas, 33⅞ × 29 in. (86 × 74 cm), Kat. 828 N
Shown in all cities

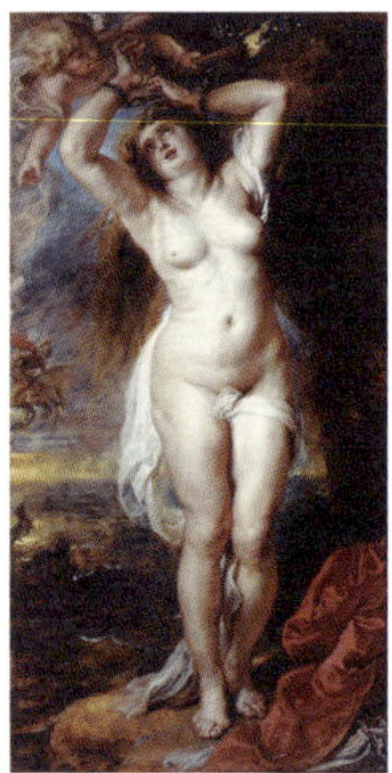

**BR 149**
**Peter Paul Rubens (Flemish, 1577–1640)**
*Andromeda*, circa 1638
oil on oak panel, 74¼ × 36¹⁵⁄₁₆ in. (188.6 × 93.8 cm) Kat. 776 C
Returned after Boston

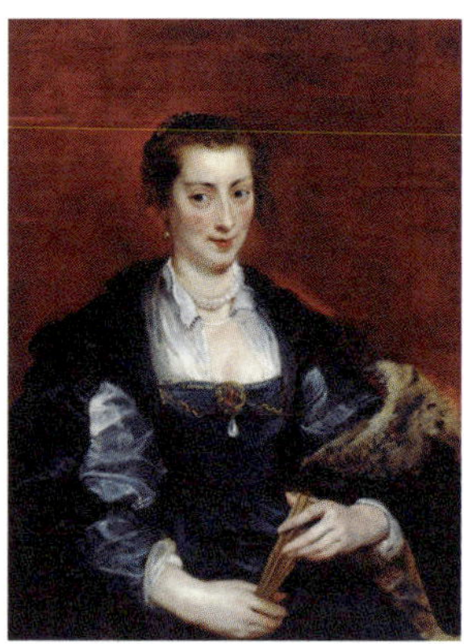

**BR 150**
**Peter Paul Rubens (Flemish, 1577–1640)**
*Portrait of a Woman* (formerly titled *Isabella Brandt*), 1622–26
oil on oak panel, 38⁷⁄₁₆ × 28¼ in. (97.7 × 71.8 cm), Kat. 762 A
Returned after Washington, DC

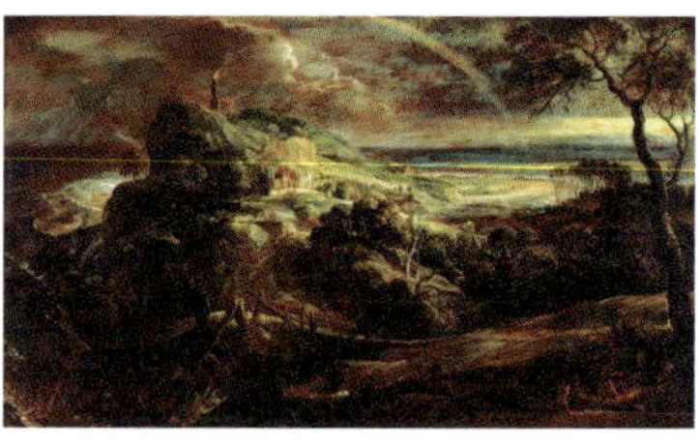

**BR 151**
**Peter Paul Rubens (Flemish, 1577–1640)**
*Landscape with the Shipwreck of Paul* (formerly titled *Landscape with the Shipwreck of Aeneas*), 1620–25
oil on canvas, 24⁵⁄₁₆ × 39½ in. (61.7 × 100.3 cm), Kat. KFMV 776 E
Shown in all cities

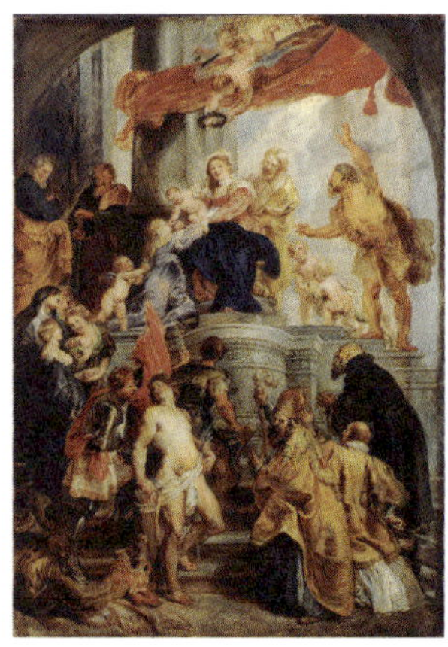

**BR 152**
**Peter Paul Rubens (Flemish, 1577–1640)**
*Madonna and Child Enthroned with Saints*, circa 1627–28
oil on oak panel, 31 × 21⅝ in. (79 × 55 cm), Kat. 780
Shown in all cities

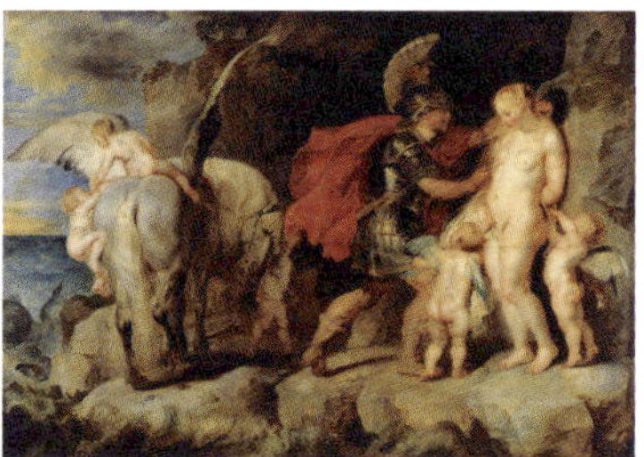

**BR 153**
**Peter Paul Rubens (Flemish, 1577–1640)**
*Perseus Frees Andromeda*, 1620–22
oil on oak panel, 39¼ × 54¹⁵⁄₁₆ in. (99.7 × 139.6 cm), Kat. 785
Returned after Washington, DC

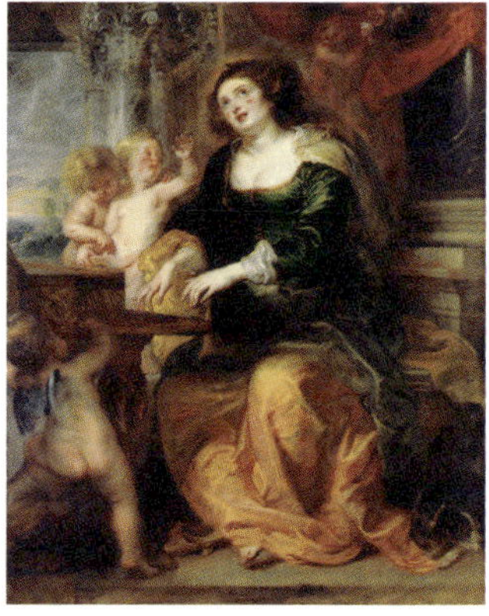

**BR 154**
**Peter Paul Rubens (Flemish, 1577–1640)**
*Saint Cecelia*, 1639–40
oil on oak panel, 71 × 56³⁄₁₆ in. (180.6 × 142.7 cm), Kat. 781
Returned after Boston

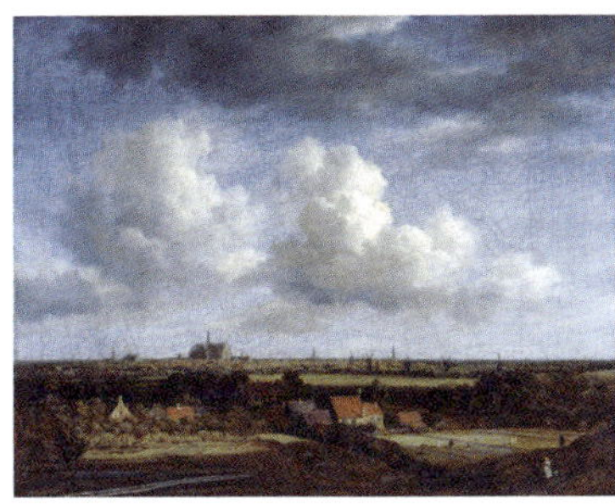

**BR 155**
**Jacob van Ruisdael (Dutch, 1628–1682)**
*Landscape with a View of Haarlem*, circa 1670
oil on canvas, 21⁵⁄₁₆ × 26⁵⁄₁₆ in. (54.1 × 66.9 cm), Kat. 885 C
Shown in all cities

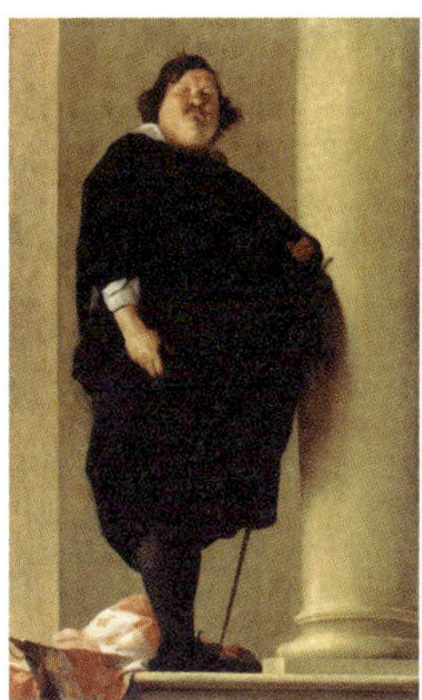

**BR 156**
**Attributed to Charles Mellin (French, 1597–1649), formerly attributed to Andrea Sacchi (Italian, 1599–1661)**
*Portrait of a Man* (formerly titled *Alessandro del Borro*), circa 1630
oil on canvas, 79¹⁵⁄₁₆ × 47⁵⁄₈ in. (203 × 121 cm), Kat. 413 A
Shown in all cities

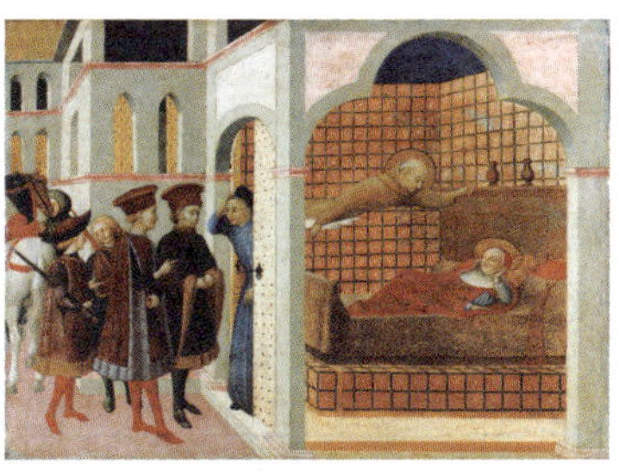

**BR 157**
**Stefano di Giovanni Sassetta (Italian, 1392–1451)**
*The Blessed Ranieri of Borgo San Sepolcro Appears to a Roman Cardinal in His Sleep* (formerly titled *Episode from the Legend of Saint Francis*), 1444
oil on poplar panel, 17¹⁵⁄₁₆ × 23⁹⁄₁₆ in. (45.5 × 59.8 cm), Kat. 1945
Shown in all cities

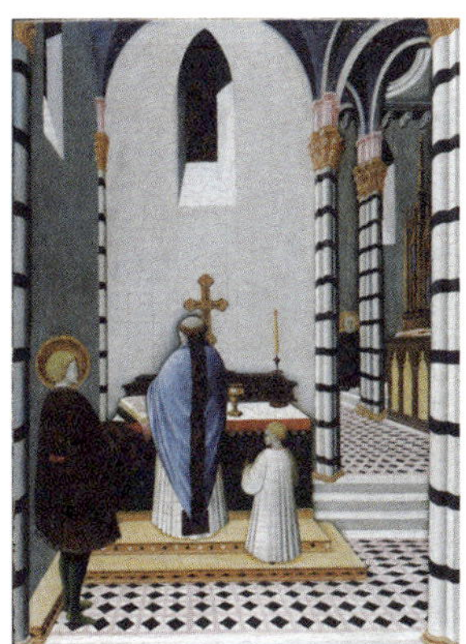

**BR 158**
**Sano di Pietro (Italian, 1405–1481), formerly attributed to Stefano di Giovanni Sassetta (Italian, 1392–1451)**
*The Mass of Saint Anthony Abbot*, circa 1435
oil on poplar panel, 18⁷⁄₁₆ × 13 in. (46.8 × 33.4 cm), Kat. 63
Returned after Boston

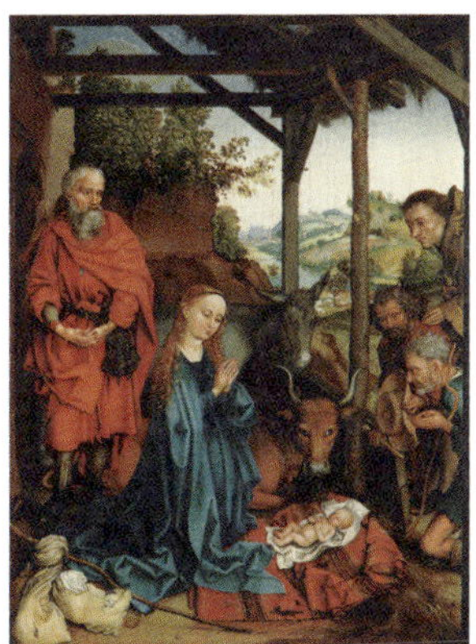

**BR 159**
**Martin Schongauer (German, 1430/50–1491)**
*The Nativity*, circa 1475
oil on oak panel, 15³⁄₁₆ × 11 in. (38.6 × 27.9 cm), Kat. 1629
Returned after Boston

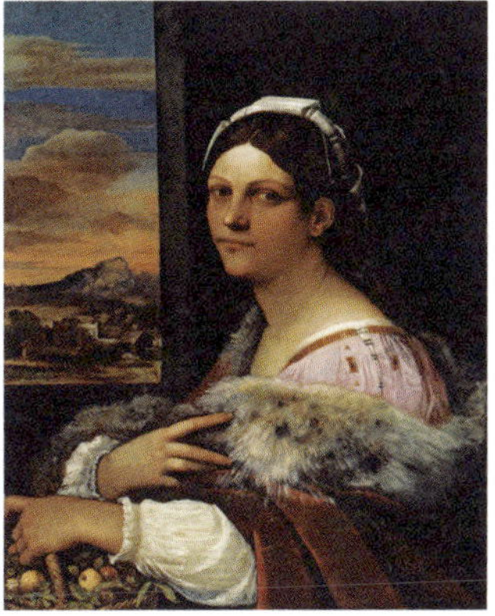

**BR 160**
**Sebastiano del Piombo (Italian, 1485–1547)**
*Portrait of a Young Roman Woman*, circa 1512–13
oil on poplar panel, 30⁹⁄₁₆ × 24 in. (77.7 × 61.3 cm), Kat. 259 B
Returned after Boston

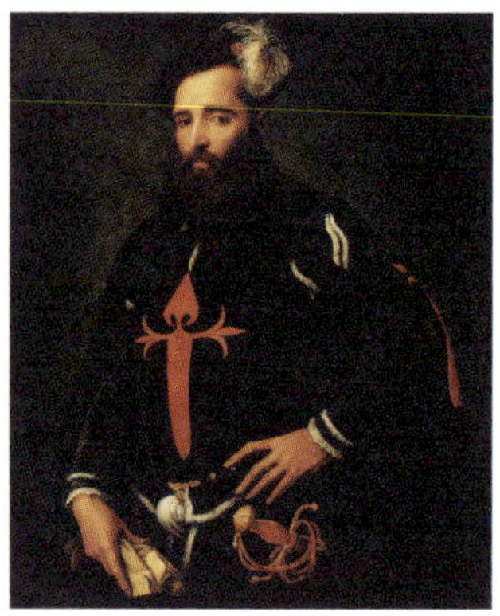

**BR 161**
**Niccolò dell'Abate (Italian, 1509/12–1571), formerly attributed to Sebastiano del Piombo (Italian, 1485–1547)**
*Portrait of a Knight of the Order of Santiago*, 16th century
oil on canvas, 43 11/16 × 35 13/16 in. (111 × 91 cm), Kat. 259 A
Shown in all cities

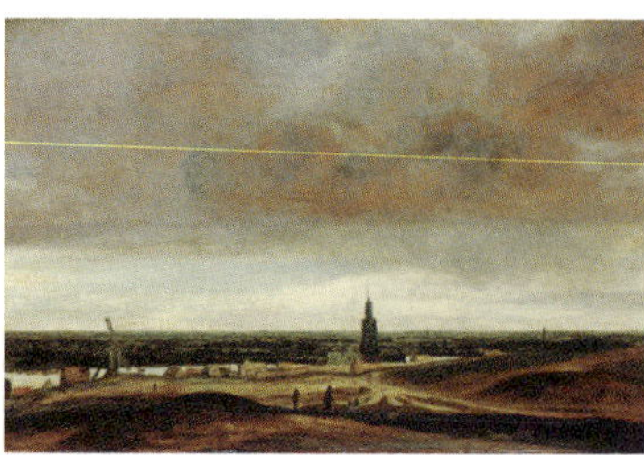

**BR 162**
**Hercules Seghers (Dutch, 1589/90–before 1640)**
*View of Rhenen*, 1620–30
oil on oak panel, 16¾ × 26 1/16 in. (42.6 × 66.2 cm), Kat. 808 A
Shown in all cities

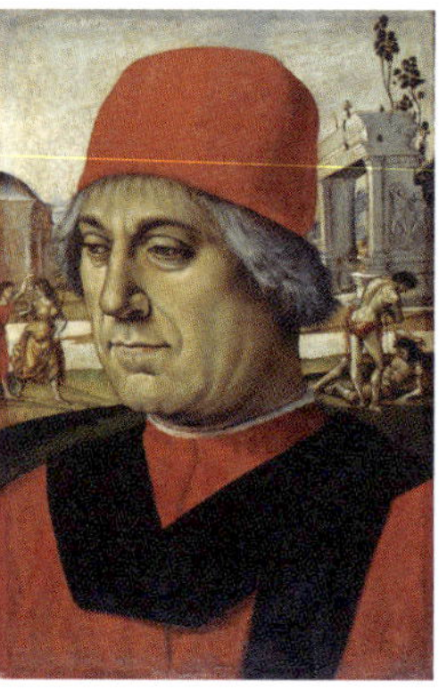

**BR 163**
**Luca Signorelli (Italian, 1441–1523)**
*Portrait of an Elderly Man*, circa 1492
oil on poplar panel, 19 11/16 × 12⅝ in. (50 × 32 cm), Kat. 79 C
Returned after Boston

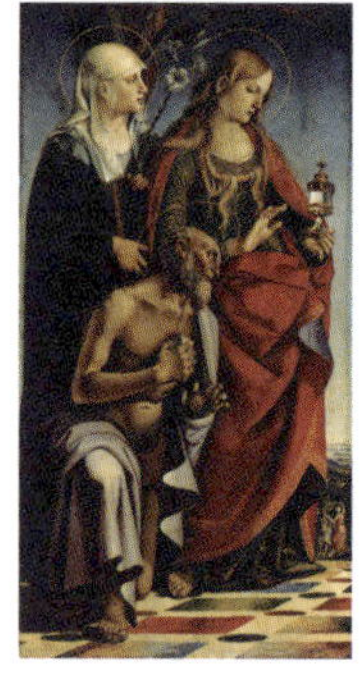
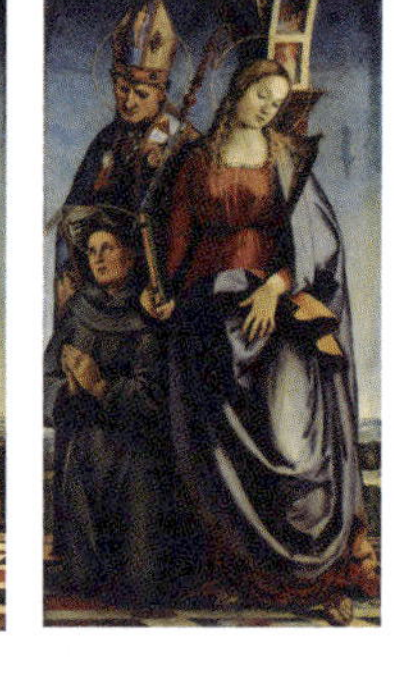

**BR 164**
**Luca Signorelli (Italian, 1441–1523)**
*Two Side Panels of an Altarpiece: Saint Eustachia, Mary Magdalene, and Saint Jerome* (left panel) and *Saint Augustine, Saint Anthony of Padua, and Saint Catherine of Alexandria* (right panel), circa 1498
oil on poplar panel, each panel 57 11/16 × 29¾ in. (146.5 × 75.5 cm), Kat. 79
Returned after Washington, DC

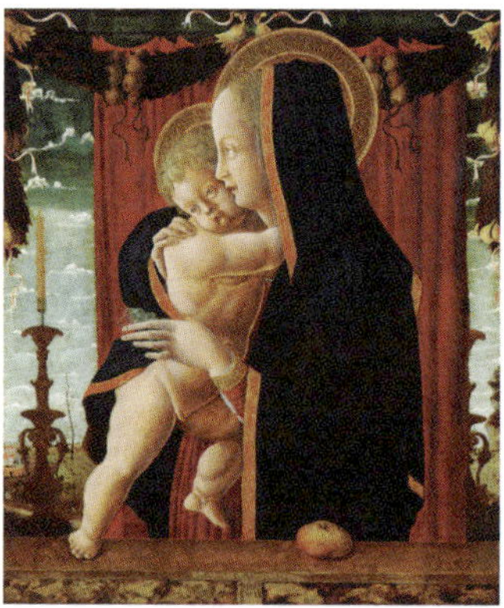

**BR 165**
**Francesco Squarcione (Italian, 1397–1468)**
*Madonna and Child*, circa 1455
tempera on poplar panel, 32 5/16 × 27⅜ in. (82 × 69.5 cm), Kat. 27 A
Returned after Boston

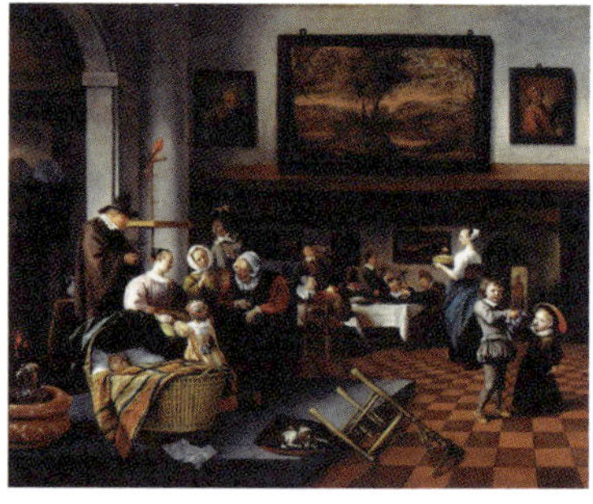

**BR 166**
**Jan Steen (Dutch, 1625/26–1679)**
*"So de Oude songen, so pypen de Jongen"* (formerly titled *Baptismal Party*), 1665–70
oil on canvas, 33½ × 39 9/16 in. (85.1 × 100.5 cm), Kat. 795 D
Shown in all cities

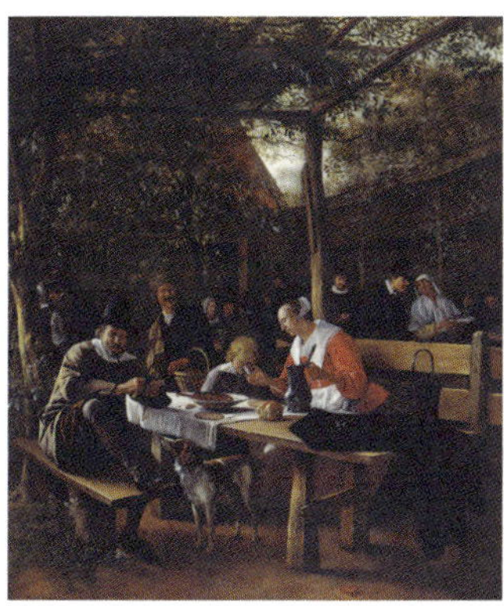

**BR 167**
**Jan Steen (Dutch, 1625/26–1679)**
*The Tavern Garden* (or *The Garden of the Inn*), 1661–63
oil on canvas, $27\frac{7}{16} \times 23\frac{1}{16}$ in.
(69.7 × 58.6 cm), Kat. 795
Shown in all cities

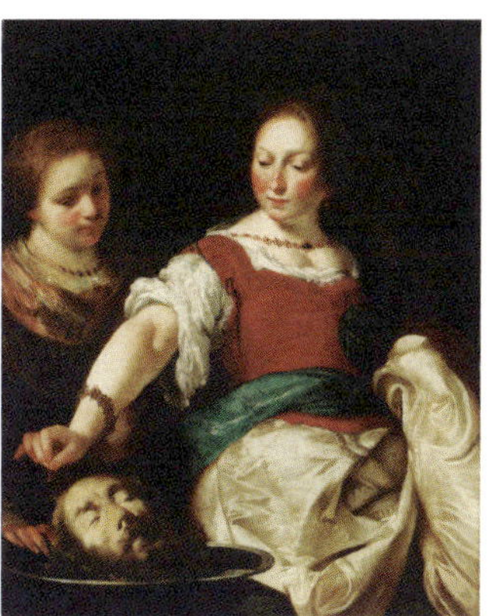

**BR 168**
**Bernardo Strozzi (Italian, 1581–1644)**
*Salome with the Head of John the Baptist* (formerly titled *Judith with the Head of Holofernes*), after 1630
oil on canvas, $49\frac{13}{16} \times 37$ in.
(124 × 94 cm), Kat. KFMV 1727
Shown in all cities

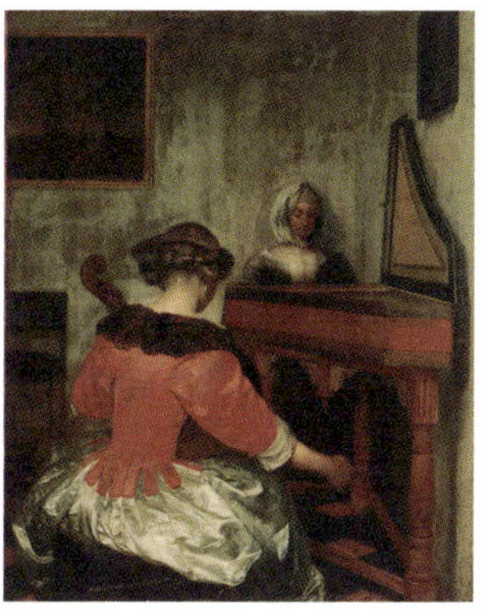

**BR 169**
**Gerard ter Borch (Dutch, 1617–1681)**
*The Concert*, circa 1675
oil on oak panel, $22\frac{1}{16} \times 17\frac{5}{16}$ in.
(56 × 44 cm), Kat. 791 G
Returned after Boston

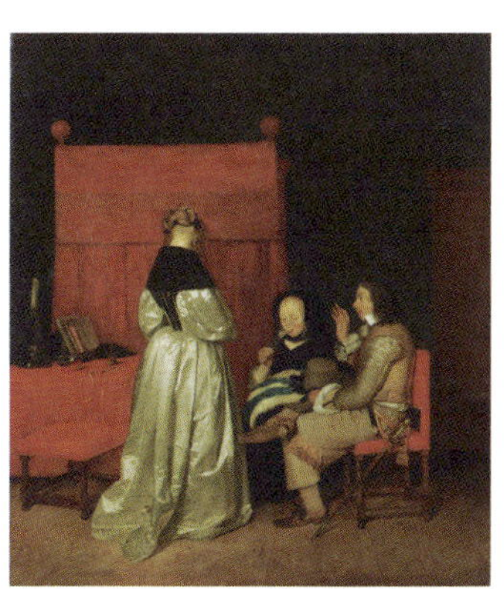

**BR 170**
**Gerard ter Borch (Dutch, 1617–1681)**
*Gallant Conversation* (formerly titled *Fatherly Advice*), 1654–55
oil on canvas, $28 \times 24\frac{7}{16}$ in.
(71.4 × 62.1 cm), Kat. 791
Shown in all cities

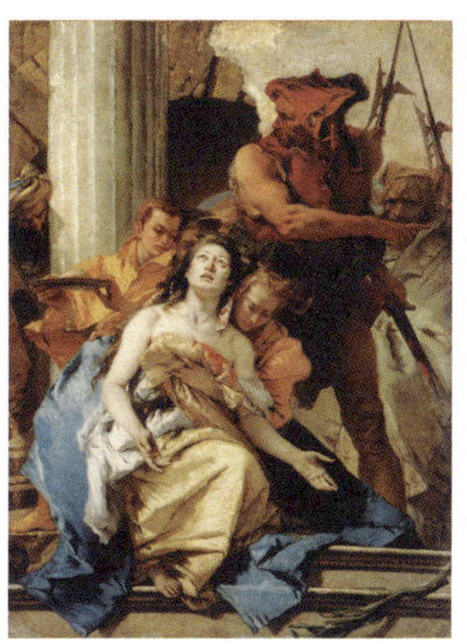

**BR 171**
**Giovanni Battista Tiepolo (Italian, 1696–1770)**
*Martyrdom of Saint Agatha*, circa 1750
oil on canvas, $72\frac{7}{16} \times 51\frac{9}{16}$ in.
(184 × 131 cm), Kat. 459 B
Shown in all cities

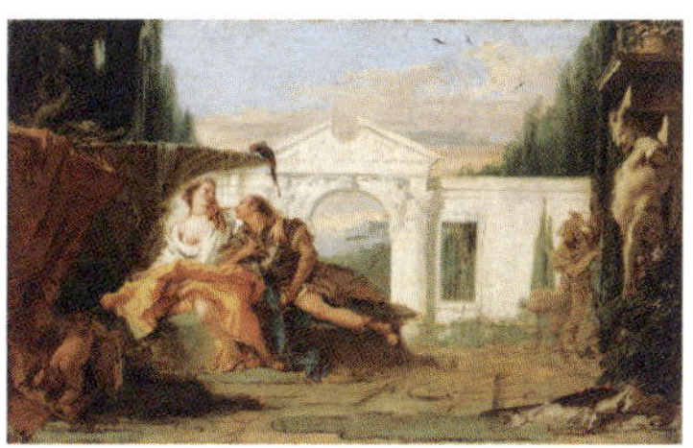

**BR 172**
**Giovanni Battista Tiepolo (Italian, 1696–1770)**
*Rinaldo in Armida's Enchanted Garden*, circa 1755–60
oil on canvas, $15\frac{3}{8} \times 24\frac{7}{16}$ in.
(39 × 62 cm), Kat. 459 D
Shown in all cities

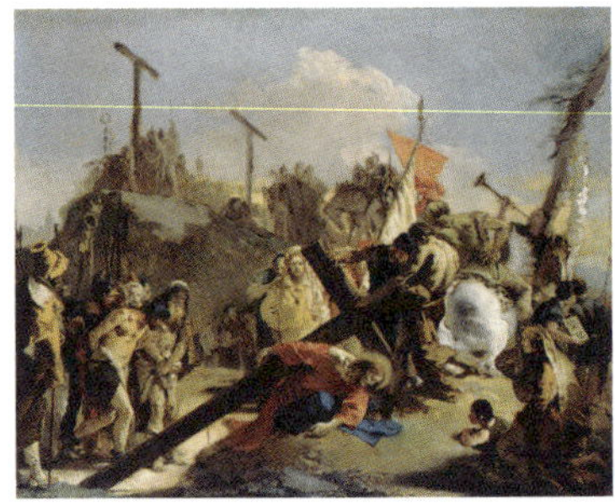

**BR 173**
**Giovanni Battista Tiepolo (Italian, 1696–1770)**
*Christ Bearing the Cross* (formerly titled *Via Crucis*), circa 1738
oil on canvas, 20½ × 24¹³⁄₁₆ in.
(52 × 63 cm), Kat. 459 C
Shown in all cities

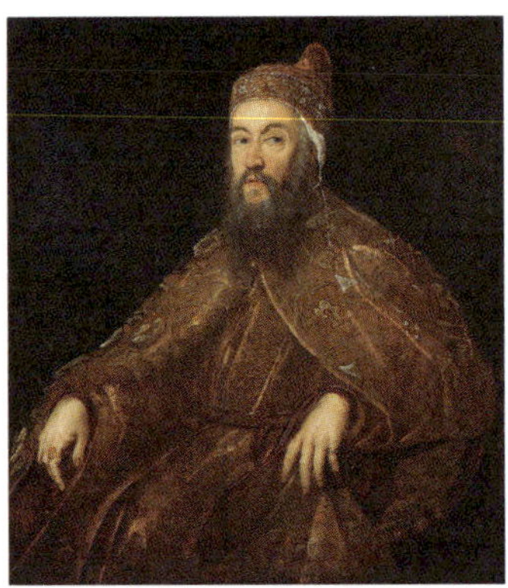

**BR 174**
**Workshop of Jacopo Tintoretto (Italian, 1518–1594), formerly attributed to Jacopo Tintoretto**
*Doge Alvise Mocenigo*, circa 1577
oil on canvas, 43⁵⁄₁₆ × 37⅜ in.
(110 × 95 cm), Kat. 2145
Shown in all cities

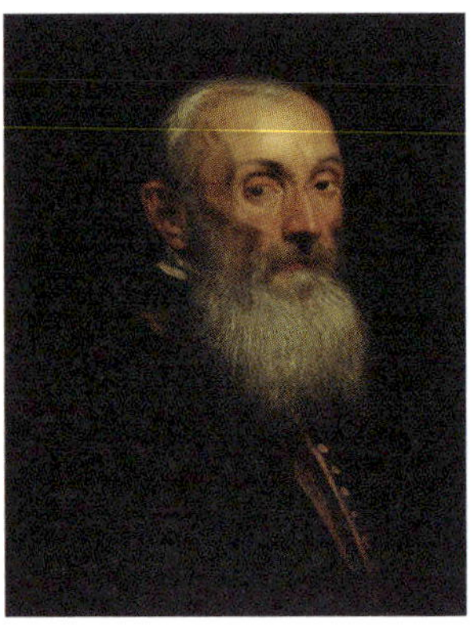

**BR 175**
**Jacopo Tintoretto (Italian, 1518–1594)**
*Giovanni Mocenigo* (formerly titled *Portrait of a Man with a Long White Beard*), before 1580
oil on canvas, 22¹³⁄₁₆ × 17⁵⁄₁₆ in.
(58 × 44 cm), Kat. 298 B
Shown in all cities

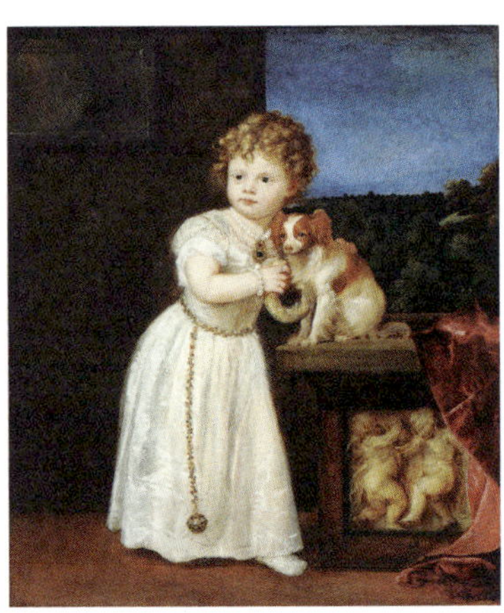

**BR 176**
**Titian (Italian, circa 1488–1576)**
*Clarissa Strozzi at Two Years Old*, 1542
oil on canvas, 47¹⁵⁄₁₆ × 41³⁄₁₆ in.
(121.7 × 104.6 cm), Kat. 160 A
Shown in all cities

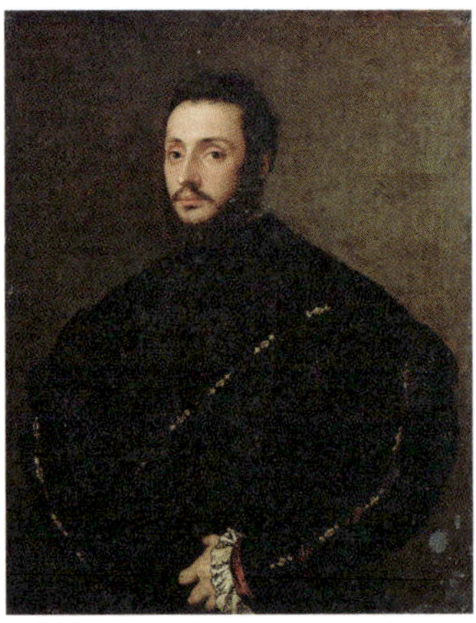

**BR 177**
**Titian (Italian, circa 1488–1576)**
*Portrait of a Young Man*, circa 1525
oil on canvas, 37 × 28⅜ in.
(94 × 72 cm), Kat. 301
Shown in all cities

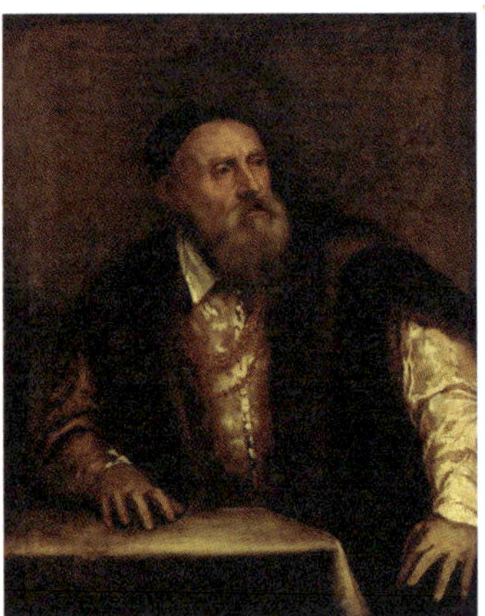

**BR 178**
**Titian (Italian, circa 1488–1576)**
*Self-Portrait*, circa 1560
oil on canvas, 39⁷⁄₁₆ × 30⁵⁄₁₆ in.
(100.1 × 77 cm), Kat. 163
Shown in all cities

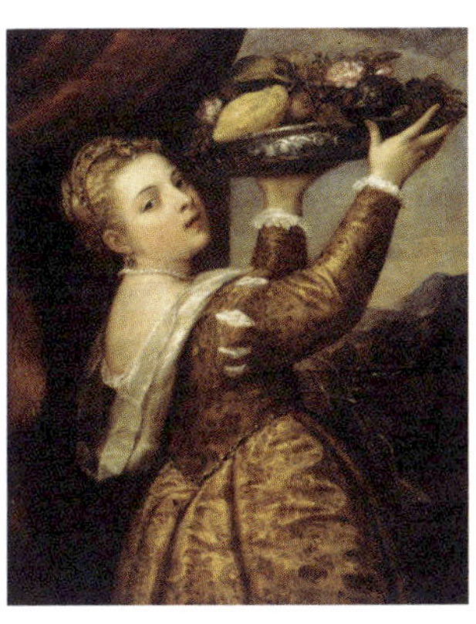

**BR 179**
**Titian (Italian, circa 1488–1576)**
*Girl with a Platter of Fruit* (formerly titled *Titian's Daughter Lavinia*), circa 1555
oil on canvas, $41\frac{13}{16} \times 33\frac{3}{8}$ in.
(106.2 × 84.8 cm), Kat. 166
Shown in all cities

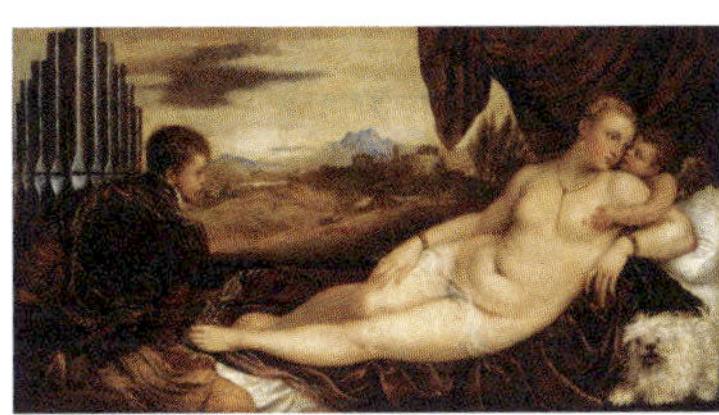

**BR 180**
**Titian (Italian, circa 1488–1576)**
*Venus with the Organ Player*, 1550–52
oil on canvas, $45\frac{1}{4} \times 82\frac{11}{16}$ in.
(115 × 210 cm), Kat. 1849
Shown in all cities

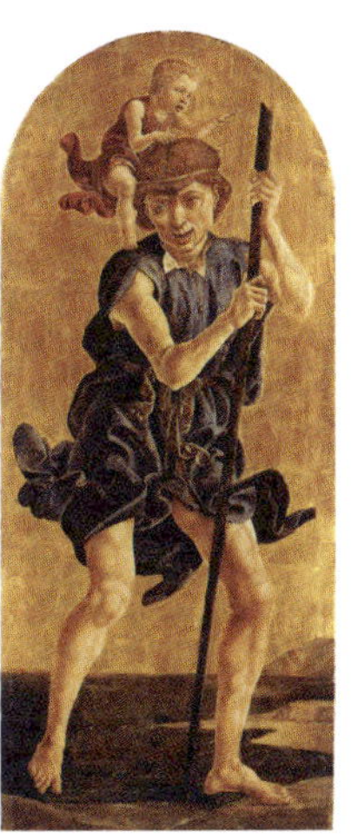

**BR 181**
**Cosmè Tura (Italian, circa 1430–1495)**
*Saint Christopher*, circa 1460–65
oil on poplar panel, $30\frac{1}{4} \times 13\frac{7}{16}$ in.
(76.9 × 34.1 cm), Kat. 1170 C
Returned after Boston

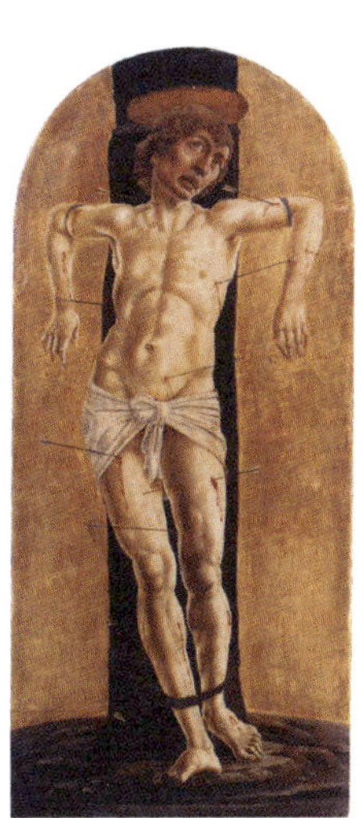

**BR 182**
**Cosmè Tura (Italian, circa 1430–1495)**
*Saint Sebastian*, 15th century
oil on poplar panel, $29\frac{3}{4} \times 13$ in.
(75.6 × 33.3 cm), Kat. 1170 B
Returned after Boston

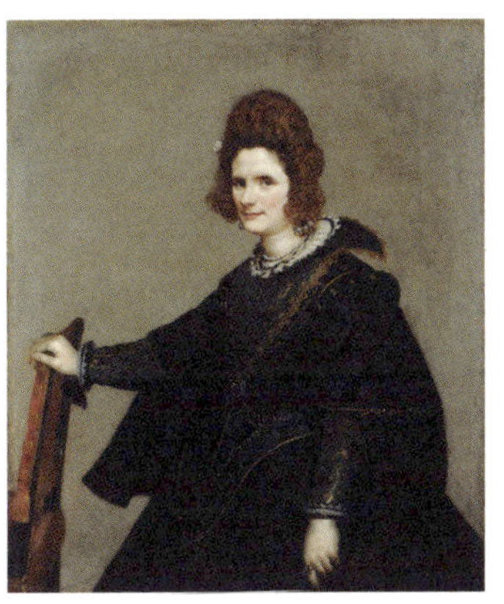

**BR 183**
**Diego Rodríguez de Silva y Velázquez (Spanish, 1599–1660)**
*Portrait of a Lady* (formerly titled *Countess Olivares*), circa 1631–40
oil on canvas, $48\frac{11}{16} \times 40\frac{1}{16}$ in.
(123.7 × 101.7 cm), Kat. 413 E
Shown in all cities

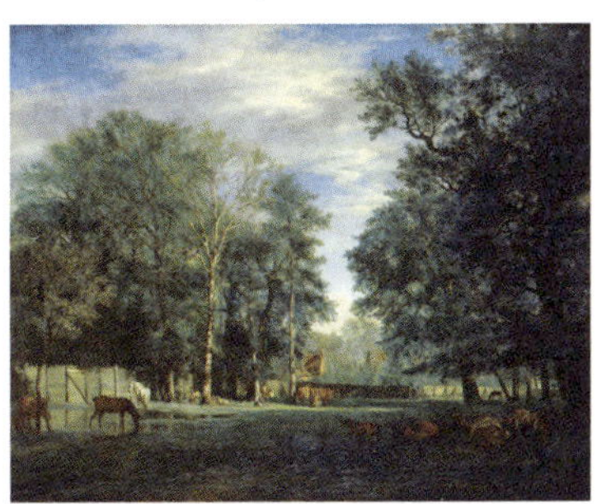

**BR 184**
**Adriaen van de Velde (Dutch, circa 1636–1672)**
*The Farm*, 1666
oil on canvas mounted on wood panel, $24\frac{13}{16} \times 30\frac{11}{16}$ in.
(63 × 78 cm), Kat. 922 C
Shown in all cities

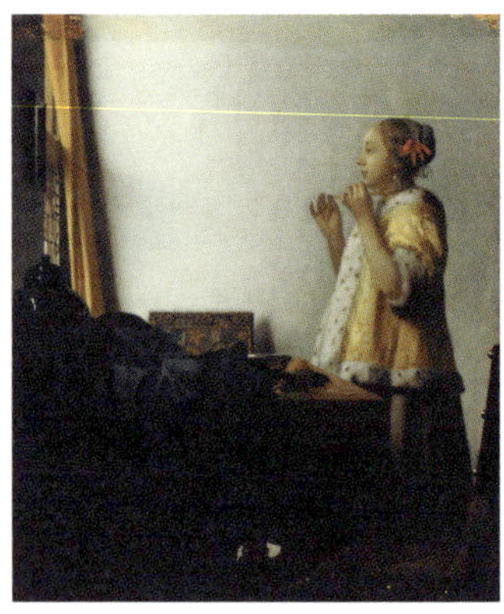

**BR 185**
**Jan Vermeer (Dutch, 1632–1675)**
*Lady with a Pearl Necklace*, 1663–65
oil on canvas, 22 1/16 × 18 11/16 in.
(56.1 × 47.4 cm), Kat. 912 B
Shown in all cities

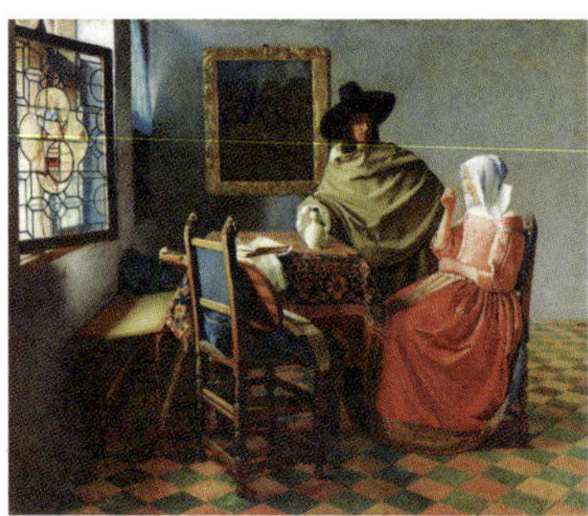

**BR 186**
**Jan Vermeer (Dutch, 1632–1675)**
*Lady and Gentleman Drinking Wine* (formerly titled *A Taste of Wine*), 1658–60
oil on canvas, 26 5/8 × 31 5/16 in.
(67.7 × 79.6 cm), Kat. 912 C
Returned after Boston

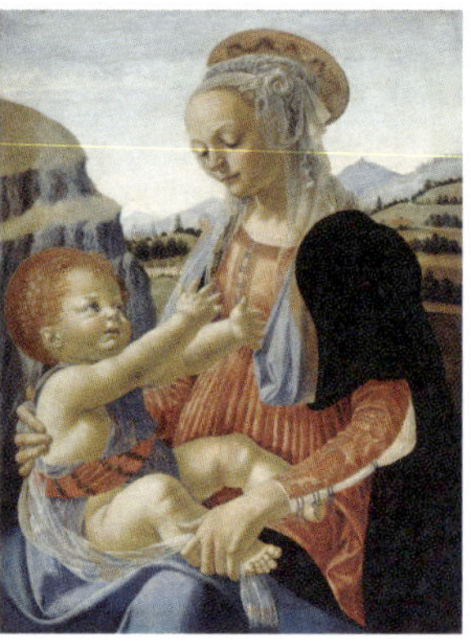

**BR 187**
**Andrea del Verrocchio (Italian, 1435/36–1488)**
*Madonna and Child*, circa 1470
oil on poplar panel, 29 13/16 × 21 1/2 in.
(75.8 × 54.6 cm), Kat. 104 A
Returned after Washington, DC

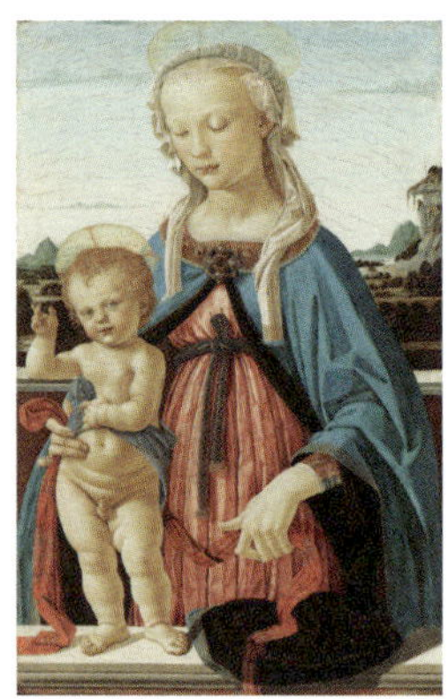

**BR 188**
**Andrea del Verrocchio (Italian, 1435/36–1488)**
*Madonna and Child*, circa 1473
tempera and gold on poplar panel, 29 13/16 × 18 7/8 in. (75.8 × 47.9 cm), Kat. 108
Returned after Boston

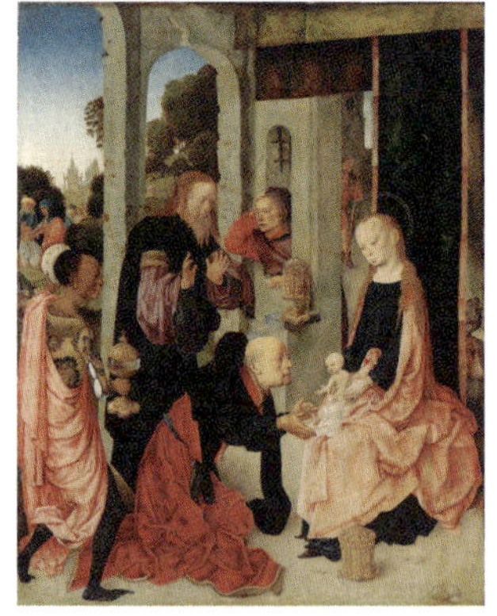

**BR 189**
**Master of the Virgo inter Virgines (Dutch, fl. circa 1480–95)**
*Adoration of the Magi*, circa 1485
oil on oak panel, 24 13/16 × 18 7/8 in.
(63 × 48 cm), Kat. 1672
Shown in all cities

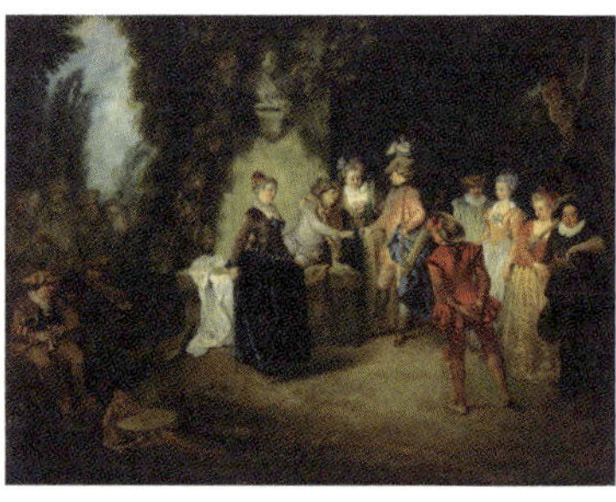

**BR 190**
**Jean-Antoine Watteau (French, 1684–1721)**
*The French Comedians*, 1715–17
oil on canvas, 15 1/4 × 19 1/16 in.
(38.8 × 49.4 cm), Kat. 468
Shown in all cities

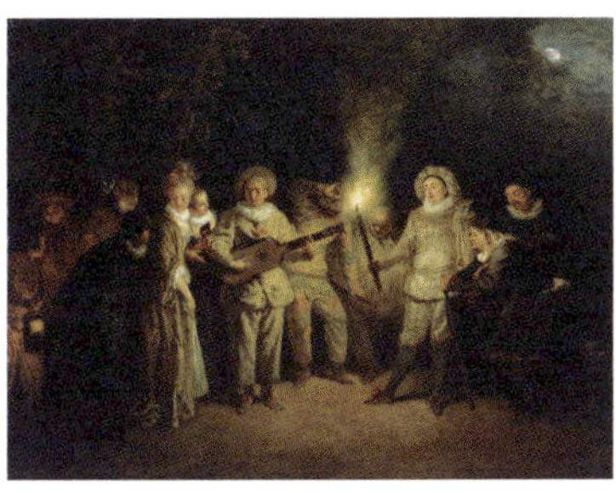

**BR 191**
**Jean-Antoine Watteau (French, 1684–1721)**
*The Italian Comedians*, 1715–17
oil on canvas, 15³⁄₁₆ × 19⁵⁄₁₆ in. (38.5 × 49.1 cm), Kat. 470
Shown in all cities

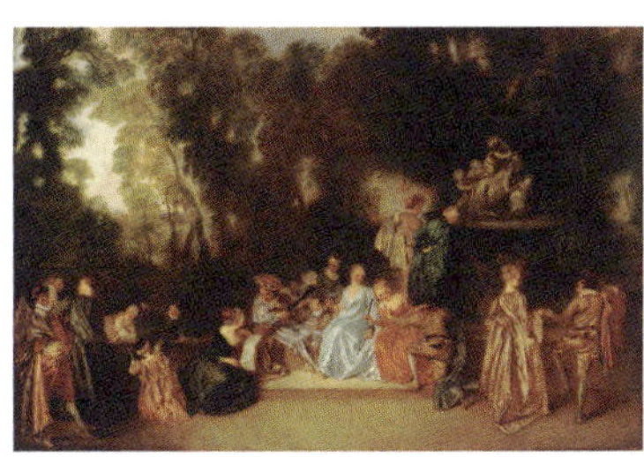

**BR 192**
**Jean-Antoine Watteau (French, 1684–1721)**
*Company Outdoors* (or *Outdoor Festival*), circa 1718–21
oil on canvas, 45¹⁄₁₆ × 65¹³⁄₁₆ in. (114.5 × 167.2 cm), Kat. 474 B
Shown in all cities

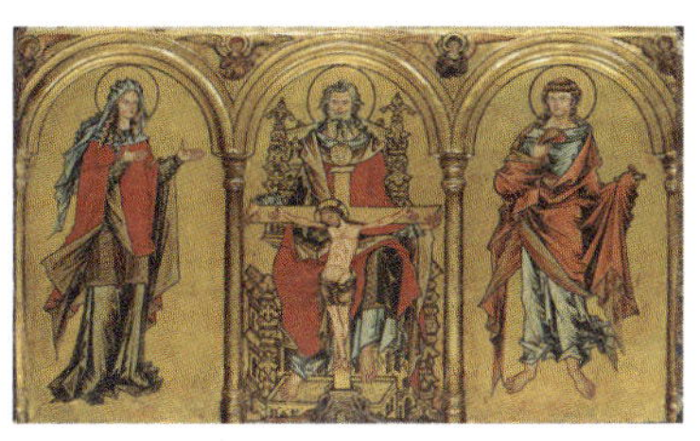

**BR 193**
**Westphalian School**
*The Trinity with the Virgin and Saint John*, circa 1260
oil on oak panel, 28³⁄₁₆ × 48⁵⁄₁₆ in. (71.6 × 122.7 cm), Kat. 1216 B
Returned after Washington, DC

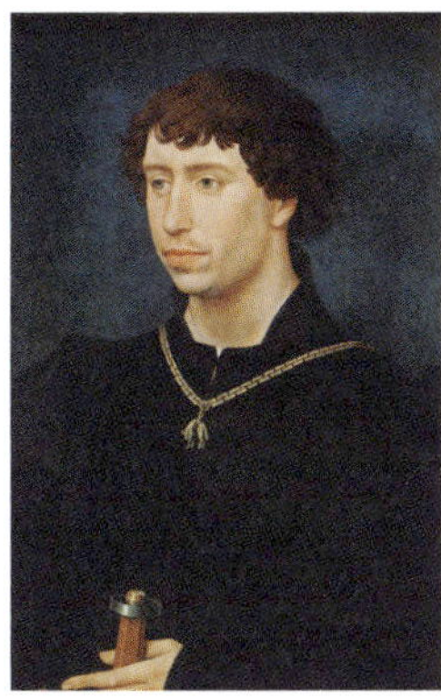

**BR 194**
**Workshop of Rogier van der Weyden (Flemish, 1399–1464), formerly attributed to Rogier van der Weyden**
*Charles the Bold, Duke of Burgundy*, circa 1460
oil on oak panel, 19⁵⁄₁₆ × 12⁵⁄₈ in. (49 × 32 cm), Kat. 545
Returned after Boston

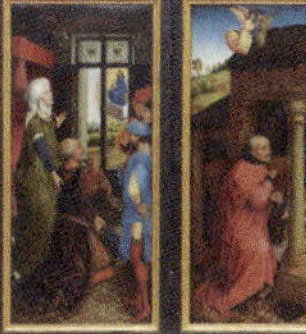

**BR 195**
**Rogier van der Weyden (Flemish, 1399–1464)**
*The Middleburg Altarpiece (Bladelin Altarpiece): Emperor Augustus and the Tiburtine Sibyl* (left wing), *The Nativity* (center), *The Magi* (right wing), circa 1450
oil on oak panel, central panel 35¹³⁄₁₆ × 35¹⁄₁₆ in. (91 × 89 cm), wings each 36¹³⁄₁₆ × 16⁷⁄₁₆ in. (93.5 × 41.7 cm), Kat. 535
Returned after Washington, DC

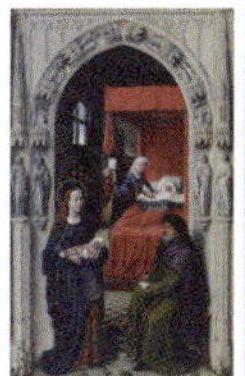
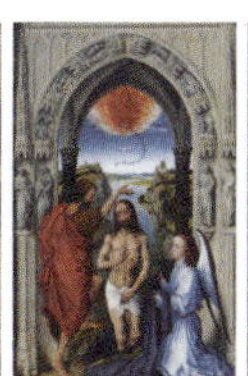
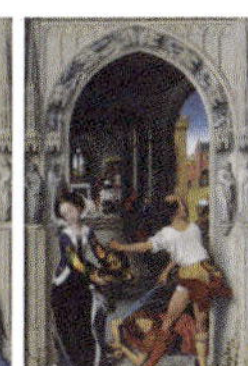

**BR 196**
**Rogier van der Weyden (Flemish, 1399–1464)**
*The Saint John Altarpiece*, circa 1455–60
oil on oak panel, each panel 31 × 19³⁄₈ in. (78.7 × 49.2 cm), Kat. 534 B
Returned after Washington, DC

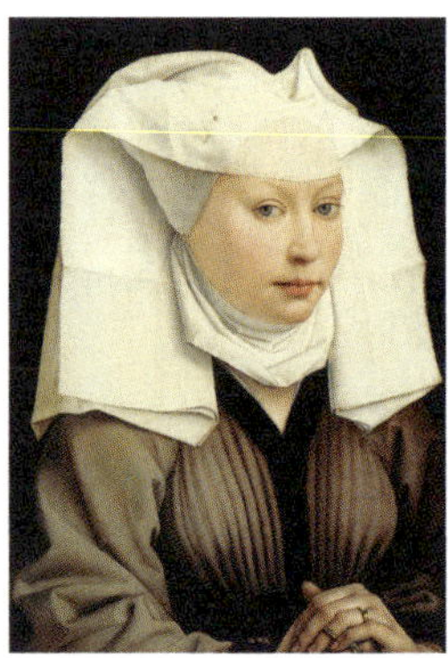

BR 197
**Rogier van der Weyden (Flemish, 1399–1464)**
*Portrait of a Young Woman*, circa 1440
oil on oak panel, 19⁷⁄₁₆ × 12¹⁵⁄₁₆ in. (49.3 × 32.9 cm), Kat. 545 D
Returned after Boston

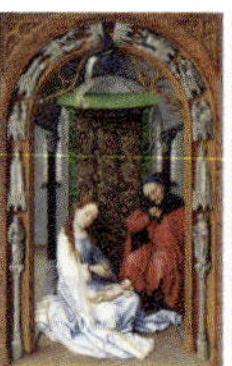
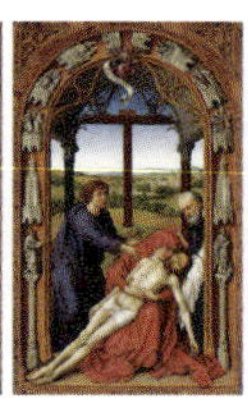

BR 198
**Rogier van der Weyden (Flemish, 1399–1464), formerly attributed to School of Rogier van der Weyden**
*The Miraflores Altarpiece* (formerly titled *Joys and Sorrows of Mary*), before 1445
oil on oak panel, each panel 29¼ × 17¹¹⁄₁₆ in. (74.3 × 45 cm), Kat. 534 A
Shown in all cities

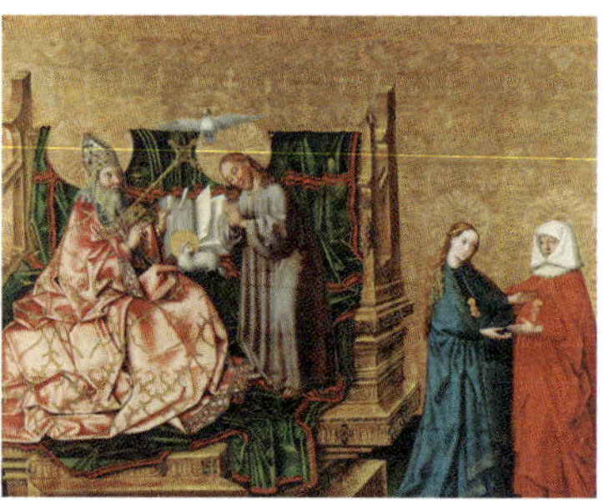

BR 199
**Konrad Witz (German, 1400/10–1444/46)**
*The Counsel of Salvation* (formerly titled *The Decision on the Redemption of Man*), circa 1445
oil on fir panel, 53¼ × 64⁷⁄₁₆ in. (135.3 × 164 cm), Kat. 1673
Returned after Boston

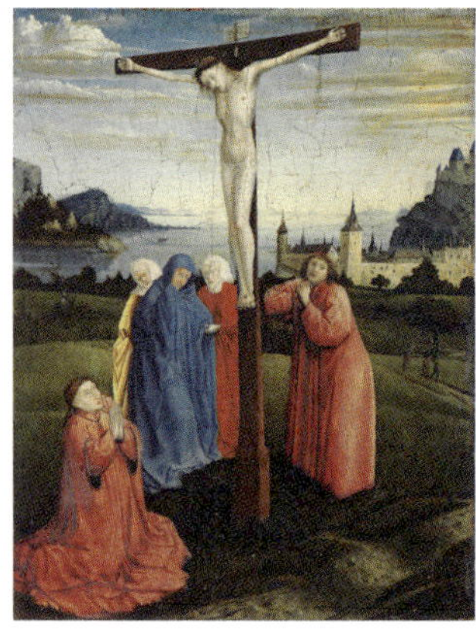

BR 200
**Attributed to Konrad Witz (German, 1400/10–1444/46)**
*The Crucifixion*, circa 1440–50
oil on panel transferred to canvas, 13⅜ × 10¼ in. (34 × 26 cm), Kat. 1656
Returned after Boston

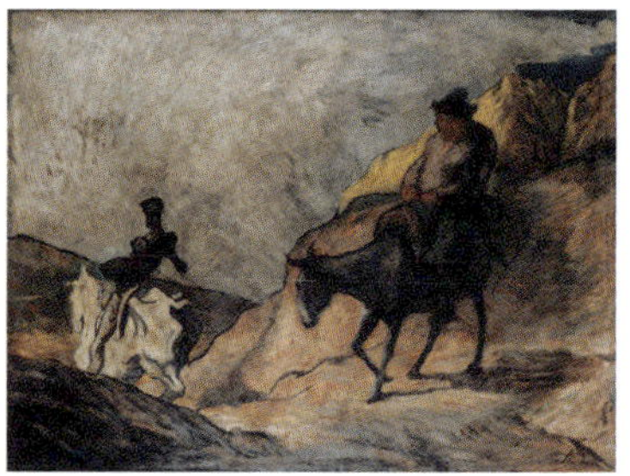

BR 201
**Honoré Daumier (French, 1808–1879)**
*Don Quixote and Sancho Panza*, 1866–68
oil on canvas, 30¹¹⁄₁₆ × 40³⁄₁₆ in. (78 × 102 cm),
Alte Nationalgalerie, A I 976
Returned after Boston

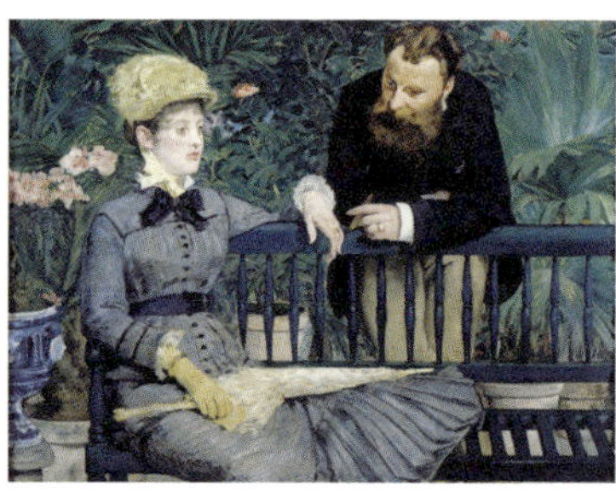

BR 202
**Édouard Manet (French, 1832–1883)**
*The Winter Garden* (or *The Greenhouse*), 1878–79
oil on canvas, 45¼ × 59¹⁄₁₆ in. (115 × 150 cm),
Alte Nationalgalerie, A I 550
Shown in all cities

## DOCUMENTS RELATED TO THE 1945 TRANSFER OF THE "202"

KATHRYN GRIFFITH

In early November 1945, an order to ship to the United States "at least 200 German works of art of greatest importance" was disseminated among various divisions of the Office of Military Government, US Zone (OMGUS) and the US Army.[1] At the highest level, the order was signed by General Eisenhower (doc. 1). This action was originally discussed by American officials at the Potsdam Conference in July 1945. The White House had announced the transfer in a press release dated September 26, 1945, but no order was issued at the time. At least some of the Monuments Men were aware of the proposal to remove German art before the November order, but they had hoped that no action would be taken. In Wiesbaden, Captain Farmer received the order via a hand-delivered teletypewriter exchange (TWX) from the US Seventh Army (doc. 2).[2] As he described in his memoir, this order spurred Farmer to summon his fellow Monuments Men to draft the Wiesbaden Manifesto (doc. 3).[3]

The precise timeline of these events is difficult to determine from surviving documents.

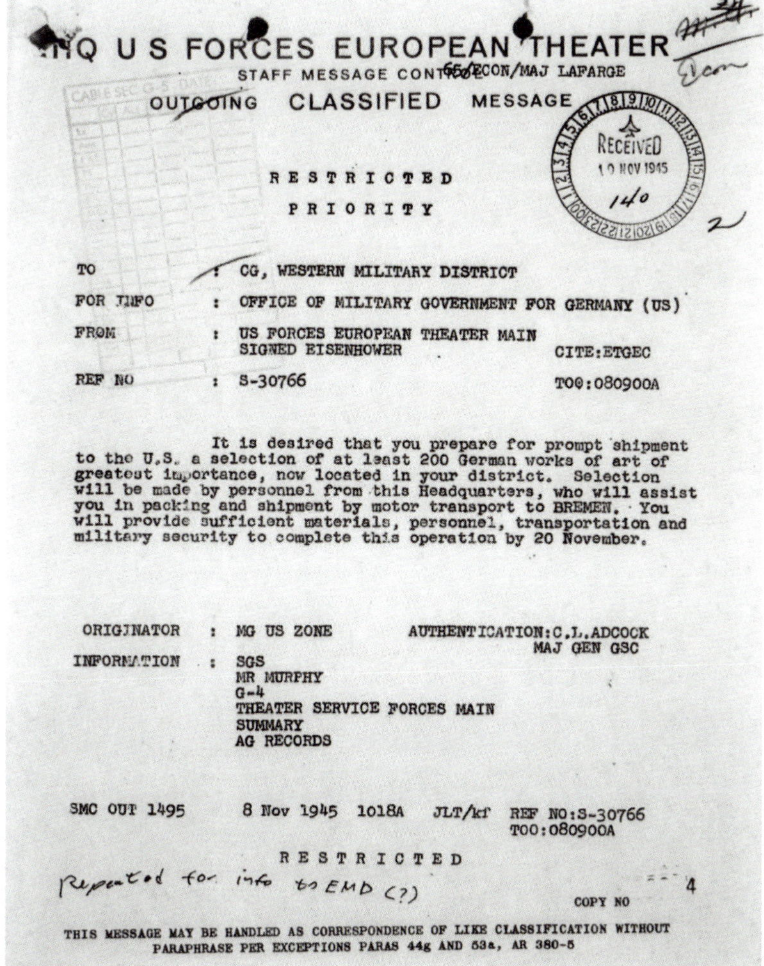

HQ U S FORCES EUROPEAN THEATER
STAFF MESSAGE CONTROL 65/ECON/MAJ LAFARGE
OUTGOING CLASSIFIED MESSAGE

RECEIVED 10 NOV 1945 140

R E S T R I C T E D
P R I O R I T Y

TO : CG, WESTERN MILITARY DISTRICT
FOR INFO : OFFICE OF MILITARY GOVERNMENT FOR GERMANY (US)
FROM : US FORCES EUROPEAN THEATER MAIN SIGNED EISENHOWER CITE:ETGEC
REF NO : S-30766 TOO:080900A

It is desired that you prepare for prompt shipment to the U.S. a selection of at least 200 German works of art of greatest importance, now located in your district. Selection will be made by personnel from this Headquarters, who will assist you in packing and shipment by motor transport to BREMEN. You will provide sufficient materials, personnel, transportation and military security to complete this operation by 20 November.

ORIGINATOR : MG US ZONE AUTHENTICATION:C.L.ADCOCK MAJ GEN GSC
INFORMATION : SGS
MR MURPHY
G-4
THEATER SERVICE FORCES MAIN
SUMMARY
AG RECORDS

SMC OUT 1495 8 Nov 1945 1018A JLT/kf REF NO:S-30766 TOO:080900A

R E S T R I C T E D

Repeated for info to EMD (?)

COPY NO 4

THIS MESSAGE MAY BE HANDLED AS CORRESPONDENCE OF LIKE CLASSIFICATION WITHOUT PARAPHRASE PER EXCEPTIONS PARAS 44g AND 53a, AR 380-5

Doc. 1. Order for the shipment of German works of art, from "US Forces European Theater Main signed Eisenhower" to "Commanding General, Western Military District," ref. no. S-30766, November 8, 1945. Folder 24 Cables, Outgoing, General Records, Records Concerning the Central Collecting Points ("Ardelia Hall Collection"): OMGUS Headquarters Records, 1938–1951 (National Archives Microfilm Publication M1941, Roll 21), Records of US Occupation Headquarters, Record Group 260, National Archives at College Park, College Park, MD

Doc. 2. Order from "7th US Army" to "Office Military Government for Stadtkreis, Wiesbaden," DUAU V DVAA NR T1086 PP. Out-Shipment 1 (November 19, 1945), Cultural Object Movement and Control Records, 1945–1952, Records Concerning the Central Collecting Points ("Ardelia Hall Collection"): Wiesbaden Central Collecting Point, 1945–1952 (National Archives Microfilm Publication M1947, Roll 32), Records of US Occupation Headquarters, Record Group 260, National Archives at College Park, College Park, MD

To:
Capt. Farmer

VVV 96

EAIN

DUAU V DVAA NR T1086 P P

FROM 7TH U S ARMY

TO OFFICE MIL GOVT FOR STADTKREIS , WIESBADEN

GR NC R E S T R I C T E D

BT

HIGHER HEADQUARTERS DESIGES THAT IMMEDIATE PREPARATIONS BE MADE FOR PROMPT SHIPMENT TO THE UNITEK OF A SELECTION OF AT LEAST TWO ZERO ZERO GERMAN WORKS OF ART OF GREATEEST IMPORTANCE X MOST OF THESE ARE NOW IN ART COLLECTING POINT WIESBADEN X SELECTIONS WILL BE MADE BY PERSONNEL FROM HEADQUARTERS CMA US FORCES CMA EUROPEAN THEATER WHO WILL ASSIST IN PACKING AND SHIPMENT BY MOTOR TRANSPORT TO BREMEN X FROM CG SEVENTH ARMY TO DIRECTOR CMA OFFICE OF MILITARY GOVERNMENT FOR STADTKREIS WIESBADEN CMA REF NO ABLE THREE THREE ZERO TWO SEVEN X YOU WILL PROVIDE SUFFICIENT MATERIAL AND PERSONNEL X THIS HEADQUARTER IS TO BE INFORMED BY TELEPHONE OF PROGRESS AND ANTICIPATED REQUIREMENTS X OPERATION TO BE COMPLETED BY TWO ZERO NOVEMBER X TRANSPORTATION AND MILITARY SECURITY DURING TRANSIT WILL BE PROVIDED BY THIS HEADQUARTERS X

BT 091520

POKED REM 1730
AAEAINOT

Received
13 Nov 45
1400 hrs

Versions of the same order signed by different commands and received by different divisions are dated between November 6 and November 9, 1945. In the receipt for the transfer of custody of the "202" from the Wiesbaden CCP to Lamont Moore, Farmer gave the date of the order from the Seventh Army as November 9,[4] but, in his later "Status of the Collecting Point Report," he indicated that that same order was received on November 13.[5]

Extant copies of the Wiesbaden Manifesto are consistently dated November 7, though this date has been questioned.[6] It is possible that an earlier copy of the order reached Wiesbaden prior to the communication from the Seventh Army, and the manifesto was dated to coincide with the initial gathering of MFAA officers.[7] Nevertheless, the original manifesto was given to Major Bancel LaFarge, MFAA chief, who decided not to send it up the chain of command. A firm *terminus ante quem* can be established by copies of the manifesto mailed by Captain Edith A. Standen, dated December 1.[8] It became public in January 1946, when former Monuments officer Charles Kuhn, who had returned to civilian life, published it in the *College Art Journal*.[9]

Doc. 3. The Wiesbaden Manifesto, from "US Forces, European Theater, Germany," November 7, 1945. Shipment of Works of Art to the United States ("202"), July 1945–October 1946, Records Concerning the Central Collecting Points ("Ardelia Hall Collection"): Wiesbaden Central Collecting Point, 1945–1952 (National Archives Microfilm Publication M1947, Roll 70), Records of US Occupation Headquarters, Record Group 260, National Archives at College Park, College Park, MD

File: Wiesbaden HQ.

COPY

U.S. FORCES, EUROPEAN THEATER
GERMANY

7 November 1945

1. We, the undersigned, Monuments, Fine Arts and Archives Specialist Officers of the Armed Forces of the United States, wish to make known our convictions regarding the transportation to the United States of works of art, the property of German institutions or nationals, for purposes of protective custody.

2. a. We are unanimously agreed that the transportation of these works of art, undertaken by the United States Army, upon direction from the highest national authority, establishes a precedent which is neither morally tenable nor trustworthy.

b. Since the beginning of United States participation in the war, it has been the declared policy of the Allied Forces, so far as military necessity would permit, to protect and preserve from deterioration consequent upon the processes of war, all monuments, documents, or other objects of historic, artistic, cultural, or archaeological value. The war is at an end, and no doctrine of "military necessity" can now be invoked for the further protection of the objects to be moved, for the reason that depots and personnel, both fully competent for their protection, have been inaugurated and are functioning.

c. The Allied Nations are at present preparing to prosecute individuals for the crime of sequestering, under the pretext of "protective custody", the cultural treasures of German-occupied countries. A major part of the indictment follows upon the reasoning that even though these individuals were acting under military orders, the dictates of a higher ethical law made it incumbent upon them to refuse to take part in, or countenance, the fulfillment of these orders. We, the undersigned, feel it our duty to point out that, though as members of the armed forces, we will carry out the orders we receive, we are thus put before any candid eyes as no less culpable than those whose prosecution we affect to sanction.

3. We wish to state that from our own knowledge, no historical grievance will rankle so long, or be the cause of so much justified bitterness, as the removal, for any reason, of a part of the heritage of any nation, even if that heritage may be interpreted as a prize of war. And though this removal may be done with every intention of altruism, we are none the less convinced that it is our duty, individually and collectively, to protest against it, and that though our obligations are to the nation to which we owe allegiance, there are yet further obligation to common justice, decency, and the establishment of the power of right, not of expediency or might, among civilized nations.

COPY

/s/ Stephen Kovalyak
/t/ STEPHEN KOVALYAK
1st Lt. Inf., 0314411
(U.S. Zone)

/s/ Patrick J. Kelleher
/t/ PATRICK J. KELLEHER
Capt., TC, 01944717
Office of Military
Government for Land
Great Hesse

/s/ Lamont Moore
/t/ LAMONT MOORE
2nd Lt., AUS, 02011967
Office of Military
Government (U.S. Zone)

/s/ Samuel Ratensky
/t/ SAMUEL RATENSKY
1st Lt., AUS, 02025813
Office of Military
Government for Land
Great Hesse

/s/ Charles P. Parkhurst, Jr.
/t/ CHARLES P. PARKHURST, Jr.
Lt., (jg), USNR, 298080
Office of Military
Government (U.S. Zone)

/s/ Sheldon W. Keck
/t/ SHELDON W. KECK
2nd Lt., AUS, 020255318
Office of Military
Government for Stadt-
kreis and Landkreis
Marburg

/s/ Edith A. Standen
/t/ EDITH A. STANDEN
Capt. WAC, L 117136
Office of Military
Government
(U.S. Zone)

/s/ Walter I. Farmer
/t/ WALTER I. FARMER
Capt., CE. 01108653
Office of Military
Government for Stadt-
kreis Wiesbaden

/s/ Walker K. Hancock
/t/ WALKER K. HANCOCK
Capt., Inf., 0515311
Office of Military
Government for
Stadtkreis and Land-
kreis Marburg

/s/ Julius H. Buchman
/t/ JULIUS H. BUCHMAN
Capt., FA, 01171068
Office of Military
Government for Stadt-
kreis Frankfurt

/s/ Frederick C. Shrady
/t/ FREDERICK C. SHRADY
2nd Lt., AUS, 02025212
Office of Military
Government for Land
Great Hesse

/s/ Richard H. Kuhlke
/t/ RICHARD H. KUHLKE
1st Lt., Ord., 01556305
Office of Military
Government for Stadt-
kreis Frankfurt

-2-

NOTES

1. See documents in the folder Shipment of Works of Art to the United States ("202"), July 1945–October 1946, NARA, M1947, Roll 70.
2. The organization of the US military government in Germany in November 1945 requires some clarification here. Eisenhower's order was directed to the "Commanding General, Western Military District." At the end of the war, the US Zone in Germany was divided into Eastern and Western military districts. The Western Military District was the responsibility of the US Seventh Army. Wiesbaden fell within this district, and the local arm of the military government was designated Office of Military Government for Stadtkreis Wiesbaden. Farmer, as director of the CCP, reported to this office, and it was listed as his assignment under his signature in the Wiesbaden Manifesto.
3. Farmer 2000, pp. 55–57.
4. Walter I. Farmer, "Shipping List and Transfer of Custody," November 19, 1945, Out-Shipment 1 (November 19, 1945), NARA, M1947, Roll 32.
5. Walter I. Farmer, "Status of the Collecting Point Report," December 3, 1945, Monthly Report on Monuments Fine Arts and Archives Seventh United States Army Land Greater Hesse November 1945, NARA, M1941, Roll 32.

COPY

| | |
|---|---|
| /s/ Everett P. Lesley, Jr.<br>/t/ EVERETT P. LESLEY, JR.<br>Capt., CAC, 01531907<br>The General Board, U.S.<br>Forces, European<br>Theater | /s/ Theodore A. Heinrich<br>/t/ THEODORE A. HEINRICH<br>2nd Lt., AUS, 02015985<br>Office of Military<br>Government for Regie-<br>rungsbezirk Kassel |
| /s/ Clyde K. Harris<br>/t/ CLYDE K. HARRIS<br>1st Lt., CE, 01116157<br>Office of Military<br>Government for Regie-<br>rungsbezirk Hessen | /s/ Doda Conrad<br>/t/ DODA CONRAD<br>1st Lt., AUS, 01691535<br>Office of Military<br>Government (U.S.) |
| /s/ Edwin C. Rae<br>/t/ EDWIN C. RAE<br>Capt., AC, 01543246<br>Office of Military<br>Government for Bavaria | /s/ William A. Lovegrove<br>/t/ WILLIAM A. LOVEGROVE<br>1st Lt., CMP, 01797674<br>Office of Military<br>Government (U.S. Zone) |
| /s/ Edward J. Lutrur<br>/t/ EDWARD J. LUTRUR<br>Capt., QMC, 01575023<br>Office of Military<br>Government for Regie-<br>rungsbezirk Niederbayern<br>and Oberpfalz | /s/ Walter W. Horn<br>/t/ WALTER W. HORN<br>1st Lt., Inf., 01326328<br>Office of Military<br>Government (U.S. Zone) |
| /s/ J. T. Forey<br>/t/ J. T. FOREY<br>1st Lt., CE, 01113367<br>Office of Military<br>Government for Regie-<br>rungsbezirk Oberbayern | /s/ Robert A. Koch<br>/t/ ROBERT A. KOCH<br>1st Lt., AUS, 02011971<br>Office of Military<br>Government for Wurt-<br>temberg - Baden |
| /s/ Dale V. Ford<br>/t/ DALE V. FORD<br>2nd Lt., CE, 01112695<br>Office of Military Government<br>for Landkreis Heilbronn | /s/ Thomas C. Howe, Jr.<br>/t/ THOMAS C. HOWE, Jr.<br>Lt. Comdr., USNR, 237822<br>Office of Military<br>Government (U.S. Zone) |

-3-

6. See Tanja Bernsau's essay, pp. 43–45. In his report on the transfer of the "202" Lamont Moore wrote that he and Colonel McBride visited the Wiesbaden CCP on November 7 and conferred with Farmer and Captain James Rorimer about packing supplies for the transfer. Moore, Farmer, and Captain Patrick Kelleher began selecting paintings on November 9, and actual packing began on November 12. The paintings departed on November 19 (Lamont Moore, "Report on the Shipment of Paintings," December 14, 1945, Shipment of Works of Art to the United States ("202"), July 1945–October 1946, NARA, M1947, Roll 70). Major Bancel LaFarge reported that he and Lt. Commander Thomas C. Howe, Jr. made an inspection visit to the Wiesbaden CCP on November 11 and 12 (Bancel LaFarge, Weekly Intelligence Report, November 14, 1945, Folder 6 [Miscellaneous Reports], 1945, NARA, M1941, Roll 10).
7. Major Bancel LaFarge, MFAA chief, recorded the order (which he dated November 7 and November 8) in two brief reports. Bancel LaFarge, "10 Day War Diary," November 9, 1945, Folder 6 [Miscellaneous Reports], 1945, NARA, M1941, Roll 10, and "Weekly Intelligence Report," November 14, 1945 (cited above).
8. Standen sent identical letters to Monuments Men and fellow signatories, each enclosing additional copies of the

COPY

The following officers have expressed agreement with the sentiments of this paper but do not feel at liberty to sign any statement:-

JAMES J. RORIMER
Capt., AUS, 0-557225
Office of Military Government
(Western District)

LESLIE J. POSTE
2nd Lt., AUS, 02025871
Office of Military Government
(Western District)

W.B. VAN NORTWICK
Capt., Inf. (Armd), 0-1108653
Office of Military Government
for Stadtkreis Wiesbaden.

The following officers have expressed similar sentiments by means of separate letters to Major L.B. La Farge:-

JOHN H. COULTER
Lt. Comdr., USNR, 13699
Office of Military Government
for Bavaria (U.S.)

CRAIG H. SMYTH
Lt., USNR, 173173
Director, Munich Collecting Point.

EDWARD E. ADAMS
CAPT., TC, 0-444317
Office of Military Government
(U.S. Zone)

HARRY D. R. GRIER
Capt., Inf., 0-1305763
Office of Military Government
for Germany (U.S.)

KURT F. HAUSCHILDT
2nd Lt., AC., 0-1540391
U.S. Headquarters Berlin District

The names listed above include 32 of the 35 MFA&A Specialist Officers now in Europe assigned to headquarters in Germany. No contact has been possible with the remaining three officers owing to the shortage of time and the distances involved.

It may also be noted that, while no attempt has been made to ascertain the opinion of the enlisted men and civilians in the Monuments, Fine Arts and Archives organization, nor of the personnel of American Monuments, Fine Arts and Archives organizations outside of Germany, all the individuals in these categories who have read this paper have expressed complete agreement with its sentiments.

-4-

Wiesbaden Manifesto. Standen wrote, “the original has been given to Maj. L.B. La Farge to use as he sees fit; he has said that it will be of great service to him but he does not feel that it can be made public. He sees no reason, however, why you should not send copies to friends, with the understanding that it is to be circulated only privately” (Edith A. Standen, letter [addressee blank], December 1, 1945, Shipment of Works of Art to the United States (“202”), July 1945–October 1946, NARA, M1947, Roll 70). Kenneth Lindsay later wrote that Standen sent the letter to all of the signatories as well as those who expressed agreement but did not sign, or who had sent separate letters to LaFarge (Lindsay 1998, p. 123, fn. 9). Several of the Standen letters are preserved in the National Archives, College Park, MD.

9. Kuhn 1946, pp. 81–82. Kuhn published only the text of the manifesto and not the signatures, perhaps out of a desire to protect his colleagues who were still active military.

# BIBLIOGRAPHY


## Archival Sources

**Detroit Institute of Art (DIA) Archives**
The Edgar P. Richardson Records, Series IX Exhibitions, 1936–1961.

Folder: Exhibitions of Paintings from the Berlin Museums, Sept. 10–26, 1948 (RCH 66/12).

Scrapbook, 1948–1950.

**The Metropolitan Museum of Art (MMA) Archives, New York**
Folder: German Paintings – Publicity, 1948, Office of the Secretary Records.

Birkmeyer, Karl M. "Report on 202 Paintings Belonging to the Berlin Museums in the United States of America," April 22, 1949. Folder: Loan Exhibitions – Held – 1948. Office of the Secretary Subject Files, 1870–1950.

**National Archives and Records Administration (NARA), College Park, MD**
Microfilm Publication M1941, Records concerning the Central Collecting Points ("Ardelia Hall Collection"): OMGUS Headquarters Records, 1938–1951, Records of US Occupation Headquarters, Record Group 260.

*Roll 10*: General Records, 1938–1948, From: (5b) [Miscellaneous MFAA reports], 1956, To: (6) [Miscellaneous reports], 1945.

*Roll 32*: Activity Reports, 1945, From: Eastern Military District, Third United States Army: Monthly report on Monuments, Fine Arts, and Archives, September–November 1945, To: Greater Hesse: Monthly report on Monuments, Fine Arts, and Archives, Western Military District, Seventh United States Army, July–December 1945.

Microfilm Publication M1947, Records Concerning the Central Collecting Points ("Ardelia Hall Collection"): Wiesbaden Central Collecting Point, 1945–1952, Records of US Occupation Headquarters, Record Group 260.

*Roll 14*: General Records, 1945–1952 [A1, Entry 492], From: Press Clippings [by Title]; To: Receipts for Cultural Objects & Loans for Exhibitions General.

*Roll 15*: General Records, 1945–1952 [A1, Entry 492], From: Receipts for Cultural Objects & Loans for Exhibitions: Major Baer; To: Reports: Weekly Summary Reports, May 1945–May 1947.

*Roll 28*: Administrative Records, 1944–1951 [A1, Entry 493], From: Personnel: Administration, Jan. 1949–June 1951; To: Policy–Scarff.

*Roll 32*: Cultural Object Movement and Control Records, 1945–1952 [A1, Entry 494], From: In-shipment 226 (May 19, 1949), To: Out-shipment 47 (Apr. 18, 1947).

*Roll 54*: Activity Reports, 1945–1951 [A1, Entry 496], From: Monthly Report: Supreme Headquarters Allied Expeditionary Force, Dec. 1944; To: Monthly Report: Wiesbaden Central Collecting Point, Dec. 1949.

*Roll 70*: Records Relating to the Status of Monuments, Museums, and Archives, 1945–1950 [A1, Entry 497]. From: State Museums Berlin: War Chronicles of the Berlin Museums, May 1946; To: War Damaged Art Applications: Abresch–Busemann.

**National Gallery of Art (NGA) Archives, Washington, DC**
Record Group 2, Records of the Office of the Director, David Finley Office Files, Series 2A1, Box 8, File: German Paintings, General Correspondence 1945–April 1947.

Record Group 17, Records of the Curatorial Departments, General Curatorial, World War II Files, 1941–1953, Series 17A5, Box 9, Folder: German Paintings, General Correspondence, 1945–April 1947.

Record Group 28, Collection of Donated Materials.

Walter I. Farmer Papers, 1935–2000. 28MFAA-C.

Press Clippings scrapbook, RG14A8, vol. 24.

**Toledo Museum of Art (TMA) Library and Archives**
Folder: Masterpieces from Berlin Museums – Negotiations and Official Documents.

Folder: Masterpieces from Berlin Museums – Catalog, *Art News Picturebook*, April 1948.

Folder: Masterpieces from Berlin Museums – Packing Lists, etc.

Folder: Masterpieces from Berlin Museums – Record of Operations.

Folder: Masterpieces from Berlin Museums – Publicity.

Folder: Masterpieces from Berlin Museums – Contributors to Bus Fund. April 14, 1949.

Scrapbook November 1938 – May 1949.

**The Getty Research Institute Special Collections, Los Angeles, CA**
Duveen Brothers records, 1876–1981 (bulk 1909–1964). Series II. Correspondence and papers. Series II.D. Correspondence with museums, 1909–1967. Box 334 [Reel 189], Folder 2, Kaiser Friedrich Museum, 1931–1939.

## Publications

**Aalders 1999**
Aalders, Gerard. *Roof: De ontvreemding van joods bezit tijdens de Tweede Wereldoorlog.* The Hague, 1999.

**Ahl 2008**
Ahl, Diane Cole. *Fra Angelico.* London and New York, 2008.

**American Association of Museums 2005**
American Association of Museums. *Vitalizing Memory: International Perspectives on Provenance Research.* Washington, DC, 2005.

**Baetjer, Rosenberg, and Cowart 2009**
Baetjer, Katherine, Pierre Rosenberg, and Georgia J. Cowart. *Watteau, Music, and Theater.* Exh. cat. New York (Metropolitan Museum of Art), 2009.

**Barron 1991a**
Barron, Stephanie. *"Degenerate Art": The Fate of the Avant-Garde in Nazi Germany.* Exh. cat. Los Angeles (Los Angeles County Museum of Art) and Chicago (Art Institute of Chicago), 1991.

**Barron 1991b**
Barron, Stephanie. "Modern Art and Politics in Prewar Germany." In **Barron 1991a**, pp. 9–24.

**Barron 1991c**
Barron, Stephanie. "The Galerie Fischer Auction." In **Barron 1991a**, pp. 134–69.

**Barron 1997**
Barron, Stephanie. *Exiles and Emigrés: The Flight of European Artists from Hitler.* Exh. cat. Los Angeles (Los Angeles County Museum of Art), Montreal (Montreal Museum of Fine Arts), Berlin (Neue Nationalgalerie), 1997.

**Bartsch 1870**
Bartsch, Adam. *Le peintre graveur.* Vol. 17, No. 13. Leipzig, 1870.

**Bayerische Staatsgemälde-Sammlungen 1948**
Bayerische Staatsgemälde-Sammlungen. *Meisterwerke des Kaiser-Friedrich-Museums Berlin.* Exh. cat. Munich (Haus der Kunst), 1948.

**Bernsau 2013**
Bernsau, Tanja. *Die Besatzer als Kuratoren? Der Central Collecting Point Wiesbaden als Drehscheibe für einen Wiederaufbau der Museumslandschaft nach 1945.* Berlin, 2013.

**Blass-Simmen, Rowley, and Villa 2018**
Blass-Simmen, Brigit, Neville Rowley, and Giovanni C.F. Villa, eds. *Bellini / Mantegna: Capolavori a confronto. Presentazione di Gesù al Tempio.* Exh. cat. Venice (Fondazione Querini Stampalia), 2018.

**Boskovits and Brown 2003**
Boskovits, Miklós, and David Alan Brown. *Italian Paintings of the Fifteenth Century. The Collections of the National Gallery of Art.* Washington and New York, 2003.

**Bradsher 1999**
Bradsher, Greg. *Holocaust-Era Assets: A Finding Aid to Records at the National Archives at College Park, Maryland.* Washington, DC, 1999.

**Brinkmann et al. 2007–08**
Brinkmann, Bodo, et al. *Cranach.* Exh. cat. Frankfurt (Städel Museum) and London (Royal Academy of Arts), 2007–08.

**Brinkmann et al. 2011**
Brinkmann, Bodo, et al. *Konrad Witz.* Exh. cat. Basel (Kunstmuseum Basel), 2011.

**Brown and Van Nimmen 2005**
Brown, David Alan, and Jane Van Nimmen. *Raphael and the Beautiful Banker: The Story of the Bindo Altoviti Portrait.* New Haven, 2005.

**Butterfield 2019**
Butterfield, Andrew, ed. *Verrocchio: Sculptor and Painter in Renaissance Florence.* Exh. cat. Washington, DC (National Gallery of Art), 2019.

**Caglioti and De Marchi 2019**
Caglioti, Francesco, and Andrea De Marchi, eds. *Verrocchio, il maestro di Leonardo.* Exh. cat. Florence (Palazzo Strozzi), 2019.

**Campbell et al. 2019**
Campbell, Caroline, et al. *Mantegna & Bellini.* Exh. cat. London (National Gallery) and Berlin (Gemäldegalerie), 2019.

**Carls 1969**
Carls, Carl Dietrich. *Ernst Barlach.* London, 1969.

**Chapuis and Kemperdick 2015**
Chapuis, Julien, and Stephan Kemperdick, eds. *The Lost Museum: The Berlin Painting and Sculpture Collections 70 Years after World War II.* Exh. cat. Berlin (Bode-Museum), 2015.

**Christiansen and Weppelmann 2011**
Christiansen, Keith, and Stefan Weppelmann, eds. *The Renaissance Portrait from Donatello to Bellini.* Exh. cat. Berlin (Bode-Museum) and New York (Metropolitan Museum of Art), 2011.

**Edsel 2009**
Edsel, Robert M. *The Monuments Men: Allied Heroes, Nazi Thieves, and the Greatest Treasure Hunt in History.* New York, 2009.

**Eissenhauer 2019**
Eissenhauer, Michael, ed. *Gemäldegalerie: 200 Meisterwerke der europäischen Malerei.* Berlin, 2019.

**Evans and Weppelmann 2015**
Evans, Mark, and Stefan Weppelmann, eds. *Botticelli Reimagined.* Exh. cat. Berlin (Gemäldegalerie) and London (Victoria and Albert Museum), 2015.

**Farmer 1996**
Farmer, Walter I., and Margaret Farmer Planton. "The Wiesbaden Manifesto of 7 November 1945." *Jahrbuch Preußischer Kulturbesitz.* Vol. 33 (1996), pp. 91–119.

**Farmer 1997**
Farmer, Walter I. "Custody and Controversy at the Wiesbaden Collecting Point." In **Simpson 1997**, pp. 131–34.

**Farmer 2000**
Farmer, Walter I., Klaus Goldmann, and Margaret Farmer Planton. *The Safekeepers: A Memoir of the Arts at the End of World War II.* Berlin and New York, 2000.

**Farmer 2002**
Farmer, Walter I., Klaus Goldmann, and Margaret Farmer Planton. *Die Bewahrer des Erbes: Das Schicksal deutscher Kulturgüter am Ende des Zweiten Weltkrieges.* Berlin, 2002.

**Feliciano 1997**
Feliciano, Hector. *The Lost Museum: The Nazi Conspiracy to Steal the World's Greatest Works of Art.* New York, 1997.

**Flanner 1945**
Flanner, Janet [Genêt]. "Letter from the Rhineland." *The New Yorker.* November 17, 1945, pp. 71–74.

**Flanner 1947**
Flanner, Janet. "Annals of Crime. The Beautiful Spoils (III Monuments Men)." *The New Yorker,* March 8, 1947, pp. 38–55.

**Flanner 1957**
Flanner, Janet. *Men and Monuments.* New York, 1957.

**Franits 2004**
Franits, Wayne E. *Dutch Seventeenth-Century Genre Painting: Its Stylistic and Thematic Evolution.* New Haven, 2004.

**Friemuth 1989**
Friemuth, Cay. *Die geraubte Kunst: Der dramatische Wettlauf um die Rettung der Kulturschätze nach dem Zweiten Weltkrieg (Entführung, Bergung und Restitution europäischen Kulturgutes 1939–1948). Mit dem Tagebuch des britischen Kunstschutzoffiziers Robert Lonsdale Charles.* Braunschweig, 1989.

**Garas 2003**
Garas, Klára. "Quadal [Chwátal], Martin Ferdinand." Grove Art Online. 2003; Accessed 13 Nov. 2019. https://doi.org/10.1093/gao/9781884446054.article.T070295.

**Gemäldegalerie 1950–51**
Gemäldegalerie. *Meisterwerke aus den Berliner Museen: Deutsche, italienische und altniederländische Malerei des 13.–16. Jahrhunderts.* Exh. cat. West Berlin (Museum Dahlem), 1950–51.

**Gemäldegalerie 1951–52**
Gemäldegalerie. *Meisterwerke aus den Berliner Museen: europäische Malerei des 17. und 18. Jahrhunderts.* Exh. cat. West Berlin (Museum Dahlem), 1951–52.

**Gemäldegalerie 1953**
Gemäldegalerie. *Verzeichnis der Kunstwerke des Kaiser-Friedrich-Museums-Vereins, die dem Museum Dahlem 1953 als Leihgabe übergeben wurden.* Exh. cat. West Berlin (Museum Dahlem), 1953.

**Gemäldegalerie 1978**
Gemäldegalerie. *Catalogue of Paintings 13th–18th Century, Picture Gallery, Staatliche Museen Preußischer Kulturbesitz, Berlin,* 2nd ed. Berlin, 1978.

**Goldmann 1997**
Goldmann, Klaus. "Laudation für Walter I. Farmer in Fürth am 10. Mai 1997." *Eleusis.* Vol. 3 (1997), pp. 7–11.

**Grasselli and Rosenberg 1984**
Grasselli, Margaret Morgan, and Pierre Rosenberg. *Watteau, 1684–1721.* Exh. cat. Washington, DC (National Gallery of Art), Paris (Grand Palais), and Berlin (Schloss Charlottenburg), 1984.

**Groves 1972**
Groves, Naomi Jackson. *Ernst Barlach: Life in Work: Sculpture, Drawings and Graphics, Dramas, Prose Works and Letters in Translation.* Königstein im Taunus, 1972.

**Haberstock 1967**
Haberstock, Karl. *Hundert Bilder aus der Galerie Haberstock.* Berlin and Munich, 1967.

**Hakanson 1948**
Hakanson, Joy. "All Chicago Throngs to See Berlin Art Treasures." *Detroit News.* August 1, 1948.

**Hamlin 1946a**
Hamlin, Gladys E. "German Paintings in the National Gallery: Official Statement." *College Art Journal.* Vol. 5, No. 2 (January 1946), pp. 75–77.

**Hamlin 1946b**
Hamlin, Gladys E. "European Art Collections and the War." *College Art Journal.* Vol. 5, No. 3 (March 1946), pp. 219–28.

**Hammond 1946**
Hammond, Mason. "The War and Art Treasures in Germany." *College Art Journal.* Vol. 5, No. 3 (March 1946), pp. 205–18.

**Hartwieg 2018**
Hartwieg, Babette. "Le 'Presentazioni di Gesù al Tempio' di Andrea Mantegna e di Giovanni Bellini: genesi delle opere e paragone tecnologico." In **Blass-Simmen, Rowley, and Villa 2018**, pp. 75–94.

**Held 1980**
Held, Julius S. *The Oil Sketches of Peter Paul Rubens: A Critical Catalogue.* Princeton, 1980.

**Hildebrand 1989**
Hildebrand, Martin. "Wie ein deutsches Fort Knox der Kunst. Zur Geschichte des amerikanischen Central Collecting Point im Museum Wiesbaden (2)." *Wiesbadener Kurier,* August 16, 1989.

**Hildebrand 1995**
Hildebrand, Martin. "Als Nofretete in Wiesbaden war. Zur Geschichte des amerikanischen Central Collecting Points im Museum (Teil 1)." *Wiesbadener Leben: Die Monatszeitschrift unserer Stadt.* Vol. 44, No. 3 (1995), pp. 26–31.

**den Hollander and Müller 2009**
den Hollander, Pieter, and Melissa Müller. "Jacques Goudstikker, 1897–1940." In Melissa Müller and Monika Tatzkow, *Lost Lives, Lost Art: Jewish Collectors, Nazi Art Theft, and the Quest for Justice,* pp. 216–31. New York, 2009.

**Hope et al. 2003**
Hope, Charles, et al. *Titian.* Exh. cat. London (National Gallery), 2003.

**Howe 1946**
Howe, Thomas Carr. *Salt Mines and Castles: The Discovery and Restitution of Looted European Art.* Indianapolis, 1946.

**Humfrey 2007**
Humfrey, Peter. *Titian: The Complete Paintings.* Ghent, 2007.

**Jaffé et al. 2007**
Jaffé, David, et al. *Samson and Delilah: A Rubens Painting Returns.* Exh. cat. Antwerp (Rockoxhuis) and Vienna (Liechtenstein Museum), 2007.

**Jawlensky et al. 1998**
Jawlensky, Maria, et al. *Alexej von Jawlensky. Catalogue raisonné, Vol. 4: The Watercolours and Drawings 1890–1938, with Addenda to the Catalogue of the Oil Paintings.* London, 1998.

**Just and Lohmann-Siems 1971**
Just, Klaus Günther, and Isa Lohmann-Siems. *Ernst Barlach 1870 / 1970.* Bonn-Bad Godesberg, 1971.

**Karlsgodt 2011**
Karlsgodt, Elizabeth Campbell. *Defending National Treasures: French Art and Heritage under Vichy.* Stanford, 2011.

**Karrels 2017**
Karrels, Nancy. *Provenance: A Forensic History of Art.* Exh. cat. Champaign, IL (Krannert Art Museum and Kinkead Pavilion), 2017.

**Kelch 1986**
Kelch, Jan, ed. *Der Mann mit dem Goldhelm: eine Dokumentation der Gemäldegalerie in Zusammenarbeit mit dem Rathgen-Forschungslabor SMPK und dem Hahn-Meitner-Institut Berlin.* West Berlin, 1986.

**Klipstein 1955**
Klipstein, August. *The Graphic Work of Käthe Kollwitz: Complete Illustrated Catalogue.* New York, 1955.

**Kokoschka 1974**
Kokoschka, Oskar. *My Life.* London, 1974.

**Koop 2006**
Koop, Volker. *Besetzt: Amerikanische Besatzungspolitik in Deutschland.* Berlin, 2006.

**Kuhn 1946**
Kuhn, Charles L. "German Paintings in the National Gallery: A Protest." *College Art Journal.* Vol. 5, No. 2 (January 1946), pp. 78–82.

**Kühnel-Kunze 1950**
Kühnel-Kunze, Irene. "Einleitung." In **Gemäldegalerie 1950**, pp. 4–7.

**Kühnel-Kunze 1984**
Kühnel-Kunze, Irene. "Bergung – Evakuierung – Rückführung: Die Berliner Museen in den Jahren 1939–1959." *Jahrbuch Preußischer Kulturbesitz.* Sonderband 2 (1984), pp. 1–533.

**Lane 2009**
Lane, Barbara G. *Hans Memling: Master Painter in Fifteenth-Century Bruges.* London, 2009.

**Lee and Riddleberger 1946**
Lee, Rensselaer W., and James W. Riddleberger. "Letter to the Secretary of State." *College Art Journal.* Vol. 5, No. 2 (January 1946), pp. 83–84.

**Lillie 2003**
Lillie, Sophie. *Was einmal war: Handbuch der enteigneten Kunstsammlungen Wiens.* Vienna, 2003.

**Lindsay 1998**
Lindsay, Kenneth. "Official Art Seizure under the Military Cloak." *Art, Antiquity and Law.* Vol. 3, No. 2 (June 1998), pp. 119–36.

**Longhi 1952 (1975)**
Longhi, Roberto. "Il 'Maestro di Pratovecchio.'" *Paragone Arte.* Vol. 3, No. 35 (1952), pp. 10–37 (reprinted in *Fatti di Masolino e di Masaccio e altri studi sul Quattrocento: 1910–1967. Edizione delle opere complete di Roberto Longhi. Vol. 8/1.* Florence, 1975, pp. 99–122).

**Longhi 1952 (1985)**
Longhi, Roberto. "Quadri italiani di Berlino a Sciaffusa (1951)." *Paragone Arte.* Vol. 3, No. 33 (1952), pp. 39–46 (reprinted in *Critica d'arte e buongoverno. Edizione delle opere complete di Roberto Longhi. Vol. 13.* Florence, 1985, pp. 311–317).

**Lugt 1921**
Lugt, Frits. *Les marques de collections de dessins & d'estampes: marques estampillées et écrites de collections particulières et publiques: marques de marchands, de monteurs et d'imprimeurs: cachets de vente d'artistes décédés: marques de graveurs apposées après le tirage des planches: timbres d'édition, etc.: avec des notices historiques sur les collectionneurs, les collections, les ventes, les marchands et éditeurs, etc.* Amsterdam, 1921.

**von Lüttichau 2014**
von Lüttichau, Mario-Andreas. "'Crazy at Any Price' The Pathologizing of modernism in the run-up to the 'Entartete Kunst' exhibition in Munich in 1937." In **Peters 2014a**, pp. 36-51.

**Martineau 1992**
Martineau, Jane, ed. *Andrea Mantegna.* Exh. cat. London (Royal Academy of Arts) and New York (Metropolitan Museum of Art), 1992.

**McBride 1948**
McBride, Harry A. "Masterpieces on Tour." *National Geographic Magazine.* Vol. 94, No. 6 (December 1948), pp. 717–50.

**Meyer 2000**
Meyer, Ruth K. "The Roberts Commission." In **Farmer 2000**, pp. 123–43.

**Michaelis 1995**
Michaelis, Rainer, ed. *Staatliche Museen zu Berlin. Dokumentation der Verluste. Band I. Gemäldegalerie.* Berlin, 1995.

**Mihan 1944**
Mihan, George. *Looted Treasure: Germany's Raid on Art.* London, 1944.

**Mochon 1991**
Mochon, Anne. *Alexej Jawlensky: From Appearance to Essence.* Exh. cat. Long Beach, CA (Long Beach Museum of Art), 1991.

**Monnet 1976**
Monnet, Jean. *Mémoires.* Paris, 1976.

**Mosse 1991**
Mosse, George L. "Beauty without Sensuality: The Exhibition *Entartete Kunst.*" In **Barron 1991a**, pp. 25–31.

**Musée du Petit Palais 1951**
Musée du Petit Palais. *Chefs-d'œuvre des Musées de Berlin.* Exh. cat. Paris (Petit Palais), 1951.

**Museum Wiesbaden 1988**
Museum Wiesbaden. *Alo Altripp: ein Wiesbadener Maler.* Exh. cat. Wiesbaden (Museum Wiesbaden), 1988.

**Museum zu Allerheiligen Schaffhausen 1951**
Museum zu Allerheiligen Schaffhausen. *Meisterwerke europäischer Malerei: deutsche, italienische und altniederländische Malerei des 14.–16. Jahrhunderts mit Hauptwerken des Kaiser-Friedrich-Museums, Berlin.* Exh. cat. Schaffhausen (Museum zu Allerheiligen Schaffhausen), 1951.

**Natter 2002**
Natter, Tobias G., ed. *Oskar Kokoschka: Early Portraits from Vienna and Berlin, 1909–1914.* Exh. cat. New York (Neue Galerie) and Hamburg (Hamburger Kunsthalle), 2002.

**Nicholas 1994**
Nicholas, Lynn H. *The Rape of Europa: The Fate of Europe's Treasures in the Third Reich and the Second World War.* New York, 1994.

**Palais des Beaux-Arts 1950**
Palais des Beaux-Arts. *Chefs-d'œuvre des Musées de Berlin.* Exh. cat. Brussels (Palais des Beaux-Arts), 1950.

**Peters 2014a**
Peters, Olaf, ed. *Degenerate Art: The Attack on Modern Art in Nazi Germany, 1937.* Exh. cat. New York (Neue Galerie), 2014.

**Peters 2014b**
Peters, Olaf. "From Nordau to Hitler: 'Degeneration' and Anti-Modernism between the Fin-de-Siècle and the National Socialist Takeover of Power." In **Peters 2014a**, pp. 16–35.

**Petropoulos 1996**
Petropoulos, Jonathan. *Art as Politics in the Third Reich.* Chapel Hill, NC, 1996.

**Petropoulos 2000**
Petropoulos, Jonathan. *The Faustian Bargain: The Art World in Nazi Germany.* Oxford, 2000.

**Prelinger 1992**
Prelinger, Elizabeth. *Käthe Kollwitz.* Exh. cat. Washington, DC (National Gallery of Art), 1992.

**Rand 2006**
Rand, Richard. *Claude Lorrain: The Painter as Draftsman; Drawings from the British Museum.* Exh. cat. San Francisco (Fine Arts Museums of San Francisco) and Williamstown, MA (Sterling and Francine Clark Art Institute), 2006.

**Reed 2003**
Reed, Victoria S. *In Pursuit of the Past: Provenance Research at the Princeton University Art Museum.* Exh. cat. Princeton (Princeton University Art Museum), 2003.

***Rettet die Berliner Museen* 1954**
*Rettet die Berliner Museen: eine Denkschrift des Kaiser-Friedrich-Museums-Vereins.* West Berlin, 1954.

***Returned Masterworks* 1949**
*Returned Masterworks/Zurückgekehrte Meisterwerke aus dem Besitz Berliner Museen, 1949.* Exh. cat. Wiesbaden (Central Collecting Point, Landesmuseum), 1949.

**Rijksmuseum 1950**
Rijksmuseum. *120 beroemde schilderijen uit het Kaiser-Friedrich-Museum te Berlijn.* Exh. cat. Amsterdam (Rijksmuseum), 1950.

**Roethlisberger 1961**
Roethlisberger, Marcel. *Claude Lorrain: The Paintings.* 2 vols. New Haven, 1961.

**Röttgen 1961**
Röttgen, Herwarth. "Zwei noch umstrittene Zuschreibungen an Konrad Witz." *Jahrbuch der Berliner Museen.* Vol. 3 (1961), pp. 76–93.

**Rowley 2018**
Rowley, Neville. "Fortuna e sfortune della 'Presentazione di Gesù al Tempio' di Andrea Mantegna ora alla Gemäldegalerie di Berlino." In **Blass-Simmen, Rowley, and Villa 2018**, pp. 51–61.

**Rowley 2020**
Rowley, Neville. "Das James-Simon-Kabinett: Zur Geschichte eines Raumes in Wilhelm Bodes 'Renaissance-Museum.'" In *James Simon: Briefe an Wilhelm von Bode 1885–1927*, ed. Olaf Mattes, pp. 31–59. Vienna, 2020.

**Ruda 1993**
Ruda, Jeffrey. *Fra Filippo Lippi: Life and Work with a Complete Catalogue.* London, 1993.

**Ruhemann 1968**
Ruhemann, Helmut. *The Cleaning of Paintings: Problems and Potentialities.* New York, 1968.

**Russell 1982**
Russell, H. Diane. *Claude Lorrain, 1600–1682.* Exh. cat. Washington, DC (National Gallery of Art) and Paris (Grand Palais), 1982.

**Schloss collection website**
Maintained by the government of France. https://www.diplomatie.gouv.fr/sites/archives_diplo/schloss/sommaire_ang.html.

**Schoenebeck and Bloch 1972**
Schoenebeck, Anna von, and Peter Bloch. "Zur Geschichte des Kaiser-Friedrich-Museums-Vereins." In *Kaiser-Friedrich-Museums-Verein Berlin: Erwerbungen 1897–1972*, pp. 7–10. West Berlin, 1972.

**Schumacher 2009**
Schumacher, Andreas, ed. *Botticelli: Likeness, Myth, Devotion.* Exh. cat. Frankfurt (Städel Museum), 2009.

**Schwarz 2004**
Schwarz, Birgit. *Hitlers Museum: Die Fotoalben Gemäldegalerie Linz: Dokumente zum "Fuhrermuseum."* Vienna, 2004.

**Scott 1987**
Scott, Mary Ann. *Dutch, Flemish, and German Paintings in the Cincinnati Art Museum: Fifteenth through Eighteenth Centuries.* Cincinnati, 1987.

**Shendar and Goldberg 2008**
Shendar, Yehudit, and Niv Goldbert. "The Insatiable Pursuit of Art: The Jacques Goudstikker Collection and Nazi Art Looting." In **Sutton et al. 2008**, pp. 34–52.

**Sheriff 2006**
Sheriff, Mary D., ed. *Antoine Watteau: Perspectives on the Artist and the Culture of His Time.* Newark, 2006.

**Simpson 1997**
Simpson, Elizabeth, ed. *The Spoils of War: World War II and its Aftermath; The Loss, Reappearance, and Recovery of Cultural Property.* New York, 1997.

**Spike 1993**
Spike, John T. *Italian Paintings in the Cincinnati Art Museum.* Cincinnati, 1993.

**Staatliche Museen Berlin 1957**
Staatliche Museen Berlin. *Gemälde des XIII. bis XVIII. Jahrhunderts.* West Berlin, 1957.

**Stechow 1966**
Stechow, Wolfgang. *Dutch Landscape Painting of the Seventeenth Century.* London, 1966.

**Suda and Nickel 2019**
Suda, Sasha, and Kirk Nickel, eds. *Early Rubens.* Exh. cat. San Francisco (Fine Arts Museums of San Francisco) and Toronto (Art Gallery of Ontario), 2019.

**Sutton et al. 1984**
Sutton, Peter C., et al. *Masters of Seventeenth-Century Dutch Genre Painting.* Exh. cat. Philadelphia (Philadelphia Museum of Art), West Berlin (Gemäldegalerie), and London (Royal Academy of Arts), 1984.

**Sutton 1987**
Sutton, Peter C. *Masters of 17th-Century Dutch Landscape Painting.* Exh. cat. Amsterdam (Rijksmuseum), Boston (Museum of Fine Arts), and Philadelphia (Philadelphia Museum of Art), 1987.

**Sutton et al. 2008**
Sutton, Peter C., et al. *Reclaimed: Paintings from the Collection of Jacques Goudstikker.* Exh. cat. Greenwich, CT (Bruce Museum) and New York (The Jewish Museum), 2008.

**Sutton, Wieseman, and Van Hout 2004**
Sutton, Peter C., Marjorie E. Wieseman, and Nico van Hout. *Drawn by the Brush: Oil Sketches by Peter Paul Rubens.* Exh. cat. Greenwich, CT (Bruce Museum), Berkeley (Berkeley Art Museum and Pacific Film Archive), and Cincinnati (Cincinnati Art Museum), 2004.

**Tisa Francini, Heuss, and Kreis 2001**
Tisa Francini, Esther, Anja Heuss, and Georg Kreis. *Fluchtgut – Raubgut: Der Transfer von Kulturgütern in und über die Schweiz 1933–1945 und die Frage der Restitution.* Zurich, 2001.

**Wheelock et al. 2004**
Wheelock, Arthur K., Jr., et al. *Gerard ter Borch.* Exh. cat. Washington, DC (National Gallery of Art) and Detroit (Detroit Institute of Arts), 2004.

**Winter 2008**
Winter, Petra. "'Zwillingsmuseen' im geteilten Berlin: Zur Nachkriegsgeschichte der Staatlichen Museen zu Berlin 1945 bis 1958." *Jahrbuch der Berliner Museen.* New series, Vol. 50 (2008), pp. 1–235.

**Winter 2013**
Winter, Petra. "Vom Kläger zum Beklagten? Der Direktor der Gemäldegalerie Ernst Heinrich Zimmermann." In Jörn Grabowski und Petra Winter, eds., *Zwischen Politik und Kunst: die Staatlichen Museen zu Berlin in der Zeit des Nationalsozialismus*, pp. 271–285. Cologne, 2013.

**Yeide 2009**
Yeide, Nancy H. *Beyond the Dreams of Avarice: The Hermann Goering Collection.* Dallas, 2009.

**Yeide et al. 2001**
Yeide, Nancy H., Konstantin Akinsha, and Amy L. Walsh. *The AAM Guide to Provenance Research.* Washington, DC, 2001.

**Zimmermann 1954**
Zimmermann, E. Heinrich. "Botticellis Berliner Madonna." *Berliner Museen.* New series, Vol. 4, Nos. 3–4 (1954), pp. 26–28.

**Zulauf 1995**
Zulauf, Jochen. *Verwaltung der Kunst oder Kunst der Verwaltung: Kulturverwaltung, Kulturförderung und Kulturpolitik des Landes Hessen 1945–1960.* Wiesbaden, 1995.

**Zuschlag 1991**
Zuschlag, Christoph. "An 'Education Exhibition': The Precursors of *Entartete Kunst* and Its Individual Venues." In **Barron 1991a**, pp. 82–103.

# PHOTO CREDITS

**Sold and Stolen: The Use and Abuse of Paintings in Nazi Germany and During World War II**

Fig. 3 Staatliche Museen zu Berlin—Gemäldegalerie / Jörg P. Anders

**Walter Farmer and the Central Collecting Point in Wiesbaden**

Fig. 1 Binghamton University Libraries' Special Collections and University Archives, Binghamton University
Fig. 5 Photo: Sim Smiley, Academic Historical Research
Fig. 6 Photo: Sim Smiley, Academic Historical Research
Fig. 7 Photo: Sim Smiley, Academic Historical Research
Fig. 9 Photo: Sim Smiley, Academic Historical Research

**Making Art History: The Masterpieces' Postwar Tour**

Fig. 1 © Washington Star
Fig. 3 Staatliche Museen zu Berlin—Gemäldegalerie / Jörg P. Anders
Fig. 4 Staatliche Museen zu Berlin—Gemäldegalerie / Christoph Schmidt
Fig. 5 From the Toledo Museum of Art Archives
Fig. 7 From the Toledo Museum of Art Archives
Fig. 8 From the Toledo Museum of Art Archives
Fig. 9 From Chicago Tribune. © 1948 Chicago Tribune. All rights reserved. Used under license.
Fig. 11 From the Toledo Museum of Art Archives

**The Road (Back) to Berlin: The Endless Journey of the "202"**

Fig. 1 Staatliche Museen zu Berlin—Gemäldegalerie / Christoph Schmidt
Fig. 2 Staatliche Museen zu Berlin—Gemäldegalerie / Christoph Schmidt
Fig. 3 bpk Bildagentur / Zentralarchiv, Staatliche Museen, Berlin, Germany / Gustav Schwarz / Art Resource, NY
Fig. 4 bpk Bildagentur / Gemäldegalerie, Staatliche Museen, Berlin, Germany / Dietmar Katz / Art Resource, NY
Fig. 5 Staatliche Museen zu Berlin—Gemäldegalerie / Christoph Schmidt
Fig. 6 bpk Bildagentur / Zentralarchiv, Staatliche Museen, Berlin, Germany / Art Resource, NY
Fig. 7 bpk Bildagentur / Zentralarchiv, Staatliche Museen, Berlin, Germany / Walter Steinkopf / Art Resource, NY
Fig. 8 Staatliche Museen zu Berlin—Gemäldegalerie / Christoph Schmidt
Fig. 9 bpk Bildagentur / Zentralarchiv, Staatliche Museen, Berlin, Germany / Reinhard Friedrich / Art Resource, NY
Fig. 10 bpk Bildagentur / Zentralarchiv, Staatliche Museen, Berlin, Germany / Reinhard Friedrich / Art Resource, NY
Fig. 11 bpk Bildagentur / Zentralarchiv, Staatliche Museen, Berlin, Germany / Jörg P. Anders / Art Resource, NY
Fig. 12 Skulpturensammlung und Museum für Byzantinische Kunst, Staatliche Museen zu Berlin / Antje Voight
Fig. 13 Staatliche Museen zu Berlin—Gemäldegalerie / Christoph Schmidt

**What's Past is Prologue: Provenance Research in American Museums**

Fig. 1 The Art Institute of Chicago / Art Resource, NY
Fig. 6 Courtesy of Sotheby's Images

**Catalogue**

Cat. 1 © 2019 Fondation Oskar Kokoschka / Artists Rights Society (ARS), New York / ProLitteris, Zürich
Cat. 2 © 2019 Artists Rights Society (ARS), New York
Cat. 4 © 2019 Artists Rights Society (ARS), New York / VG Bild-Kunst, Bonn
Cat. 8 Staatliche Museen zu Berlin—Gemäldegalerie / Jörg P. Anders
Cat. 9 Staatliche Museen zu Berlin—Gemäldegalerie / Christoph Schmidt
Cat. 10 Staatliche Museen zu Berlin—Gemäldegalerie / Jörg P. Anders
Cat. 11 Staatliche Museen zu Berlin—Gemäldegalerie / Jörg P. Anders
Cat. 22 © Estate of Alo Altripp

**Paintings from the Berlin Museums Checklist**

BR 1–7, 9, 11–16, 21–22, 25, 27–28, 30, 34, 36–38, 41, 43–45, 49–53, 55–56, 58–59, 62, 64, 67–68, 70–73, 76–79, 81, 88–106, 113, 116, 119, 124, 126–127, 129–130, 136, 148–150, 153–158, 161, 163–164, 166–167, 169–173, 175, 177–182, 184, 189–193, 199–200
Staatliche Museen zu Berlin—Gemäldegalerie / Jörg P. Anders

BR 8, 10, 18–20, 23–24, 26, 29, 33, 35, 39–40, 42, 48, 54, 57, 60–61, 63, 65–66, 69, 74, 83–87, 107–112, 114–115, 117–118, 120–122, 125, 128, 131–135, 137–147, 152, 162, 165, 174, 176, 183, 185–188, 194–195, 197
Staatliche Museen zu Berlin—Gemäldegalerie / Christoph Schmidt

BR 17, 31, 46–47, 123, 160, 196, 198
Staatliche Museen zu Berlin—Gemäldegalerie / Volker-H. Schneider

BR 32, 75, 80, 82, 151
Kaiser Friedrich Museumsverein, Förderverein der Gemäldegalerie und Skulpturensammlung / Jörg P. Anders

BR 159, 168
Kaiser-Friedrich Museumsverein, Förderverein der Gemäldegalerie und Skulpturensammlung / Christoph Schmidt

BR 201–202
Alte Nationalgalerie, Staatliche Museen zu Berlin / Jörg P. Anders

# INDEX